Dennis Wegner
The Underspecification of Past Participles

studia grammatica 83

Herausgegeben von Manfred Bierwisch,
Hans-Martin Gärtner und Manfred Krifka

unter Mitwirkung von
Regine Eckardt (Konstanz) und Paul Kiparsky (Stanford)

Dennis Wegner

The Underspecification of Past Participles

On the Identity of Passive and Perfect(ive) Participles

DE GRUYTER

ISBN 978-3-11-073648-9
e-ISBN (PDF) 978-3-11-061614-9
e-ISBN (EPUB) 978-3-11-061366-7

Library of Congress Control Number: 2018963416

Bibliografic information published by the Deutsche Nationalbibliothek
The Deutsche Nationalbibliothek lists this publication in the Deutschen Nationalbibliografie; detailed bibliografic data are available on the Internet at http://dnb.dnb.de.

© 2020 Walter de Gruyter GmbH, Berlin/Boston
This volume is text- and page-identical with the hardback published in 2019.
Typesetting: Integra Software Services Pvt. Ltd.
Printing and binding: CPI books GmbH, Leck

www.degruyter.com

This book is dedicated to the fond memory of
Erika Wegner,
whose confidence in me has accompanied me through this project,
and Matthias Steger,
whose drive and devotion I will never cease to admire.

Acknowledgements

This book is a revised version of my doctoral dissertation submitted to the University of Wuppertal, Germany, in March 2017 and defended in July 2017. I am genuinely thankful to the many supportive and kind people who have guided me through this project and would like to devote the first words of this work to them.

My deepest gratitude is due to Gisa Rauh, whose confidence in my academic path I strongly felt from the very first class I took with her and whose lectures turned out to be invaluable. Her unwavering support went well beyond everything I could ever have wished for and her devotion to the completion of this project was immeasurable. In a similar vein, I am sincerely grateful to Carsten Breul for providing me with a job, offering me the possibility to write a dissertation and contributing his advice as my supervisor (and beyond).

Furthermore, I am deeply indebted to Thilo Tappe and Leah Bauke for being the kind and benevolent people they are. They did not just manage to supplement my linear vision with hierarchy by virtue of introducing me to the field of syntax, but also always had an open ear and provided valuable feedback for my ideas and problems. Additionally, I am very thankful to Horst Lohnstein for showing an interest in my work and gladly participating in my dissertation committee in addition to the aforementioned people. I am also grateful to Holden Härtl for welcoming me to the University of Kassel with open arms.

I would also like to thank the audiences of the numerous conferences at which I was allowed to present parts of the research that eventually culminated in this book. In particular, I would like to express my gratitude to Ida Larsson, Theresa Biberauer, Berit Gehrke, Elena Anagnostopoulou, Tillmann Pross and Josep M. Fontana for their valuable comments and interest in my work.

Moreover, I am grateful to the editors of *Studia Grammatica*, Manfred Bierwisch, Hans-Martin Gärtner, and Manfred Krifka, for including my work in the series and to Daniel Gietz and Albina Töws at De Gruyter for guiding me through the publishing process.

Writing this book would not have been possible without the support of my colleagues, friends and family. I thank from the bottom of my heart my mother Elke and my grandparents Erwin, Hedwig and Heinrich. Finally, I am eminently grateful to Andrea for having accompanied me throughout this project, her patience and understanding as well as putting things into perspective every now and then. Thank you!

Contents

Acknowledgements — VII

Abbreviations — XI

1	**Introduction — 1**	
1.1	Preliminary remarks — 3	
1.2	The framework — 14	
2	**Empirical data — 34**	
2.1	Participial morphology — 34	
2.1.1	Germanic languages — 38	
2.1.2	Romance languages — 45	
2.1.3	Slavic languages and beyond — 51	
2.2	The distributional and categorial flexibility of past participles — 55	
2.2.1	Periphrastic occurrences — 56	
2.2.2	Adnominal use — 63	
2.2.3	Additional modes of occurrence — 69	
2.2.4	Questions of category — 73	
2.3	Auxiliary selection and the verbal semantics of past participles — 79	
2.4	Past participial polymorphy — 87	
2.4.1	Morphological distinctions and substantial non-identity — 89	
2.4.2	Agreement morphology in periphrastic instances — 95	
2.4.3	Subtle differences — 99	
2.5	Divergent realisations of past participles — 101	
2.5.1	The Perfect(ive) Participle Paradox — 102	
2.5.2	Infinitivus pro Participio — 106	
2.5.3	Participium pro Infinitivo — 114	
2.5.4	Deponent verbs — 119	
2.6	Implications from the historical development of past participles — 121	
3	**Past participial (non-)identity in the literature — 134**	
3.1	The ambiguity of past participles — 135	
3.2	Identity in form equals identity in meaning — 141	
3.2.1	The tense/aspect hypothesis — 144	

3.2.2	The argument structure hypothesis —— 151
3.2.3	The amalgamation hypothesis —— 158
3.2.4	The semantic vacuity hypothesis —— 162
3.3	Challenges and opportunities of (non-)identity —— 166

4 A compositional approach to the identity of past participles —— 171
4.1   The basic meaning of past participles and what the auxiliaries contribute —— 173
4.1.1   The argument structural effect —— 173
4.1.2   The aspectual contribution —— 181
4.1.3   The contribution of the auxiliaries —— 184
4.2   The syntax and semantics of past participles —— 195
4.2.1   The basics: the formation of past participial periphrases —— 198
4.2.2   The periphrastic passive —— 219
4.2.3   The analytic perfect —— 242
4.2.4   Grasping divergent realisations and polymorphy —— 274
4.3   Bare instances and the category of past participles —— 295
4.3.1   Bare past participles in resultative and eventive configurations —— 295
4.3.2   Categorial considerations —— 317

5 Conclusion —— 321

References —— 329

Index —— 353

Abbreviations

ACC	accusative case
Ag	Agent
BNC	British National Corpus
C-I	conceptual-intentional interface
COCA	Corpus of Contemporary American English
Comp	complement (of a head)
CxG	Construction Grammar
DA	designated argument
DAT	dative case
def-perf	defective perfectivity
DM	Distributed Morphology
E	Event time
EA	external argument
EF	Edge Feature
EM	External Merge
E-Perfect	existential perfect
EPP	Extended Projection Principle
Exp	Experiencer
FL	Faculty of Language
GEN	genitive case
HPSG	Head-Driven Phrase-Structure Grammar
IA	internal argument
iF	interpretable feature
iF[val]	valued interpretable feature
IM	Internal Merge
IPFV	imperfective
IPP	Infinitivus pro Participio
LF	logical form
LFG	Lexical Functional Grammar
ME	Middle English
MidD	Middle Dutch
ModD	Modern Dutch
ModE	Modern English
MP	Minimalist Programme
NEUT	neutral
NOM	nominative case
OE	Old English
OHG	Old High German
PASS	passive
Pat	Patient
PF	phonological form
PFV	perfective
PPI	Participium pro Infinitivo
PPP	Perfect(ive) Participle Paradox

PRF	perfect
PTCP	(past) participle
R	Reference time
S	Speech time
S-M	sensory-motor interface
SMT	Strong(est) Minimalist Thesis
Spec	specifier (of a head)
SUP	supine
Th	Theme
TSit	Time of the Situation
TT	Topic Time
TU	Utterance Time
~~uF~~	checked uninterpretable feature
*u*F	uninterpretable feature
*u*F[ ]	unvalued uninterpretable feature
*u*F[val]	valued uninterpretable feature
U-Perfect	universal perfect

1 Introduction

Participles have been the odd man out ever since the most ancient exponents of traditional grammar and – despite rapid progress in virtually all of the (sub-)disciplines of linguistic inquiry, especially since the late 1950s – have retained this status up to the most modern instantiations of linguistic frameworks. In spite of numerous insightful approaches, one of the main mysteries concerning participles is whether they constitute a designated linguistic category or are to be included within the category of verbs or adjectives. What is clear is that participial forms range between these two categories – *prima facie*, they appear to be categorially underspecified. In addition to such categorial questions, the class of participles is internally heterogeneous, traditionally distinguished into present and past (or 1st and 2nd) particles in Germanic and Romance languages. While present participles are rather simple in only ever giving rise to simultaneous active meaning (e.g. expressing progressive aspect with or without the help of the auxiliary *be* in English), past participles fulfil two quite distinct functions. This functional diversity intuitively appears to necessitate yet another distinction: passive vs. perfect(ive) participles. The fact that the past participles used to fulfil these two functions take on an identical morphophonological form (consider the suffix *-en* in *Marty has beaten Rust* and *Rust was beaten by Marty*) in Germanic and Romance languages suggests that this functional distinction does not bear any grammatical substance. Further support for this comes from the fact that passive and perfect(ive) participles may diachronically be traced back to one and the same source. In fact, the morphophonological identity is so pervasive that it strongly suggests that any more detailed scrutiny is superfluous. However, what sheds substantial doubt on this premature evaluation is that the two kinds of past participles may occur in the context of distinct auxiliaries (*have* and *be* in English) and exhibit quite distinct meanings (temporal/aspectual vs. diathetic) for which it is hard to identify a common semantic basis. Additionally, the fact that they historically share the same source may not be taken at face value as the forms need not have retained a substantial syntacticosemantic identity despite their identity in form. As a matter of fact, it is still entirely unclear whether the distinct kinds of past participle – despite apparently exhibiting homophonous forms in all of their uses – should be considered distinct as traditionally assumed or whether the two functions, indeed, stem from one and the same lexical entry. While the former view has to face the challenge of providing an explanation for why these two forms are 'accidentally homophonous', the latter approach crucially has to identify what that basic meaning is from which the two major functions may be derived with (or without) the help of the syntactic context.

Reminiscent of what is observable in the context of categorial indeterminacy, the underlying question thus boils down to one of underspecification. Are there two kinds of past participles that are specified for distinct features (the ambiguity approach), potentially even in so far as to – in its most radical instantiation – dispose the auxiliaries of any substantial semantic contribution whatsoever? Or is there only one past participial marker that is – to a certain extent – underspecified with respect to fulfilling its two main functions (the identity approach)? The latter view crucially entails that certain aspects of the semantic contribution responsible for expressing the distinct functions are shifted off to the auxiliaries or other contextual factors.

Some preliminary steps have been made into both of these conceivable directions of past participial (non-)identity, i.e. the ambiguity as opposed to identity of these elements,[1] offering interesting opportunities. However, a proper account of past participial (non-)identity is still searched for in vain. This is particularly surprising since this basic question crops up in virtually every work primarily concerned with passive and/or perfect(ive) participles. Additionally, the settlement of this central issue bears a range of potential insights not only for a theory of periphrases, i.e. auxiliaries and how they aid their secondary predicates, but also for modes of encoding aspectual information and diathesis. Furthermore, it provides theoretical implications for the organisation of the lexicon and how syntax makes the most of what it is given. The present work attempts to close the void posed by the issue of past participial (non-)identity by approaching it from a cross-linguistic perspective. In fact, it will rely on insights gained from cross-linguistic data, although the approach to be laid out will focus on English and German, where the null hypothesis is that it properly grasps the workings of other languages exhibiting (at least shallow) past participial identity as well.[2] Since both these empirical insights as well as theoretical considerations clearly point in the direction of substantial past participial identity in Germanic and Romance, the present work will provide arguments for the identity view. Accordingly, the thesis

---

[1] Note that 'past participial (non-)identity', of course, only refers to the alleged identity of past participial formation for elements eventually taking on a passive and perfect(ive) function and not of the underlying (verbal) lexemes involved. While the perfect participle *beaten* and the passive participle *seen* clearly do not share a verbal meaning, they may well turn out to be subject to the same kind of past participial formation.

[2] These two languages sufficiently draw the distinctions most important for the current investigation: auxiliary alternation, the presence of a designated passive auxiliary that is not BE, and the presence of lexical dative case, all three of which are present in German but not in English.

to be pursued holds that passive and perfect(ive) participles can be traced back to one and the same instance of past participial formation, occasionally requiring contextual support in order to be able to express a certain function. Before laying out the plans intended to settle the issue of past participial (non-)identity, a few preliminary remarks are in order.

1.1 Preliminary remarks

In the face of the general scholarly uncertainty pertaining to the class of participles it does not come as a surprise that this has been and still is mirrored in a lot of terminological confusion circling around the concept, especially with regard to its hyponym 'past' participle. As a matter of fact, while the denomination of present participles is rather fixed (though these are also commonly referred to as 'progressive participles' in languages in which this aspectual meaning may unanimously be attributed to them, e.g. English),[3] their 'past' correspondents are referred to by a variety of distinct designations in linguistic research. The most common term for this class is 'past participle', yet they are also referred to as 'perfect(ive) participles',[4] as 'passive participles' or, predominantly in German linguistics, as 'second participles'. An immediate issue arising here is that most of these terms are used ambiguously: while 'past participle' and 'perfect(ive) participle' may refer to both the whole class of active as well as passive elements, especially the latter term is also used to refer solely to active instances, while the term 'passive participle' is typically – but not exclusively – restricted to refer to the subclass of passive instances. The term 'second participle' or 'participle II', on the other hand, is on a par with the traditional hyperonymic use of 'past participle' yet does not bring with it the terminological bias of entailing any inherent (temporal/aspectual or diathetic) meaning. An additional attempt at imposing neutral terminology is to be

---

[3] The present participle (or participle I) does not play much of a role in the present work, even though some cross-linguistic differences as well as similarities are certainly striking. For instance, German – unlike English – does not allow these to occur in periphrases (consider *Der Mann ist rennend*, lit. the man is running), which is sometimes taken to suggest that these elements are not participial at all (see, amongst others, Valentin 1994: 43f.). On the other hand, German and English share that present participial formation is monomorphemic (invariably built with -*ing* or -*end*, respectively), while its past or second participial counterpart is polymorphemic (e.g. -*ed* and -*en* English, -*en* and -*t* typically accompanied by the prefix *ge*- in German) (cf. Faucher 1994: 1).

[4] The notation 'perfect(ive)' will be used in order to leave open whether we are talking about a tense (perfect) or an aspect (perfective) until this issue is explicitly discussed in Chapter 4.2 below.

found in the fact that this class is sometimes also referred to by highlighting its morphological derivation as '*-en* forms' in English. However, in spite of its mnemonic convenience, this is not much of a sensible solution given that it does not equally pertain to (roughly) equivalent elements in other languages (cf. Huddleston 2002: 83fn4)[5] and is – although marking the only dedicated way – not even the sole (let alone most wide-spread) means of morphological realisation.

The traditional terminology of present (*participium praesentis*) as distinguished from past participles (*participium praeteriti*) has long been criticised as inadequate (see, amongst others, Heyse 1886 [1838]: I, 686). One of the main reasons for this is that both present as well as past participles may well also be combined with past and present tense, respectively, as observable in *John was leaving* and *Johann wird geschlagen* ('John is being hit.', lit. John becomes hit) (cf. Marillier 1994: 19f.). An alternative possibility advocated by Heyse (1886 [1838]: I, 686) is to opt for the aspectual opposition of imperfective (*participium imperfecti*) vs. perfective participles (*participium perfecti*). This, however, also turns out to be problematic, as it forces the exclusion of passive participles and hence suggests non-identity. This is for instance observable on the basis of the latter example in which the action of *hitting* is by no means finished even though a past participle is used (cf. Marillier 1994: 22, 29). Therefore, the traditional terminology (past participles, perfect(ive) participles) is both biased and corrupted in that it presupposes the elements that it designates to exhibit semantic content that may *a priori* not clearly be identified with it as not all of the exponents are either past or perfect(ive).[6] This inadequacy of both the aspectual (imperfective vs. perfective) as well as the temporal (present vs. past) opposition comes to the fore more clearly in German than in English due to differences in auxiliary selection. Thus the semantically neutral terms, most prevalent in German linguistics, 'first participle' (1P/PI) and 'second participle' (2P/PII) appear to be preferable.[7] However, since a neutral term is not very insightful and a terminological revision based on the findings of the present work is pending, we will keep with the

---

[5] The notation 'fn' in references within the text refers to a given footnote in the respective work, while 'en' is used to refer to an endnote.

[6] Huddleston (2002: 78) attempts to justify the designation 'past participle' by claiming that "the inclusion of 'past' in the name does not imply that the past participle is itself a tensed form: it is a participle which occurs in constructions with the past tense auxiliary **have**" (emphasis in original). This is a highly dubious decision since the meaning entailed by the terminology should actually hold for all of the exponents it exhibits (yet not all past participles occur with *have*), a criterion that holds for virtually every clear-cut scientific term.

[7] This semantically neutral terminology comes close to attempts at morphological designations shortly discussed (and criticised) above (e.g. *-ing* vs. *-en* in English or *-end* vs. *ge-* in German) (cf. Kathol 1994: 239fn4).

tradition of using the term 'past participle', though not presupposing any inherent content for this term. This means that, for the time being, we restrict ourselves to what de Saussure (1916) calls the *signifiant* without yet devising any *signifié*. Eventually, then, we will use the traditional term past participle out of convenience and the general consensus to use this term for all non-present participles.

As we could just see, one of the indeterminacies inherently connected to past participles is the issue of whether what is expressed (at least in the active variants) is tense (past/perfect) or aspect (perfective). Comrie (1985: 6) distinguishes these two concepts as follows: tense "locate[s] the situation somewhere on the time line [while aspects refers to] [t]he internal temporal contour of a situation" (see also Comrie 1976; Lindstedt 2000: 368; Dahl & Velupillai 2013a). Accordingly, tense is for instance supposed to denote that a situation lies in the past or present, while aspect contributes whether it is ongoing or completed. What is generally undisputed is that past participles are dependent non-finite elements (usually introduced in the context of an auxiliary or as adjuncts). Nevertheless, participles have to encode some tense-linguistic information or otherwise the observable differences between bare occurrences like *der ankommende Zug* ('the arriving train', ongoing action) and *der angekommene Zug* ('the train that has arrived', lit. the arrived train, completed action)[8] cannot be explained (cf. Struckmeier 2007: 19). The precise nature of this information as either aspect or (secondary) tense is what remains unclear. Struckmeier (2007: 19) subscribes to the aspect-view of past participles. This perspective is shared by Lübbe & Rapp (2011: 266), who claim (at least for German) that the crucial difference between finite verbs and participles is that the former mark tense but not aspect morphologically, while the latter are inherently tenseless but mark aspect. Under this view, the present participle designates imperfective aspect, while the past participle entails perfective aspect.[9] As already briefly pointed out above, a possible argument against the aspectual view is that the past participle may easily be combined with imperfective aspect as well, as observable in the English sentence *Since last week, she has been writing the*

---

8 The abbreviation 'lit.' (literally) is used to indicate glossed word-by-word translations in the main text.
9 Note, however, that it is assumed here that the participles – although crucially not being marked for tense – nevertheless may be interpreted for tense as they adapt to the tense of their clause, where present participles denote co-occurrence, while past participles are taken to denote precedence (cf. Lübbe & Rapp 2011: 297). This idea may already be found in Paul (1957), although Belitschenko (1980: 376) points out that it is not clear how this co-occurrence or anteriority is determined, i.e. what constitutes its basis.

article (cf. Larsson 2009: 76) as well as in periphrastic passives. On the other hand, the resolute reluctance to show up in finite contexts without the help of some other tensed elements, i.e. the inability to introduce tense all by itself, intuitively appears to dismiss the possibility that past participles are encoded for tense (cf. Drijkoningen 1989: 73). While there may be room for tense information in non-finite elements as well (secondary tense), the ability to occur in present passives supports the intuition that tense is not inherently stored in past participles (cf. Grewendorf's 1995: 82f. criticism of Zeller's 1994: 99 tense-account). Bybee (1985: 160), however, points out that the participial denotation "seems to resemble a tense more than an aspect, since it does not affect the internal temporal contours of the situation". This brief venture into the intricate discussion of the temporal as opposed to aspectual properties of past participles indicates how difficult it is to get to their basic meaning. In fact, particular care is in order as it is always possible that particular properties attributed to past participles actually stem from their compositional interaction with certain grammatical environments such as auxiliaries. Perfect meaning, for instance, is made up compositionally, which means that it is necessary to determine what is contributed by the auxiliary as well in order to find out what it is exactly – be it temporal or aspectual, if anything – that the past participle contributes.

The observation that (past) participles are dependent elements that are either introduced in the context of auxiliaries, copulas or as adjuncts partly accounts for their categorial indeterminacies. Dionysios Thrax in his ancient grammar, the *Tékhnē grammatikē*, defines participles as a part of speech (a lexical category) exhibiting adjectival as well as verbal properties (cf. Davidson 1874: 336). This flexibility is mirrored in their realisation as distinct syntactic categories: participles fulfilling adjectival functions may prototypically be found in attributive positions (e.g. in *the written book*)[10] and (arguably) in copular structures (*John is gone*), while verbal uses usually occur as periphrastic structures (*John has married Holly*). The lexical categorial flexibility is unequivocally represented in the Latin designation *participium*, which stems from the Ancient Greek *metochikon* and means 'to take part in', namely in both the verbal as well as the adjectival category (cf. Valentin 1994: 33). The German (somewhat archaic) designation 'middle word' (*Mittelwort*) follows the same intuition of positioning participles in-between two linguistic categories (cf. Marillier 1994: 19). In fact, "[t]he most heavily debated matter concerning participles is their *hybrid* nature:

---

[10] The adjectival character of participles in attributive position is clearly marked by agreement morphology in languages like German: *das geschriebene Buch* ('the written book', lit. the written-NOM.SG.N book). However, not all past participles may show up attributively and exhibit inflectional morphology (cf. Poitou 1994: 110).

they exhibit both verbal and adjectival properties" (Helland & Pitz 2012: 103). In other words, there quite generally is an "ongoing unraveling of the 'mixed' syntactic and semantic properties of deverbal categories such as participles" (Sleeman 2011: 1570). Accordingly, the eponymous uncertainty of the participial category led to a large variety of distinct proposals regarding the question of whether they should be treated as exponents of a designated linguistic category, or rather simply as verbs or adjectives.[11] This question boils down to one concerning the discrepancy between parts of speech (or lexical categories) and syntactic categories.[12] While participles were long treated as a designated lexical category based on their habit of comprising both verbal as well as adjectival morphology, more recent work rather assumes that they are derivative (usually deverbal) elements, as for instance observable in Curme (1935: 210) and Bloch (1947: 401) (cf. Blevins 2003: 763). Although categorial matters will repeatedly turn up again in the present work, for the time being we will simply follow the latter intuition. Accordingly, it is assumed that the elements belonging to the lexical category of verbs when being enhanced by participial morphology may exhibit more or less adjectival properties depending on the syntactic context in which they occur.

The fact that past participial (non-)identity has not yet been investigated in a principled fashion is particularly surprising in the face of the enormous amount of literature on both passive and perfect. In fact, the "passive is one of the most commonly analysed constructions within linguistics" (Ackerman & Webelhuth 1998: 11), granting important insights into essential concepts like movement and argument structure and eventually even invigorating whole frameworks (most clearly Transformational Grammar) (cf. Horgan 1978: 65). The complex syntacticosemantic nature of the perfect similarly gave rise to numerous insightful accounts and the preliminary discussion on whether the perfect is a tense or an aspect shows that there are still a lot of issues revolving around the perfect that are far from understood and thus pose major problems to contemporary theories (cf. Zeller 1994: 79). Despite this high degree of attention attributed to the two constructions, the issue of past participial (non-)identity is typically only treated in passing and – although a rather limited number of preliminary discussions exists – principled investigations are virtually non-existent. This shows that past participial (non-)identity is in fact "a widely ignored phenomenon" (Abraham 2006b: 464f.). Any attempt to dismiss this issue by claiming that past participles

---

[11] See Weber (2002: 195–200) for an overview of the historical development of the perception of participles in linguistic research (predominantly in German philology).
[12] See Rauh (2017) for a concise demarcation of lexical as opposed to syntactic categories. An introductory differentiation of the two terms may be found in Forsgren (2000: 668).

are clearly non-identical runs into the problem of not being able to account for why the passive and perfect(ive) participles are "systematically encoded by the same verb form" (Wunderlich 1997: 2). Supposing that they must be identical, on the other hand, raises the question of what the basic meaning of that form is then, no principled answer for which may easily be given. Moreover, the latter assumption demands an explanation for why there appear to be exceptions to this formal identity (see Chapter 2.4 below). This shows that "the consistent identity of the past participles in periphrastic passives and perfects is unexpected and in need of an explanation" (Ackema 1999: 88).

In order to be able to provide a principled account of past participial (non-)identity, once the distinct shapes and functions of past participles (primarily but not exclusively in Germanic and Romance) have been laid out, a major focus will be on the search for a potential basic meaning of the past participle. As a means to find out whether there is substantial evidence against there being a single underlying past participle and, if the answer turns out to be negative, to get a hold of its semantic ingredients, we will review potential exceptions to the assumption of formal identity. Furthermore, contexts in which the passive and perfect(ive) participles show a substantially different behaviour will be scrutinised. Let us briefly turn to some examples of both of these, i.e. regular exceptions to formal identity and divergent realisations of past participles in particular contexts.

Exceptions of the former kind most prominently arise with respect to agreement phenomena,[13] as observable in the Icelandic example in (1), adapted from Thráinsson (2007: 9).

(1) a. Maður   var   bitinn   af   hundi.
       the.man was   bite.PTCP.M.SG   by   the.dog
       'The man was bitten by the dog.'
    b. Hundurinn hefur bitið   manninn.
       the.dog   has   bite.PTCP   the.man
       'The dog has bitten the man.'

---

13 Additionally, we will also see exceptions in terms of slightly different morphological forms for distinct participial functions (e.g. *rotten* vs. *rotted*) (cf. Embick 2003: 155). These, however, do not concern the opposition of perfect and passive participles, but rather (stative) adjectival and (eventive or resultative) verbal items, only the latter of which turn out to be participles in the strict sense.

The past participle in the periphrastic passive in (1a) exhibits agreement morphology, unlike its perfect counterpart formed with an equivalent of *have* in (1b), which is formed with an invariant (neuter) counterpart. Something similar is also observable in Swedish, yet with the interesting difference that the invariant form, often referred to as 'supine', is built with the help of a designated participial marker, as observable in (2), adapted from Larsson (2009: 2).

(2) a. Brevet var skrivet av någon annan.
    the.letter.N.SG *was* write.PTCP.N.SG *by somebody else*
    'The letter was written by somebody else.'
 b. Hon har skrivit brevet.
    she has write.SUP *the.letter*
    'She has written the letter.'

Given that *skrivit* ('written') in (2b) features a participial marker not to be found in the passive participial paradigm, Swedish apparently is a promising candidate for a Germanic language employing substantially non-identical forms. In other language families like Slavic, this is actually the typical pattern. In Bulgarian, for instance, we equally find two morphologically distinct participles employed in passive and perfect contexts, both of which are bound to exhibit agreement and are formed with one and the same auxiliary, namely an equivalent of *be*, as may be seen in (3), taken from Broekhuis & Migdalski (2003: 2f.).

(3) a. Paulina e pročela knigata.
    Paulina.F.SG *be*.3.SG read.PRF.PTCP.F.SG *the.book*
    'Pauline has read the book.'
 b. Knigata e pročetana ot Ivan.
    the.book.F.SG *be*.3.SG read.PASS.PTCP.F.SG *by Ivan*
    'The book is read by Ivan.'

Besides the properties of bare occurrences like those in (4) below (cf. Breul 2014: 465; Breul & Wegner 2017: 6f.), the arguably most compelling insights for the determination of the basic meaning of past participles and the contribution of the auxiliaries comes from divergent realisations like those in (5). The latter examples exhibit relevant phenomena highlighting the crucially distinct behaviour of passive and perfect(ive) where (5a) and (5b) are taken from Breul (2014: 452) and (5c) as well as (5e) stem from Bader & Schmid (2009: 176) and den Dikken & Hoekstra (1997: 1058), respectively.

(4) a. *Eaten*, the shark does not terrify them anymore.
  b. *Built* in the suburbs, the house is supposed to become part of a housing estate.

(5) a. She created the roadside garden because of a desire to return something to others. And *return/returned something she has*.
  b. It will never be known how Jarman was caught, but **catch/caught he was*, and condemned to hang.
  c. Marie wusste, dass Peter das Buch *hat lesen*
    Mary knew that Peter the book has read.INF
    müssen/*gemusst.
    must.INF/must.PTCP
    'Mary knew that Peter had to read the book.'
  d. Peter wusste, dass das Unheil kommen **sehen/gesehen wurde.*
    Peter knew that the disaster come.INF see.INF/see.PTCP became
    'Peter knew that the disaster was anticipated.'
  e. Hy soe it dien/ dwaan wollen ha.
    he would it do.PTCP/ do.INF want.PTCP have.INF
    'He would have liked to do it.'

As observable in (4), the (bare) adverbial use of a past participle gives rise to a passive interpretation yet necessitates an auxiliary to express an active perfect. The examples in (5a) and (5b) show the possibility of what is called the 'Perfect Participle Paradox' (PPP) and the ungrammaticality of the corresponding use of an infinitive (or plain) form in the context of passive participles (cf. Breul 2014: 450–454). Leaving matters of word order aside for the time being, the examples in (5c) and (5d) show a phenomenon of *ge*-languages like German and Dutch that resembles the PPP in terms of the possibility of using an infinitival form where we would normally expect a past participle, the so-called 'Infinitivus pro Participio' (IPP) effect. This, once again, only appears to be licit in perfect (viz. only with equivalents of *have*), but not in passive contexts. What we can see in (5e) appears to be the mirror image of those IPP-constructions in terms of there being two participial forms in the context of just a single equivalent of *have* in languages like Frisian, which is typically referred to as 'Participium pro Infinitivo' (PPI) or 'parasitic participles' ever since den Dikken & Hoekstra's (1997) seminal paper. While we most certainly cannot provide an in-depth analysis of each of these phenomena in the languages in which they occur, aspects like these will be taken into consideration in order to reach a more profound understanding of the (non-)identity of past participial morphology.[14] Additionally, evidence from the diachronic development of past participles will be considered as a potential impetus for past participial (non-)identity.

After reviewing the relevant synchronic data and briefly turning to diachronic developments, what will eventually be pointed out is that the assumption of past participial identity has a sound empirical basis in those (Germanic and Romance) languages that do not make a substantial morphological distinction. Hence, influenced by the discussion of problems and merits of previous theories to past participial (non-)identity, a novel approach to the identity of past participles will be proposed. In an attempt to account for the wide range of past participial occurrences and their flexible semantics, the basic ingredients of the past participial marker will be assumed to be of a two-fold character. On the one hand, past participial morphology brings with it the lexical marking of the external argument (if present) for existential binding. This operation renders the external argument inoperative for syntactic purposes unless there is independent help by an element that may introduce it as an adjunct (*by*-phrases and their cross-linguistic equivalents) or an auxiliary that may license arguments marked this way (usually *have* and its cross-linguistic equivalents). On the other hand, the past participial marker contains aspectual information, namely defective (or aktionsart/event-structure sensitive) perfectivity, which may or may not induce completion (i.e. perfectivity) depending on the properties of the underlying verb. This will be shown to account for auxiliary alternation in those languages that entertain it by virtue of necessitating no additional aspectual information with telic unaccusative (i.e. simple, anticausative change of state) predicates, which are thus selected by the ('semantically vacuous') auxiliary BE.[15] Based on the sense of completion

---

[14] Note that I typically follow the general habit of talking about 'affixes' and 'affixation' just out of convenience and not as to presuppose an affix- as opposed to a word-based system. Although this issue will briefly be tackled in 1.2, the present work will not rely on either one of those two opposing views for the theoretical analysis that will be worked out, i.e. what will be proposed here is generally applicable to both kinds of approaches.

[15] Small capitals (e.g. HAVE, BE) will henceforth be used to indicate (rough) cross-linguistic equivalents. The particular lexical items of individual languages will, on the other hand, be given in italics (*have*, *be*). Referring to rough equivalents (or cognates), of course, does not entail that these elements cannot substantially differ in their morphosyntactic as well as phonological properties, while at least some functional and often also etymological similarities can be attested.

brought in by the combination of aspectual information and verbal aktionsart, posteriority may be introduced via implication and a proper perfect reading comes about. With other kinds of predicates, though, the aspectual information is unable to induce a sufficient amount of perfectivity (as the predicate either does not induce a change of state or is too complex by virtue of containing a cause), which may be made up for by the overt introduction of posteriority (on HAVE).[16] This, in turn, allows for completion to come about by implication (though not necessarily forcing it, as observable with universal perfect readings like *Jack has loved Kate ever since he laid eyes on her*). In HAVE-only languages, both of these ingredients may be spelled out (*The man has arrived*). The weak sense of defective perfectivity does not only come to the fore with universal perfect readings. It also accounts for why a seemingly simultaneous interpretation may be derived in certain bare cases (consider *Carried by his mother, the baby felt safe*). Accordingly, the two-fold ingredients are taken to be constitutive for adjectival instances of past participles as well, although these arguably undergo an additional lexical operation. This operation takes care of marking an internal argument (crucially one that does not carry inherent case) for λ-abstraction and hence grants the direct attribution of a property to a referent, which in turn may have some semantic effects (occasionally forcing resultant state readings). These ingredients will be argued to do justice to the intricate properties of past participles in identity languages.

In order to tackle the underlying questions of past participial (non-)identity in a comprehensive as well as profound fashion, the discussion will proceed in the following manner. The present first chapter is concerned with laying out the groundwork and already provided justifications for why the present investigation is fruitful and clarified some major terminological issues. What remains to be done in the remainder of this chapter is a brief discussion of the most important presuppositions of the framework that will be used here. Therefore, the central operations and properties of a minimalist framework will be introduced in Chapter 1.2. A special focus of this discussion will be on relevant issues concerning the syntax-morphology interface and whether disposing of a designated morphological level (as in Distributed Morphology) at the expense of lexicalism

---

[16] In other words, the past participial aspectual information only suffices to induce proper perfectivity in cases like *Das Mädchen ist verschwunden* ('The girl has disappeared.', lit. the girl is disappear.PTCP), but crucially not in cases like *Die Kirche hat gebrannt* ('The church has burned.') or *Die Mutter hat ihre Tochter getragen* ('The mother has carried her daughter.', lit. the mother has her daughter carry.PTCP), where it is only imposed via implication.

is a sensible undertaking against the backdrop of the present purposes. Additionally, a classification of verbs will be laid out on the basis of a brief discussion of their syntactic and semantic properties. The second chapter will then give an overview of the data relevant for providing a principled account of past participial (non-)identity. Accordingly, Chapter 2.1 will present the most important aspects of (past) participial morphology from a cross-linguistic perspective. Section 2.2 will be concerned with various distributions and categorial instantiations of past participles, prior to a brief investigation of the main facts about auxiliary selection and what they tell us about past participial semantics in Chapter 2.3. The subsequent Chapter 2.4 will discuss morphological distinctions within single languages. These are most prominently observable in Slavic, but also occur in Germanic in the context of the Swedish distinction between past participles and supines as well as in differences with respect to past participial agreement in Romance and (North) Germanic. The remainder of Chapter 2 will then focus on the search for a potential past participial basic meaning on the basis of divergent participial realisations and some diachronic insights. Accordingly, Chapter 2.5 will discuss relevant data provided by various synchronic phenomena, some of which we could briefly see above, and Chapter 2.6 will eventually take into consideration the diachronic perspective by briefly laying out some aspects of the historical development of past participles. Equipped with this array of relevant insights, the remaining thing to do before being able to attempt to get to grips with the issue of past participial (non-)identity is to provide an (approximately) exhaustive discussion of potentially fruitful previous approaches. This will be carried out in Chapter 3, which provides a concise overview of the distinct approaches to past participial (non-)identity that have been pursued in the literature and consequently attempt to work out their main flaws and opportunities. Based on the discussion in the previous sections, Chapter 4 will present a novel approach to past participles. Accordingly, the compositional distribution of meaning in past participial constructions will be worked out in 4.1, where a focus will thus be on the basic meaning of past participles and the semantic contribution of the auxiliaries. Section 4.2 will attempt a syntactic as well as semantic analysis of past participles and the passive and perfect periphrases they give rise to, i.e. it will investigate how the properties of a single past participial form allow us to derive the proper perfect and passive semantics and how this is to be represented syntactically. The subsequent Chapter 4.3 will extend the scope of the approach to bare (i.e. auxiliaryless) instances of past participles with the aim of showing that the basic past participial properties also shine through in these cases although certain additions may be necessary to do justice to all bare cases. As the discussion of bare instances is intertwined with categorial issues, it will eventually take us back to the seemingly everlasting mystery of past participial category and some preliminary conclusions on how the categorial flexibility may be accounted for. The final fifth chapter of the present work will eventually provide an overview of the main conclusions, tie together loose ends and point to promising fields of future research.

1.2 The framework

Even though the main proposals and conclusions to be laid out below are by no means incompatible with a wide variety of different theoretical frameworks, their technical implementation will be attempted for the most recent instantiation of mainstream generative grammar: a minimalist framework. Accordingly, we will mainly operate within the confines of the Minimalist Programme (henceforth MP), as proposed by Chomsky (1993 *et seq.*). The central assumption of this programme is linguistic minimalism, which consists of a methodological as well as an ontological dimension (cf. Martin & Uriagereka 2000: 1). Methodological minimalism is "common practice to all disciplines" (Gallego 2010: 2) and has already been a part of linguistic research at the very beginning of generative grammar. It simply holds that a theory should strongly adhere to William of Occam's fundamental principle *pluralitas non est ponenda sine necessitate* (Occam's Razor). While this merely advocates that one should always prefer a simpler explanation that does without superfluous elements, ontological minimalism is the real innovation of the MP (cf. Gallego 2010: 3). Applied to linguistic research, it boils down to a strong claim about the design of the innate Faculty of Language (FL), namely "the expression of the idea that language communicates with external systems of human biology in an optimal way" (Gallego 2010: 3). In other words, the programme's[17] main aim is to work out in how far the Strong(est) Minimalist Thesis (SMT), "which holds that language is an optimal solution to interface conditions that FL must satisfy" (Chomsky 2008: 135), can be approximated.

In an attempt to do justice both to methodological as well as ontological minimalism, minimalist frameworks rely only on a highly restricted set of

---

[17] A point often stressed by proponents of the MP is that it is not a theory but a programme (cf. Hornstein 2001: 21). In contrast to a fully-blown theory, linguistic minimalism should hence solely be seen as a research guide (cf. Boeckx 2006: 84), making it more flexible and less vulnerable, a point that is still dwelled upon in Chomsky (2013: 38). Accordingly, the SMT is merely regarded as an ideal that is not expected to be met fully and for which it still remains to be determined precisely in how far it can be approached (cf. Chomsky 2008: 135).

indispensable operations, most importantly the basic structure-building operation Merge, which comes in various kinds, and the feature-checking/-valuation mechanism Agree. The former either glues together two elements that are not in any relation with one another yet (i.e. are 'external' to each other – External Merge or EM) or two objects where one is already included in the other (i.e. one is 'internal' to the other – Internal Merge or IM) (cf. Chomsky 2013: 40). In addition to those two applications of the same operation, Merge has been argued to come in two types depending on whether it elicits a symmetric set (set Merge) {α, β} (hence entirely equivalent with {β, α}) or an (asymmetric) ordered pair (pair Merge) <α, β> (cf. Chomsky 2013: 45f.). The latter option was initially introduced as a way to technically allow for adjunction (cf. Chomsky 2004: 117f.), but was recently argued to potentially also account for the concatenation of heads, taken to boil down to a presyntactic morphological rule in Epstein, Kitahara & Seely (2016). The recursive (and cost-free) application of the operation of Merge yields infinitely complex (and infinitely many) structures. In order for this not to lead to extensive overgeneration, deficient structures are usually filtered out at the interfaces to externalisation (the sensory-motor interface S-M) and meaning (the conceptual-intentional interface C-I). This is most strictly imposed whenever the configuration is not capable of properly taking care of feature valuation, viz. if uninterpretable (typically unvalued) features remain unchecked. The latter is taken care of by the operation Agree, "consisting of matching (simple nondistinctness) under minimal search and valuation of features unvalued in the lexicon" (Chomsky 2013: 42). Accordingly, this operation relates features in a minimal search domain, say $uF[]$ and $iF[val]$ yielding $\text{\sout{u}}F[val]$. If the features in question do not already share a local domain, internal Merge may trigger 'movement' (i.e. inserting a copy of the suitable counterpart of a given $uF[]$ in order to check it) so as to make sure that the derivation does not crash at the interfaces. Thus, movement is necessarily feature-based.[18]

A pressing question in this context is whether this also holds for labelling. This mechanism determines whether α or β in a set {α, β} constitutes the head and has been one of the primary concerns of minimalist research in recent years. One

---

[18] Note that this somewhat oversimplifies things as movement may also serve symmetry-breaking in order to assure labelling, as for instance proposed in Moro (2000) and investigated in Bauke (2014) and Ott (2012) (see also Chomsky 2013). However, given that label determination is commonly taken to be contingent on the feature interaction of the elements within a given set (cf. Chomsky 2008: 141; Cecchetto & Donati 2010: 245; 2015: 39), as briefly laid out in the next paragraph, this source for movement may also be taken to be feature-based.

of the crucial questions here is whether it is only relevant at the interfaces, i.e. imposed by requirements of logical form (LF) and phonological form (PF), or also part of narrow syntax. Approaches of the former kind (cf. e.g. Chomsky 2000: 133 and Moro 2000) crucially suffer from the problem of not being able to account for "why labeling plays a role at **both** interfaces in the same relevant way" (Bauke 2014: 9; emphasis in original). Additionally, it may be shown that labelling is an indispensable requirement for the formation of complex structures in that the derivation has to figure out which of the two elements in a combination provides the constitutive grammatical properties.[19] This, however, need not entail that labels are overt elements that are explicitly created at the level of narrow syntax. Rather than label creation, label determination is arguably based on label identification (cf. Collins 2002; Seely 2006; Chomsky 2004; *et seq.*) and thus contingent on a search mechanism, namely Minimal Search (cf. Chomsky 2013: 46). Cecchetto & Donati (2015: 39) primarily tie label identification to probing (as effected by the operation Agree): "[t]he label of a syntactic object {α, β} is the feature(s) that act(s) as a probe for the merging operation creating {α, β}" (cf. also Chomsky 2008: 141; Cecchetto & Donati 2010: 241). This is taken to also account for the wide-spread validity of earlier head-based labelling algorithms (see Chomsky 2008; Narita 2011: 18). These are grounded on the observation that it is always the element taken from the lexicon that provides the label in an {H, α} configuration, which is tied to probing by virtue of the claim that 'words' – unlike morphemes and phrases (or labels) – bear a designated (edge) feature (cf. Cecchetto & Donati 2015: 33).[20] Recent approaches, on the other hand, have denied the existence of a substantial grammatical basis for the concept of 'word' altogether. While we cannot do justice to the elaborate debate concerning lexicalist as opposed to anti-lexicalist positions, let us briefly dwell on the major distinctions between the two and some reasons for why the present work endorses the former.

In its most radical instantiation, a lexicalist framework entails that what enters the syntactic derivation are terminal elements that come equipped with phonological information and bear a fixed internal structure that may not be altered by syntax (cf. Williams 2007: 353f.). Crucially, then, lexicalist approaches

---

[19] Cecchetto & Donati (2015: 33) point to the indispensability of both internal, i.e. syntactically induced, as well as external, i.e. interface-based, labelling. See also Irurtzun (2007) and Gallego (2010: 14) for a number of phenomena in which label determination is vital.
[20] Cecchetto & Donati (2015: 33) explicitly refrain from calling this feature 'edge feature' due to the theoretical burden that this notion brings with it (especially in terms of its supposed non-deletability).

assume that word-formation applies in a designated component, i.e. "[m]orphology comes first and assembles morphemes into words, while syntax, which comes later, assembles the output of morphology (words) into phrases and sentences" (Cecchetto & Donati 2015: 7). This stands in strong opposition to anti-lexicalist approaches which instead argue for "Syntactic Hierarchical Structure All the Way Down" (Harley & Noyer 1999: 3). According to this maxim, the rules that make phrases out of words equal those that make words out of morphemes (cf. Cecchetto & Donati 2015: 7). While there are numerous distinct formalisations of this idea (see e.g. Borer's 2003; 2004; 2005a; b, 2013; exo-skeletal approaches or nanosyntactic approaches like Ramchand 2008; Caha 2009), the arguably most common version is typically referred to under the heading of Distributed Morphology (henceforth DM) (see, amongst many others, Halle & Marantz 1993; 1994; Embick 1997; 2004; Siddiqi 2009). The main assumption of DM is that there is no designated level of morphological computation, and morphology is rather distributed over distinct levels of representation (cf. Embick & Noyer 2007). Given the extensive amount of similarities between morphology and syntax (cf. e.g. recursion in compounding and word-internal structural ambiguity), i.e. the fact that "there are systematic correspondences between word syntactic and phrasal syntactic structures" (Ackema & Neeleman 2007: 328), this *a priori* falls out naturally. Accordingly, Ackema & Neeleman (2007: 328) claim the following:

> At first sight, the fact that syntax and morphology share vocabulary and principles undermines a model in which the two are distinct, because it seems we then need to duplicate the relevant vocabulary and principles in the two separate systems, which is conceptually inelegant.

Especially in a minimalist framework, then, the idea that the same mechanisms are responsible for the formation of words and phrases is *per se* desirable, yet there are some theoretical as well as empirical issues questioning anti-lexicalism in general and DM in particular (cf. Cecchetto & Donati 2015: 9).[21]

One of the central characteristics of anti-lexicalist frameworks, eponymous for *Distributed* Morphology, is their distribution of morphology over three distinct lists: grammatical, semantic and phonological features are not stored in a

---

[21] We can just briefly point to some general problems here. For discussion, see for instance Ackema & Neeleman (2007), Julien (2007), Embick & Noyer (2007), Williams (2007), Harley (2014) and the responses to it, e.g. Alexiadou (2014) and Borer (2014), as well as Panagiotidis (2002) and Rauh (2016).

designated lexical item, but distributed to syntax (viz. a store of syntactically relevant formatives), LF and PF (cf. Halle & Marantz 1993). The core of a given 'lexical' element is a specific kind of syntactic formative, an acategorial 'root'. In terms of categorial specifications, a root may for instance be introduced in the context of a functional head or categoriser, say *n*, *a* or *v*, which *per se* leads to categorial variability. Although occasionally denied (cf. Barner & Bale 2002: 777), this induces extensive overgeneration (cf. Rauh 2016: 37fn12). Categorial variability also raises problems in that the meaning of a given root should be constant across distinct functional surroundings, contrary to fact (cf. Rauh 2016: 39). Evans (2000: 107f.) for instance shows this with respect to the verbal use of kinship terms like *mother, father* or *uncle someone*, which crucially induce quite distinct meanings when introduced in the domain of a verbal categoriser.[22] In addition to their acategorial nature, roots are also taken to be maximally underspecified in terms of their grammatical properties, which are bound to be determined by their syntactic environment (cf. Borer 2014).[23] This, however, is no less problematic due to the fact that there are idiosyncratic properties like gender specifications, conjugation or declension classes, which are syntactically relevant but associated with their listemes regardless of their syntactic environment (cf. Rauh 2016: 37, 41f.). Such pieces of information, which are arguably first and foremost responsible for purposes of organisation in terms of storing, need to be associated with individual roots. The point that there is syntactically relevant information that needs to be associated with particular items and hence may not stem from their syntactic environment may also be made with respect to diachronic developments. As for instance observable in the development of impersonal passives and the gradual loss of dative case in Old English (cf. Allen 1995: 446, 451), there are (syntactically relevant) diachronic changes that apply to specific items one after the other rather than to whole classes at once. This necessitates that individual syntactic formatives be allowed to store idiosyncratic grammatical information.

Besides these problematic aspects of a root-based approach, another justification for why the present work does not adopt an anti-lexicalist framework (but rather opts for a moderate lexicalist system to be sketched shortly) concerns the fact that the latter obscures the notion of identity. This mainly follows from the

---

[22] The same point may be made for a variety of denominal verbs like *boat, dog, form* or *snail someone* as well, according to Rauh (2016: 39f.).

[23] Note that there are also approaches that grant roots some grammatical properties, e.g. argument structural information concerning the realisation of the internal argument (cf. Harley 2014: 255), which is, however, strongly denied for instance in Borer (2014: 356) and Alexiadou (2014).

overarching importance of numerous kinds and combinations of functional heads that conspire to embed roots. Focussing on the participial domain, differences in the behaviour of various kinds of (past) participles are assumed to stem from distinct structural embeddings rather than differences in the properties of the participial morpheme itself. While the relevant morpheme is thus arguably identical, the immediate morphosyntactic context into which it is introduced strongly determines the grammatical behaviour and interpretation of the participial form. Accordingly, the morpheme itself gains its properties through the functional context into which it is inserted, i.e. the functional context specifies the underspecified participial marker (cf. Embick 2003; 2004; Abraham 2006b: 491–494).[24] What is not clear at all in these cases is whether the observable distinctions really follow from properties crucially related to the participial morphology or rather stem from independent properties of the structural context (say the presence of an eventive head leading to a verbal reading and introducing an empty subject). In other words, the notion of identity loses much of its relevance in anti-lexicalist accounts, which renders it difficult to pursue the thesis that passive and perfect participles are in fact identical. More radically speaking, a strict anti-lexicalist approach seems to be (at least representationally) inferior by virtue of obscuring syntacticosemantic similarities by distributing these over numerous functional heads. While this of course need not pertain to all anti-lexicalist accounts, i.e. a thorough demarcation of the contributions and how these relate to participial morphology may well make up for this, it points to the dangers of such approaches.

These preliminary observations shall suffice to justify the decision to maintain a certain form of lexicali sm for the present purposes. However, in order to keep track of the SMT and to do justice to the large amount of similarities between morphology and syntax, instead of adopting a strictly lexicalist framework, we will follow Ackema & Neeleman's (2007) and Williams' (2007) intuition of two designated systems that largely share the same machinery: word syntax and phrasal syntax (see also Hale & Keyser's 1991; 1993; 2002; distinction between L- and S-Syntax). As Ackema & Neeleman (2007: 328) propose, "[t]hese submodules can have their own vocabulary and principles, but as a matter of course they also inherit the vocabulary and principles of the bigger module [(i.e. syntax)] in which they are contained." This allows us to do justice to

---

[24] This basic idea actually also carries over to the present approach, but with the vital distinction that there is a single participial marker that exhibits specific properties of both a passive and a perfect(ive) kind in specific functional environments.

the null hypothesis that the two systems are the same in so far as their basic machinery is concerned, i.e. the basic operations of syntax (most importantly Merge and Agree) are also usable for the derivation of words. Additionally, however, it also allows for a certain amount of differences and supposedly concedes some substance to the concept of 'word'. Eventually, then, we retain a lexicalist account while also acknowledging the similarities between the structure of words and phrases. As numerous phenomena show that the phonological specification of a given structure has to follow its syntactic composition, we need to enrich this kind of lexicalist account by means of allowing for phonological late insertion (thus leaving room for additional mechanisms like impoverishment and ornamental morphology). Even though it crucially remains to be worked out how exactly word and phrasal syntax differ, for our purposes all that matters is that the output of the former serves as the input for the latter, an asymmetrical relation (cf. Williams 2007: 356). In other words, word syntax provides terminals – potentially endowed with a certain kind of 'edge' feature in the sense of Cecchetto & Donati (2015: 33) – that serve as the input for the phrasal system. These items are subject to atomicity and may hence not be internally meddled with by the phrasal system: "the word system is subject to a condition of 'immediate resolution' (locality, or word-internal atomicity) which is irrelevant in the phrasal system" (Williams 2007: 356). The assumption that the word system supplies the terminal elements to be worked with in the phrasal system demands that there be a designated application of Transfer. This raises further issues like the question of what triggers this kind of (intermediate) 'spell-out' (or what renders complex words usable for phrasal syntax) and whether even simple words have to pass through this level of computation before being inserted into phrasal syntax. This most certainly is a fairly non-standard take on the morphology-syntax interface. However, given the apparent drawbacks of anti-lexicalism and the structural similarities of syntax and morphology, it appears to be sensible to pursue a moderate reconciliation of the opposing poles of (radical) lexicalism in the traditional sense (with designated morphological mechanisms) and anti-lexicalism (as in DM).[25] Crucially, none of the major propositions to be made about the basic thesis of the present work relies on the workings of this theoretical framework, whose feasibility remains to be scrutinised in future research.

---

[25] Note that it may well turn out to be the case that what is involved in word formation is indeed pair rather than set Merge (cf. Epstein, Kitahara & Seely 2016), which would then have to be taken to target morphemes rather than fully-fledged terminals (at least in word syntax).

The conception of words being generated in a designated syntactic component (word syntax) and then being passed on to phrasal syntax by Transfer suggests that words are phases. Introduced as a means to account for the cyclic nature of syntactic derivations, the concept of phases holds that the syntactic objects constructed by Merge "at some point in the derivation, are transferred to the two interfaces" (Chomsky 2005: 16). This ties in neatly with the general theses of the MP in that CP and vP (or v*P) are taken to constitute phases, which leads to a cyclic transfer of their complements, thus significantly reducing memory load (cf. Chomsky 2007: 24). Although the implementation of this concept is still highly controversial and even its general feasibility remains contested, this idea shows the merits of a principled investigation in MP in that it allows us to take into consideration third-factor effects in our attempts to explain the mechanisms of language (cf. Chomsky 2007: 5). In spite of the general appeal of its central assumptions, the programmatic nature of the MP still shines through abundantly and unfortunately manifests in many circular arguments concerning basic theoretical notions like the Extended Projection Principle (EPP) and the Edge Feature (EF) as well as general open questions like what ends a derivation in an unrestricted cost-free Merge-framework, to name just a few cases in point. Accordingly, we will pass many problematic aspects of the current mainstream minimalist framework when attempting to lay out a novel approach to the identity of past participles in Chapter 4. For instance, there apparently is still no agreement on the nature of distinct kinds of features, say strong uF triggering movement and weak features allowing for long-distance valuation (e.g. with long-distance agreement in Icelandic). Furthermore, there apparently is the unexpected need to allow for default valuation of certain features (as we will see in the context of default case in ditransitives and default agreement in impersonal passives) despite the apparent lack of a theoretical justification. Additionally, there are quite general theoretical issues like the mysterious nature of head-movement and whether it applies in syntax or at PF (cf. Bauke 2014: 252–268, Chomsky 2015: 15), the discussion of restrictions concerning the direction and multiplicity of Agree (see Zeijlstra 2012), and whether feature-valuation is restricted to pairs of unvalued uninterpretable and valued interpretable features (see Pesetsky & Torrego 2002; 2006; 2007), amongst many others. In spite of these open questions and controversies, the general principles and workings of a minimalist framework are worthwhile and provide promising insights into the properties of language and its interaction with other mental structures.

Abstracting away from the featural representation and interaction, a standard structure within the confines of a minimalist framework may be found for exemplification in (6).

(6)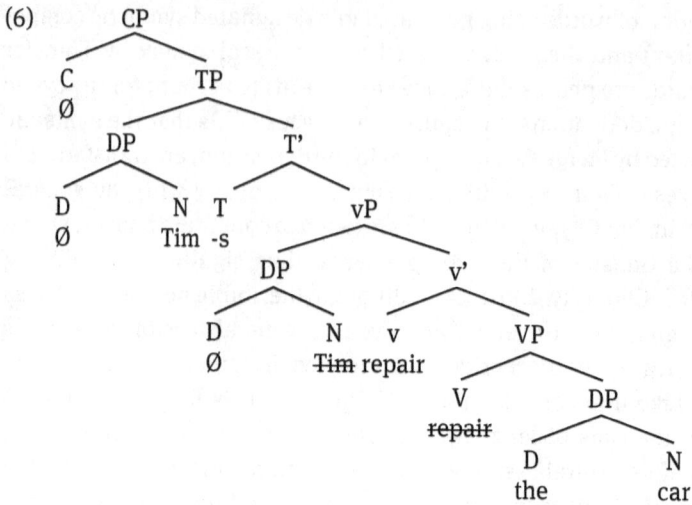

This structure represents the outcome of the recursive application of Merge at the level of (phrasal) syntax to derive the simple sentence *Tim repairs the car*. It features syntactic as well as phonological instances of 'movement'. In terms of the former, internal Merge of the external argument DP is necessary to assure that a copy of this argument receives structural case in Spec, T and the lexical verb is moved to the functional projection v via head-movement (potentially to obtain causative properties). A phonological instance of movement may be found in the PF-operation of lowering the tense affix to v. Additionally, there are numerous instances of featural interaction (i.e. Agree) that are not represented in the present case but below (by including all the relevant features and their values), e.g. subject-verb agreement (triggered by T) and the assignment of structural case from v to the object-DP.

Based on the criticism levelled at the syntactic reality of roots and the decision to take a lexicalist stance (though one featuring a designated 'word syntax'), functional heads serving as categorisers are taken to be relevant only for category conversion, but crucially not to specify acategorial roots. This presupposes that lexical items are associated with parts of speech. The traditional assumption here, as for instance still held in Cecchetto & Donati (2015: 14) is that "a word (be it a functional or an open class word) is intrinsically endowed with a categorial feature and can always transmit this feature to the structure in which it is inserted". However, as pointed out by Rauh (2000a; 2000b; 2010: 144), categorial features actually stem from sets of characteristics which (more or less prototypically) allow us to associate a given lexical item with a certain part of speech, rendering designated categorial features in the lexicon redundant. This has important repercussions for syntax in that syntactic categorial labels may then be taken to stem from the formal features the syntactic objects include, i.e. "feature representations which have the status of complex syntactic-category labels" (Rauh 2010: 144).[26] For the purposes of the present (lexicalist) approach, let us maintain that past participles do not consist of roots from which either verbs or adjectives are derived. Rather, we will assume that (past) participles are first and foremost verbs, i.e. they come equipped with verbal properties. Depending on the presence of a functional head which grants to directly modify a nominal governor, they may, however, occur in adjectival distributions (occasionally forfeiting some of their verbal characteristics). Given the primacy of their verbal nature, it is not surprising that the properties of the underlying verbal forms are constitutive of their distribution (as for instance observable with auxiliary alternation). Hence, it is indispensable to provide a clear-cut picture of the distinct verbal classes. The dimensions of difference that are essential for the current investigation are the verbal event structure (including aktionsart) as well as the verbal argument structure, which are also usually assumed to be the constitutive ingredients for positing distinct classes.[27]

The most general typology of verbs that one may posit concerns their arity, i.e. the number of arguments a given verb takes. We may distinguish between the one-place or intransitive predicates in (i) and (ii), the two-place or transitive predicates in (iii) and the three-place or ditransitive verbs in (iv). For the languages most relevant to the current investigation (i.e. those of Germanic and Romance), additional options in terms of arity are excluded. Factoring out controversial cases like verbs taking prepositional complements, we may take for granted the canonical patterns of structures projected by verbal predicates in (i) to (iv). These are accompanied by some German and English predicates for expository purposes, but are assumed to hold for all Germanic and Romance languages alike.

---

[26] Accordingly, the categorial labels used in the structure in (6) and below are merely included for representational clarity and do not entail the presence of a designated label. Rather, we will generally assume a bare phrase structure (cf. Chomsky 1995a), although this is not representationally adopted for the sake of clarity.

[27] This can for instance be seen in the traditional distinction of prototypical atelic unergatives possessing only an external argument and their telic unaccusative counterparts possessing only an internal argument.

(i) Unaccusative[28]

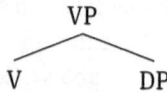

German: *ankommen* ('arrive'), *verschwinden* ('disappear'), *landen* ('land'), *fallen* ('fall'), *abfahren* ('depart'), *einschlafen* ('fall asleep'), *schmelzen* ('melt'), *brechen* ('break'), *sinken* ('sink'), *abbrennen* ('burn down'), *glücken* ('succeed')

English: *arrive, disappear, land, fall, depart, melt, break, sink*

(ii) Unergative

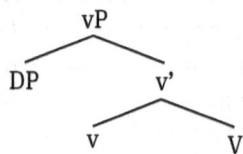

German: *arbeiten* ('work'), *tanzen* ('dance'), *schwimmen* ('swim'), *laufen* ('walk'), *rennen* ('run'), *telefonieren* ('call'), *putzen* ('clean')

English: *work, dance, swim, walk, run, call, clean*

(iii) Transitive

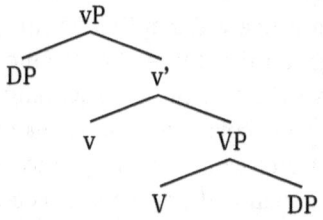

German: *reparieren* ('repair'), *bauen* ('build'), *unterstützen* ('support'), *tragen* ('carry'), *treffen* ('meet'), *sehen* ('see'), *beneiden* ('envy'), *kennen* ('know'), *freuen* ('delight'), *entzücken* ('enrapture'), *bedrücken* ('depress'), *bekommen* ('receive'), *verlieren* ('lose'), *erkennen* ('recognise'), *beinhalten* ('contain'), *kosten* ('cost'); *widersprechen* ('dissent'), *helfen* ('help'), *gedenken* ('commemorate')

English: *repair, build, support, carry, meet, see, envy, know, delight, enrapture, depress, receive, lose, recognise, contain, cost, help, commemorate*

---

28 Note that many of the predicates in (i) to (iv) have counterparts that belong to a different class: *schmelzen/melt* in (i), *putzen/clean* in (ii), and *kaufen/buy* in (iv) may for instance also be found as members of the class in (iii).

(iv) Ditransitive

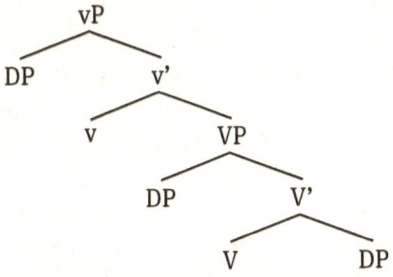

German: *schenken* ('give as a present'), *geben* ('give'), *reparieren* ('repair sth. for sb.'), *kaufen* ('buy'), *erteilen* ('grant'), *servieren* ('serve'), *reichen* ('pass')
English: *give, buy, grant, read, serve, pass*

The distinction of intransitive verbs into the two-classes given in (i) and (ii) may be traced back to Perlmutter's (1978) seminal Unaccusativity Hypothesis. While certain flaws remain,[29] the general validity of a distinction of intransitive verbs along the lines of (i) and (ii) is fairly uncontroversial. In the unaccusative instances given in (i), the exponents feature a single Theme-argument, licensed in the complement position of a lexical verb (V). Since a v-layer cannot be introduced with such predicates, the internal argument (IA) remains without structural (accusative) case and thus has to move to Spec, T.[30] The unergative cases in (ii), on the other hand, comprise a single external argument (EA), viz. an Agent-argument introduced in the specifier position of the functional projection v (based on Larson's VP shell analysis 1988; for ditransitives as well as Kratzer's 1996; introduction of a VoiceP). As we will see shortly, there are countless instances of intransitives that cannot be grouped as simply with either one of the two classes. This requires the boundaries of the class of unergatives to be drawn in a somewhat more flexible fashion. First, however, let us take the general distinction between unaccusatives and unergatives for granted for now and first turn to elements featuring more than one argument.

The ditransitives in (iv) – though providing interesting insights in terms of case assignment, especially concerning interesting cross-linguistic differences

---

29 Most importantly, it is often the case that different diagnostics have to be employed to distinguish the two classes and there are so-called unaccusativity mismatches both cross-linguistically as well as within a given language (see Levin & Rappaport Hovav 1995; Alexiadou et al. 2004; for discussion).
30 This is traditionally captured in Burzio's (1986) Generalization, which correlates the ability to assign a subject θ-role with the ability to assign accusative case (cf. Burzio 1986: 182f.).

like the lexical (dative) or default (accusative) case assigned to the indirect object – are fairly straightforward in terms of the arguments and their semantic mapping. Here, typically a Theme is assigned to Comp, V, an Agent to Spec, v and a Recipient, Goal or Beneficiary to Spec, V. The transitives in (iii), on the other hand, are quite flexible in terms of which semantic roles they assign. The prototypical pattern here is that – keeping more fine-grained distinctions like Patients aside – a Theme is merged in Comp, V and an Agent in Spec, v, where both arguments receive structural case (the IA receives accusative case *in situ*, the EA nominative case after moving to Spec, T). This is for instance the case with the Agent-Theme verbs *reparieren/repair, bauen/build*, and *unterstützen/support*. While there are also cross-linguistic differences imposed by the availability of dative case to be returned to shortly, the class of structural case assigning NOM-ACC predicates is actually quite flexible itself when it comes to possible patterns of θ-role distribution. This is for instance observable with psych verbs, which differ in their mappings of Experiencer and Theme-stimulus (see, amongst many others, Belletti & Rizzi 1988; Dowty 1991; Pesetsky 1995). Verbs like *sehen/see, beneiden/envy*, and *kennen/know* bear an Exp-Th grid. Opposed to these there are cases apparently featuring Th-Exp assignments, where the former marks the cause for the latter's experience, as instantiated in *freuen/delight, entzücken/enrapture*, and *bedrücken/depress*.[31] This unexpected mapping of θ-roles to argument positions with psych-verbs is underlined by alternations like *The doctor worried Max* and *Max worried* (cf. Reinhart 2002: 245). In those cases, the linking of Theme and Experiencer appears to be arbitrary and thus crucially questions Baker's (1988) Uniformity of Theta Assignment Hypothesis,[32] although this problem has often been attempted to be resolved by resorting to a cause being mapped to Spec, v rather than an Experiencer (cf. Belletti & Rizzi 1988; Pesetsky 1995; Reinhart 2002). As the discussion of such intricate problems of mapping semantic roles to argument positions exceeds the scope of the present work, we will simply acknowledge it here. In a similar vein (and hence also not explicitly discussed here) are the characteristics of somewhat symmetric verbs like *beinhalten/contain, kosten/*

---

31 The conceptual basis for these distinctions seems to be the following: Exp-Th verbs focus on a perception being applied to some object, whereas Th-Exp verbs present an external cause that triggers some experience.

32 This hypothesis suggests that "[i]dentical thematic relationships between items are represented by identical structural relationships between those items" (Baker 1988: 46).

cost, apparently containing two Themes, but assigning the one defined by the other to Spec, v. These are problematic in that it is not intuitively clear why one of the roles is being mapped to Spec, v. In the former case of *beinhalten/contain*, this might potentially stem from the lexical heritage of these verbs as once actively involving an argument carrying out the event. In cases like *kosten/cost*, things cannot be easily done away with, but it may be argued that these are special in establishing a particular kind of equative relation, for which it is rather unclear which thematic roles are involved and how they are mapped.[33] In contrast to such problematic instances, the linking of Recipient and Theme with verbs like *bekommen/receive* and *erhalten/obtain* falls out fairly naturally in that the former potentially causes a transition by providing a goal. In addition to these instances featuring structural case assignment, the fact that German employs inherent case gives rise to transitives that pattern with the ones in (iii) structurally, but comprise an IA that is marked for dative or genitive case. Exponents of this class are predicates that take an Agent- and a Beneficiary- or Theme-argument, the latter of which is lexically associated with inherent case, dative case with predicates like *widersprechen* ('dissent'), *helfen* ('help'), and genitive case in instances like *gedenken* ('commemorate').

This leaves the two problematic classes of verbs in (v) and (vi), referred to as Theme-unergatives and two-place unaccusatives, respectively, by Reinhart (2002: 237, 245). As the configuration of the former conforms with that of the prototypical unergatives in (ii), only the configuration of two-place unaccusatives is represented below.[34]

(v) Theme-unergatives
German: *blühen* ('bloom'), *brennen* ('burn'), *funktionieren* ('function'), *glühen* ('glow'), *ruhen* ('rest'), *schwitzen* ('sweat'), *leiden* ('suffer'), *fehlen* ('lack'); *begeistern* ('delight'), *erstaunen* ('astonish'), *entzücken* ('enrapture'), *bedrücken* ('depress')
English: bloom, burn, glow, rest, sweat, suffer, delight, astonish, enrapture, depress

---

[33] All that matters for us here is that these do not give rise to passive readings, because they do not involve an EA that carries a sufficient amount of Proto-Agent features (cf. Dowty 1991). We will turn to this below.
[34] See also Gunkel (2003: 77–81) for further German verbs of the class in (v) that he refers to as HAVE-Theme verbs (*haben-Thema Verben*) as well as additional instances of the cases in (vi), featuring a dative argument.

(vi) Two-place unaccusatives

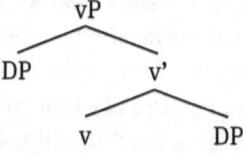

German: einleuchten ('be understandable'), bevorstehen ('be imminent'), drohen ('impend'), entsprechen ('resemble'), zusagen/gefallen ('appeal to'), gehören ('belong to'), genügen ('suffice'); entgehen ('elude'), gelingen ('succeed'), unterlaufen ('occur'), entfallen ('escape'), widerfahren ('befall'), geschehen ('happen')[35]
English: *resemble, suffice, lack; elude, escape, befall*

The predicates in (v) are unexpected to give rise to an unergative configuration because their sole argument interpretively resembles a Theme. However, a subset of the verbs in (v) allows for transitive counterparts which crucially map the sole argument of their unergative variants to the EA-position (Spec, v), e.g. *begeistern/ delight, erstaunen/astonish, entzücken/enrapture*.[36] This – along with the atelic nature shared with prototypical instances of unergatives (unlike unaccusatives) – suggests that there may also be non-agentive instances of unergatives, e.g. *brennen/burn, funktionieren/function, glühen/glow, schwitzen/sweat* and *leiden/suffer*. This ties in with the traditional habit of grouping predicates such as *lachen/laugh, husten/cough, glühen/glow*, and *glitzern/sparkle* with an unergative configuration. Potashnik (2012: 262) distinguishes Agent-unergatives (*run, march*), Experiencer-unergatives (*worry, scare*), both to be grouped with (ii) in the present classification, and emission verbs (*glow, shine*),[37] part of the class in (v) here, arguing that all map an EA to Spec, v. The latter verbs of emission arguably instantiate most clearly what the class of verbs in (v) shares: Theme-unergatives like those in (v) are "internally caused verbs" (Levin & Rappaport Hovav 1995: 92), i.e. they comprise a cause which is mapped to Spec, v despite not exhibiting agentive properties.

The English two-place unaccusatives in (vi) (e.g. *escape, suffice, lack*) feature an argument not marked for structural case in Spec, V and crucially do not

---

35 Further examples of this controversial class are the following: *behagen* ('to please'), *widerstreben* ('to jib'), *zustehen* ('to be entitled'); *auffallen* ('to strike'), *zukommen* ('to receive'), *glücken* ('to succeed'), *missraten* ('to turn out badly'), *passieren* ('to happen to').
36 It is occasionally put into question whether the unergative variants of these predicates exist at all or whether there always has to be an object, where the implicit claim is that acceptable occurrences come about via ellipsis.
37 See Levin & Rappaport Hovav (1995: 281) for numerous instances of such 'verbs of emission'.

introduce a cause (cf. Reinhart 2002: 237). Their German counterparts, on the other hand, mark their second IA, similarly introduced in Spec, V with dative case. Contrary to what is commonly expected from unaccusatives, these predicates come in two kinds depending on their verbal aktionsart. The first sub-class, consisting of predicates like *gefallen* ('appeal to') and *drohen* ('impend') features atelic verbs. The members of this class are to be distinguished from transitive Experiencer-verbs like *quälen* ('worry') (cf. Marelj 2013: 149f.).[38] Further members of this class are predicates like *einleuchten* ('be understandable') and *bevorstehen* ('be imminent'). The second sub-class shares the properties of θ-role assignment, but comprises telic verbs like *entfallen* ('escape'), *widerfahren* ('befall'), and *geschehen* ('happen'). According to Fanselow (2000; 2003) and Wegener (1998) for German, all of these Experiencer-object verbs licensing dative case may be shown to be unaccusative. This is structurally accounted for – as in (vi) – by the assumption that this class features a VP-internal nominative Th- and an Exp-argument (cf. Fadlon 2014: 26), the latter of which is also taken to be introduced VP-internally here. Reminiscent of the verbs in (i), then, this class of predicates shares the habit of doing without a functional projection v. In other words, by means of being unaccusative, the configuration in (vi) – just like the one for the prototypical unaccusatives in (i) – is taken to lack a causative ingredient (cf. Pesetsky 1995; Reinhart 2002: 237),[39] which is expected to be present in the transitive and unergative configurations in (iii), (iv) and (ii), (v), respectively. Unlike one-place unaccusatives, on the other hand, it also consists of atelic instances like *gehören* ('belong') and *entsprechen* ('resemble'), which do not feature a prototypical Exp, but rather mark possession and equivalence.[40] This shows that the neat aktionsart-based distinction of the intransitive verbs in (i), i.e. unaccusatives, and those in (ii) and (v), i.e. Ag- and Th-unergatives, does not carry over to the other classes, viz. at least not to the two-place unaccusatives in (vi) and certainly also not to the transitive predicates in (iii) (consider telic *lose* and atelic *carry*).

The classification just laid out is summarised in the table in (vii), with a special focus on verbal aktionsart (Table 1).

---

[38] This distinction may be traced back to Pesetsky's (1995) criticism of treating instances like the Italian *preoccupare* and *piacere* and their English equivalents *worry* and *appeal* as members of a single class, as proposed by Belletti & Rizzi (1988) for English and Grewendorf (1989) for German.

[39] Pesetsky (1995) points out that accusative Exp-object verbs feature a cause introduced in a position higher than Exp, whereas this is absent in two-place unaccusatives .

[40] Thus, a more fine-grained analyses is called for. See e.g. Landau (2010), where it is claimed that stative dative and accusative Exp-object verbs are unaccusative but eventive ones have an Ag or cause above their Exp.

(vii) **Table 1:** Classification of verbs

	1-place		2-place		3-place
	Unaccusative	Unergative	Two-place unaccusative	Transitive	Ditransitive
Telic	ankommen, verschwinden, schmelzen, brechen; arrive, disappear, melt, break		entgehen ('elude'), gelingen ('succeed'), unterlaufen ('occur'), entfallen ('escape'), widerfahren ('befall') (all DAT); elude, escape, befall	verlieren, erkennen, schmelzen, brechen, reparieren, bauen; lose, recognise, melt, break, repair, build	geben, kaufen, erteilen, servieren (all DAT); give, buy, grant, serve
Atelic		tanzen, schwimmen, putzen, blühen, schwitzen, begeistern; dance, swim, clean, bloom, sweat, astonish	einleuchten ('be understandable'), bevorstehen ('be imminent'), drohen ('impend'), zusagen/gefallen ('appeal to'), entsprechen ('resemble') (all DAT); resemble, suffice, lack	unterstützen, tragen, treffen, sehen, widersprechen (DAT), helfen (DAT), gedenken (GEN); support, carry, meet, see, dissent, help, commemorate	

Two remarks are in order here. The first of these concerns the structure of the table. Here, translations are only provided if a corresponding verb in the other language is not given as part of the same column. Additionally, the presence of inherent case is indicated for those individual entries that license an argument that carries it. As is well-known, this possibility is restricted to German instances since English has historically lost its dative case. The second remark is more substantial in that it concerns the association of (di-)transitive verbs into the telic and atelic columns, which is generally based on whether a given predicate is semantically associated with a sense of completion (see, e.g., Garey 1957; Krifka 1998). The situation is clear in this respect with the class of verbs that is traditionally called achievements (cf. Vendler 1967), i.e. verbs like *verlieren/ lose* which bring with them an internal endpoint. However, several of the verbs usually termed accomplishments, e.g. *bauen/build* and *reparieren/repair*, allow for atelic interpretations with plural subjects. Thus, an event like *build* is considered to be atelic in sentences like *John built houses*, whereas it is telic if its (incremental) object allows for delimitation (*John built the house*) (cf. Vendler 1967). For simplicity's sake, accomplishments are simply regarded as telic instances in the table, even though their ambivalence needs to be recognised. The remaining two kinds of Vendler's (1967) traditional distinction of verbal aktionsart, i.e. states and activities, are considerably less problematic in that they are uniformly atelic. For our purposes in the present work, it is often not necessary to resort to the specifics of Vendler's (1967) four-fold distinction but instead it typically suffices to take into consideration the telicity of a given predicate. Although this already gets us quite far (e.g. concerning auxiliary alternation), we will eventually have to resort to more fine-grained event structural considerations, most importantly whether a given predicate involves a BECOME- and/or a CAUSE-operator, for the proper determination of past participial behaviour. These issues will be addressed in Section 4, which lays out a novel approach to the identity of past participles.

The presuppositions just laid out allow us to investigate in a principled fashion the underlying question of whether passive and perfect(ive) participial forms in languages realising them homophonously are also substantially identical and hence to be treated under a single moniker, e.g. as past participles. In terms of the central tenets of the minimalist framework used in the present work, an affirmative outcome of the present investigation to a certain extent bears the potential to underline the MP's main thesis. If the two kinds of past participles turn out to be identical, they need to feature (partly abstract) information of an aspectual kind but also induce a reduction in argument structure. These components then conspire and interact with contextual properties to allow for a whole range of different readings and distributions. This is in line with the SMT and actually provides a prime example for the assumption that syntax makes the most of what it is handed by the lexicon, hence exploiting the flexibility of past participles by employing them (occasionally aided by functional elements) in quite a range of different uses. A negative outcome, on the other hand, would indicate that the lexicon is quite unrestricted in terms of storing additional information and FL allows for a high degree of (accidental) homophony even in cases in which the forms in question are arguably rather closely related.

*

Before we venture into the empirical reality of past participles, let us briefly recapitulate the main presuppositions laid out in the present chapter. As we have seen, a lot of confusion surrounds the notion of 'participle', a term that traditionally pointed to its dependent nature and was defined by its categorial indeterminacy, and its hyponym 'past participle'. While present participles are a rather coherent class, past participles functionally split up into passive and perfect(ive) participles, typically giving rise to homophonous exponents. While the two are commonly summed up under the heading of *past* participle, it is still entirely unclear whether the members of this class share information of a temporal, aspectual or diathetic nature. As a matter of fact, it is still far from settled whether there is a shared syntacticosemantic basis at all and whether passive and perfect(ive) participles are substantially different or rather turn out to be identical. The latter issue is what will principally be investigated in the present work, i.e. the main question to be answered is whether perfect(ive) and passive participles, crucially exhibiting morphological identity in Germanic and Romance, may indeed be traced back to one and the same past participial form or whether the two are merely (accidentally) homophonous. In order to properly carry out this investigation, we will mostly take into consideration empirical data from Germanic and Romance languages, the large majority of which exhibit morphological identity, although there are certain (alleged as well as substantial) exceptions to this. Such exceptions will have to be reviewed and correlated with languages regularly exhibiting substantial non-identity in the past participial domain (e.g. Slavic languages like Bulgarian). Additionally, the two kinds of past participles exhibit differences in terms of their willingness to participate in divergent realisations that arise in specific contexts. Alongside implications drawn from the historical development of past participial constructions, these data will allow us to determine whether passive and perfect(ive) participles may sensibly be taken to be substantially non-identical or have to be traced back to a single past participial element. Subsequently, previous approaches to past participial (non-)identity will be reviewed and a novel theory, based on the idea that past participles are substantially identical and bring in the suppression of an EA as well as aspectual information (defective perfectivity), will be proposed. This approach will be based on a large amount of cross-linguistic findings, but mainly be laid out for English and German, which will be discussed in detail (even though the null hypothesis is that it holds cross-linguistically). The theory used to cope with these purposes ranges within the confines of a minimalist framework which observes the basic ideas of lexicalism while acknowledging the (word-)syntactic reality of word-formation and incorporating phonological late insertion. An essential ingredient for the determination of past participial capabilities will eventually be found in the (aktionsart and event structural) properties of the underlying verb.

2 Empirical data

The current chapter will lay out the empirical groundwork for the discussion at hand by providing an overview of occurrences of past participles and several aspects particularly relevant for the issue of past participial (non-)identity. In order to do so, the present section is structured as follows. The subsequent subsection 2.1 will dive into the distinct patterns of past participial morphology from a cross-linguistic perspective and thus start the present chapter off with a short investigation of how past participial constructions are formed. Accordingly, the subchapters 2.1.1 and 2.1.2 will put a special focus on Germanic and Romance languages, while a brief (yet essential) look over the rim of the tea cup grants some insights into the properties of non-identical past participles in other, most importantly Slavic, languages in Chapter 2.1.3. Section 2.2 will be devoted to the (intertwined) distributional and categorial flexibility of past participles, and Chapter 2.3 provides some preliminary insights into auxiliary selection and its relation to the semantics of past participles. Chapter 2.4 will zoom in on past participial polymorphy by considering languages that exhibit – more as well as less substantial – distinct morphological means of realising perfect(ive) and passive participles. These are arguably quite substantial in Slavic languages like Bulgarian and the North Germanic language Swedish, but less so in contexts of participial agreement in Romance and the other North Germanic languages. Section 2.5 presents a range of morphologically divergent realisations in specific past participial contexts, which provide important insights on the inherent meaning of past participles. The final subchapter 2.6 will eventually add a diachronic perspective to the synchronic data presented before by briefly focussing on the historical development of past participles and what it may tell us about past participial (non-)identity.

2.1 Participial morphology

While a uniform (and cross-linguistically valid) theory of participles is rendered highly unlikely by their diverse grammatical properties and the various types of exponents they exhibit in different languages (cf. Wunderlich 1997: 1),[1] extensive similarities suggest that a contrastive analysis of past participles is in fact

---

[1] As Haspelmath (1994: 152f.) points out, participles commonly appear in the languages of Europe and Asia as well as (somewhat less regularly) in Africa, but rarely do they occur in languages of the Americas and Oceania. Strikingly, only languages exhibiting adjectives feature

quite fruitful. This becomes immediately obvious with Germanic and Romance languages, which encode the passive and perfect analytically and do so with the help of "the same form of the main verb, namely the past participle" (Ackema & Marelj 2012: 228). In spite of this astonishing similarity, the way of forming the past participle may differ considerably even within a given language family, as in Germanic, where English *seen* merely makes use of the suffix -*en*, while its German counterpart *gesehen* requires the additional prefix *ge*-. This allows for interesting contrastive investigations, e.g. of whether the additional morphological ingredient provides meaning or is just a semantically vacuous diachronic remnant of participle formation. In a similar vein, the forms carrying past participial morphology may have to occur with distinct auxiliaries in periphrastic uses, as observable with respect to the analytic perfect in HAVE-only languages as opposed to those showing auxiliary alternation (HAVE vs. BE). In addition to such contrastive issues, however, language-internal investigations are not to be neglected. As a matter of fact, the formal identity of past participles in Germanic and Romance should not be taken at face value as it is allegedly challenged by a variety of empirical data, e.g. the occurrence of agreement morphology on passive but not on perfect(ive) participles in Icelandic. Furthermore, it is worthwhile to consider data from languages that analytically encode passive and perfect but regularly do so with the help of morphophonologically non-identical participial forms (e.g. Slavic languages like Bulgarian and Slovenian). In addition to the two periphrastic options of expressing passive and perfect with the help of morphophonologically identical (Germanic and Romance) or distinct (Slavic) past participial forms, it is necessary to acknowledge a further instance of cross-linguistic variability. This additional possibility boils down to expressing the two concepts synthetically (i.e. with an inflected form) rather than analytically (i.e. with a periphrastic construction). Strikingly, perfect and passive are always expressed by distinct means in languages that instantiate them with synthetic forms (cf. Ackema 1999: 87f.).[2] For expository purposes, let us briefly turn to the general typological patterns of the two functions that past participles express.

Turning first to the past participle's capacity of expressing diathesis, it has repeatedly been pointed out that the passive is always marked in a morphological

---

participles, i.e. the appearance of adjectives is a necessary – yet not a sufficient – condition for exhibiting participles (cf. Haspelmath 1994: 152f.).

2 Ackema (1999: 87f.) claims that all of the languages that make use of periphrases to encode passive and perfect show morphologically identical exponents. This generalisation may be traced back to his primary focus on Germanic and Romance but does not carry over to Slavic, for instance.

way, i.e. "passive constructions without passive morphology do not exist" (Haspelmath 1990: 27; see also Abraham 2006a: 2).[3] The precise means of how the passive is cross-linguistically encoded, however, differ considerably (cf. Abraham 2006a: 5). The by far most common way of expressing the passive is by means of attaching an additional stem affix, followed in frequency by the periphrastic way of using a combination of auxiliary verb and participle (cf. Haspelmath 1990: 28). Further strategies employed by the world's languages are attaching an extra-inflectional affix (e.g. in Danish and Icelandic), exhibiting differential subject person markers or replacing stem affixes, and the use of a particle (cf. Haspelmath 1990: 28–30). What is even more surprising than the fact that synthetic passives are most common is that exhibiting a passive at all is also a relatively marginal phenomenon (cf. Haspelmath 1990: 28).[4] Furthermore, although this is not a prerequisite, most of the languages that do exhibit a passive utilise its morphological marker(s) in other functions as well (e.g. reflexive, reciprocal, anticausative and potential passive) (cf. Haspelmath 1990: 32). According to Abraham's (2006a: 1f.) correlation, for instance, passive morphology was introduced to serve information structural purposes, but has been opened up to fulfil other uses once this initial function could also be expressed by freedom of word order in German and Russian. The 'epiphenomenal' function of passive markers most important for our present purposes, of course, is that of expressing the perfect (cf. Abraham 2006b: 463).

The typological patterns of the perfect largely hinge on the specific definition that is adopted.[5] In fact, what needs to be distinguished is a 'proper' perfect (e.g. the present perfect in English) and perfective aspect (e.g. in Latin or Russian). While the perfective merely has to induce the completion of a situation, a proper perfect is supposed to exhibit a range of basic perfect readings (the universal, experiential, and resultative perfect) (cf. Pancheva 2003: 293; Mittwoch 2008: 323f.). There is the general tendency that the latter occurs periphrastically, whereas the former is realised synthetically, but this is not absolute, i.e. cases of aspectual perfectives being

---

[3] This is challenged by Dryer (1982: 54f.), who claims that languages sometimes also allow for not marking it morphosyntactically at all. This assumption strongly hinges on adopting a broad definition of 'passive', though.

[4] As Haspelmath (1990: 28) puts it, although "it is still widely believed that the unmarked case is for a language to have a passive [...] one can say that it is more likely for a language to lack a passive than to have one".

[5] As Klein (1994: 111) emphasises, "[m]any languages have an inflectional or a periphrastic verb form called 'perfect' [yet this] does not mean [...] that these forms have the same meaning". In fact, many uses of the term stem from inconsiderate application of the concept in semantically distinct contexts (cf. Lindstedt 2000: 365).

expressed periphrastically may also be found (cf. Dahl & Velupillai 2013b, c). On the other hand, it is a matter of debate whether a proper perfect may also be expressed solely synthetically (see Iatridou et al. 2001 and below for approaches that hold against this assumption). Given these observations, what is clear is that the perfect vs. perfective distinction often cannot properly be drawn along the lines of periphrastic vs. synthetic. Iatridou et al. (2001: 218fn50) still distinguish two classes of perfect formation: synthetic perfects (e.g. Classical Greek, Latin, and Turkish) and analytic/periphrastic perfects (e.g. Romance, Slavic, Germanic, Modern Greek).[6] Exponents of the latter kind, however, crucially cannot consistently be said to involve a proper perfect. What is intuitively appealing, eventually, is that the different semantics of the perfect as opposed to mere perfective marking substantially hinge on the interpretive possibilities offered by the periphrasis in question. This is suggested in Iatridou et al. (2001: 216), where the morphosyntactic composition of the analytic perfect is held responsible for the availability of a specific meaning variant of the perfect, viz. the universal perfect.[7] These possibilities are arguably closely related to the particular auxiliaries involved.

A periphrastic perfect may cross-linguistically be made up out of the combination of a main verb and a particle meaning 'already' or a construction featuring verbs meaning 'finish' or 'cast aside' (cf. Lindstedt 2000: 366f.; Bybee & Dahl 1989: 67f.). Most important for our purposes here, though, are the strategies of deriving the perfect from a possessive construction (usually formed with HAVE) and a past participle, and the combination of the latter with an element that starts out as a copula (typically BE). Strikingly, as pointed out by Benveniste (1960/1966), entertaining HAVE + past participle presupposes the possibility of BE + past participle (cf. Leiss 1992: 166f.). In other words, while there are Indo-European languages that show the combination of BE + past participle but not HAVE + past participle (e.g. Russian), there is not a single exponent of a language exhibiting HAVE + past participle but not BE + past participle (cf. Leiss 1992: 166f.). However, the latter is not necessarily perfect-forming in these languages anymore. German, Danish, French and Italian still employ both HAVE and BE for periphrastic perfects,

---

[6] According to Iatridou et al. (2001: 218fn50) we may also find covert periphrasis, where an auxiliary is incorporated into the verb form as in Tajik. This emphasises that there are additional complicating factors that even render a neat distinction into analytic and synthetic expression problematic.

[7] In fact, Iatridou et al. (2001) claim that the universal perfect may only be found in languages that are able to form a periphrastic perfect based on an imperfective participle, something we will return to below.

i.e. exhibit auxiliary alternation.⁸ English, Swedish, Spanish and Portuguese, on the other hand, only use HAVE for perfect formation, while BE is reserved for other purposes. Quite generally, a HAVE-perfect is far from common, virtually confined to Romance and Germanic, Modern Greek and Albanian (cf. Łęcki 2010: 145–147).

The auxiliary BE may not only occur in periphrastic perfects (in languages showing auxiliary alternation), but is also found as the passive auxiliary in languages like English. An alternative option is that there is a designated passive auxiliary, as observable with *werden* ('become') in German and *blive* ('become') in Danish. Languages showing auxiliary alternation but lacking a designated passive auxiliary use BE both as a passive auxiliary as well as the (unaccusative) perfect auxiliary, as for instance observable in French (cf. van den Wyngaerd 1988: 164). Beside WERDEN⁹ (e.g. in German, Danish, and Persian) and BE (e.g. in English, Russian, and Romance), we may also find the equivalents of elements corresponding interpretationally to English *get* (e.g. in Celtic and Tzeltal) and *go* (e.g. in Hindi and Persian) as passive auxiliaries (cf. Roberts 1987: 42). Anderson (2000: 813f.) finds additional passive-inducers in elements roughly equivalent to *come, suffer, receive, eat*, and the Vietnamese verbs *bi* ('suffer something unpleasant') and *duoc* ('undergo something not unpleasant').

Now that the basic typological facts and tendencies of perfects and passives and their ingredients, viz. past participles and auxiliaries, have briefly been introduced, the remainder of the present chapter will be devoted to particular instantiations of past participles and their auxiliaries. Although a primary focus will lie on Germanic and Romance languages – investigated in Chapters 2.1.1 and 2.1.2 respectively – there will also be room for a short look at some other, most importantly Slavic, languages in Chapter 2.1.3.

2.1.1 Germanic languages

While it is the most accurately researched language in the world, the first Germanic language we will turn to, namely English, is rather plain and not very insightful when it comes to its morphological realisation of past participles. The central observation here is that the passive and the perfect use of the past

---

8 Note that we will follow the common tradition of using the term 'auxiliary alternation' solely for contexts of composite tense, viz. crucially not applying it to refer to distinctions between passive auxiliaries.

9 As there is no passive-forming counterpart in English, we will resort to German *werden* ('become') when attempting to refer to its rough equivalents, thus designating these as WERDEN.

participle are both formed with -(e)n (cf. Radford et al. 2009: 137), as observable in (7).

(7) a. Rustin has seen Maggie.
b. Maggie was seen (by Rustin).

Resorting to the suffix -(e)n is just a fairly minor possibility in English, though. The only reason for calling past participles '-(e)n forms' is that it is the only strategy that is exclusive to past participles (cf. Aronoff 1994: 23fn33). In fact, the default exponent of past participial formation is identical to the past tense form -ed, which entails that *loved, kissed,* and *hated* are ambiguous between a (simple) past and past participial reading. In addition to these default cases, there are also lexically marked (or irregular) verbs, where there is a variety of options for deriving a past participle, e.g. by ablaut (*sung*) or combinations of several strategies (*broken, thought*) (cf. Aronoff 1994: 23).[10] These forms also often exhibit formal identity with their past tense alternants (cf. Kjellmer 2003: 17), although crucially not in the case of -(e)n.[11] Given the variety of morphological means to derive past participles, past participial markers cannot be said to be simply suffixal (cf. Aronoff 1994: 23f.) a nd thus the designation '-(e)n participle' is just an abstract (or generalised) way of referring to a morphological marker that may be realised in numerous ways (see, for instance, Roberts 1987: 18). Despite these internal complications, only exhibiting a designated suffix in irregular and reusing the past tense morpheme in regular cases renders the English past participial morpheme quite simple.

In terms of auxiliary selection, the English past participle is no less straightforward. While earlier stages of English still featured auxiliary alternation (cf. Radford 1997: 212), Modern English basically only shows *have* when forming the analytic perfect, whereas *be* is confined to passive cases. The passive may actually also be expressed with the help of an alternative auxiliary, i.e. *get*,[12] but

---

10 As Carstairs-McCarthy (1994: 739) points out, forms like *given* and *spoken* also differ in terms of the former apparently being derived from the simple present (**gaven*) while the latter stems from the simple past form (**speaken*). Additional, there is the possibility of zero derivation as in *cut* (cf. Carstairs-McCarthy 2005: 17).
11 Bloch (1947: 403) attempts to assign possible past participial forms to seven inflectional classes. See also Bertacca (2010: 142–144) for a list of possible morphological exponents of past participles grouped in terms of their identity with the simple past and the number of bases present in the paradigm.
12 It is questionable though, whether *get* really is an auxiliary, as it does not pass the prototypical tests of auxiliarity (cf. Wanner 2009: 17). We will mostly abstract away from *get* throughout the present work.

this apparently only has a stylistic motivation (cf. Wanner 2009: 85). The precise trigger for auxiliary insertion in English remains to be discussed, yet it is clear that one of its causes in Germanic and Romance generally is the need to introduce finiteness, i.e. while a "finite verb need not be accompanied by an auxiliary, [...] a participle cannot normally stand on its own" (Wanner 2009: 15).

While other Germanic languages like German and Dutch share with English that a morphophonologically identical participial form is employed in the periphrastic passive and perfect (cf. Abraham 2006a: 7), a major difference comes to the fore in terms of morphological realisation. As a matter of fact, both German and Dutch, in addition to the strategy of employing the suffix -(e)n, are also able and typically bound to mark the past participle by the use of the additional past participial prefix ge-. This is observable in (8) and (9) for German and Dutch, respectively.

(8) a. Rustin hat Maggie gesehen.
       Rustin has Maggie see.PTCP
       'Rustin has seen Maggie'
    b. Maggie wurde   (von Rustin) gesehen.
       Maggie became   by   Rustin see.PTCP
       'Maggie was seen (by Rustin).'

(9) a. Rustin heeft Maggie gezien.
       Rustin has   Maggie see.PTCP
       'Rustin has seen Maggie.'
    b. Maggie werd   (door Rustin) gezien.
       Maggie became by Rustin   see.PTCP
       'Maggie was seen (by Rustin).'

Reminiscent of English, German also exhibits two suffixes -*t* (regular) and -*en* (irregular), where the latter pattern may be supplemented by additional phonological changes. The major difference of German in contrast to English is that the former forms past participles "simultaneously by the prefix *ge* and the suffix *t*" (Ackerman & Webelhuth 1998: 148). While the realisation of the morphological marker *ge-* is mandatory for both regular as well as irregular forms (cf. Smolka et al. 2007: 327), it is contingent on specific phonological environments, viz. "[i]ts distribution is, without exception, prosodically conditioned" (cf. Smolka et al. 2007: 327). This can for instance be seen with participles derived from verbs that already have a prefix, e.g. **geerlebt* (vs. *erlebt* 'experienced') and those that bear final stress like **gemarschiert* (vs. *marschiert* 'marched') (cf. Wolff 1981: 3; Neubauer & Clahsen 2009: 406; Vater 2013). Nevertheless, elements without *ge-* are easily identifiable (and thus interpretable) as past participles. In fact, they behave absolutely parallel in terms of grammatical features to those that permit the prefix (cf. Struckmeier 2007: 15). This might have to be explained from a diachronic perspective, i.e. while the prefix historically bore an aspectual or temporal meaning, its modern counterpart does not exhibit such properties and only fulfils a prosodic function (cf. Struckmeier 2007: 36). This would explain why not only intra- but also cross-linguistic past participle formation without *ge-* does not induce any differences (cf. Struckmeier 2007: 16).[13] The assumption of a semantically vacuous prefix points towards parallel introduction of the two parts of past participle marking, e.g. in terms of circumfixation, since only a single function is expressed (cf. Blevins 2003: 746).

Just like in English and the other languages of modern Germanic, a given verb may not bear participial morphology and finite inflection simultaneously, i. e. participles are non-finite (cf. Ackema 1999: 141). The function of supplying finiteness is once more fulfilled by the auxiliaries. In the case of the German periphrastic perfect, there is auxiliary alternation between *haben* ('have') and *sein* ('be'), while the passive is primarily formed with *werden* ('become'). Ditransitives may also occur with *bekommen* ('receive') or *kriegen* ('get'), the latter of which merely is a colloquial variant of the former (cf. Siewierska 1984: 134). One complicating factor in this respect is that *sein* ('be') may also give rise to so-called stative passives (as opposed to eventive ones formed with *werden* 'become'), as in a *Die Armee ist besiegt* ('The army is defeated.').

The past participles in Dutch strongly resemble those of German in their morphophonological realisation as well as auxiliary selection. In terms of the latter, Dutch uses *worden* ('become') as the designated passive auxiliary, and *hebben* ('have') and *zijn* ('be') for perfect formation, although the latter also forms stative passives. While the strong morphophonological similarities allow us to skip a detailed treatment of past participial formation in Dutch, slight differences in contrast to German appear in the context of *ge-* prefixation. Whereas the distribution of *ge-* in German is governed by prosodic factors, the realisation of *ge-* in Dutch depends primarily on morphological aspects (cf. Sybesma & Vanden Wyngaerd 1997: 215f.). Therefore, Dutch *gemarcheerd* is grammatical, whereas its German counterpart **gemarschiert* (vs. *marschiert* 'marched') is not (cf. Vater 2002: 355fn1). The participial prefix is also available in the Germanic languages Afrikaans, West Flemish and Yiddish, which will not be discussed in detail here.

---

[13] This is disputed by Sybesma & Vanden Wyngaerd (1997: 209f.), who argue for Dutch (and Mandarin Chinese) that the prefix is responsible for bringing in 'realisation' of an endpoint. Note further that the so-called Infinitivus pro Participio (see Chapter 2.5.2) only occurs in languages exhibiting *ge-* (cf. Ørsnes 2008: 124–126).

Like English (and Frisian), the North Germanic languages, i.e. Swedish, Norwegian, Danish, Icelandic, and Faroese, do without a participial prefix. Nonetheless, the patterns of morphophonologically realising past participles are somewhat more elaborate in the Scandinavian languages, which deserve some special attention concerning their participial make-up as well as auxiliary selection. In terms of the latter, the perfect is formed only with HAVE in Swedish (*ha*), Icelandic (*hafa*), Faroese (*hava*), Norwegian (*har*), while Danish exhibits auxiliary alternation between HAVE and BE (*ha* and *være*) (cf. Lockwood 1977: 74f.; Thráinsson 2007: 11; Larsson 2009: 143). The passive is formed with the help of a designated auxiliary that is equivalent to German *werden* ('become'),[14] namely Swedish *bli*, Icelandic *verða*, Faroese *verða* or *blíva*, Norwegian *verte* or *bli*,[15] and Danish *blive* (cf. Lockwood 1977: 74f.; Strandskogen & Strandskogen 1995 [1986]: 39; Åfarlí 1992: 9f.).[16] Additionally, *vera* ('be') is used to form the dynamic passive in Icelandic (cf. Thráinsson 2007: 10), whereas BE gives rise to stative passives in the other Scandinavian languages.[17]

In terms of past participial morphology, the Scandinavian languages exhibit peculiarities in both the passive and the perfect. With respect to passivisation, it can be observed that alongside the canonical ways of forming a periphrastic passive with BE or WERDEN, there is a synthetic alternative. Danish, Swedish and Norwegian exhibit a synthetic passive with the extra-inflectional suffix *-s* (cf. Larsson 2009: 12) and Faroese and Icelandic form one with *-st* (cf. Lockwood 1977: 75; Haspelmath 1990: 29). The analytic and synthetic strategies of passivisation in Swedish are shown in (10), taken from Larsson (2009: 12).

(10) a. Barnen   blev   hämtade av sin   moster.
     the.children became picked.up by POSS.REFL *aunt*
     'The children were picked up by their aunt.'

---

14 We abstract away here from additional possibilities like forming the passive with an equivalent of English *get* (e.g. Swedish and Norwegian *få*) (cf. Larsson 2009: 409, Klingvall 2011: 55fn3).
15 The existence of *varda* alongside *bliva*, where the former is typically used in eventive passives, is also observable in older Swedish and certain varieties of present-day Swedish (cf. Larsson 2009: 12fn8).
16 While *verða* and *verte* clearly are equivalents of passive *werden*, *bliva*, *blíva*, *bli*, and *blive* are cognates of German *bleiben* ('remain'), which unlike the Scandinavian cases is not a proper auxiliary.
17 In fact, there is more to auxiliary selection in these languages as they allow for a range of resultative (or stative passive) constructions with BE, i.e. Swedish *vara*, Icelandic *vera*, Norwegian *være/vere*, and Faroese *vera*, some of which occasionally are close to proper BE-perfects (cf. Larsson 2015: 145f.; McFadden & Alexiadou 2010).

b. Barnen   hämtades   av sin   moster.
   the.children picked.up.PASS *by* POSS.REFL *aunt*
   'The children were picked up by their aunt.'

The possibility of synthetically deriving the passive in Scandinavian marks a property not found in any of the other (West) Germanic languages. An additional and particularly relevant peculiarity of North Germanic is to be found in terms of past participial morphology.

While all other Germanic languages exhibit past participles that are always identical in form in passive and perfect constructions (at least when these are formed periphrastically), there is a set of North Germanic languages that challenge the traditional generalisation by exhibiting shallow differences in morphology. In fact, the Scandinavian languages exclusively exhibit past participial agreement morphology in periphrases (cf. Benincà 1989: 6). This is regularly observable in Swedish and Icelandic (cf. Sigurðsson 1989: 323–325; Svenonius 2012: 2), optionally available in Danish, and also found in Norwegian, where it generally shows up in Nynorsk, but not in Bokmål (cf. Larsson 2009: 19; Klingvall 2011: 53fn2).

Whenever there is a structurally case marked subject with which it may agree, the past participle used in Icelandic BE-passives exhibits agreement morphology. This comes in the form of a suffix, namely *-s*, *-ir*, *-ir*, *-n*, *-ið*, or *-in*, following the participial marker (strong *-in* or weak *-ð*) (cf. Svenonius 2012: 1; Thráinsson 2007: 9). Past participles used in perfect contexts, on the other hand, are invariable. They come in a form identical to a singular neuter realisation and do without any additional agreement marker, i.e. they do not inflect for agreement (cf. Thráinsson 2007: 9; Svenonius 2012: 1). This is observable in (11), adapted from Thráinsson (2007: 9).

(11) a. Hundurinn   hefur   bitið   manninn.
       the.dog   has   bite.PTCP   *the.man*
       'The dog has bitten the man.'
    b. Maður   var   bitinn   af hundi.
       the.man.NOM.M.SG *was* *bite*.PTCP.M.SG *by the.dog*
       'The dog was bitten by the dog.'

Similar observations may be made in Norwegian. While past participles in dialects corresponding to Bokmål do not show agreement morphology (cf. Åfarli 2009: 168), those that correspond to Nynorsk show subject agreement in non-HAVE contexts, as observable in (12), partly adapted from Åfarli (1992: 11f.).

(12) a. Han har drept   hesten.
       he   has kill.PTCP *the.horse*
       'He has killed the horse.'
   b. Hesten   vart   drepen.
      the.horse.NOM.M.SG *became* *kill*.PTCP.M.SG
      'The horse was killed.'

The examples in (12) show that past participles in HAVE-perfects are invariable, whereas periphrastic passives formed with *verte* ('become') include past participles that overtly agree with the syntactic subject.

The data in (13), partly taken from Larsson (2009: 19f.), indicate that the situation is somewhat more complicated in Danish in two respects.

(13) a. Glassene   er   vasket/   vaskede.
       the.glas.NOM.N.PL *are* *wash*.PTCP/ *wash*.PTCP.N.PL
       'The glasses are washed.'
   b. Glassene   blev   vasket/   *vaskede.
       the.glas.NOM.N.PL *were* *wash*.PTCP/ *wash*.PTCP.N.PL
       'The glasses were washed.'
   c. Kvinderne har   vasket/   *vaskede glassene.
       the.women have washed.N.SG/ *washed*.PL *the.glasses*
       'The women have washed the glasses.'

On the one hand, it is striking that there is optionality when it comes to employing agreement in Danish (cf. Larsson 2009: 19). On the other hand, the realisation of agreement morphology is restricted to so-called stative passives like the one in (13a), but consistently ruled out in the eventive passive formed with WERDEN in (13b) and the perfect formed with HAVE in (13c). As we will see below, this difference potentially stems from the adjectival nature of the participial forms used in the resultative constructions commonly called stative passives.

Finally, Swedish presents a particularly interesting case of morphophonological non-identity with respect to the realisation of the invariant form, as observable in (14), taken from Klingvall (2011: 54).

(14) a. Boken   blev   skriven/   *skrivet   av Johanna.
       the.book.C.SG *became* *write*.PTCP.C.SG *write*.PTCP *by Johanna*
       'The book was written by Johanna.'
   b. Johanna har   skrivit   en bok.
      Johanna has   write.SUP *a book*
      'Johanna has written a book.'

Reminiscent of the other Scandinavian languages, the Swedish passive features a past participle that agrees with the surface subject in number and (in the singular) gender (cf. Larsson 2009: 19). Hence, the past participle of *skriva* ('write') in (14a) carries agreement morphology expressing the singular and common gender ('utrum'). This is once more absent in HAVE-perfect counterparts, as in (14b), where the participial form always remains invariant (cf. Platzack 1989: 305). Swedish, however, differs from any other Germanic (as well as Romance) language with respect to the morphological make-up of the invariant form. In fact, this form is not simply identical to a form (usually the neuter singular) employed in the participial paradigm, but actually marks a designated form, the so-called supine.[18] Morphologically speaking, the supine is realised with the suffix *-it* (*skrivit* 'written'), while the past participle is formed with *-et* (*skrivet* 'written') on the basis of strong verbs (cf. Klingvall 2011: 57f.). Yet this distinction is not restricted to strong verbs, but sometimes also surfaces with weak verbs in the spoken language, where "[t]he final *-t* is left out in the perfect form but retained in the past participial form" (Klingvall 2011: 58). It remains to be discussed in Chapter 2.4 below whether this morphophonological non-identity is substantial or "the supine is [just] the non-agreeing form of the past participle" (Platzack 1989: 305).

2.1.2 Romance languages

Focussing on an insightful cross-section of Romance languages, i.e. French, Italian, Spanish, Catalan, Portuguese, and Romanian, it becomes obvious that most of the basic properties are quite similar to Germanic when it comes to the realisation of past participles. These are also formed by suffixation (accompanied by an occasional stem change) and – apart from variation in terms of agreement morphology – employ identical forms to express the analytic passive[19] and the periphrastic perfect. Hence, the Italian and French examples in (15) and (16) are quite similar to those in the previous section (see Ackema 1999: 87 for similar examples).

---

18 Note that the invariant forms in the other Scandinavian (and Romance) languages are occasionally also called supines (cf. Thráinsson 2007: 9). As the situation in Swedish may turn out to be substantially different, we have to beware of such terminological fuzziness and reserve the use of the term for designated forms as in Swedish.

19 Note that we will not consider the supposedly synthetic passives of Romance, as for instance observable in the Spanish *se*-construction, as their status and qualification as real passives is far from clear (cf. Lyons 1995: 78).

(15) a. Maria ha   baciato   Gianni.
       Mary   has   kiss.PTCP John
       'Mary has kissed John.'
    b. Gianni viene   baciato   da Maria.
       John   comes[20]   kiss.PTCP   by Mary
       'John is (being) kissed by Mary.'

(16) a. Marie a   embrassé   Jean.
       Mary   has kiss.PTCP   John
       'Mary has kissed John.'
    b. Jean est embrassé par Marie.
       John is   kiss.PTCP by Mary
       'John is (being) kissed by Mary.'

Italian forms regular past participles with -*ato*, -*ito*, -*uto*, and irregular ones with -*o*, -*so*, -*sto*, -*tto* typically accompanied by changes to the verb stem (cf. Peyronel & Higgins 2006: 85f.), while French employs the regular suffixes -*é*, -*i*, or -*u* and in irregular cases resorts to -*u*, -*s*, -*t* or suppletion (cf. Hawkins 1985: 172, Bourns 2013: 67). These two languages furthermore share with their Romance relatives Occitan and Piedmontese that they resort to HAVE and BE – *avere* and *essere* in Italian as well as *avoir* and *être* in French – to form analytic perfects (cf. Lois 1990: 245). Periphrastic passives, on the other hand, are usually formed with BE (cf. Rowlett 2007: 226f.; Peyronel & Higgins 2006: 86).

In addition to the set of languages exhibiting auxiliary alternation, there are those that may be defined as HAVE-only languages, namely Spanish, Catalan, Portuguese, Romanian, and Walloon (cf. Lois 1990: 245; Muxí 1996: 138). In unison with the general Romance pattern, past participial inflection boils down to suffixation: e.g. by -*ado* and -*ido* in Spanish (cf. Pountain & Kattân-Ibarra 1997: 62), or -*at*, -*ut*, -*s*, -*t*, -*it*, -*ât* in Romanian (cf. Gönczöl-Davies 2008: 99f.). While the analytic perfect may only be formed with HAVE (*haber* in Spanish, *haver* in Catalan, *ter*/*have* in Portuguese, *avea* in Romanian), the periphrastic passive is usually realised with BE (*ser* in Spanish, *ser*/*ésser* in Catalan, *ser* in Portuguese, *fi* in Romanian) (cf. Pountain & Kattân-Ibarra 1997: 112f.; Squartini 1998: 163; Wheeler, Yates & Dols 1999: 309, 506; Lois 1990: 235f.; Hutchinson & Lloyd 1996: 95; Alkire & Rosen 2010: 276; Pană Dindelegan 2013: 226). The Catalan

---

[20] Italian primarily exhibits the auxiliary *essere* ('be') in passive contexts, but may also employ *venire* ('come') and *andare* ('go') (cf. Siewierska 1984: 134). As *essere* is ambiguous in that it also gives rise to adjectival readings (similar to the situation in German) (cf. Siewierska 1984: 134), *venire* ('come') is used here.

examples in (17), loosely based on Smith (1995: 271), provide another case in point of the formal identity of Romance past participles.

(17) a. Ella ha escrit el llibre.
    she has write.PTCP the book
    'She has written the book.'
  b. El llibre és escrit per Lucía.
    the book is write.PTCP by Lucía
    'The letter is (being) written by Lucía.'

However, the Italian, French and Catalan instances of past participles that are inflectionally identical in their uses as passive and perfect(ive) participles are not entirely representative. As a matter of fact, reminiscent of Scandinavian, the Romance languages regularly exhibit past participles carrying agreement morphology (cf. Belletti 2006: 495). The default case in Romance is that past participles that occur in a periphrastic perfect with HAVE are invariant, whereas those that occur with another auxiliary, i.e. typically BE, exhibit agreement with the surface subject. This is observable in the Spanish and Romanian examples in (18) and (19), adapted from Pountain & Kattân-Ibarra (1997: 112) and Soare (2007: 174).

(18) a. Un amigo mío ha escrito una carta.
    a friend mine has write.PTCP a letter
    'A friend of mine has written a letter.'
  b. Una carta fue escrita por un amigo mío.
    a letter.NOM.F.SG was write.PTCP.F.SG by a friend mine
    'A letter was written by a friend of mine.'

(19) a. Am cules căpșuni.
    have pick.PTCP strawberries
    'I have picked strawberries.'
  b. Căpșunile sînt culese.
    the.strawberries are picked.PTCP.PL
    'The strawberries are (being) picked.'

There is more to past participial agreement in Romance than this contrasting juxtaposition of HAVE-perfect and BE-passive, though. In fact, there are two observations to be made in this context that are particularly relevant for the present investigation. First, unlike in the North Germanic languages, past participial agreement is not restricted to passive contexts but may also occur in analytic perfect constructions formed with BE.[21] Second, a subset of the Romance languages exhibits past participial object-agreement in a restricted set of periphrastic perfects formed with HAVE. French and Italian examples of the former, i. e. agreement in the context of an analytic BE-perfect, can be found in (20) and (21), taken from Friedemann & Siloni (1997: 71).

(20) a. Johnny a ouvert/ *ouverte la porte.
       Johnny has open.PTCP/ *open*.PTCP.F.SG *the*.F.SG *door*.F.SG
       'Johnny has opened the door.'
   b. Cornelia est *arrivé/ arrivée.
       Cornelia is arrive.PTCP/ *arrive*.PTCP.F.SG
       'Cornelia has arrived.'

(21) a. Johnny ha aperto/ *aperta la porta.
       Johnny has open.PTCP/*open*. PTCP.F.SG *the*.F.SG *door*.F.SG
       'Johnny has opened the door.'
   b. Cornelia è *arrivato/ arrivata.
       Cornelia is arrive.PTCP/ *arrive*.PTCP.F.SG
       'Cornelia has arrived.'

As observed in Lois' (1990) seminal paper, the second capacity, i.e. the presence of past participial agreement in the context of HAVE, quite neatly correlates with the availability of auxiliary alternation. The languages that have just been shown to lack auxiliary alternation between HAVE and BE in periphrastic perfects, i.e. Spanish, Catalan, Portuguese, Romanian, and Walloon, accordingly never exhibit past participle agreement with their respective variant of HAVE (cf. Lois 1990: 245; Muxí 1996: 138). Those Romance languages that do, on the other hand, are the ones that feature auxiliary alternation, namely French, Italian, and Occitan (cf. Lois 1990: 245).[22] Instances of past participial agreement in the context of the HAVE-perfect may thus be found in French and Italian examples like those in (22) and (23), taken from Franco (1994: 247), Bjorkman (2011: 155) and Belletti (2006: 500).

---

[21] Note, however, that some such cases may also be found in Norwegian, which allows for a BE-perfect in certain dialects, where the past participles feature agreement morphology, as we will see in Chapter 2.4 below.

[22] Piedmontese is not mentioned here as it exhibits auxiliary alternation but does not allow for past participial object-agreement (cf. Lois 1990: 245). Lois (1990: 244) acknowledges this and points out that the availability of auxiliary alternation is a necessary, but not a sufficient condition for participial agreement with HAVE-perfects.

(22) a. Jean l'   a   peint/   peinte.
       *Jean it.F has paint.*PTCP/ *paint.*PTCP.F
       'Jean has painted it.'
   b. La maison que les filles on   peint/   peinte.
      *the house   that the girls have paint.*PTCP/ *paint.*PTCP.F
      'The house that the girls have painted.'

(23) a. Gianni l'   ha   *mangiato/ mangiata.
       *Gianni it.F has eat.*PTCP/   *eat.*PTCP.F
       'Gianni has eaten it.'
   b. I   libri   che ho   letto/   *letti.
      *the books.M that have.1.SG read.*PTCP/ *read.*PTCP.M.PL
      'The books that I have read.'

These examples show that there are two exceptional contexts in which a past participle governed by HAVE may show object-agreement: cliticised direct objects and *wh*-fronted direct objects (cf. Rowlett 2007: 226f.). This is primarily observable in the written language in French, where past participial agreement in the spoken language is typically – yet unlike in (22) – veiled behind homophony and "often neglected, i.e. the masculine form is used in contexts where a feminine form would be required in written French" (Müller et al. 2006: 82). Whereas participial agreement is thus optional in these cases in French (cf. Franco 1994: 247), things are a bit different in Italian. In fact, Italian is more strict in that participial agreement with direct object clitics is obligatory for clitics that bear 3rd person specifications, as in (23a), while optionality is observable with respect to all other person specifications (cf. Belletti 2006: 495f.). Past participial agreement is hence also observable in the context of cliticised direct objects, but absent in the context of *wh*-movement in Italian, as can be seen in (23b). This shows that the range of possibilities need not necessarily be shared by all languages generally allowing for past participial agreement in the context of HAVE.

Before concluding the present introduction of the basic aspects of Romance past participial morphology most relevant for the present work, let us briefly turn to the central ancestor of the Romance languages: Latin. This Italic language exhibits a number of interesting morphosyntactic differences that need to be taken into consideration. First of all, Latin features fully-fledged aspectual marking in terms of overtly distinguishing imperfective (capiebat, lit. seize. ipfv) and perfective (cepit, lit. seize.pfv) forms synthetically (cf. Haspelmath 2000: 656). When it comes to the passive, however, synthetic forms may only be formed with imperfective (capiebatur, lit. seize.pass.ipfv) but crucially not with perfective aspect (cf. Vincent 1987: 242). The latter is instead formed periphrastically by combining the auxiliary esse ('be') with a participial element (typically formed with -t or -s) as in captum esse (lit. seize.pass.pfv be) (cf. Haspelmath 2000: 656). The different strategies of forming the passive are repeated in the overview in (24), based on Haspelmath (2000: 656).

(24)   active   passive
      imperfective *capiebat capiebatur*
      perfective   *cepit*   *captum est*

This two-fold means of expressing voice and aspect in the passive paradigm could be referred to as a mixed system due to the fundamentally different strategies (synthesis vs. periphrasis) involved. This is unlike anything we have encountered thus far in Romance and Germanic in terms of the availability of designated (im)perfective markers and their synthetic realisation in the active as well as the imperfective passive cases. The only phenomenon remotely similar is the occurrence of synthetic passives in Scandinavian, which however is not a necessity but coexists alongside the more typical periphrastic paradigms here.

It should not be surprising that past participial agreement morphology is generally available in Latin (consider the masculine, feminine, and neuter singular cases *captus, capta, captum*, for instance). There are basically two reasons for this. First, the traditional definitions of participles stem from Ancient Greek and Latin, where they are described as exhibiting both verbal as well as adjectival properties (cf. Embick 2000: 185f.). The latter primarily boils down to exhibiting agreement morphology. Second, the Romance languages, are direct descendants of Latin and hence unanimously retained past participial agreement in the context of their respective equivalent of BE. Another property that is shared with Romance is that agreement morphology may be realised on both the auxiliary and its auxiliate, as in *Feminae captae sunt* ('The women have been seized.') as opposed to *Femina capta est* ('The woman has been seized.'). Both the past participle and the auxiliary agree with the same object here.

In order to be able to adequately investigate the question of past participial (non-)identity, we have been concerned with a brief introduction of past participial morphology and its most important properties in Germanic as well as Romance (including its central ancestor Latin) in the present chapter. As we will see in the next subsection, a brief discussion of the general properties of past participial morphology in languages outside of the realm of Romance and Germanic grants us an insightful look over the rim of our tea cup.

2.1.3 Slavic languages and beyond

There is good reason for the fact that most linguists attempt generalisations about the assumed cross-linguistic identity of past participles only with regard to Germanic and Romance and do not (explicitly) extend their claims to the effect that they are assumed to hold universally. It is first and foremost the Slavic languages that provide a number of contexts clearly ruling out such an extension.

With respect to the passive, the underlying structures found in Slavic are quite similar to the ones in Germanic and Romance in that they are periphrastically formed and consist of BE and a participial form (cf. Siewierska 1988: 245). Interesting distinctions arise, however, in that Slavic exhibits 'aspectual languages'. These overtly mark (im)perfectivity reminiscent of Latin. While there is the tendency to use a perfective verb to form a periphrastic passive, the latter may usually be formed with both aspectual options (cf. Siewierska 1988: 247). This flexibility, however, is not a necessity, as observable in Russian, which is usually taken to be restricted to forming its periphrastic passive with perfective verbs (cf. Basilico 2008: 1730; but see Borik & Gehrke to appear for some evidence against this), and Polish, which does not combine a perfective verb with the passive (cf. Siewierska 1988: 247).

Crucially, the Slavic languages are not uniform in terms of expressing the perfect. The East (e.g. Russian and Ukranian) and most of the West Slavic languages (e.g. Polish) do not exhibit a perfect auxiliary anymore,[23] but instead mark perfectivity solely synthetically (cf. Migdalski 2006: 49, 266). These are hence not very insightful for the present purposes, quite unlike their South Slavic counterparts (e.g. Bulgarian, Slovenian and Macedonian), which resort to periphrases both in the context of expressing the perfect as well as the passive. While this marks a direct correlation with Romance and Germanic, most of these relevant Slavic languages differ from exponents of the former two language families by exhibiting separate participial forms to derive the passive and the perfect. The latter is typically – yet not always, as we will see right away – made up by the so-called *l*-participle (cf. Spencer 2001: 291).[24]

First turning to those Slavic languages most similar to Romance and Germanic, let us briefly regard some Slavic exponents in which the morphological distinction between passive and perfect participles increasingly – yet to

---

[23] In general, there is a "decline of the compound tenses in East and West Slavic [which] affects both the present perfect and the pluperfect" (Migdalski 2006: 49).
[24] Reminiscent of the term '*-en* form' for past participles, this notation points to the *l*-participle's reluctance to be attributed any constant meaning, e.g. also expressing passives in some Slavic languages (cf. Spencer 2001: 311).

different degrees – converges. This is the case in Kashubian and Macedonian, which are special in terms of using HAVE to form the periphrastic perfect (cf. Migdalski 2006: 129).[25] All other Slavic languages that are able to form a composite perfect, on the other hand, only use BE (usually in the context of the *l*-participle) to derive it (cf. Migdalski 2006: 129). Whenever BE is used, the participle in question inflects for gender and number and agrees with the surface subject (cf. Spencer 2001: 291). Reminiscent of North Germanic and Romance, those that make use of HAVE, on the other hand, feature a participial form that does not show any agreement morphology (cf. Migdalski 2006: 129). This is illustrated in the Macedonian examples in (25), taken from Migdalski (2006: 136).

(25) a. Ja   imam   skinato   mojata nova košula.
   her.CL.ACC have.1.SG tear.PTCP my.the new shirt.F.SG
   'I have torn my new shirt.'
  b. Novata košula mu   e   skinata.
   new.F shirt.F.SG him.CL.DAT be.3.SG tear.PTCP.F
   'His/her new shirt is torn.'

The example in (25a) shows that the default (neuter) realisation of the past participle (typically formed with *-en/-t*) occurs in the context of *ima* ('have'), whereas past participial agreement appears on the same kind of participle in the context of *sum* ('be') in (25b) (cf. Migdalski 2006: 129–131). However, the situation in Macedonian is obscured by a number of factors. First of all, while Macedonian appears to increasingly become a HAVE-only language (cf. Migdalski 2006: 134), this process is far from complete (cf. Graves 2000: 481–484). In fact, it is also possible to form a BE-perfect by combining *sum* ('be') with a random past participle, although using the *l*-participle in such contexts is considerably restricted due to competition with the passive (cf. Graves 2000: 480–484, 493).

The only other Slavic language featuring a properly grammaticalised HAVE-perfect is Kashubian. This language presents some interesting differences, though, namely in terms of instantiating a fully-fledged auxiliary alternation (cf. Migdalski 2006: 129f.). The auxiliary *bëc* ('be') is used to form the perfect with

---

[25] Note that structures suspiciously similar to the HAVE-perfect arise in several other Slavic languages, for instance Polish, Czech, Serbian, and Bulgarian (cf. Migdalski 2006: 154–157). These, however, differ from proper HAVE-perfects in numerous regards (the participial agent need not be the same as the subject of the clause, there is object agreement, the participle may not be modified by adverbs, HAVE is not properly bleached semantically, etc.) and may actually be exposed to be stative perfects (cf. Migdalski 2006: 154–157). Hence, a grammaticalised HAVE-perfect is indeed restricted to Macedonian and Kashubian (cf. Migdalski 2006: 129).

unaccusatives, whereas *miec* ('have') is used with unergative and transitive predicates (cf. Migdalski 2006: 130). As we can see in (26), taken from Stone (2002: 777) and Migdalski (2006: 130), while agreement morphology is present on the past participle (formed with *-en/-t*) in the context of BE, it is absent with HAVE.

(26) a. Ta białka   je   precz jidzenô.
       this woman.F.SG *be*.3.SG *away go*.PTCP.F.SG
       'This woman has gone away.'
   b. Jô móm   tą   białkã   bité.
       I have.1.SG *this*.F *woman*.F.SG *beat*.PTCP
       'I have beaten this woman.'

The past participle employed in these perfect cases also surfaces in periphrastic passives and, additionally, an *l*-participle may be used in passive as well as perfect periphrases (cf. Migdalski 2006: 131f.). This suggests that participial distinctions are increasingly lost, a potential reason for which may be found in language contact with German and its use of the same type of participle in the two kinds of constructions (cf. Migdalski 2006: 132). Eventually, then, while Macedonian also comes fairly close to this (generally allowing everything but the combination of an *l*-participle with HAVE), Kashubian properly employs full interchangeability of participial forms unlike any other Slavic language (cf. Migdalski 2006: 132). Strikingly, with respect to the realisation of agreement morphology in the context of BE but not HAVE, the observable facts remain the same regardless of which participle is used.

While Macedonian and Kashubian exhibit intricate (yet insightful) properties due to their (ongoing) development of a HAVE-perfect, the situation in Bulgarian and Slovenian is fairly straightforward. They only feature the auxiliary BE (*sum* in Bulgarian, *biti* in Slovenian), which is used to derive the passive and the perfect, and distinguish between two participial forms: the *l*-participle and the 'passive' participle (formed with *-en/-t*) (cf. Pancheva 2003: 296; Marvin 2003: 141fn1). Whereas the former gives rise to the composite perfect in Bulgarian, the latter is used in passive contexts, as observable in (27), taken from Broekhuis & Migdalski (2003: 2f.).

(27) a. Paulina   e   pročela   knigata
       Paulina.F.SG *be*.3.SG *read*.PRF.PTCP.F.SG *the.book*
       'Pauline has read the book.'
   b. Knigata   e   pročetana   ot Ivan.
       the.book.F.SG *be*.3.SG *read*.PASS.PTCP.F.SG *by Ivan*
       'The book is read by Ivan.'

As we can see here, Bulgarian crucially differs from the Germanic and Romance languages in that distinct passive and perfect participial forms[26] are employed (though recall the potential exception Swedish) in the context of a single auxiliary, namely BE (cf. Migdalski 2010: 131). Furthermore, what is not equalled in any Germanic or Romance language is that the participial form, no matter which, generally agrees with its surface subject in both the analytic perfect as well as the periphrastic passive (cf. Spencer 2001: 291f.; Broekhuis & Migdalski 2003: 3).

Eventually, the distinction between perfect and passive participles must indeed be hard-coded within the participial forms (cf. Savova 1989: 68). This follows rather naturally from the fact that Bulgarian uses only one – potentially semantically vacuous and solely finiteness-inducing – auxiliary, namely BE, which cannot signal whether a passive or perfect interpretation is expressed. Accordingly, the preliminary prediction is that languages which cannot signal any difference on the basis of the auxiliary (featuring BE in all of their contexts) are bound to resort to substantial morphological non-identity. Those languages that have several auxiliaries (say HAVE, BE, WERDEN) at their disposal in the domain of the analytic passive and the periphrastic perfect, on the other hand, typically do with at least formally identical past participles.[27]

Now that the essential properties of participial morphology in Slavic have been succinctly introduced against the backdrop of differences with Germanic and Romance, let us in conclusion take into consideration two further languages to see some additional patterns of how the passive and the perfect may be expressed with the help of participial forms.

Quite closely related to the observations that pertain to Bulgarian (and other Slavic languages only featuring BE) are the properties exhibited by Modern Hebrew. This Semitic language also lacks HAVE and instead only possesses *haya* ('be'), which is used in the context of passives as well as in order to form complex tenses including the perfect. What is striking here in terms of morphology, rather reminiscent of the picture in Bulgarian, is that the participial forms entertained in complex tenses and passives do not fall together. The combination of a perfective version of *haya* ('be') and an active participle suffices to give rise to a complex tense. In order to form the passive, however, *haya* ('be') needs to be accompanied by an explicitly marked passive participle, which entails that any

---

[26] The *l*-participle forms the perfect but carries perfective (*obiknala*, lit. love.PFV.PTCP), imperfective (*običala*, lit. love.IPFV.PTCP) or neutral (*pila*, lit. drink.NEUT.PTCP) morphology (cf. Iatridou et al. 2001: 208–210).

[27] See Wegner (2017) for a preliminary discussion of the parameterisation of past participial (non-)identity.

combination of a passive participle + *haya* ('be') leads to a passive reading (cf. Friedemann & Siloni 1997: 88; Gzella 2011: 443). Additionally, imperfective uses of the passive can be formed synthetically, i.e. may do without a form of BE unless the latter is supposed to introduce perfectivity (cf. Berman 1980: 32f.). In terms of agreement, things are quite similar to Bulgarian, since both the participle and the auxiliary exhibit agreement with the surface subject (cf. Berman 1980: 25, 32; Siloni 1997: 16, 119; Friedemann & Siloni 1997: 79).

As a final case in point, let us sneak a peek at the most important exponent of the Hellenic languages. Modern Greek possesses synthetic (im)perfective marking, but still forms its perfect with έχω ('have'), which is regarded a chief influence to Macedonian's development towards a HAVE-perfect (cf. Graves 2000: 483). While this compound tense may only be derived from perfective verbs,[28] the Greek passive is formed synthetically (cf. Lindstedt 2000: 372; Iatridou et al. 2001: 220f.). This entails that Greek is not all that interesting with respect to our underlying question concerning the (non-)identity of past participles. However, Greek will recur as a point of interest due to its capacity of morphologically deriving distinct types of passives by morphologically distinct means. In fact, verbal passives are synthetically derived with the help of 'non-active' morphology, while adjectival passives are derived with the help of the auxiliary *i'me* ('be') and an element that behaves like an adjective in terms of exhibiting agreement (cf. Anagnostopoulou 2003: 7). This discrimination is one of the matters we turn to in the next section on the variety of distributions and functions of past participles.

2.2 The distributional and categorial flexibility of past participles

The distributional and categorial flexibility of past participles is virtually unequalled by any other inflectional form. While present participles actually come fairly close, the most prominent past participial capacity of occurring in passive and perfect periphrases immediately shows that the latter indeed is more flexible. As a matter of fact, elements carrying past participial morphology appear in further kinds of periphrastic constructions, pre- and postnominal positions, as part of adverbial sentential modifiers, and in the context of

---

[28] This will become important in the discussion of the analytic perfect in Chapter 4.2.3, since the absence of a perfect with imperfective morphology precludes a universal perfect interpretation (cf. Iatridou et al. 2001: 206).

(raising-)verbs demanding adjectival complements (e.g. *seem* and *remain*). It is essential to treat these different occurrences together in order to do justice to the diverse properties of past participles as a whole (cf. von Stechow 1998: 1). Thus, the present section attempts to provide a concise overview of the distinct uses of past participial forms and their basic properties. This investigation will mostly be restricted to a small set of languages since an in-depth cross-linguistic investigation would by far exceed the scope of the present chapter, which serves to lay out the empirical basis for the approach to be introduced below. Accordingly, we will primarily – though by no means exclusively – be concerned with German and English. These languages are quite suited in that they display distributional properties that largely carry over to the other Germanic and Romance languages. Additionally, they are sufficiently different in terms of the distinction between resorting to auxiliary alternation as opposed to HAVE-only.

The discussion of the distributional characteristics of past participles automatically leads us to the strongly intertwined issue of which category past participles belong to. In principle, the participial forms in the distinct configurations differ in terms of the amount of verbality as opposed to adjectivity they exhibit. Past participles occupying the prenominal position in English (*the written book*), for instance, are quite strongly pushed to the adjectival end of the spectrum, whereas those in eventive periphrastic passives (*The dog was chased by the cat.*) are clearly verbal. Such data raise the question of whether there is any substance to the claim that verbal and adjectival past participles are non-identical, i.e. derived by distinct means. This, then, instantiates a second dimension of past participial (non-)identity, namely one of a categorial kind (verbal vs. adjectival) as opposed to the issue of functional (non-)identity that the present work is primarily concerned with. A tentative answer to the former intricate issue will be provided in the last part of the current chapter.

In order to do justice to its purposes, the present chapter attempts to lay bare the distinct past participial occurrences and their categorial properties by proceeding along the lines of the following structure. The major uses of past participles will be laid out in Chapter 2.2.1 on periphrastic occurrences, 2.2.2 on adnominal uses, and 2.2.3 on additional modes of occurrence. The subsequent Section 2.2.4 will then be concerned with basic considerations of the category of past participles.

2.2.1 Periphrastic occurrences

Past participles may occur as parts of different kinds of periphrastic constructions in Germanic and Romance. Typically, yet not always, these include overtly distinct periphrasts which signal the expression of different functions. Accordingly, past participial constructions featuring HAVE express the perfect, whereas those featuring BE in English are restricted to instantiating the passive. The latter, however, is typically assumed to come in two kinds: the prototypical eventive passive and the so-called stative passive. Examples for these three basic kinds of past participial periphrases may be found in (28).

(28) a. Justin Vernon has written a song.
　　b. The song was sung by him.
　　c. The song is well-written.

Let us briefly discuss the main properties of these distinct periphrastic constructions in turn.

The combination of a past participle and the perfect auxiliary HAVE may elicit interpretationally distinct types of the perfect. The major kinds of the perfect in English (see, for instance, McCawley 1971; Comrie 1976; Binnick 1991) are summarised in (29).[29]

(29) a. He has been in love since 2010.
　　b. He has read Chomsky's *Syntactic Structures* more than once.
　　c. He has lost his key.

The example in (29a) evokes what is called the 'universal perfect' (or U-Perfect), which "conveys the meaning that the predicate holds throughout some interval stretching from a certain point in the past up to the present" (Iatridou et al. 2001: 191). In the case at hand, this entails that the situation of 'being in love' holds from the denominated point in time ('in 2010') up until the present (cf. Iatridou et al. 2001: 191). The sentence in (29b) elicits the prototypical instance of what is typically referred to as the 'experiential perfect', which assigns a certain (reiterable) experience ('reading a book') to the subject (cf. Iatridou et al. 2001: 191). This reading may in principle also be derived from (29a), where it entails that ever since the designated point in time, there was at least one interval during which the subject could be said to experience 'being in love' (cf. Iatridou et al. 2001: 191). These two kinds of perfect hence differ in terms of whether the situation holds throughout the entire interval or merely for one or several sub-intervals.

---

29 Another type is the so-called 'perfect of recent past' (or 'hot news perfect') as in *She has just arrived at home*, which will, however, not play any role in the present work (cf. Iatridou et al. 2001: 192, Rothstein 2008: 111).

What we find in (29c) is the 'perfect of result' (or 'resultative perfect'), which may only be formed on the basis of telic events and is restricted to hold only as long as the given (resultative) situation pertains (cf. Iatridou et al. 2001: 192, Mittwoch 2008: 323). This entails that we may not use (29c) as a perfect of result anymore once the object in question has been found, where the experiential reading is forced instead (cf. Iatridou et al. 2001: 192).

A dividing line is typically drawn between the U-Perfect and what is called the 'existential perfect' (or E-Perfect), which serves as a cover term including the experiential and resultative readings (cf. Iatridou et al. 2001: 192). A matter of controversy for a proper definition of the perfect is whether it has to be able to express the U-Perfect or whether it suffices for it to induce the E-Perfect readings (see Dahl & Velupillai 2013b for the latter view). Additionally, it is debatable whether the two major readings are induced merely by pragmatic differences or actually have a semantic basis (see Pancheva 2003: 280f. for an overview of previous approaches). Below, we will assume that the perfect includes a fixed set of ingredients that elicit distinct interpretations on the basis of the properties of the predicate involved as well as adverbial modification, if present (cf. Iatridou et al. 2001: 194–198).

The second prototypical use of past participles in Germanic and Romance is, of course, the eventive passive. It arises in the context of BE in languages that do not have an auxiliary exclusively reserved for eventive passives, like English in (30a), and with WERDEN in those that do, like German in (30b).

(30) a. Lester Nygaard was arrested (by Bill Oswalt).
 b. Lester Nygaard wurde   (von Bill Oswalt) festgenommen.
    *Lester Nygaard became (by   Bill Oswalt) arrest.*PTCP
    'Lester Nygaard was arrested (by Bill Oswalt).'

These cases exemplify the traditional passive function of blocking the semantic subject from being realised in subject position, although it may be introduced in the form of an agentive *by*-phrase (cf. Wanner 2009: 3).[30] Instead, the underlying object, if present, is promoted to the syntactic subject position in personal passives or the latter simply remains vacant, as is the case in the impersonal passive *Es wird getanzt* ('There is dancing.', lit. it is dance.PTCP) (cf. Rapp 1997: 124). The availability of the latter is, however, subject to cross-linguistic variation and thus available in German but not in English.

---

30 Ward et al. (2002: 1428) distinguish passives that possess an agentive *by*-phrase from those that do not by using the terms 'long passives' and 'short passives'.

2.2 The distributional and categorial flexibility of past participles — 59

These two major uses of the past participle in a HAVE-only language like English, i.e. HAVE-perfect and eventive passive, are supplemented by an additional perfect-variant in languages that show auxiliary alternation. In addition to perfect formation with HAVE, these languages form a perfect with BE, e.g. the *sein*-perfect in German in (31).

(31) Marie ist angekommen.
      Mary is arrive.PTCP
      'Mary has arrived.'

The perfect with BE may typically only be formed with unaccusatives in languages employing auxiliary alternation, where HAVE takes care of transitives and unergatives. This is particularly interesting since verbs of the former kind may usually not be passivised (cf. Rapp 1997: 125).

An additional periphrastic variant available in both English as well as German is the so-called stative passive, as in (32).

(32) a. Tywin ist geschlagen.
         Tywin is beat.PTCP
         'Tywin is beaten.'
     b. Tywin is beaten.

The stative passive attributes a property, namely a state that usually is the result of a dynamic event, to a referent (cf. Maienborn 2007: 106, Müller 1999: 291). It is generally assumed to be formed only with verbs that also allow for an eventive passive (cf. Helbig & Buscha 1970: 175). Nevertheless, clearly delineating the stative passive from the *sein*-perfect in German often turns out to be problematic (cf. Leiss 1992: 171). As a matter of fact, not all verbs partaking in the perfect formed with BE stand in complementary opposition to those in the stative passive (cf. Höhle 1978: 41–43). This is primarily observable with verbs that participate in the causative-inchoative alternation, but may also be seen with proper unaccusatives in German.[31] Hence, verbs that may occur in both

---

[31] Inchoative variants of the verbs participating in the causative alternation are also analysed as unaccusatives. However, whereas the former readily give rise to stative passives, the latter are usually exempt from these in English, unlike in German: consider *Das Mädchen ist verschwunden* (lit. the girl is disappear.PTCP), which is ambiguous between a perfect ('The girl has disappeared.') and a stative passive interpretation. Since stative passives thus do not force an agentive (implied) subject, the term is a bit of a misnomer (cf. Haider 1986: 32fn6).

constructions give rise to ambiguity (cf. Rapp 1997: 172). This is observable in (33) (cf. Wunderlich 1997: 24f.).

(33) Die Vase ist zerbrochen.
    the vase is break.PTCP
    'The vase has broken.' (perfect) vs. 'The vase is broken.' (stative passive)

Although the reality of a substantial difference is occasionally contested (see Leiss 1992: 164), the wide-spread alternative is to take it seriously. Proponents of this view usually assume that the stative passive boils down to a copular structure including an adjectival form derived from a past participle (see, amongst others, Lenz 1993; Kratzer 2000; Rapp 1997; 1998; Zimmermann 1999; Maienborn 2007: 106). This is quite unlike the *sein*-perfect, which is taken to comprise an auxiliary and a verbal participle (cf. Wunderlich 1997: 24f.). The ambiguity between a *sein*-perfect and a stative passive interpretation may for instance be resolved by adverbial modification. The *sein*-perfect allows for the adverbial modifier *schon oft* ('already often'), which reiterates the participial event (cf. Wunderlich 1997: 24f.). Stative passives, on the other hand, combine with *immer noch* ('still'), which shows that the resultative state they denote may last (cf. Thieroff 1994: 104f.).[32]

Since English also employs BE for expressing the eventive passive, ambiguity with the stative passive is wide-spread.[33] This becomes obvious in (34) on the basis of the ambiguity between the eventive passive reading in (34a) and the stative passive interpretation in (34b) (cf. Ward et al. 2002: 1436).

(34) They were married.

   a. 'They were married last week in London.'
   b. 'Hardly anyone knew that they were married – that they had been for years.'

The differentiation between a stative and an eventive passive is substantially supported by cross-linguistic data from languages like German, Dutch, and

---

[32] Additional diagnostics for the reality of this distinction may for instance be found in Maienborn (2007: 89–102).
[33] In languages with auxiliary alternation in the perfect, yet still resorting to BE for eventive as well as stative passives, ambiguity is ubiquitous. This is for instance observable in Italian: *La nave è affondata* (lit. the ship is sink.PTCP), which expresses a perfect, an eventive passive, and a stative passive (cf. Remberger 2006: 122).

Danish, where the two are distinguished by employing distinct diagnostics (cf. Wanner 2009: 19–21). As we have seen in our very brief digression to Greek, further support comes from the observation that there are languages in which eventive passives are synthetic while stative passives are analytic (cf. Anagnostopoulou 2003: 5f.). It is thus not surprising that the assumption "that the English passive participle leads a double life" (Israel et al. 2000: 104) is generally accepted.

Another periphrastic instantiation of past participial forms is provided by a sub-kind of the eventive passive, the so-called 'recipient passive' or 'dative passive' in German. This construction is identifiable on the basis of using the auxiliary *bekommen* ('receive') or *kriegen* ('get') instead of the usual eventive passive auxiliary *werden* ('become') (cf. Kathol 1994: 238f.), as in (35) (see also Müller 2007: 296).

(35) Der Junge bekommt/ kriegt die Fernbedienung weggenommen.
      the boy   receives/ gets   the remote.control take.away.PTCP
      'The boy gets the remote control taken away from him.'

The present example shows that the traditional term 'recipient passive' – stemming from prototypical cases like *Walter bekam ein Buch geschenkt* ('Walter was given a book as a present.', lit. Walter became a book give.PTCP) – does not quite fit, since it is not necessarily implied that someone receives something (cf. Müller 2007: 296). The alternative term 'dative passive' is more appropriate then, as the predicate has to be able to assign dative case in order to be able to show up in this construction (cf. Müller 2007: 298). This case is filtered out in dative passives, according to Fanselow (1987: 165).

While English due to its historical collapse of dative and accusative case does not exhibit a dative passive, a potential remnant may be found in the form of the *get*-passive, as observable in (36) (see also Wanner 2009: 86).

(36) John was/got arrested.

As this structure is virtually identical to the eventive passive formed with *be* (and hence by no means as insightful as the dative passive in German), we will simply follow Wanner (2009: 85f.) in assuming that the two are merely stylistic variants of distinct formal status.[34]

One final periphrastic formation that has to be taken into consideration is the so-called stative perfect. While stative passive constructions are cross-

---

[34] However, see König & Gast (2009: 125f.) for some additional semantic differences.

linguistically usually formed with BE, German also exhibits a stative construction in the context of HAVE, as observable in (37) (see also Hole 2002: 1).

(37) Sie hat die Augen verbunden.
      She has the eyes bandage.PTCP
   a. 'She has bandaged the eyes.'
   b. 'Her eyes are bandaged.'

While we might expect that the combination of *haben* ('have') and the past participle automatically induces a transitive perfect reading as in (37a), what we find here is the additional possibility to interpret this structure in a stative way, i.e. corresponding to (37b) (cf. Schlief 2012: 300). Abraham (1986: 105–107) leads the peculiarity of this configuration back to the alternation between *haben* ('have') as a main verb and an auxiliary, reminiscent of the copula (i.e. main verb) analysis of BE in the case of the stative passive. In a similar vein, Schlief (2012: 322f.), following and supporting Rothstein (2007), analyses the construction as a predicative structure including an adjectival participle. Such analyses are supported by the finding that this construction serves as a precursor – lacking a semantically bleached auxiliary – in the development of a HAVE-perfect (cf. Migdalski 2006: 157).[35]

As we have just seen, past participles may be realised in periphrastic (or predicative) distribution in a range of distinct configurations. A schematic overview of these different uses is provided in the representational overview in (38).

(38) prototypical perfect   prototypical passive

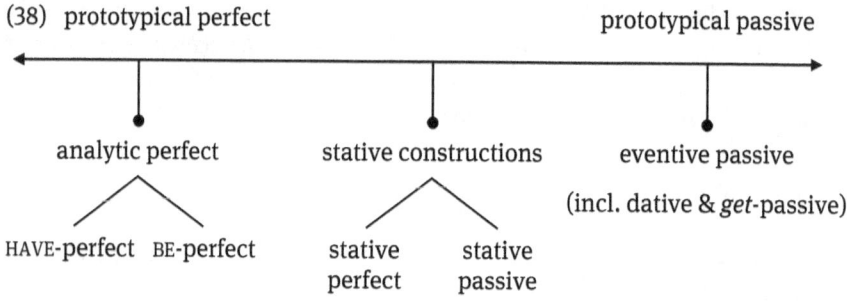

Abstracting away from shallow morphological distinctions in terms of agreement, what is striking about these periphrastic constructions in Germanic and

---

[35] Note that such constructions are also found in Latin: *Habemus oppidum obsessum* (lit. have.1.PL town.ACC.M.SG besiege.PTCP.ACC.M.SG) (cf. Hoekstra 1986a: 98).

Romance is their consistent morphological identity (cf. Müller 2002: 4f.).[36] Nevertheless, the stative configurations, on the one hand, and the eventive passive and perfect, on the other, appear to differ in terms of the category of the past participial elements involved. Before we set out to discuss such categorial issues, let us take a look at the use of past participles in adnominal distribution in the following Chapter 2.2.2 as well as additional uses in Section 2.2.3.

2.2.2 Adnominal use

In addition to their periphrastic uses, past participles also regularly appear as adjuncts in adnominal positions, i.e. as pre- or postnominal modifiers. Quite generally, periphrastic and adnominal occurrences share that they are governed locally, either by the auxiliary or copula in periphrastic instances or by the nominal expression in pre- and postnominal uses (cf. Eisenberg 1994: 86). In adnominal uses, this nominal element serves as an internal argument of the past participle, which in turn does not license but only modify it (cf. Müller 2007: 227f.).[37] What is striking here, is that not all of the readings we have seen so far in the context of periphrastic occurrences may also be evoked by (both kinds of) adnominal uses. In fact, the requirement for an independently licensed nominal entity that serves as an internal argument for the past participle makes clear that not all of the participles occurring in periphrastic constructions are also allowed to show up adnominally. Other than that, these constructions are quite flexible and hence often perceived as quite complicated (cf. von Stechow 1998: 4).

The English examples in (39) show the grammaticality of past participles derived from transitive verbs as opposed to those based on unergatives in prenominal positions. This is a consequence of the aforementioned requirement for an internal argument to be part of the semantic structure of the participles (cf. Meltzer-Asscher 2012: 178).

---

[36] Note that we will see some alleged exceptions in the distinction of stative and resultative passives in Chapter 2.4.3 below (cf. Embick 2004: 357–359). This basically boils down to the distinction between proper adjectives and deverbal adjectival participles and hence need not primarily concern us, though.

[37] The use of the term 'argument' (be it internal or external) is thus restricted here (and occasionally below) in the sense that it does not tell us anything about the properties of a given nominal expression, but rather describes how a participial element semantically relates to the referent that it modifies.

(39) a. the shaved boy
b. the (well-)written letter
c. *the slept children

The prenominal occurrences and their periphrastic counterparts are always morphophonologically identical in English, a language very poor in inflectional morphology. German, on the other hand, indicates categorial differences between the two uses since prenominal occurrences of past participles take up number and case agreement morphology, i.e. they inflect just like proper adjectives (cf. Dammel 2012: 249). This is observable in (40).

(40) a. das geschriebene Buch
the.N.NOM.SG *write*.PTCP.NOM.SG *book*.N.NOM.SG
'the written book' (or 'the book written')
b. die geschriebenen Bücher
the.N.NOM.PL *write*.PTCP.NOM.PL *book*.N.NOM.PL
'the written books' (or 'the books written')

German thus has entirely given up inflectional properties on past participles (apart from the past participial morphology itself) in periphrastic uses, while retaining them in prenominal occurrences (cf. Dammel 2012: 247). This is not unexpected given that the prenominal position is prototypically reserved for adjectival material and the past participle's use as a non-finite verb in (eventive) periphrases most strongly deviates from this (cf. Dammel 2012: 267). As we could see in North Germanic and Romance, however, this distinction does not cross-linguistically pertain, since agreement morphology need not be restricted to prenominal uses.

Although their outward appearance suggests that past participles in prenominal distribution are fully-fledged adjectival elements, their verbal heritage typically cannot be denied. Accordingly, Wunderlich (1997: 1) claims that the attributive use is "a construction in which the participle behaves as a mixed category: internally as a verb but externally as an adjective". For English, this is sometimes challenged on the basis of the past participial inability to occur with agentive *by*-phrases in prenominal positions, which need to be realised as postnominal constructions instead, as in (41) (cf. Lundquist 2013: 13f.).

(41) a. the (*by John) broken (*by John) window
b. the window broken by John

(42) a. das von John zerbrochene Fenster
the by John break.PTCP window
'the window broken by John'
b. *das Fenster zerbrochen von John
the window break.PTCP by John

The German equivalent in (42) readily allows for prenominal *by*-phrases in attributive distribution (cf. Rapp 2001: 395),[38] while postnominal occurrences are generally ruled out. Accordingly, past participles in prenominal positions cannot generally be said to forfeit their verbal properties just because they do not allow for PP-modifiers in languages like English (cf. Lundquist 2013: 13f.).

Without going into specifics, additional support for the presence of verbal characteristics retained by prenominal past participles comes from attributive occurrences like those in (43) (cf. Laskova 2007: 134; Haspelmath 1994: 162).

(43) a. the evacuated house
b. Das von seiner Mutter getragene Kind
the by it mother carry.PTCP child
'the child carried by his mother'

With respect to (43a), Laskova (2007: 134) points out that there are two readings: a stative one according to which the house is in an evacuated state, and an eventive one that entails that there was some entity evacuating the house. While this conclusion is debatable for English, the German example in (43b) expresses an ongoing event rather than a resultative state. As long as we want to take seriously the widely-acknowledged correlation between verbal and eventive, on the one hand, as well as adjectival and stative participles (cf. Haspelmath 1994: 159), on the other, the ambiguity of such occurrences provides evidence against the exclusively adjectival nature of prenominal past participles (cf. Laskova 2007: 132f.).[39]

---

38 In fact, the attributive construction may almost arbitrarily be enlarged in German, as observable in *der gestern von mir in mühevoller Arbeit geschnitzte Engel* ('the angel that was carved in laborious work by me yesterday', lit. the yesterday by me in laborious work carve.PTCP angel) (cf. Welke 2008: 128). Even combinations of a dative object and a *by*-phrase are possible: *das ihm vom Meister geputzte Fenster* ('the window that has been cleaned for him by the foreman', lit. the him by.the foreman clean.PTCP window) (cf. Wunderlich 1997: 2).
39 The flexibility in German prenominal past participles leads Wunderlich (1997: 30) to point out that "they sometimes get perfect reading, sometimes passive reading, and sometimes both".

Leaving questions of past participial category to be addressed in Chapter 2.2.4, let us briefly turn to the question of which kinds of past participles may occur in prenominal position and why. As briefly pointed out above, one of the characteristics of adnominal past participles is that they have an internal argument. Hence, while past participle formation is not subject to restrictions, formation of an attributive past participle is. The fact that the nominal referent modified by the past participle may not serve as its external argument suggests that past participles are inherently object-oriented (cf. Marillier 1994: 21). Since this is merely a formal requirement, a subject, if semantically present, may still be realised in the form of a BY-phrase (as in German), unless there are independent restrictions (as in English prenominal positions).

This inherent orientation also allows for a neat distinction of past and present participles. In German, the latter are confined to prenominal and adverbial positions (cf. Wunderlich 1997: 27), while such a restriction does not exist in English (consider *Forrest is running* vs. **Forrest ist laufend*, lit. Forrest is running). Hence, the terminology 'present participle' and 'past participle' suggests more similar properties than are actually observable (cf. Faucher 1994: 1). What both kinds of participles share, however, is that they have to semantically relate to the nominal referent that they modify in adnominal use: in the present participle, the latter serves as the external argument (if present, otherwise as the internal argument), while in the past participle, as we have seen, it is necessarily interpreted as an internal argument (cf. Gunkel 2003: 87–90). Accordingly, while the past participle is always object-oriented (cf. Marillier 1994: 21), the present participle is subject-oriented (cf. Haspelmath 1994: 164; Lübbe & Rapp 2011: 262). A fruitful correlation is that in the case of the present participle subject-orientation is tied to imperfective aspect, while the past participle's object-orientation is tied to perfective aspect (cf. Lübbe & Rapp 2011: 282). However, as we have briefly seen, a strict aspectual value of prenominal participles is challenged by eventive occurrences, which may induce an imperfective reading. Hence, whereas the present participle consistently expresses an ongoing event (cf. Weber 2002: 208), the past participle usually focusses on a result, although the latter focus may be dropped in eventive passives (cf. Gunkel 2003: 89f.). Lübbe & Rapp (2011: 269–272) attempt to account for the flexible behaviour of prenominal past participles by focussing on their event structural properties: on the basis of (homogeneous) atelic predicates, the participial perfectivity remains weak in that only one out of several (sub-)events is brought to an end, whereas (heterogeneous) telic predicates may readily be brought to an end. This accounts for why a neat aspectual distinction may not be observed for cases like *eine liebende Frau* ('a loving wife') vs. *ein geliebter Mann* ('a loved man'), where both express an ongoing process (cf. Marillier 1994: 22). This, once again, emphasises that present participles are more consistent than past participles (cf. Eisenberg 1994: 71).[40]

As we have seen, German exclusively allows for prenominal instances of past participles, which are rather restricted in English. In order to make up for this, English often resorts to postnominal occurrences. While postnominal modifiers are rather marked in Germanic, cross-linguistically they are anything but unusual, as a look at Romance languages (e.g. French and Spanish) makes clear, where they are typically more productive than their prenominal counterparts (cf. Alexiadou et al. 2007: 288). This also holds for English, where the postnominal distribution is about as flexible as the prenominal position in German and may house a large class of past participles as well as some adjectives. In fact, while the verbs that allow for postnominal occurrences are virtually the same as those that participate in prenominal uses, the class of unaccusatives is often reluctant to occur in prenominal position[41] in English, where a large range of modifiers (e.g. *by*-phrases) are principally excluded from this position. The flexibility of postnominal cases is observable in (44).

(44) a. the dog chased by the cat around the house at 12 o'clock
 b. the book bought by Alex for Anni's birthday
 c. *the boy slept in the garden

The ungrammaticality of (44c) as opposed to (44a) and (44b) once more shows the object-orientation of adnominal past participles, as induced by the necessity to be governed by a nominal element serving as an internal argument.

On the basis of the large number of characteristics shared with the prenominal occurrence, the two adnominal distributions are often assumed to stem from one and the same underlying structure. Kayne (1994) for instance claims that these structures are derived from relative clauses via extraction of either the participle and its modifiers (prenominal: [$_{DP}$ the [$_{CP}$ recently sent$_i$ [book t$_i$]]]) or the noun (postnominal: [$_{DP}$ the [$_{CP}$ book$_i$ [t$_i$ sent t$_i$ to John]]]) (cf. Sleeman 2011: 1583). In a similar vein, Cinque (1999; 2003; 2005a, b) assumes that both pre- and postnominal past participles are introduced by functional projections in the nominal domain and moved to distinct positions (cf. Sleeman 2011: 1583). We will leave the question of a unitary (see also Laskova 2007: 125f.) as opposed to a

---

[40] Wunderlich (1997: 29) puts it as follows: "[Participles I] have nothing of the Janus-face of participles II, shifting between perfect and non-perfect, between passive and non-passive, and between verbal and adjectival."
[41] This also holds for the closely related stative passives formed with unaccusatives: ??*The girl is disappeared.*

non-unitary (as for instance assumed in Sleeman 2011: 1570) analysis pending for the time being. However, let us briefly turn to whether the differences in distributional flexibility and interpretation of the pre- as opposed to the postnominal position may be traced back to the past participial forms involved. This is usually suggested by proponents of the view that prenominal uses are adjectival past participles and those in postnominal 'relative clauses' are verbal.[42] While we have already seen an argument against this, an additional point may momentarily be made against such a neat distinction. As a matter of fact, the stative vs. eventive opposition observable in pre- and postnominal past participles is mirrored by the interpretations introduced by adjectival instances, as in *the visible stars* vs. *the stars visible*. Whereas the prenominal variant attributes a permanent property to the nominal governor, its postnominal counterpart denotes a temporary property (cf. König & Gast 2009: 180). This suggests that the difference in meaning does not primarily stem from the adjectival or participial elements involved but rather is largely contingent on their constructional embedding. Accordingly, both pre- as well as postnominal occurrences are generally subject to different degrees of limitations imposed by their distribution.

This concludes our brief introduction of the general aspects of adnominal occurrences of past participles. These may be defined as bare (or auxiliaryless) participial instances that occur as nominal modifiers. Since they are introduced in the context of an independently licensed nominal element, they underlie certain restrictions, most importantly the need to involve an internal argument. These occurrences are sometimes shallowly different from periphrastic occurrences in terms of featuring adjectival morphology. Additionally, a stative character is generally attributed to certain distributions (prenominals in English), but not others (postnominals in English or prenominals in German, the latter of which are ambiguous). However, this arguably does not stem from a strict categorial difference in the past participial form (adjective vs. verb) but rather from its structural embedding. In addition to a brief attempt at their derivation in Section 4.3, we will return to such occurrences in Chapter 4.1 below, as they arguably allow for a rather unadulterated perspective on the basic properties of past participles due to the fact that they are not affected by auxiliaries. A preliminary conclusion that may for instance be drawn in this context is that "the meaning of the passive does not depend on the auxiliary *per se*" (Wanner 2009: 18). This view is shared by Wunderlich (1997: 22), who claims that in

---

[42] Note that this comes at the price of allowing bare past participles to occur in clausal functions without a finite verb (cf. Wanner 2009: 110–112). Additionally, assuming that these are verbal in nature brings with it stipulating a designated means of relating the nominal governor to the participle's internal semantic role.

contrast to perfect information, "passive should already be implemented in the participles as an option [as] it is hard to see how the attributive construction could demote an argument by itself".

2.2.3 Additional modes of occurrence

In addition to their prototypical appearance in periphrastic constructions as well as their ability to occur as pre- and postnominal attributes, past participles also show up in a quite flexible distribution, namely as adverbial (or bare[43] past participial) clauses. By virtue of containing a non-finite predicate but no finite auxiliary, these are "non-finite and hence restricted to subordinate position" (Ward et al. 2002: 1430). Besides this shared characteristic, they are less (or not at all) contingent on the local presence of a nominal referent that they may modify. In this respect, they are crucially different from periphrastic uses (where the participial form can only be introduced in the context of an auxiliary or copula) and adnominal occurrences (where the participial form can be shown to be subject to restrictions imposed by the superordinate nominal expression).

Adverbial past participial uses are typically only quite loosely integrated into a given sentential structure. Based on this distinctive characteristic, they are sometimes even terminologically distinguished from (periphrastic and adnominal) participles by calling them converbs, which are described as "verb forms used for adverbial subordination" (Haspelmath 1994: 153). In this use, it is often not at all or only quite loosely determined which entity is specified by the past participle (cf. Klein 1999: 69). Conventional examples of such adverbial uses of past participles may be found in (45) (see also Wanner 2009: 84f.).

(45) a. *Looked at from an economic perspective*, the proposal is promising.
    b. *Viewed collectively*, these findings seem to suggest ...

Such uses are primarily found in the written language, especially in academic discourse (cf. Wanner 2009: 84f.). While the examples in (45) are fairly closely related to the main clause in that its subject serves as the adverbial participle's internal argument, this is not a necessity. The examples in (46), for instance, differ from past participial instances more tightly woven into the overall clause

---

[43] The term 'bare' is employed here (and below) in order to convey that no auxiliary is around, i.e. it crucially does not tell us anything about the absence of nominal arguments, unlike in Breul & Wegner (2017: 5f.).

structure by allowing for an 'overt surface subject' (cf. Ward et al. 2002: 1430), which is bound to be instantiated by the internal argument, though.[44]

(46) a. *All things considered,* we're lucky not to have been sued for a lot more.
   b. People really are inconsiderate – *present company excepted.*
   c. *My house wrecked by a tornado* is something I don't ever want to see.
   d. *Their vehicle immobilised by the mud,* they had to escape on foot.

With respect to their argument structure, what is particularly interesting about the adverbial clauses considered so far is that all of the past participles are underlyingly passive. In fact, they either refer, i.e. directly relate, to an argument of the main clause, which they interpretively take as their internal argument, as in (45), or they explicitly realise their internal argument, as in (46). With the latter kind, a 'pertinence relation' is established to a participant in the main clause (cf. Helland & Pitz 2012: 96). Given these slight differences, Helland & Pitz (2012: 94) distinguish the two kinds of bare past participial clauses with the terms 'open adjuncts', as in (45) and 'closed adjuncts', as in (46).[45] What these crucially share is an object-orientation, reminiscent of what we could observe in adnominal uses. A subject-orientation or an active interpretation, on the other hand, is barred as the external argument may never be realised and a perfect interpretation cannot persistently be granted, as observable on the basis of the concurrency in (45). Accordingly, Bresnan (1982: 81f.fn5) reaches the conclusion that "[p]assive participles can (and often must) occur without the passive auxiliary *be*, but perfect participles never occur without *have*". This correlation becomes clearly observable in the sets of examples in (47) and (48), adopted from Urushibara (1997: 133) and Breul (2014: 465).

(47) a. (*Being*) *used* by the millions, the spelling checker has proved to be very helpful.
   b. *(*Having*) *used* a spelling checker, John was able to submit a typo-free paper.

---

[44] Similar examples may also be found in German: *Den/?der Rasen gemäht, begann er die Hecke zu schneiden* ('The lawn mowed, he began cutting the hedge.', lit. *the*.ACC/NOM *lawn mow*.PTCP, *began he the hedge to cut*).

[45] Note that examples like the one in (46c) may not properly be termed 'adjuncts' as they mark the use of an adverbial complement, rather than an adverbial adjunct clause (and hence may for instance not be omitted).

(48) a. *Eaten,* the shark does not terrify them anymore.
   b. *Having eaten,* the shark does not terrify them anymore.

As Breul (2014: 465) points out, an "auxiliaryless [instance] can only be interpreted as a passive participle; it would need an accompanying perfect auxiliary in order to be interpreted as a perfect participle".

In addition to these passive instances, unaccusative past participles are readily able to surface. This is observable in the English examples in (49), taken from Ward et al. (2002: 1429) and retrieved from the Corpus of Contemporary American English (COCA) and the British National Corpus (BNC) (see also Breul & Wegner 2017: 6f.).

(49) a. *Now fallen on hard times,* he looked a good deal older.
   b. *Returned, seconds later, to sanity,* she heard, in this order, Stevie's light cry of surprise, the mozo's reassurance, laughter, silence, a gasp, laughter again, a long silence.
   c. *Arrived at the office,* the publisher sent down for him by Laurence, the boy with spots.

Reminiscent of Lübbe & Rapp's (2011: 269–272) aspectual take on attributive past participles, these inherently telic predicates may only give rise to perfective interpretations. As expected, this carries over to the other Germanic and Romance languages, as observable with French and Norwegian in (50), adapted from Helland & Pitz (2012: 94).

(50) a. *Hjemvendt fra den glade by,* lot han bygge ei stue på
      return.PTCP from the joyous city, let he build a house at
      Bjørnstad.
      Bjørnstad
   b. *Rentré de la ville joyeuse,* il fit construiere une
      return.PTCP from the city joyous he let build a
      maison à Bjørnstad.
      house at Bjørnstad
      'Having returned from the joyous city, he had a new house built at Bjørnstad.'

Eventually, then, the properties of bare past participial clauses are quite similar to adnominal uses in terms of which verbs are allowed to occur. This is also observable with respect to the ungrammaticality of unergative cases like those in (51).

(51) a. *Slept in the garden, the boy was found by the postman.
   b. *Functioned all year, the computer suddenly didn't work anymore.

In fact, the similarities between adnominal and adverbial participles are so striking that at least open adjuncts may often readily be analysed as pre- or postposed adverbial clauses that are derived from adnominal cases. The most important difference between adnominal and adverbial instances is that the latter are more flexible with respect to not having to be introduced in the local domain of a nominal element that may serve as the participle's internal argument. In fact, as we have seen in the case of closed adjuncts (often also termed absolute clauses), the internal argument may supposedly be realised by the past participle. This stands in contrast to adnominal cases and open adjuncts, where the participial form is just semantically related to a nominal referent. Given these characteristics and its loose integration into a given clause, it is not surprising that the adverbial use is the most flexible bare participial occurrence.

A more marginal use of the past participle may be found in what Emonds (2013: 58) terms 'indirect passives', as exemplified in (52) (cf. Emonds 2013: 59).

(52) a. The players had/heard many insults [shouted at them (by irate fans)].
   b. We got/wanted the free samples [handed to us (personally)].

According to Emonds (2013: 62, 66f.), these are to be analysed as verbal passives, which may hence not only occur with *be* and *get* but also with *have, want, need, see* and *hear*. While we cannot zoom in on the specifics of this phenomenon here, it may be pointed out that the participial constructions involved strongly resemble those that act as postnominal modifiers. Crucially, the past participles in these constructions take the clause's object as their internal argument, although their other arguments can be introduced by prepositional phrases. The major difference with respect to postnominal occurrences, however, is that the participial constructions in indirect passives are required by the main verbs in question.

To put forth one final case in point for the distributional flexibility of past participles, let us turn to the occurrence of past participles as complements of *seem* and *remain*. Past participles may occur in the context of these raising verbs but are subject to particular restrictions when doing so, as observable in (53), adapted form Lundquist (2013: 14f.).

(53) a. This song seems very well-written (*by Ludovico Einaudi).
   b. The window remained broken (*by John) for many days.

Reminiscent of what we have seen in the context of stative perfects and stative passives, past participles used as complements of *seem* and *remain* may only be interpreted in a stative fashion, i.e. behave like fully-fledged adjectives (cf. Lundquist 2013: 14f.).[46] Therefore, these are regularly considered to be suitable testing grounds to uncover the properties of adjectival (as opposed to verbal) past participles.

What we could see in the discussion of bare uses of past participles is that there is no reason to assume that these differ along the lines of perfect and passive. Rather, they exhibit fairly consistent behaviour in terms of their argument structure. However, a distinction that regularly comes up in the context of bare past participial occurrences (and is often tied to the presence or absence of a resultative reading) is one between stative and eventive forms. As this is usually tied to the categorial difference between adjectival and verbal forms, we will now briefly turn to some categorial considerations in conclusion of the current chapter.

2.2.4 Questions of category

The past participial flexibility to occur in the context of auxiliaries and copulas (periphrastically), as nominal modifiers (adnominally), in adverbial clauses, as well as in other adjectival distributions (e.g. embedded under main verbs like *seem* and *remain*) is commonly taken to be tightly interwoven with issues of a categorial kind. An indeterminacy in terms of category has, as already mentioned, been one of the defining characteristics ascribed to the lexical category of participles ever since their very first grammatical descriptions (cf. Davidson 1874: 336). Once a focus on syntax was adopted (i.e. since the beginnings of structuralism with Boas 1911; Harris 1946; 1951; 1954; amongst many others), however, it was observed that past participles do not simply fall into two syntactic categories, i.e. a prototypical adjectival (attributive) and verbal (periphrastic) distribution. Rather, there is both a general tendency to assume that certain periphrastic instances (stative constructions) go back to adjectival participles and that prototypically adjectival distributions like the attributive position may also house verbal participles (cf. Lübbe & Rapp 2011: 261f.). Accordingly, Struckmeier (2007: 20f.) claims that the complex properties of participles bar a

---

46 There are further adjectival distributions in which past participles may occur, e.g. the copredicative function in *Er fährt betrunken Auto* ('He drives the car while being drunk.', lit. he drives drink.PTCP car) (cf. Dammel 2012: 247). Such cases cannot be discussed here, but appear to boil down to stative participles used as manner adverbs.

'simple' analysis according to which attributive participles are adjectives and periphrastic ones are verbs; rather, participles come in two variants both in their attributive as well as periphrastic use. Without going into specifics, the present chapter is supposed to provide a tentative answer to the question of whether there is substantial evidence for the existence of a categorial non-identity of past participle and whether it bears semantic consequences.

As indicated before, past participles are usually viewed as deverbal elements (cf. Huddleston 2002: 78). These may retain more or less of the verbal properties of their base, but never exhibit all the prototypical characteristics of the respective category: verbal participles lack typical inflectional properties like tense and person, while adjectival participles typically cannot deny their verbal heritage (cf. Lenz 1993: 63f.). How many verbal properties are retained crucially depends upon which construction the past participle in question occurs in (cf. Larsson 2009: 13f.). Quite generally, perfect participles are taken to be verbal, whereas passives are less clearly so (cf. Ross 1972: 316) and arguably split up into adjectival and verbal participles (cf. Ackema 1999: 152). The assumption that participial occurrences in the analytic perfect are verbal is usually grounded on their ability to realise all of the underlying verb's arguments and their invariant nature in the context of HAVE (cf. von Stechow 1998: 4, 16; Valentin 1994: 41f.; Migdalski 2006: 125). However, as briefly considered already, this should not be taken lightly, as there are BE-perfects (primarily in Romance), which readily take up adjectival inflection in the form of agreement morphology.[47] While the situation with respect to categorial issues is thus not as straightforward as usually assumed, clear instantiations of a difference come to the fore in the context of passive participles. These are taken to be either verbal or adjectival ever since Wasow (1977: 338–340), who assumed that the two differ in that participial formation may either happen in the lexicon or in syntax (cf. Levin & Rappaport 1986: 623). While many subsequent approaches (see, amongst others, Abney 1987; Embick 2004; Kratzer 1994; 2000; von Stechow 1995; 1996; 1998) rather traced the difference back to distinctions in internal structure (cf. Klingvall 2011: 57), the general differentiation is still regularly acknowledged. Ever since Wasow (1977: 338–340), a range of diagnostics has been used to distinguish the distinct types of past participles.[48]

---

47 Moreover, these are arguably less eventive by virtue of usually featuring unaccusative predicates, which do not include external arguments and boil down to simple anticausative changes of state (rather than complex events).

48 Note that the brief overview of some common diagnostics provided here is largely adopted from Laskova (2007: 127–132), Larsson (2009: 14–18), and Maienborn (2007: 91–96) yet definitely does not aim to be exhaustive.

2.2 The distributional and categorial flexibility of past participles

The most common semantic criterion to distinguish verbs from adjectives is to determine whether they are eventive or stative (cf. Levin & Rappaport 1986: 625; Ward et al. 2002: 1437–1439). However, a potential problem is acknowledged by Ward et al. (2002: 1437–1439) in terms of the deficiencies of correlating eventive and stative with verbal and adjectival: "adjectival and verbal passives cannot be distinguished simply by asking whether the interpretation is stative or dynamic [as] verbal passives may [well] have a stative meaning". Hence, this criterion alone is not sufficient to properly account for the differences between verbal and adjectival past participles (cf. Lundquist 2013: 19). Fortunately, in addition to this underlying semantic distinction, morphosyntactic diagnostics may be used to test for the grammaticality of an adjectival and/or verbal past participle in a particular context.

The most commonly used diagnostic for adjectival status is the combinability with the adjectival prefix *un-* (see e.g. Siegel 1973; Wasow 1977; Levin & Rappaport 1986; Bresnan 1995). This is generally based on the observation that there simply are no verbs like **untouch* or **uninhabit*, while these may easily occur in adjectival form (cf. Laskova 2007: 128).[49] Verbal status, on the other hand, is often tied to the possibility to take an adjunct BY-phrase, i.e. the ability to introduce an agent (cf. Abraham 2006b: 499). Applying these tests to the prototypical verbal and adjectival distribution in English, as in (54a-c), points to their potential value, whereas (54d) raises problems.

(54) a. Marty has (*un)seen Ledoux.
  b. The (un)seen child hid behind the counter.
  c. The child (*un)seen (by his father) hid behind the counter.
  d. Unseen by his father, the child hid behind the counter.

Whereas the adjectival prefix is illicit in the prototypically verbal HAVE-perfect in (54a) and usually not allowed in postnominal positions as in (54c), it may readily occur in the prototypically adjectival prenominal position in (54b). A strongly related means to uncover adjectival behaviour is the formation of adjectival compounds like *well-written*, *deeply-rooted* and *densely-populated*, which is also not possible with verbal participles and hence elicits similar results in (54). An agentive BY-phrase, on the other hand, is independently ruled out in active perfects like (54a) and prenominal positions like (54b), but may readily occur in postnominal positions, as in (54c). The participial distributions in (54a)

---

[49] It occurs in verbs like *untie* and *unhorse*, but clearly has a different meaning here (Ward et al. 2002: 1437). In fact, "the prefix carries the meaning of a reversal of an action, rather than negation" (Migdalski 2006: 126fn67).

and (54c) are hence properly predicted to be verbal, whereas (54b) is predicted to be adjectival. The adverbial participial clause in (54d) is problematic, though, in that it allows for both diagnostics to be applied at the same time and hence shows that these diagnostics are anything but absolute (see also Lenz 1993: 57f.; Meltzer-Asscher 2011: 819f.; Larsson 2009: 23f.).

An additional diagnostic for past participial verbality concerns the ability to realise direct objects (cf. Emonds 2000; Laskova 2007: 128).[50] Examples for employing this property as a test may be found in (55), partly adopted from Huddleston (2002: 79) and enriched by a bare participial clause and a prenominal instance from German.

(55) a. He quickly spent the money given him by his uncle.
　　 b. The lawn mowed, the gardener went home.
　　 c. Das　　dem　　　Mann　　　geschenkte　　　Buch　war sehr dick.
　　　　 the　 the.DAT　man.DAT　give.PTCP　　　 book　was very thick
　　　 'The book given to the man was very thick.'

The examples in (55a) and (55b) show that the English postnominal and adverbial uses of past participles are verbal. Furthermore, the example in (55c) shows that prenominal participles in German may additionally realise indirect objects marked for dative case, which arguably adds to the severe doubts one may have about the strictly adjectival nature of prenominal positions.

In order to isolate adjectival uses, there are various tests using adverbial modifiers, for instance the degree modifiers *more* or *most* as well as *very* and *too*, which may only be combined with adjectives (cf. Laskova 2007: 128; Ward et al. 2002: 1436). These are regularly employed to distinguish stative and eventive passives in English, as observable in (56) (see also Emonds 2006: 176; Ward et al. 2002: 1436; Huddleston 2002: 79).[51]

(56) a. *Turkey is more avoided by tourists than other countries.
　　 b. *The plants were very/too watered by the gardener.
　　 c. The boy was very frightened.
　　 d. The boy was too frightened to move.

---

[50] However, Quintin (1994: 96f.) assumes that adjectives may also take arguments. See Levin & Rappaport (1986: 656–658) and Lois (1990: 248–250) for discussions on differences between adjectival and verbal θ-role assignment.

[51] Note that the modifier *very much*, on the other hand, is taken to combine only with verbal participles, as observable in *Elizabeth was very much annoyed (by Darcy)*, taken from Huddleston (2002: 78f.).

2.2 The distributional and categorial flexibility of past participles

These examples show that an eventive passive interpretation, as suggested by the presence of the *by*-phrase in (56a-b), arguably featuring a verbal participle, may not combine with *more, very* and *too*. This is flawless with adjectival participles in stative passives, on the other hand, as in (56c-d). As these modifiers are contingent on gradability, their proper combinability entails that there is an adjectival element, whereas lack thereof does not tell us anything (cf. Ward et al. 2002: 1436; Huddleston 2002: 79).

The most obvious overt means to distinguish adjectival from verbal past participles is considering the explicit expression of agreement morphology, of course. While adjectival forms are usually expected to overtly exhibit agreement with the elements they modify, non-finite verbal forms are expected to lack overt agreement morphology.[52] Nevertheless, many Romance languages have their passive participles agree in all of their occurrences (cf. Emonds 2013: 69). This behaviour is largely shared by the North Germanic languages. Additionally, German exhibits past participial agreement only in prenominal positions (even with those clearly interpreted in an eventive fashion), but not elsewhere (cf. Emonds 2013: 69). In contrast to these intricate observations, the situation should generally be as in Danish, where passive participles in the context of the copula BE (i.e. in stative passives) show agreement, whereas those in eventive passives in the context of WERDEN do not (cf. Lundquist 2013: 29en5). Additional challenges for taking agreement as a trustworthy diagnostic stem from perfect participles. These largely behave as expected in cross-linguistically being invariant in the context of HAVE, but strangely enough also exhibit object-agreement in BE-perfects in Italian and French. Additionally, as we have seen, there are also exceptions to the invariance of past participles in the context of HAVE in Romance. The distribution of agreement morphology is thus often unexpected and definitely does not generally conform with the prediction that verbal participles (e.g. in the BE-perfect) consistently lack agreement morphology whereas adjectival participles (e.g. in stative passives) uniformly exhibit it. Rather, it is largely dependent on the specific distributional surrounding, though certainly not just in general terms like periphrastic vs. adnominal, but contingent on which kind of periphrast is used or how closely (semantically and locally) a given participle is tied to the element it modifies.

This leaves the question of whether the assumption of a substantial grammatical differentiation of verbal and adjectival past participial forms is

---

[52] Quite generally, as Emonds (2013: 68f.) points out, verbal and adjectival agreement differ in that the latter "often include[s] gender but very rarely person, while verbal agreements are the opposite".

sensible at all.[53] For our purposes here, it suffices to assume that this is indispensable by virtue of taking seriously the combinability with prototypical adjectival morphology (e.g. the prefix *un-*) as well as the necessity for certain past participles to be able to directly relate to a given nominal expression (in adnominal and stative passive cases). Hence, we will follow the proposal (see Lieber 1980; 1983; Bresnan 1982: 23f., 28–30; Levin & Rappaport 1986: 646f.; Kratzer 1994) that past participles may combine with an (empty) adjectival morpheme, which allows them to morphosyntactically behave like an adjective.[54] This, however, cannot force a purely adjectival interpretation, as many verbal properties may still shine through even in prototypically adjectival environments. This assumption is supported by the observation that past participles which occur without any disambiguating factors often give rise to ambiguity between a verbal and an adjectival reading (cf. Lenz 1993: 41).[55]

This concludes our very short discussion of the basic properties of past participial category. Most importantly, the preliminary conclusion to be kept in mind for the discussion of past participial (non-)identity is the following. When a verbal element undergoes past participial formation, it loses some of its core verbal properties (e.g. finiteness, the ability to participate in person agreement, and arguably also the capability to realise an external argument), but in return often gains some adjectival properties (e.g. the possibility to exhibit gender and number agreement). This tendency may furthermore be supported by adding adjectival morphology, which allows a participial element to directly relate to a nominal referent and grants it the freedom to take part in adjectival word-formation processes like *un-*affixation. While the presence of the latter demands a stative interpretation, this need not be the case with all 'adjectival' past participles, as for instance observable in German prenominal instances (and arguably also in English postnominal cases).

---

[53] Recall that this cannot be denied for Greek, where adjectival passives are formed analytically with BE and show agreement, while verbal participles are formed synthetically (cf. Anagnostopoulou 2003: 6f.).

[54] There are alternative approaches (see e.g. Williams 1981; Struckmeier 2007: 36f.) assuming that adjectival participles are directly derived from verbal stems (cf. Borer 1998: 89). However, as we will see in Chapter 4.3, the properties of the participial marker shine through even in adjectival instances, which challenges this.

[55] Coussé (2011: 611) claims that such cases are inherently ambiguous, as "supported by the conversational maxims of quantity that state that a contribution should only be as informative as is required to fulfill the goal of the conversation". This allows her to assume that "disambiguation [is not achieved] by means of contextual information as a categorical but rather as a gradual process" (Coussé 2011: 629f.).

Important to note in this context is that participles are not considered to be exponents of an underived (lexical) part of speech category, but rather derivative of verbs. The properties these verbal forms gain when they take up past participial morphology are subsumed under the label 'past participle'. This hence dissolves into a decisive set of formal features, rendering a designated categorial label grammatically redundant (cf. Rauh 2000a; 2000b; 2010: 144). The same holds for the addition of adjectival properties, which in principle allow for a stative interpretation, but cannot guarantee that no verbal properties are retained in interpretation. In fact, an eventive interpretation may well be regularly possible in spite of the presence of these formal properties. We will return to these intricate questions in Chapter 4.3 on bare instances of past participles and their categorial specifications.

What matters most for the discussion of past participial (non-)identity is that we may also take into consideration past participles in distributions other than their prototypical instantiations in analytic perfects and periphrastic (eventive) passives when attempting to find out about their basic properties. Of course, these occasionally have to be handled with care, though, as some of their properties potentially stem from their adjectival morphology.

2.3 Auxiliary selection and the verbal semantics of past participles

As the previous sections have shown, auxiliaries tend to play a vital role in the context of past participles. This is for instance observable in the fact that the use of a combination of the perfect auxiliary HAVE and a past participle is bound to elicit a perfect reading, whereas the German passive auxiliary *werden* ('become') in combination with a past participial form can only give rise to an (eventive) passive reading.[56] Depending on which of these two auxiliaries is used, we thus do not only get a different meaning in terms of whether or not a perfect reading is induced, but the respective difference also brings with it crucial changes for whether or not restrictions on the expression of argument structure are imposed. The precise contribution of the auxiliary in question, which may well house all or none of the relevant semantics and might even differ individually in this respect, should not be addressed before predictions about the basic meaning of past

---

56 Struckmeier (2007: 44f.) describes this by (preliminarily) associating the features [±perfective] and [±deletion of the external argument] with the distinct periphrastic constructions housing past participles.

participles have been made (see Section 4.1). What is trivially true, however, is that auxiliaries correlate with particular verbal properties. Whereas this is often quite straightforward and does not deserve much of a detailed discussion in the context of passive periphrases, the situation is different with perfect auxiliaries in languages that exhibit auxiliary alternation (HAVE vs. BE) in the composite perfect. The underlying aim of the present section therefore boils down to roughly determining which verbal properties are relevant in order to predict that a certain auxiliary surfaces in the context of a particular participial construction. Being careful not to dive in too deeply into the matter at hand, a salient issue that needs to be tackled in this context is whether auxiliary selection is cross-linguistically fixed or rather allows for parametric variation in Germanic and Romance.

While we will try not to make any specific claims about the contribution of the auxiliaries in participial constructions, a brief look at the properties generally attributed to them is worthwhile. This is mainly due to the fact that it points us to the observable differences between eventive passives formed with BE and WERDEN, on the one hand, and dative passives, on the other. Even though their specific characteristics largely remain mysterious, what is typically acknowledged is that auxiliaries differ from their main verb counterparts in terms of the semantic contribution they make, i.e. "auxiliaries typically show semantic depletion" (Anderson 2000: 813). This is for instance observable in the case of the auxiliary HAVE, which has diachronically lost its inherent meaning of possession via grammaticalisation despite arguably retaining certain argument structural properties (cf. Anderson 2000: 813; Haider 1986: 19). However, a strong sense of semantic bleaching is typically not assumed to be shared by all auxiliaries, which accordingly differ in terms of which properties of their main verb ancestors are retained. This becomes observable in the context of the (ditransitive) WERDEN-passive and the dative passive, formed with *bekommen* ('receive') or *kriegen* ('get') in German, as in (57).

(57) a. Dem   Jungen   wird   die Fernbedienung weggenommen.
       the.DAT boy.DAT   becomes   the remote.control take.away.PTCP
       'The remote control is (being) taken away from the boy.'
   b. Der   Junge   kriegt die Fernbedienung weggenommen.
       the.NOM boy.NOM   gets   the remote.control take.away.PTCP
       'The boy gets the remote control taken away from him.'

The passive auxiliary WERDEN (and BE, in languages that do not have a passive auxiliary exclusively used in this context) arguably does not have any effect on the expression of argument structure in the sense that it generally occurs in periphrastic eventive passives. These are primarily contingent on the presence of an external argument that bears a sufficient amount of Proto-Agent properties (cf. Dowty 1991), as explicated in Chapter 4.2.2 below. The auxiliaries in German dative passives crucially differ from this by virtue of exhibiting additional requirements. In fact, the auxiliaries *bekommen* ('receive') and *kriegen* ('get') arguably impose thematic restrictions that are similar to those of their main verb counterparts (cf. Haider 1986: 19; Bader & Häussler 2013: 135f.). On the one hand, the argument that is eventually realised as the nominative subject, as in (57b), thematically starts out as the argument that would otherwise be realised as a (dative) indirect object by the embedded verb, as in (57a) (cf. Haider 1986: 21).[57] On the other hand, this argument is licensed by the auxiliary, which apparently only works out if the semantics of the verbal stem are in some way compatible with the auxiliary. While this compatibility is not only granted with prototypical Recipients, as the example in (57b) emphasises, semantic restrictions are responsible for the ungrammaticality of examples like **Er bekam ein Fahrrad geklaut* (lit. he received a bicycle steal.PTCP) and **Er bekam die Lösung verschwiegen* (lit. he received the solution keep.secret.PTCP) (cf. Bader & Häussler 2013: 135). Eventually, the lexical history of the auxiliaries *bekommen* ('receive') and *kriegen* ('get') still shines through in terms of imposing semantic restrictions (cf. Bader & Häussler 2013: 137; Alexiadou, Anagnostopoulou & Sevdali 2014: 17).

Given these differences in how much semantic information is retained, setting up a clear-cut class of auxiliaries typically turns out to be problematic, which led Haider (1986: 4) to assume that there is a class in-between full verbs and auxiliaries, so-called 'parasitic verbs'. An alternative possibility is to simply entertain a rather weak definition in which only a 'certain amount' of semantic depletion is characteristic of auxiliaries (cf. Siewierska 1984: 128f.). What is generally striking is that auxiliaries are always traced back to elements that contain only a fairly small amount of semantic content. This is most clearly observable with BE, which in its main verb use as a copula only establishes a relation between a property and a subject referent as in *Andy Burrows is a musician* (cf. Maienborn 2007: 106). The case of WERDEN in German is quite similar in that it basically behaves like a copula that marks a transition when used as a main verb, as in *Sie wurde Schriftstellerin* ('She became an author.', lit. she

---

[57] An additional variant of the dative passive is formed with *erhalten* ('obtain'). Rapp (1997: 119) also mentions *gehören* ('belong') as a semantically contentful auxiliary in German, as in *Sie gehört (von ihren Eltern) hinausgeworfen* ('She needs to be thrown out by her parents.', lit. she belongs by her parents throw.out.PTCP). König & Gast (2009: 131) call this type of passive auxiliary 'modal passive' and point to its use in prohibitive contexts in legal language. We will abstract away from such specialised instances here.

became author). In a similar vein, HAVE just marks possession, yet this is often present only in a weak sense, rendering HAVE compatible with a wide range of complements (cf. Cowper 1989b: 86f.). With *bekommen* ('receive') and *kriegen* ('get'), as we have just seen, things are different in that the meaning of receiving something is often still present, even though (57b) shows that its use as an auxiliary has already been widened considerably.

Unlike HAVE-only languages like English and Spanish, languages exhibiting auxiliary alternation, e.g. German and Italian, provide interesting insights concerning the selection of auxiliaries when forming the analytic perfect, as observable in (58) from German.

(58) a. Marty ist angekommen.
       Marty is arrive.PTCP
       'Marty has arrived.'
   b. Marty hat getanzt.
      Marty has dance.PTCP
      'Marty has danced.'

The auxiliary selection of HAVE or BE in these cases is usually taken to be primarily contingent on the argument structure of the underlying verb. As Bjorkman (2011: 147) puts it, "auxiliary selection generally tracks *argument structure*: transitive and unergative predicates select HAVE, while unaccusative (and passive) predicates select BE". This behaviour is often traced back to the main verb counterparts of these auxiliaries: HAVE is assumed to be inherently transitive due to its possessive main verb heritage (cf. Roberts 1984: 218f.),[58] whereas BE (just like its copular counterpart) is inherently unaccusative[59] and may hence only realise a single argument by virtue of being unable to assign accusative case (cf. Haider 1984: 28–30).

An approach to auxiliary alternation that exclusively relies on argument structure, however, has to face some grave challenges in the context of intransitive verbs. This becomes observable in the context of German examples like the one in (59).

(59) Ich *habe/bin (nach Hause) gerannt.
     I   have/am to   home run.PTCP
     'I have run (home).'

---

[58] See Hale & Keyser (1993: 54f.) for an account of why unergatives pattern with transitives.
[59] Consider default case assignment in copular cases like *Er ist ein Student* ('He is a student.', lit. he is a.NOM student.NOM), where structural (accusative) case may not be assigned (cf. Schütze 2001: 224; Breul 2008: 240f.).

The verb *rennen* ('run') in (59) – despite being expected to be unergative – consistently occurs with BE, which marks an exceptional behaviour shared by verbs of (manner of) motion (cf. Müller 1999: 307f.). The same behaviour carries over to verbs like *gehen* ('walk'), *laufen* ('walk'), *marschieren* ('march'), *fahren* ('drive'), *fliegen* ('fly'), *springen* ('jump'), and *stiefeln* ('walk steadily') (cf. Gillmann 2011: 213f.; Pollard 1994: 281).

While the cases just mentioned consistently take BE in all of their uses and regardless of whether an endpoint is overtly realised (e.g. as a directional PP), there are also (manner of) motion verbs that alternate between BE and HAVE depending on their contextual embedding.

(60) a. Rory hat/*ist getanzt.
       Rory has/is   dance.PTCP
       'Rory has danced.'
    b. Rory *hat/ist in   den Raum getanzt.
       Rory has/is   into the room dance.PTCP
       'Rory has danced into the room.'

As observable in the German examples in (60), the past participle of *tanzen* ('dance') takes HAVE in the absence of an endpoint, whereas it is forced to take BE when denoting a directed motion, i.e. in the context of a directional modifier (cf. Kathol 1991: 122f.).[60] Accordingly, as Ackema (1999: 111) puts it, these "unergative verbs show unaccusative behaviour when accompanied by a directional prepositional or adverbial predicate".

Something similar may for instance be seen in the context of *schwimmen* ('swim'), *klettern* ('climb'), and *joggen* ('jog'), which differ in terms of also allowing BE in the unmodified case, though (cf. Teuber 2005: 176f.; Gillmann 2011: 213). The use of HAVE, however, is only possible if an activity-reading is to be effected, where the motion is inherently 'undirected'.

(61) a. Rory hat/ist geschwommen.
       Rory has/is swim.PTCP
       'Rory has swum.'

---

[60] We will remain agnostic about the direction of auxiliary selection in the present chapter, leaving this matter for the formal treatment in Chapter 4.2. The traditional assumption (see Bech 1983 [1955]: 15f., 25; Gunkel 2003: 66) holds that the participial form is governed by the auxiliary, whereas more recent proposals question this (see Wurmbrand 2012a, where there is room for parametric variation concerning which element values which).

b. Rory *hat/ist zum Beckenrand geschwommen.
   *Rory has/is to.the pool.edge swim.*PTCP
   'Rory has swum to the pool edge.'

Teuber (2005: 176f.) with regard to ambivalent cases like the one in (61a) sees auxiliary alternation as depending on whether the process is focussed, in which case we get an atelic reading and a tendency towards using HAVE, or whether there is a change in position, which means that telicity is induced and we tend towards using BE (cf. Gillmann 2011: 213).

In general, the exceptional class of (manner of) motion verbs in German comes in three kinds: BE-only cases as in (59); using BE when there is an endpoint and HAVE elsewhere as in (60); and HAVE + BE, where the latter is the only option in cases with an overt endpoint, as in (61). Such intricate properties are usually attempted to be grasped by means of resorting to terminativity or telicity, i.e. aktionsart properties (see for instance den Dikken 1994: 77), in languages like German, Dutch, Italian, and French (cf. Sorace 2000: 875–878). Teuber (2005: 176f.), for instance, ascribes the feature [+term] to (inherently unergative) intransitive verbs like the one in (59). Wunderlich (1997: 13) formalises this by means of the (arbitrary) feature [+perf], which is assigned to all intransitive verbs that select *sein* ('be') (cf. Wunderlich 1997: 4). Something similar is also observable in Abraham (1986: 111–113), where auxiliary selection is tied to mutativity, which boils down to distinguishing non-terminative (durative) from terminative (mutative) verbs. The BE-only class is thus primarily accounted for by means of lexicalisation in terms of grammatical features being conventionally associated with the predicates in question in these approaches.

Assigning a designated feature autonomously signalling the inherent telicity of a given verb might be desirable with verbs like *rennen* ('run') and *gehen* ('walk') that invariably select BE, but does not account for the variable behaviour in cases like *tanzen* ('dance') in (60). With these, specific contextual factors have to be held responsible, i.e. they switch between HAVE- and BE-selection by virtue of being "sensitiv[e] to features that telicise the predicate" (Sorace 2000: 875). Languages that show auxiliary alternation differ in terms of how systematically this sensitivity is observed. Dutch, for instance, systematically employs *zijn* ('be') rather than *hebben* ('have') in any context telicised by a directional modifier, while Italian only shows the shift in auxiliary selection with a subset of manner of motion verbs and French does not shift the auxiliary in such contexts at all and thus unanimously sticks with *avoir* ('have') (cf. Sorace 2000: 875). This shows that auxiliary selection – despite generally being stable cross-linguistically – exhibits an extensive degree of parametric variation in the context of unergative predicates.

The class of verbs like *schwimmen* ('swim') in (61) ranges between the two extremes in that the exponents come in two kinds: the regular unergative case that is insensitive to directional modification as opposed to the lexicalised directed motion as mirrored by the examples in (59). Accordingly, these arguably are subject to homonymy and potentially indicate that a proper lexicalisation is not yet complete.[61]

Semantically, the close relation between telicised unergatives and unaccusatives is actually not entirely unexpected, since both bring with them a 'resultative subsituation' (cf. Bjerre & Bjerre 2007: 49). While certain languages (e.g. Dutch) consistently obey this correlation, others (e.g. French) do not observe it at all. German (like Italian), although typically following this correlation, additionally has lexicalised a range of these verbs to the effect that they do not need the result to be overtly brought in anymore. Here, BE is employed without there being any explicit telicisation, something that is illicit in Dutch (cf. Sorace 2000: 875). In other words, the latter class behaves in an irregular fashion, while those manner of motion verbs overtly modified by a directional phrase at least partly act according to rule. Accordingly, in addition to our general account based on argument structure and aktionsart properties occasionally cropping up, we need to leave some room for lexicalisation. Eventually, then, as Wunderlich (1997: 12) puts it, "[t]he selection of *sein* is partly semantically based, but partly also lexicalized in unpredictable ways".[62] Gillmann (2011: 227) assumes that this lexicalisation may well be predicted in terms of the frequency of use of a given verb in a telic context, according to which motion verbs regularly used in a directional way tend to undergo lexicalisation. This is clearly the case with *laufen* ('walk') and *rennen* ('run'), as in (59), which are typically directed towards some goal. On the other hand, those verbs that are rarely used in a telic context as *joggen* ('jog') and *tanzen* ('dance'), as in (60), have not been influenced by such a lexicalisation (cf. Gillmann 2011: 227). An additional factor might be the normative influence of using BE with verbs of motion, which might motivate extensions to other contexts as well.[63]

---

[61] What is striking is that the three classes of (manner of) motion verbs apparently behave alike in bare uses. As the following cases of a German prenominal construction make clear, the occurrence of a directional modifier is required regardless of the extent of lexicalisation: *das *(zum Ausgang) gerannte/getanzte/geschwommene Mädchen* (lit. the to.the exit run.PTCP/dance. PTCP/swim.PTCP girl).

[62] The same point is made by Kathol (1991: 122f.): "German auxiliary selection is not fully reducible to semantic properties but has to a certain extent been lexicalized and no longer serves to necessarily indicate semantic distinctions".

[63] Evidence for the rather cumbersome nature of auxiliary selection in the context of unergatives may not only be found synchronically in the large amount of dialectal variation, but also

An additional case exemplifying the importance of aktionsart in the context of auxiliary alternation may be found in the telic and atelic two-place unaccusatives like the German ones in (62).

(62) a. Das Kleid hat ihr gefallen.
   the dress has her appeal.to.PTCP
   'The dress has appealed to her.'
 b. Die Lösung ist ihm entfallen.
   the solution is him escape.PTCP
   'The solution has escaped him.' (or 'He has forgotten the solution.')

The selection of HAVE or BE in the context of such two-place unaccusatives may not be traced back to a difference in terms of whether an external argument is around, but rather stems solely from a difference in terms of telicity. While HAVE is selected in case the predicate is atelic, as in (62a), BE occurs in telic changes of state like (62b).

The shallow overview laid out in the current chapter has shown that auxiliary selection largely correlates with the argument structural properties of the verbal stem, which need to be compatible with the (remnant) properties of the selected (or selecting) auxiliary. This usually suffices to account for why the auxiliaries BE and WERDEN only go together with predicates that realise an internal argument. In the case of BE this is not only observable in passive occurrences, where the external argument has been suppressed, but also with unaccusatives in languages employing auxiliary alternation in the composite perfect. The perfect auxiliary HAVE, on the other hand, occurs in the context of (di-)transitive and unergative predicates, i.e. arguments introducing an external argument. However, as was just pointed out in the context of auxiliary alternation, argument structure alone is often not sufficient to properly predict auxiliary selection. Rather, more fine-grained event structural properties usually pertaining to the aktionsart of the verbal phrase have to be taken into consideration as well. This becomes obvious on the basis of different kinds of two-place unaccusatives as well as, even more importantly, the intricate properties exhibited by (manner of) motion verbs.[64]

---

diachronically in that the matter of which auxiliary to use with unergatives is usually quite a late one grammaticalisation-wise, as we will see below.

64 In addition to the 'exceptional' (manner of) motion verbs, something similar may be found in southern varieties of German, where verbs of (maintenance of) position like *sitzen* ('sit'), *stehen* ('stand'), and *liegen* ('lie') occur with BE in periphrastic perfects (cf. Gillmann 2015: 341). Just like in the case of (manner of) motion predicates, this is unexpected since these predicates are

While we will postpone the evaluation of the precise consequences for the basic contribution of past participial morphology, what is undeniably clear is that the semantic properties of the verbal stem play an essential role with regard to the behaviour of past participial forms. The relevant dimensions that we will have to consider are argument structure, on the one hand, and event structure (or aktionsart), on the other. With respect to the former, the most important aspect of difference is whether a given predicate comprises an external argument (transitive, unergative) or not (unaccusative). The latter, on the other hand, appears to relate primarily to telicity, although more-fine grained properties like the presence of a simple change of state will in fact turn out to rather be what we are after.[65] These observations will be revisited and discussed in some more detail in Section 4.1 on the basic meaning of past participles.

2.4 Past participial polymorphy

The empirical data considered in Chapter 2.1 laid bare that the morphophonological identity of passive and perfect participles attested in Germanic and Romance does not necessarily carry over to other languages. Clear instances of exceptions are provided by Slavic languages like Bulgarian and Slovenian, which make a substantial morphophonological distinction between perfect and passive participles despite also forming the two periphrastically. This shallow non-identity in the context of two kinds of periphrases that resort to one and the

---

unergative. However, what is striking is that these are homophonous in southern varieties (unlike in standard and northern varieties) between an atelic reading in which a position is maintained and an inchoative one in which the referent moves into this position (cf. Kaufmann 1995: 409f.). Hence, *Ich bin gesessen* (lit. I am sit.PTCP) is ambiguous between 'I have sat' and 'I have sat down', where BE-selection has apparently been generalised from inchoative to atelic variants (cf. Diedrichsen 2002: 44). This might lexically be instated by associating an endpoint with a maintenance of position, which allows the argument to be conceptualised as a Proto-Patient, in analogy with (manner of) motion verbs.

65 This criterion appears to be challenged by durative predicates like *bleiben* ('remain') and *sein* ('be'). These may in fact be conceptualised as changes of state, though: the former denotes a change between two identical states (cf. Strobel 2007: 109) and the latter marks a change of state by virtue of attributing a property to a referent. Additionally, there are idiosyncratic cases like *ausschlafen* ('sleep in') and *abnehmen* ('decrease'), which appear to denote a change of state but nevertheless go with HAVE, supposedly since the auxiliary selection is idiosyncratically determined by the underlying verb and not its (telic) particle (cf. Strobel 2007: 114). As Strobel (2007) shows on the basis of quantitative considerations, such exceptions are extremely rare in German.

same auxiliary, namely BE, is arguably mirrored by substantial syntacticosemantic non-identity. Yet, we need not move away from the language families that we are primarily interested in, namely Germanic and Romance, to find potential cases of substantial non-identity. In fact, Swedish – in spite of possessing the perfect auxiliary HAVE and thus principally distinguishing perfect and passive periphrases by employing distinct auxiliaries – also uses a participial marker for perfect(ive) participles that is morphologically distinct from the one used in passive periphrases. This form is commonly referred to under the heading of the designation 'supine'. While this term is often applied to invariant (i.e. nonagreeing) participial forms, in Swedish things are different in that supines are not part of the participial paradigm. Such issues will be discussed in Section 2.4.1, which is thus devoted to the substantial non-identity that rather clearly manifests itself in Slavic, but may potentially also be found in Swedish (see Wegner 2017). This discussion of the properties of languages potentially exhibiting substantial non-identity arguably provides important clues regarding the question of whether the morphophonological past participial identity in Germanic (with the potential exception of Swedish) and Romance is likely to be mirrored by substantial syntacticosemantic identity.

An important ingredient for the determination of the latter furthermore is to consider potential language-internal exceptions to the observable shallow identity in Germanic and Romance, namely the occurrence of agreement morphology. This boils down to answering the underlying question of whether the appearance of agreement morphology challenges the assumption of past participial identity. Participial agreement arises in Romance but is also regularly attested in North Germanic, as we have briefly seen in Chapter 2.1. As briefly hinted at before, the essential observation in this context is that the occurrence of agreement morphology is not tied to a principled dissection between perfect and passive, but rather is contingent on particular properties of the morphosyntactic configuration. These and corresponding issues will be addressed in Chapter 2.4.2, which thus shifts the focus to the realisation of cross-linguistic occurrences of past participial agreement.

Additionally, there are more subtle morphological distinctions in the domain of past participles, which will briefly be discussed in Chapter 2.4.3. These, however, do not deserve much attention in the present work as they relate to the difference between adjectival and verbal instances (consider the case of *rotten* vs. *rotted*, for instance) rather than splitting up into perfect(ive) and passive participles.

2.4.1 Morphological distinctions and substantial non-identity

Languages that encode both the passive and the perfect synthetically are universally subject to substantial non-identity, i.e. never employ the same form to express both functions (cf. Ackema 1999: 87f.). Focussing on the periphrastic formation of past participial constructions instead and thus also leaving aside somewhat mixed cases like Latin,[66] interesting exponents of languages making a principled distinction between perfect and passive participles can be found in Slavic. As we could already see in Chapter 2.1.3 with respect to the example repeated here as (63), Bulgarian makes a morphological distinction between the *l*-participle used to express the composite perfect and a designated passive participle.

(63) a. Paulina   e   pročela   knigata
        Paulina.F.SG be.3.SG read.PRF.PTCP.F.SG the.book
        'Pauline has read the book.'
    b. Knigata   e   pročetana   ot Ivan.
        the.book.F.SG be.3.SG read.PASS.PTCP.F.SG by Ivan
        'The book is (being) read by Ivan.'

Crucially, the auxiliary consistently employed in the expression of both diathesis and composite tense is BE.[67] Since the distinction between the two participial constructions has to be signalled in one way or another, yet cannot be derived from the auxiliary in Bulgarian, it actually follows logically that a principled morphological distinction is made on the participial forms. In fact, given these findings, it would be quite a stretch to assume that the *l*-participle and the passive participle are syntacticosemantically identical. Rather, it is fairly safe to claim that the two forms are substantially non-identical (cf. Savova 1989: 68). The auxiliary, on the other hand, apparently does not bring in any additional meaning in Bulgarian and is primarily responsible for the expression of finiteness.

The assumption of a substantial non-identity in Bulgarian finds support in the observation that bare uses of the *l*-participle are able to express a fully-fledged active perfect (cf. Iatridou et al. 2001: 218f.). This is for instance

---

[66] Recall that Latin synthetically encodes passive and perfective information, whereas the combination of the two can only be instantiated periphrastically.
[67] As we have seen, a combination of HAVE and the *l*-participle is possible, but merely elicits the stative perfect, which lacks a range of properties characteristically associated with a proper perfect (cf. Migdalski 2006: 154–157).

observable in postnominal occurrences, whereas it is ruled out in all of the languages that possess formally identical past participial morphology, as observable in the comparison in (64), based on Iatridou et al. (2001: 218).

(64) a. Zapoznah se sûs ženata pročela knigata.
   met.1.SG REFL with the.woman read.PRF.PTCP.F.SG the.book
   'I met the woman who has read the book.'
   b. I saw the boy *(who has) eaten the fish.

The English postnominal use in (64b) demands an object-orientation (*the fish eaten by the boy*) and may only denote either a result or concurrency. Its Bulgarian counterpart in (64a), on the other hand, shows subject-orientation and conveys a proper (present) perfect interpretation (cf. Marvin 2003: 145, 148).[68] As a matter of fact, Marvin (2003: 146f.) points out that "[i]n Bulgarian, all aspects of the Perfect meaning that are available in full clauses are also available" in such bare cases.[69]

As we could see with respect to Macedonian and Kashubian, the grammaticalisation of a HAVE-perfect apparently has quite an effect on the expression of non-identity. In fact, these Slavic languages have increasingly lost their morphological distinctions of a designated passive as opposed to a perfect participle and may already employ one and the same form to express the two functions in the context of HAVE and BE (cf. Migdalski 2006: 132). These findings might be taken to suggest the following correlation: whenever a distinction between a perfect and a passive interpretation is expressed on the basis of distinct auxiliaries (e.g. HAVE and BE), the past participial forms are (at least morphologically) identical (cf. Wegner 2017: 21). Abstracting away from supposedly shallow distinctions like those concerning the expression of agreement, there is one language in Germanic, however, that appears to challenge this claim, namely Swedish.

---

[68] Postnominal unaccusatives, e.g. in English, also look like actives and are bound to denote a resultative state. The latter, however, follows from their verbal semantics (as achievements) and the former dissolves into an underlying object-orientation since unaccusatives only introduce an internal argument (cf. Marvin 2003: 148).

[69] Note that this behaviour need not be shared by all non-identity languages. Slovenian, for instance, lacks the possibility to express a proper perfect in postnominal uses (cf. Marvin 2003: 144). This might stem from the beginning of the grammaticalisation of a HAVE-perfect in Slovenian (cf. Oštir 2010: 36). The perfect participial form of Slovenian might already have lost some of its perfect features in terms of distributing them to HAVE.

Swedish is the only language of Germanic[70] and Romance that makes use of distinct passive and perfect(ive) participles in the context of *vara/bli* ('be'/ 'become') and *ha* ('have'), respectively (cf. Klingvall 2011: 53). A straightforward example may be found in (65), based on Klingvall (2011: 54) and Platzack (1989: 305).

(65) a. Boken blev skriven/ *skrivet av Johanna.
the.book.C.SG *became write*.PTCP.C.SG *write*.PTCP *by Johanna*
'The book was written by Johanna.'
b. Johanna har skrivit en bok.
Johanna has write.SUP *a book*
'Johanna has written a book.'

An immediate observation that may be made considering the differences between the passive construction in (65a) and its perfect counterpart in (65b) concerns the fact that participial forms in the former readily take up agreement morphology, whereas those in the latter are invariant (cf. Platzack 1989: 305). However, the examples also make clear that the morphological distinction observable here may actually not be reduced to the question of whether or not agreement morphology is expressed (cf. Platzack 1989: 305). In fact, the perfect variant, the so-called supine, is not simply identical with one of the past participial forms employed in the passive, say the singular neuter form that is ruled out by the requirement for agreement in (65a) (cf. Larsson 2009: 26).[71] Instead, the two forms differ at least in the case of strong verbs, using *-it* in perfect contexts and *-et* in passive ones (cf. Klingvall 2011: 57). Accordingly, a principled distinction is made not only between *skrivit* and *skrivet* ('written') but also with other strong verbs like *sjungit* and *sjunget* ('sung') as well as *vunnit* and *vunnet* ('won') (cf. Klingvall 2011: 57f.). Additionally, a morphological distinction between the supine and the passive participle also shows for weak verbs in some dialects, where the former leaves out *-t* unlike the latter, as observable in *byggi* and *byggt* ('built'), *byti* and *bytt* ('switched') as well as *glömmi* and *glömt* ('forgotten') (cf. Larsson 2009: 419; Klingvall 2011: 58).

---

70 According to Klingvall (2011: 53fn2) a substantial distinction also crops up in some dialects of Norwegian, e.g. in Nynorsk. We will leave the properties of such additional cases to future research. See also Lie (1994).
71 As Larsson (2009: 26fn17) points out, not all Swedish varieties exhibit a distinct supine form (i.e. one that is not identical to the neuter singular form), yet Standard Swedish as well as central varieties of Swedish do.

While the evidence for a morphological distinction in Swedish is quite robust, let us now turn to the question of whether this is mirrored in substantial non-identity. In other words, is the supine a non-finite verb syntacticosemantically different from its passive participle counterpart (see Platzack 1989: 305; Larsson 2009: 26) or just a designated invariant realisation of the past participle (see Christensen & Taraldsen 1989: 71)? Proponents of the latter assume that the observable differences are quite shallow in that they only concern the presence or absence of agreement morphology (cf. Christensen & Taraldsen 1989: 71). This is explicitly denied by proponents of the former, i.e. for instance those who claim "that the Swedish supine is a specific non-finite active form of the verb" (Platzack 1989: 305). Advocates of the substantial non-identity of supines and passive participles try to adduce cases exhibiting differences in behaviour (see Platzack 1989: 306–312). A quite compelling piece of evidence comes from the occurrence of impersonal passives, as in (66), provided by Platzack (1989: 309).

(66) Det blev drucket/   *druckit hela natten.[72]
     it was drink.PTCP.N.SG/ drink.SUP all night
     'People were drinking all night.'

The impersonal passive *per definitionem* does not include any overt argument with which the participial form could agree (cf. Platzack 1989: 309). Hence, according to proponents claiming that the supine is no more than an invariant form of the participle one might expect its realisation, contrary to fact.

Additionally, there are some distinctions in terms of morphology that reach beyond the shallow difference in terms of agreement. One of these concerns the fact that only the supine can undergo synthetic passivisation as in (*har*) *skrivits* ('has been written', lit. has write.SUP.PASS) (cf. Klingvall 2011: 59). Moreover, only passive participles but not supines are able to incorporate particles, as in *Kontraktet är påskrivet* ('The contract is signed.', lit. the.contract is on.written. PTCP) (cf. Larsson 2009: 27). Furthermore, while all verbs have a supine form, some do not occur as passive participles (cf. Platzack 1989: 308), as observable in **Radioaktivt avfall war innehållet i tunnan* ('Radioactive waste was contained in the barrel.', lit. radioactive waste was contained.PTCP.N.SG in the.barrel). These differences show that there is substance to the morphosyntactic non-identity of supines and passive participles in Swedish, which according to Platzack (1989:

---

[72] Note that there might be room for agreement with the expletive here, but Platzack (1989: 309f.) additionally provides an example in which the expletive is absent and this is hence not a licit counter-argument.

308), differ in terms of verbality and exhibit distinct θ-grids. Larsson (2009: 69) additionally assumes that supines – although they are non-finite just like passive participles – carry a past tense value, whereas passive participles lack an inherent tense specification (see also Klingvall 2011: 56).

This leaves the question of whether the existence of a separate perfect(ive) participle has repercussions for the variability in terms of expressing perfect and passive, as in Bulgarian. In other words, are there contexts that clearly show that the distinction between perfect and passive is hard-coded in the participial forms even though auxiliaries suitable to signal the properties in question are generally available? An interesting observation in this context is that Swedish is special in systematically allowing for the realisation of bare supines in (finite) subordinate clauses. Some such cases may be found in (67), partly based on Christensen & Taraldsen (1989: 82en20) and retrieved from the Swedish corpus KORP (*Språkbanken*, the Swedish Language Bank).

(67) a. eftersom Pelle redan skrivit en bok
      since   Peter already write.SUP a book
      'since Peter had already written a book'
b. att Sverige vunnit med 2–0 i fotbollen mot Spanien
    that Sweden win.SUP with 2–0 in football against Spain
    'that Sweden has won 2–0 against Spain in football'
c. men om man sjungit duet med Lasse Holm i melodifestivalen
    but if one sing.SUP duet with Lasse Holm at the.melody-festival
    'but if one has sung a duet with Lasse Holm at the melody-festival'

All of these examples show that supines may readily be realised without an accompanying perfect auxiliary in subordinate clauses and still give rise to perfect readings, whereas something similar is never possible in English (cf. Svartvik & Sager 1996: 7B; Gabrielson 1967: 176). As Larsson (2009: 376f.) points out, this possibility shows quite a large amount of flexibility, i.e. "[i]t is not restricted to certain tenses, or to e.g. certain modal contexts [and] not directly dependent on the matrix tense, or even on the presence of a matrix clause".[73] Although the examples in (67) use a supine that is always morphologically distinct from the passive participle, this is not a necessity as bare realisations

---

[73] This flexibility is observable in cases like *Vilken snögubbe du (har/hade) byggt* ('What a snowman you have/had built!', lit. what snowman you have/had build.SUP), taken from Andréasson et al. (2002: 70).

of non-distinct supines like *packat* ('packed'), *besökt* ('visited'), and *tappat* ('lost') are readily possible.

Such data generally need to be handled with care, given that it is not at all clear whether they constitute substantial cases of omission or merely phonological deletion (ellipsis). However, the principled permissibility of bare supines in Swedish embedded clauses suggests that there really is a fully-fledged grammatical basis to these. This raises the question of why the possibility to omit the perfect auxiliary is not restricted to cases in which the supine is overtly distinguishable from the passive participle. A potentially fruitful response to this might go as follows: once the morphological distinction between supines and past participles had been instantiated, it soon gained grammatical substance, resulting in different feature-sets for the perfect(ive) and passive participles (thus non-identity). This crucially does not demand the consistent occurrence of an overt distinction in all cases, as observable on the basis of the ambiguity of English elements like *loved* (simple past vs. past participle).

What is quite interesting with respect to the substantial distinction in Swedish is how it diachronically came about. In a nutshell, there was originally only one past participial form (cf. Haspelmath 2000: 663), which just developed a shallow difference in that exponents used in perfect contexts did not show agreement morphology anymore once a HAVE-perfect was grammaticalised (cf. Dammel 2012: 254f.). In addition to this loss of agreement morphology, by the 18th century an additional formal distinction (the designated supine affix *-it*) had evolved and marked the emancipation of the supine out of the adjectival system, whose neutral singular form it originally stems from (cf. Dammel 2012: 255). Without going into the specifics of this development (see Larsson 2009: 420–422; Dammel 2012: 256), according to Larsson (2009: 423) the initial phonological source of the substantial distinction may be found in independent changes of the morphophonological system (vowel balance). These soon became obsolete, which allowed what formerly was a phonological alternation to be transmitted to a morphologically conditioned one with supine *-it* as opposed to past participial *-et/-en* in the 18th century (cf. Dammel 2012: 256). Accordingly, the emancipation of the designated supine suffix *-it* and the loss of *-t* in weak verbs are morphological processes supporting the distinction based on the reduction of agreement morphology with an additional formal differentiation (cf. Dammel 2012: 257). As we have just seen, the substantial non-identity in Swedish apparently piggybacks on this formal differentiation.

Eventually, the discussion of the peculiarities of the Swedish supine has shown that this North Germanic language occupies a special position in the Germanic system, given that none of the other Germanic languages makes a distinction between perfect(ive) and passive participles that goes beyond the shallow realisation of agreement morphology. The development towards a substantial distinction in Swedish is likely to have only been possible due to the phonologically-conditioned diversion of the two forms, which then could also be exploited grammatically in natural language's strive for making optimal use of its means. In the case of Swedish supines, this morphological distinction was eventually analogously generalised to all supines, which regularly allows a supine form to occur without its perfect auxiliary at least in subordinate clauses and might extend this to other uses in the future.

2.4.2 Agreement morphology in periphrastic instances

The most far-spread way in which perfect(ive) and passive participles have been shown to differ morphologically is in terms of their ability to carry agreement morphology. With respect to the underlying question of past participial (non-)identity, this capacity – at first sight at least – appears to be contingent on whether the periphrasis in question is of a perfect or a passive kind. The present section is thus devoted to the question of whether there is substance to this claim, i.e. whether the appearance of agreement morphology could challenge the assumption of substantial past participial identity.

Turning first to the North Germanic languages, what was observed in Chapter 2.1.1 is that a common property of these is that they realise agreement morphology on participial forms in passive periphrases, but not on past participles that make up the periphrastic perfect. A straightforward example for this that we have already seen above comes from Icelandic.

(68) a. Maður   var   bitinn   af hundi.
       the.man.NOM.M.SG was   bite.PTCP.M.SG by the.dog
       'The man was bitten by the dog.'
    b. Hundurinn hefur bitið   manninn.
       the.dog   has   bite.PTCP   the.man
       'The dog has bitten the man.'

As we can see here, the past participle agrees with its internal argument in eventive passive cases in Icelandic, as in (68a), whereas this is consistently ruled out whenever the past participle is part of a composite perfect with HAVE, as in (68b). Whenever agreement may not be marked, the invariant past participial form is simply identical to its neuter singular inflecting counterpart (cf. Thráinsson 2007: 9). While Icelandic (like Swedish) forces the realisation of agreement morphology in passive cases, Danish makes it optional and actually restricts it to stative passives, which arguably mark cases of adjectival participles (cf. Sigurðsson 1989: 323–325; Larsson 2009: 19). Additionally, the Norwegian dialect Nynorsk follows the Icelandic pattern in consistently forcing the occurrence of overt agreement morphology, whereas the latter is absent in Bokmål (cf. Åfarli 2009: 168; Klingvall 2011: 53fn2). As we need not go into these cases of parametric variation for the purposes of the present work, we may conclude that the empirical data from North Germanic appears to support the initial conjecture that the general presence of agreement is restricted to passive periphrases, whereas its absence is observable in the context of the analytic perfect.

Upon closer inspection, we can see that this is not particularly telling, though, given that all the Scandinavian languages that employ participial agreement in eventive constructions are HAVE-only languages. In fact, Danish is the only language that exhibits a principled auxiliary alternation between HAVE and BE, but this language unfortunately lacks the capability to employ past participial agreement other than in stative constructions. However, there is (at least) one exception in North Germanic that shows that participial agreement may in principle also surface in BE-perfects. The latter may sometimes be formed in the Norwegian variant Nynorsk, where it readily exhibits past participial object-agreement, as observable in (69), based on Christensen & Taraldsen (1989: 53, 55).

(69) a. Gjestene   er   nett *kome/   komne
       the.guests are   just arrive.PTCP/ arrive.PTCP.PL
    b. Gjestene   har   nett kome/   *komne
       the.guest   have   just arrive.PTCP/ arrived.PTCP.PL
       'The guests have just arrived.'

These examples show that forming a BE-perfect is licit in variants of Nynorsk, whereas other Norwegian dialects consistently resort to HAVE. Crucially, the former regularly exhibit number agreement, as in (69a), whereas cases featuring HAVE are bound to do without any additional inflectional morphology, as in (69b) (cf. Christensen & Taraldsen 1989: 55). Thus, rather than splitting up into passive as opposed to perfect contexts, what we can conclude with respect to the capability of overtly marking agreement is a split into invariant HAVE-contexts, on the one hand, and other periphrastic contexts, which readily mark agreement, on the other.

While periphrastic past participial agreement in Germanic may well be called marginal in that it is restricted to the Scandinavian languages and even here only rarely obligatorily entertained, it is an essential and consistently employed property of Romance. In fact, each and every Romance language features participial agreement in periphrastic contexts in which the past participle does not occur as the complement of HAVE. Crucially, reminiscent of what we have just seen with respect to Nynorsk, those Romance languages that employ auxiliary alternation in the perfect (most importantly Italian and French) also mark object-agreement in BE-perfects. This is exemplified on the basis of Italian in (70), partly based on Friedemann & Siloni (1997: 71).

(70) a. Johnny ha aperto/ *aperta la porta.
 Johnny has open.PTCP/ open. PTCP.F the.F door.F
 'Johnny has opened the door.'
 b. La porta viene *aperto/ aperta da Johnny.
 the.F door.F comes open.PTCP/ open. PTCP.F by Johnny
 'The door is (being) opened by Johnny.'
 c. Cornelia è *arrivato/ arrivata.
 Cornelia is arrive.PTCP/ arrive.PTCP.F
 'Cornelia has arrived.'

These examples show that only the past participle occurring with HAVE in (70a) is exempt from taking up agreement morphology, whereas both the periphrastic passive in (70b) as well as the analytic perfect in (70c), i.e. a BE-perfect formed on the basis of an unaccusative predicate, readily carry it. This capability is shared by the other Romance languages exhibiting auxiliary alternation (French, Occitan, Piedmontese), whereas those that do not (Spanish, Catalan, Portuguese, Romanian, Walloon) only differ with respect to never exhibiting agreement morphology in perfect contexts by virtue of always resorting to HAVE.

Actually, not even HAVE-perfects are entirely exempt from exhibiting past participial object-agreement, as already mentioned in Section 2.1. This becomes obvious when regarding the Italian example in (71a) and the French ones in (71b) and (71c), based on Franco (1994: 247), Bjorkman (2011: 155), and Rowlett (2007: 227), respectively.

(71) a. Gianni l' ha *mangiato/ mangiata.
 Gianni it.F has eat.PTCP/ eat.PTCP.F
 'Gianni has eaten it.'
 b. La maison que les filles on peint/ peinte.
 the house that the girls have paint.PTCP/ paint.PTCP.F
 'The house that the girls have painted.'
 c. Quelles maisons avez-vouz repeintes?
 which houses have-you repaint.PTCP.PL
 'Which houses did you repaint?'

In contrast to Romance languages of the HAVE-only kind, which never show exceptions in terms of barring past participial agreement in perfect contexts, those that do make a distinction between HAVE and BE in perfect periphrases may allow for exceptions in the contexts exemplified in (71) (cf. Lois 1990: 245). In fact, (71a) exemplifies a cliticised direct object which agrees with the past participle after this clitic has been displaced out of the participial domain, something that is also observable in French. In (71b) and (71c) agreement is licit in French but not in Italian. The example in (71b) shows a direct object that has been *wh*-fronted and subsequently allows for participial agreement to be established with it. In a similar vein, (71c) features a *wh*-moved direct objects with which the past participle establishes agreement (cf. Rowlett 2007: 226f.).

Based on these findings, it is safe to conclude that the occurrence of past participial object-agreement does not mark an exception to the consistent morphological identity of past participles and hence does not in any way challenge the assumption that perfect(ive) and passive participles in North Germanic and Romance are substantially identical. Rather than dividing along the lines of the function that is expressed by the periphrastic constructions, the occurrence of past participial agreement is contingent on the presence of some kind of phrasal movement of an underlying direct object (cf. Bjorkman 2011: 154). In other words, "past participle agreement is a reflex of the displacement of the nominal projection determining agreement" (Belletti 2006: 495). This characteristic is shared by passive participles (promoting an internal argument to the syntactic subject position), unaccusative perfect participles (displacing the internal argument to assure structural case-assignment), the cliticisation of a direct object as well as *wh*-movement (both of which extract the internal argument out of the participial domain) (cf. Bjorkman 2011: 154). Crucially, then, whenever the object is not displaced out of the local domain of the past participle, the overt manifestation of past participial object-agreement is barred (cf. Belletti 2006: 509f.). This also explains why object-agreement is usually not found with a form of HAVE in that the objects in these cases typically remain *in situ* and hence do not satisfy the requirement for displacement. While the technical incorporation of these finding will be postponed until Section 4.2.4, let us in conclusion briefly turn to the characteristics of agreement in non-identity languages like Bulgarian.

As mentioned before, BE-only languages like Bulgarian decisively differ from the instantiation of past participial agreement in North Germanic and Romance. Rather than exhibiting object-agreement, such non-identity languages consistently show participial agreement with the surface subject, regardless of whether this is derived from an object or marks an underived semantic subject (cf. Bjorkman 2011: 156). Accordingly, "[i]n languages like Bulgarian where the perfect auxiliary is invariably 'be', the perfect participle *always* agrees with the subject" (Iatridou et al. 2001: 235). This is exemplified in the Bulgarian transitive perfect in (72), taken from Iatridou et al. (2001: 235en52).

(72) Maria   e   pisala   (knigata).
     Maria.F is   write.PRF.PTCP.F.SG the.book
     'Maria has worked on the book.'

The general way to account for this is to assume that movement of an argument (be it internal or external) into the canonical subject position (Spec, T) is claimed to suffice to establish the agreement relation between a participle and the surface subject (cf. den Dikken 1994: 73f.). This raises the question of why this does not carry over to Romance and North Germanic. A promising insight in this respect is that Slavic allows for ubiquitous agreement with the overt subject because all of the arguments are introduced in the distinct participial phrases, whereas the past participles in identity languages cannot properly introduce their external arguments, but rather need HAVE to license them, which is why these arguments cannot establish agreement with the participle (cf. Broekhuis & Migdalski 2003: 3). While a proper technical account of these differences between the Romance and Germanic pattern of participial object-agreement and the subject-agreement in non-identity languages is pending, it is beyond the scope of the present work and will hence be left to future research.

This concludes our brief discussion of the patterns of past participial agreement in periphrases, which pointed out that these by no means challenge the assumption of past participial identity, yet nevertheless provide interesting insights into the underlying structural configurations and the general workings of (participial) agreement.

2.4.3 Subtle differences

Whereas neither a substantial morphological distinction nor shallow differences in terms of agreement morphology may be attested in English, what we find are some more subtle morphological differences in the domain of past participles. The present subsection is devoted to briefly pointing out that these do not stem from a difference between perfect(ive) and passive participles, but rather instantiate a distinction between past participles and elements that may be classified as proper adjectives but closely resemble their participial counterparts.

The examples in (73) show that stative passive constructions may occasionally closely resemble proper adjectival constructions, but exhibit subtle differences in meaning.

(73) a. The ship is sunk.
  b. The ship is sunken.

The example in (73b) may roughly be paraphrased as 'the ship is in a sunken state'. Its counterpart in (73a), on the other hand, entails that the state ('being sunk') resulted from a presupposed event and may thus be paraphrased as 'the ship is in the state of having become sunk' (cf. Embick 2003: 148). Embick (2003: 147) claims that cases like the former comprise a 'stative passive participle', whereas instances of the latter kind include a 'resultative passive participles'. Accordingly, only resultative instances "designat[e] the end state that is the result of the action or event expressed in the verb stem" (Coussé 2011: 621), whereas their stative counterparts do not semantically make recourse to a presupposed event (cf. Helland & Pitz 2012: 103f.). This difference is morphologically marked by -en in the present case as well as in *struck/stricken*, *shrunk/shrunken*, *proved/proven*, *melted/molten* and *weaved/woven*. On the other hand, this distinction may also take a different form, as observable in the pairs *blessed/blessèd* or *aged/agèd* (syllabic -*èd*) as well as *opened/open* and *emptied/empty* (zero affix) (cf. Embick 2003: 152f.). Such morphological differences, however, are relatively rare. In fact, the difference is not explicitly marked in the vast majority of cases.

Based on their differences in meaning, these different types are usually distinguished on the basis of how much verbality is involved, as observable in Aronoff (1994: 176fn36), where the difference in morphology is assumed to mark the distinction between adjectival and verbal participles. Embick (2004: 357–359) trace the eventivity of resultative passives back to the presence of the functional projection *v*, while stative passives are taken to lack this element and hence mark simple properties (or states). In order to emphasise that this distinction really is grammatically-based, Embick (2003: 153–155) adduces a number of diagnostics, e.g.the finding that *un*-affixation is only productive with resultative passive participles). A similar distinction is drawn in Kratzer (2000: 385) with the terms target state (stative) and resultant state (resultative) passives, as coined by Parsons (1990). Most importantly for the present work, the resultative passive participles pattern with what Embick (2003: 147) calls eventive passive participles, i.e. those used in eventive passives, as well as perfect participles. The stative passive participles, on the other hand, stand out by lacking verbal properties and may hence not be used in eventive configurations.[74] Additionally, they regularly exhibit an archaic form, which is why Oku (1998: 56fn11f.) assumes

---

74 Consider for instance the ungrammaticality of *The pope has blessèd him* and *He was blessèd by the pope.*

these to be stored in the lexicon rather than being productively formed. Embick (2003: 157, 2004: 364f.), on the other hand, denies this and holds the structural environment of one and the same root responsible for the distinct morphological realisation and their associated differences in meaning.

Such cases of polymorphy are not restricted to English but also occur in German, e.g. in a pair like *gewinkt/gewunken* ('waved') (cf. Bloomer 1994: 34–36). Unlike in English, however, we may not attribute any syntacticosemantic differences to such morphological doublets (cf. Bloomer 1999: 287). Rather, these are freely interchangeable and only mark distinct diachronic stages. This is occasionally also observed in English, for which Embick (2003: 152f.) points out that we need to be careful concerning polymorphy in that some idiolects may freely interchange distinct forms in all of their uses (see also Bloomer 1999: 291). Nevertheless, while the specifics of Embick's (2003; 2004) distinction may not always be shown to hold true in English, the overall tendencies of associating specific morphological realisations with particular distributions are too consistent to simply be neglected.

We will not join the intricate discussion concerning 'stative passive participles' and 'resultative passive participles' here. What is clear, though, is that this distinction does not in any way pertain to the distinction between perfect(ive) participles and passive participles but rather concerns the one between fully-fledged adjectival elements and deverbal participles. With respect to polymorphy, the only insightful point concerning our underlying question of past participial (non-)identity is that there may be diachronic changes that lead to participial variants (e.g. *kneeled* and *knelt*, *teached* and *taught*), but these are never used to mark a substantial difference between passive and perfect(ive) participles (cf. Aronoff 1994: 24).

2.5 Divergent realisations of past participles

There are contexts in which passive and perfect(ive) participles appear to differ with regard to exhibiting realisations of past participles that are in some sense divergent from the norm. These arguably have the potential of shedding light on the underlying question of past participial (non-)identity by virtue of highlighting substantial differences in behaviour. Accordingly, the subchapters 2.5.1, 2.5.2 and 2.5.3 will be concerned with what is typically referred to as 'Perfect(ive) Participle Paradox' (PPP), 'Infinitivus pro Participio' (IPP) and 'Participium pro Infinitivo' (PPI), respectively. The first two phenomena, PPP and IPP, the former surfacing in English and the latter for instance in German, share that a base (i.e. infinitival) form is realised instead of a past participle, although this is what this form is interpreted as. The contexts in which this is possible differ: the PPP occurs in cases of preposing a verb phrase and the IPP is triggered by a verbal cluster. The third divergent realisation, PPI, as instantiated e.g. in Frisian, is also contingent on the presence of a verbal cluster, but differs from the other cases by marking the insertion of two past participial forms under a single auxiliary. What makes these phenomena particularly interesting for the present purposes is that they apparently share that they are only able to surface in the context of perfect(ive) participles, as a matter of fact (almost) exclusively in the context of an equivalent of the perfect auxiliary HAVE. A corresponding passive variant featuring a divergent realisation is not available, which supposedly holds true cross-linguistically.

In addition to these principled phenomena attended to in the designated subchapters, there are also divergent realisations that may be traced back to lexical idiosyncracies. These show in the special properties of deponent verbs, which mark past participial forms that appear to have lost their participial meaning while retaining the form associated with it, as we will briefly see in Section 2.5.4.

Eventually, the divergent realisations investigated in the present chapter mark the final pieces of (synchronic) empirical evidence to be adduced. In fact, they provide a substantial foundation for the approach to be proposed below by virtue of showing that passive information is comprised in the participial element in its entirety, whereas a decisive amount of perfect information is stored in HAVE. Participial forms that participate in BE-perfects (derived from unaccusatives) apparently pattern with the former rather than the latter in that they comprise perfectivity.

2.5.1 The Perfect(ive) Participle Paradox

While the literature on the so-called Perfect(ive) Participle Paradox (PPP) is surprisingly scarce,[75] the picture drawn of it by empirical data is quite clear. This may be seen in the examples in (74), taken from Breul (2014: 451f.) and attested in the COCA and the BNC.

---

75 First discussed in Ward (1988: 192–194) and briefly addressed in Ward et al. (2002: 1381), the PPP is virtually only discussed in Oku (1996; 1998), Urushibara (1997: 138–140), and Breul (2014). Additional discussion may be found in Breul (2004: 176–178) and Breul's PPP-related query (http://linguistlist.org/issues/12/12-2826.html; summary of responses: http://linguistlist.org/issues/12/12-2972.html, accessed on February 24, 2015) on the Linguist List in 2001.

2.5 Divergent realisations of past participles — 103

(74) a. And that kind of sense [...] is exactly what is necessary for science to prosper. And *prosper, it has*, and we are still by any measure the leading scientific nation in the world.
b. "To accept such precious gifts when one has nothing to give in return is humbling," says Noonan. "The roadside garden was created because of a desire to return something to others." And *return something she has*.
c. I don't know how he found out that she belonged to that lass, but *find out he has*.

In each of these instances, the verbal phrase is moved to a clause-initial position and subsequently introduces a plain (or infinitival) form rather than the past participle to be expected by virtue of the canonical structure (cf. Breul 2014: 449). This constitutes the paradoxical character of this construction, which thus questions Akmajian and Wasow's (1975: 210f.) traditional generalisation that preposed verbs are bound to be properly inflected when introduced by HAVE or BE (cf. Oku 1996: 282). Introducing an infinitival instead of a past participial form is not the only option, though.

The corpora also provide cases like those in (75), taken from Breul (2014: 452) and attested in the COCA, in which the expected participial form occurs in cases of preposing.

(75) a. She never understood where she'd gotten the nerve to go to his room that night, but *gone she had* [...].
b. One death is a tragedy, a million deaths is a statistic. The ka must act when consensus can not [sic!] be used, and *acted she had*.

Although there is thus a certain degree of flexibility as to whether or not the PPP is employed, its principled occurrence suggests that it is, as Breul (2014: 450) puts it, a "genuinely grammatical phenomenon of present-day standard English".[76] While discourse conditions may well serve as a trigger, the PPP must have a morphosyntactic basis (cf. Oku 1996: 282–284; Urushibara 1997: 139). Nevertheless, there is considerable (idiolectal and perhaps also

---

[76] In fact, Breul (2014: 453) comes to the following conclusion: "[a]gainst the background of the very low frequency of verb phrase preposing in general, the ratio of examples that show the PPP and those that do not suggests that the PPP is a genuine morphosyntactic phenomenon, and that it is not a spurious linguistic pseudo-fact due to performance errors or typos."

dialectal) variation concerning the acceptability of the PPP which has not yet been conclusively discussed (cf. Breul 2014: 453, 464).[77]

With respect to periphrastic passives, on the other hand, there is no variation whatsoever and neither is there any paradoxical behaviour, as using the plain form is consistently barred. Simply put, "[t]here is the PPP, but there is no corresponding passive participle paradox" (Breul 2014: 453). This is observable in the grammaticality of the examples in (76), taken from Breul (2014: 454) and attested in the COCA and the BNC, which do not allow for infinitival counterparts. Accordingly, there is not a single occurrence of a plain form instead of a passive participle to be found in the corpora (cf. Breul 2014: 453).

(76) a. Al's became [...] the place for Manhattan's beau monde to be featured. And *featured they were*, the next Sunday in the style section [...].
 b. It will never be known how Jarman was caught, but *caught he was*, and condemned to hang.

In an attempt to technically account for the PPP, Urushibara (1997: 130, 141) traces its occurrence back to a lack of string-adjacency of HAVE and the head of the VP, which has as its consequence that the word-formation rule usually deriving the participial form cannot be applied. This entails that the perfective participial marker is virtually treated as a piece of what would nowadays (see Embick & Noyer 2007: 305f.) be analysed as ornamental morphology (cf. Breul 2014: 455). This, however, is problematic, as Breul (2014: 455) points out: "[o]ne would expect such a piece of ornamental morphology to be rather systematically missing in a substantial range of the present-day varieties of English and at a certain stage during first language acquisition". Both of these conjectures do not hold true, though. Breul (2014: 463) therefore proposes an alternative account and assumes impoverishment (cf. Embick & Noyer 2007: 311) to be at the core of a proper analysis of the PPP instead. Accordingly, what is proposed is the following: the participial feature typically leading to the realisation of a properly inflected past participial form may be deleted if the participle is displaced out of the local (c-command) domain of HAVE (cf. Breul 2014: 463).

While we will postpone a more fine-grained discussion of the theoretical properties of the PPP to Section 4.2.4, the most important finding for our purposes regarding past participial (non-)identity is that this kind of inserting an infinitival instead of a participial form is restricted to the HAVE-perfect. Given that

---

[77] Based on these observation, Breul (2014: 464) eventually contends that the occurrence of the PPP is optional.

the interpretation retrieved from contexts employing the PPP is still a fully-fledged perfect, the perfect auxiliary appears to be instrumental for recovering this interpretation. Accordingly, Breul (2014: 465f.) traces the possibility of the PPP back to the contribution of the auxiliary: "the recovery of the perfect tense semantics is possible due to the presence of the perfect tense auxiliary." This entails "that the feature complex which is responsible for the interpretation of a clause as having perfect tense is located either in the perfect auxiliary alone or in the perfect auxiliary in combination with the feature equipment of the participle" (Breul 2014: 465).[78] The contribution of the auxiliary – or rather lack thereof – may then also be held responsible for the absence of a passive participial counterpart to the PPP. As we have seen in Chapter 2.2 and as Breul (2014: 464f.) remarks on the basis of bare participial clauses (e.g. *Eaten, the shark does not terrify them anymore*), passive interpretations readily come about in the absence of a passive auxiliary. This suggests that passive auxiliaries do not comprise relevant passive information, which instead resides in the participle alone (cf. Wanner 2009: 15; Breul 2014: 464f.).

Eventually then, the PPP suggests that the auxiliary HAVE plays an important role in the interpretation of the perfect, since its occurrence allows the preposed participle to be realised as a plain form rather than a proper past participle. This is generally compatible with both the non-identity and the identity view. The former could simply claim that the inherent difference between the past participial forms is responsible for the distinct behaviour, while the latter has to attribute the distinction to some feature introduced by the perfect auxiliary. Given that impoverishment is available in VP-preposing contexts in English, what is curious, however, is that there apparently is no PPP in other languages using HAVE for perfect periphrases. On the other hand, its low frequency in English suggests that it might well be a grammatical fact in some other languages as well that has just not been principally observed in any language other than English yet. There is actually a closely related phenomenon that has been observed in other Germanic languages, though.

---

78 Note that impoverishment *per definitionem* applies at PF, i.e. post-syntactically. Accordingly, it may not have an effect on the interpretation that is derived at LF. Nevertheless, a restriction on the application of impoverishment is that the intended meaning still needs to be recoverable (cf. Breul 2014: 465), which arguably is only the case in participial constructions if there is an element around that properly contributes to the interpretation in question, namely HAVE in the PPP-contexts under discussion.

2.5.2 Infinitivus pro Participio

In contrast to the apparently quite marginal PPP, the Infinitivus pro Participio (IPP) is rather wide-spread in West Germanic. As the Dutch and German examples in (77), taken from Hinterhölzl (2006: 237f.), emphasise, what is characteristic about this phenomenon is quite similar to what we have seen in the context of the PPP, namely the realisation of a plain (or infinitival) form in a context in which we expect a past participle.

(77) a. dat Elsje hem een brief heeft *gewild/ willen schrijven
     that Elsje him a letter has want.PTCP/ want.INF write
  b. dass Else ihm einen Brief hat schreiben *gewollt /wollen
     that Else him a letter has write want.PTCP/ want.INF
     'that Elsa (has) wanted to write him a letter'

Instead of the past participial forms *gewild* and *gewollt* ('wanted') an infinitival form is realised in a complex verb cluster containing a modal verb or another verb selecting a bare infinitive (cf. Bader & Schmid 2009: 178f.). In other words, the IPP shows "if a restructuring verb taking a dependent infinitive as complement is used in perfect tense" (Hinterhölzl 2009: 191). The same effect pertains to Afrikaans and West Flemish, as shown in the examples in (78), adopted from de Vos (2001: 82) and Hoekstra (1997: 165).

(78) a. Hy het Jan vir haar die tuinblomme laat/ *gelaat leer ken.
     He has Jan for her the gardenflowers let.INF/ let.PTCP learn.INF know.INF
     'He let Jan teach her to know the garden flowers.'
  b. Ik hew loup/ *loupen te dromen.
     I have walk.INF/ walk.PTCP to dream.INF
     'I dreamed as I walked.'

Based on its main characteristic, this phenomenon is also fittingly referred to as *Ersatzinfinitiv* ('substitute infinitive') and has received a lot of attention in linguistic research (see, amongst others, Reis 1979; Hoeksema 1988; Askedal 1991; Vanden Wyngaerd 1994; IJbema 1997; Meurers 2000; Eisenberg et al. 2001; Bærentzen 2004; Wurmbrand 2006; Haider 2011).[79]

---

[79] Note that discussions of the IPP actually reach back to Grimm (1837), Merkes (1895), and Dal (2014 [1952]).

Reminiscent of what we have seen in the context of the PPP, there is dialectal as well as idiolectal variation concerning the application of the IPP (cf. Askedal 1991: 1fn1). In contrast to the supposed optionality of the PPP in English, however, the IPP is obligatorily employed in Standard German with the class of modals (cf. Askedal 1991: 1). With other kinds of restructuring elements (e.g. *let* 'lassen' and perception verbs like *hören* 'hear'), there is also optionality, though. Quite generally, dialectal variation to a large part appears to correlate with or depend on underlying differences concerning the acceptability of certain word orders (cf. Bader & Schmid 2009: 176).[80] The latter is occasionally also one of the factors determining whether the IPP is obligatory or facultative, which first and foremost hinges on the immediate syntactic environment, usually in terms of which restructuring element is employed, though (cf. Lange 1982: 181).[81] Abstracting away from such dialectal and idiolectal differences and word order variation for the present purposes, the IPP may provide substantial insights into questions of past participial (non-)identity.

A salient issue that crops up in the context of the IPP is whether the forms occurring instead of properly inflected past participles are real infinitives or 'hidden' participles (cf. Hinterhölzl 1998: 62). The former view (see, amongst others, Erdmann 1886; Merkes 1895; Schmid 2002: 84f.) is for instance grounded on the observation that the IPP correlates with the availability of a participial prefix (*ge-*) yet does not merely mark the realisation of a prefixless participle (the IPP of the participle *geholfen* 'helped' is *helfen*, not *holfen) (cf. Hinterhölzl 2009: 198). Approaches of the second kind may also account for this, though, by claiming that "the infinitival morphology on the restructuring verb appears as a pure default" (Hinterhölzl 2009: 199). The assumption of a 'hidden' participle actually marks the standard account (cf. Hinterhölzl 2009: 197) and is

---

80 For further dialectal differences, see e.g. Schmid (2002: 9–11), Bader & Schmid (2009), Hinterhölzl (2009), and Vogel (2009: 319). See also Haider (2011: 249–251), where the extensive variation in the context of problematic cases of the IPP is emphasised and traced back to a general ungrammaticality of cases that may only ever partially be rescued and hence allow for various (more or less accepted) possibilities in attempts at doing so. One such problematic case is the oft-cited *Skandalkonstruktion* ('scandalous construction'), as in *ohne es haben wissen zu können* ('without having been able to know it', lit. without it have know.INF to can.INF), which is peculiar in terms of word order as well as the placement of infinitival *zu* ('to') (cf. von Stechow 1990: 159f.).

81 As Ørsnes (2008: 121) points out, the IPP is occasionally also applied in constructions featuring directional adjuncts, as observable in *Er hat ins Krankenhaus gemusst/müssen* ('He had to go to the hospital.', lit. he has into.the hospital must.PTCP/must.INF), where it is optional. This ties in with Askedal's (1991: 17f.) claim that the IPP is generally less obligatory (or possible) with decreasing auxiliarity of the dependent verb.

traditionally put forth in the context of the IPP ever since the very beginnings of its investigation (see Grimm 1837: 168f.; Behaghel 1924). This view finds support in the fact that a proper perfect interpretation comes about regardless of the absence of overt participial morphology and renders it obsolete to make room for a violation of the selectional relation between a perfect auxiliary and its past participle (cf. Hinterhölzl 1998: 62; Hinterhölzl 2009: 199). Höhle (1992: 116fn3) finds additional evidence for the verbal form in IPP contexts being a cloaked past participle[82] in the fact that there are exceptions to its formal identity with the infinitive, namely prefixless participles. This is observable in Dutch where perfect uses of the copula *zijn* ('be') do not occur as the regular infinitival form instead of *geweest* ('been'), but as the alternative form *wezen* ('been') that has otherwise dropped out of use (cf. Höhle 1992: 116fn3; see also Vanden Wyngaerd 1996: 302f.; Zwart 2007: 89f.).[83] In a similar vein, the Standard German passive auxiliary *werden* ('become') is realised as the prefixless participle *worden* ('been') instead of *geworden* ('been') when occurring in a composite perfect like *Er ist geehrt worden* ('He was honored.', lit. he is honored become.PREFIXLESS-PTCP) (cf. Hinterhölzl 2009: 199).[84] Strikingly, these supposedly lexicalised occurrences of the IPP are quite exceptional – more so in German than in Dutch, which allows for a range of exceptions, as we will see shortly – in terms of arising in analytic perfects formed with BE rather than HAVE. Besides these cases, what indicates that 'hidden' participles are involved is that prefixless occurrences diachronically precede infinitival realisations in IPP-contexts (cf. Hinterhölzl 2009: 199). This leaves the question of what triggers the insertion of a plain form, which is typically tied to the role of the participial prefix *ge-*, as the IPP only exists in languages that entertain past participial prefixes (cf. Hinterhölzl 2009: 199f.). Eventually, then, for our intents in the present section, it suffices to follow the standard view according to which the insertion of default (infinitival) morphology does not necessitate that the underlying syntacticosemantic feature-set comprised is just as default (cf. Hinterhölzl 2009: 199). With respect to recovering a perfect or passive interpretation, however, the lack of participial morphology needs to be taken seriously.

---

[82] See also Hinterhölzl (1998: 62) for empirical data from West Flemish and Afrikaans supporting this view.
[83] This is observable in the colloquial Dutch example *Hij is wezen vissen* ('He has been away fishing.', lit. he is be.PREFIXLESS-PTCP fish.INF), taken from Hoekstra & van Koppen (2013: 435f.).
[84] Note that this only pertains to the auxiliary *werden* ('become') but not to its main verb counterpart: consider *Er ist krank *(ge)worden* ('He became ill.', he is ill become.PTCP). This shows that the two are lexically independent of one another, as only one of the two has a lexicalised prefixless instantiation.

Most important for the matter of past participial (non-)identity is the question of whether the IPP brings to light differences with regard to perfect (ive) and passive participles. The IPP strongly resembles the PPP by virtue of appearing in perfect, but crucially not in passive periphrases. To be precise, with the exception of the arguably lexicalised prefixless participles that we have just seen, inserting an infinitival rather than a participial form is only possible if this form is selected by HAVE. Accordingly, the principled application of the IPP is barred whenever the form in question is governed by the passive auxiliary WERDEN or the perfect auxiliary BE (cf. Haider 2003: 104, Vogel 2009: 312). This is exemplified in (79).

(79) a. dass das Mädchen lachen   *hören/   gehört   wurde
       that the girl   laugh.INF hear.INF/ hear.PTCP become
       'that the girl was heard laughing'
    b. dass das Mädchen sitzen   *bleiben/   geblieben   ist
       that the girl   sit.INF remain.INF/ remain.PTCP be
       'that the girl remained sitting'

However, the ungrammaticality of the IPP in non-HAVE contexts does not consistently hold cross-linguistically (cf. Schallert 2014: 253). In fact, the Dutch perfect auxiliary *zijn* ('be') may occasionally also allow for the IPP (cf. Haider 2003: 110). Höhle (1992: 116fn33) attributes this to lax restrictions on the applicability of the IPP, which is underlined by Ørsnes (2008: 124), who points out that the number of IPP-forming verb classes is larger in Dutch than in German. Even in some dialects of German there are apparently exceptional cases, though. Such exceptions generally only pertain to perfect contexts, i.e. there crucially is no distinction in the fact that the IPP is never allowed to occur with a given passive auxiliary (cf. Evers 2003: 82). The possibility of the IPP with BE in Dutch is observable in (80), adopted from Broekhuis & Corver (2015: 1025) and Schmid (2002: 28).

(80) a. dat Jan is *gegaan/   gaan   zwemmen
       that Jan is go.PTCP/ go.INF swim.INF
       'that Jan has started (gone) to swim'
    b. dat Jan is *gekomen/   komen   werken
       that Jan is come.PTCP/ come.INF work.INF
       'that Jan has started (come) to work'

c. dat de mensen zijn *gebleven/ blijven staan[85]
    that the people are remain.PTCP/ remain.INF stand.INF
    'that the people have continued to stand'

The examples in (80) show that the plain realisation of *gaan* ('go'), *komen* ('come'), and *blijven* ('remain') is obligatory when the element in question serves as a restructuring predicate and hence makes up a verbal cluster. What is striking about these predicates is that they have largely lost the meaning still associated with their cognates in, e.g., Standard German and English, and primarily mark inchoativity (*gaan, komen*) or continuativity (*blijven*) (cf. IJbema 1997: 42; Broekhuis & Corver 2015: 1025).[86] In fact, they are often described as aspectual in nature and hence termed 'aspectual verbs' (cf. Broekhuis & Corver 2015: 1020–1022). This aspectual contribution may be lexically associated with a sense of completion, reminiscent of what we could find in cases of exceptional auxiliary selection with (manner of) motion verbs (e.g. *gehen* 'go', *kommen* 'come') in Standard German and (maintenance of) position predicates (e.g. *stehen* 'stand', *sitzen* 'sit') in southern dialects.[87] This could eventually be constitutive for the denotation of a perfect reading, although such a claim certainly demands a fine-grained analysis of the properties of aspectual verbs and their semantic contribution in verbal clusters, which cannot be provided here. However, the assumption that an ingredient that may be conventionally associated with an aspectual predicate is responsible for the exceptional IPP-behaviour gains support from cases in which it is embedded under a modal but unexpectedly still determines auxiliary selection (*gaan* takes BE, *moeten* takes HAVE): *Hij is naar huis moeten gaan* ('He had to go home.', lit. he is to home must.PTCP/must.INF go.INF) (cf. Mortelmans, Boye & van der Auwera 2009: 22; see Reis 2001: 309 for a similar case with *blijven*). Although the aspectual verb is not directly governed by the auxiliary, the sense of completion that it is associated with apparently suffices for the verbal cluster to trigger BE-selection. Rather than marking a principled deviation from the limitation on HAVE-perfects, the acceptability of the IPP in the context of BE might thus stem from the particular properties of the predicates in these

---

85 While it is barred in Standard German, the IPP may also be found in such BE-perfect contexts in the southern dialect Bernese German as well as in West Frisian (cf. Schmid 2002: 28).

86 This for instance clearly shows in the fact that *blijven* ('remain') combines with a wide range of distinct kinds of predicates (e.g. *liggen* 'lie', *lezen* 'read', *vliegen* 'fly'), unlike in German (see also Schmid 2002: 28fn14).

87 While the exceptional behaviour of (manner of) motion verbs was explicitly discussed in Section 2.3, we only hinted at (maintenance of) position verbs in passing in footnote 64, as these do not show exceptional behaviour in Standard German, but only in southern dialects.

exceptional cases. While acknowledging some exceptions and cross-linguistic variation, we may hence keep to our underlying assumption that similar to the PPP, the IPP is restricted to HAVE-contexts.

In a nutshell, besides the restriction on occurring in the context of HAVE, there are further factors determining the instantiation of the IPP. One important factor is the complexity of the verbal domain, which has to exceed an auxiliary taking a past participle by at least embedding a verbal complement (cf. Schmid 2002: 89).[88] In other words, the intricate properties of (complex) verbal clusters (see, amongst others, Haider 1994; Evers 1975; Rutten 1991; Hinterhölzl 1999; Koopman & Szabolcsi 2000; Wurmbrand 2001; 2004) need to be accounted for in the context of the IPP (cf. Hinterhölzl 2009: 192). Additionally, the availability of a past participial prefix is commonly taken to be decisive (cf. Schmid 2002: 89), which falls out naturally given the correlation of *ge-* and the IPP. While we will once more not enter a principled theoretical discussion here, let us briefly sketch what an approach based on an incompatibility of *ge-* with verbal clusters might be based on.

As mentioned before, the IPP is restricted to languages forming their past participles with a prefix and hence never to be found in any of the other Germanic languages (e.g. English, Frisian, and Danish) (cf. Lange 1982: 174; Ørsnes 2008: 124; Hinterhölzl 2009: 191).[89] This correlation is often taken to stem from an incompatibility of a morphologically complex participial form and a complex verbal cluster (cf. Askedal 1991: 21; Hinterhölzl 2009: 200). Accordingly, Vanden Wyngaerd (1994; 1996) and Hinterhölzl (1998: 65f.; 2009: 199f.) assume that the proper realisation of past participial morphology, viz. the participial prefix that is part of it, is blocked in verbal clusters. In a similar vein, Schmid (2002: 9) claims that the "IPP appears as a 'last resort' or repair strategy only in cases in which the past participle would be 'even worse'." These approaches share that they hold the 'repair mechanism' responsible for "suppl[ying] the morphologically depleted stem with a default ending" (Hinterhölzl 2009: 209), which leads to realising an infinitival form.

---

[88] Note that there are some exceptions like simple periphrases featuring directional adjuncts, as in footnote 81. These, however, arguably feature some kind of ellipsis.

[89] There are exceptions to this neat correlation, though. Yiddish exhibits *ge-* but does not allow for the IPP (cf. Hoeksema 1988: 160fn4) and West Frisian Dutch (a Dutch dialect spoken in North Holland) does not employ *ge-* but shows the IPP (cf. Schmid 2002: 91fn57). The latter may, however, stem from language contact and the influence of Standard Dutch, thus potentially not providing real counter-evidence (cf. Schmid 2002: 91fn57). If this holds true, the availability of *ge-* is a necessary but not a sufficient condition (cf. Schmid 2002: 90f.).

Hinterhölzl (2006; 2009: 200) assumes that past participial morphology is morphosyntactically complex, consisting of a participial pre- as well as suffix, introduced by independent functional heads. Regardless of whether both of these participial ingredients need to be present at the level of syntax, we will simply assume that the complex nature of past participles in *ge*-languages raises morphological problems at the level of vocabulary insertion for the time being. Accordingly, there is a structural incompatibility between a morphologically complex past participle and its realisation within a complex verbal cluster, supposedly reinforced by the need to induce cluster-internal conformity, as we will see in the next section. This incompatibility is attempted to be resolved by spelling out an infinitival form instead. Reminiscent of Breul's (2014) PPP-account, this may be traced back to an instance of impoverishment. In the context of the PPP it is the displacement of the participial form out of the local domain of the perfect auxiliary that eventually allows for it to be spelled out without its proper morphological designation. In the case of the IPP, on the other hand, it is the morphological reluctance to realise the past participial morphology given that this includes the complex process of circumfixation (i.e. both a prefix as well as a suffix). Therefore, just like in the context of the PPP, the specific structural conditions eventually allow for – in fact in this case occasionally even force – the impoverishment of participial morphology in IPP-contexts.[90] This entails that there is no need for postulating a designated morphosyntactic 'repair mechanism' (see Hinterhölzl 2009: 191) in this context. A technical instantiation as to how this plays out will be discussed (briefly) in Chapter 4.2.4 below.

With regard to what the IPP may tell us about the issue of past participial (non-)identity, we could just see yet another phenomenon that does not principally draw the line between passive and perfect, but rather lines up periphrases with the perfect auxiliary HAVE against perfect as well as passive ones featuring BE and WERDEN. Eventually, similar to what we have encountered in the context of the PPP, this suggests – as for instance claimed on the basis of IPP-data by Höhle (1992: 116) and Broekhuis & van Dijk (1995: 44–47) – that perfect information is not (entirely) stored in the past participial form.[91] Just like in the context of the

---

90 We will not discuss the intricate structural requirements for the application of impoverishment in IPP-contexts, as this would force us to open Pandora's box in terms of dialectal variation and complex verb clusters. What matters most for our purposes in the present work is that semantic recoverability is a necessary, but not a sufficient condition for the application of the IPP (just like the PPP), which is why the IPP is usually restricted to HAVE-perfects.

91 Vogel (2009: 315) even takes the occurrence of the IPP (and its interpretational equivalence to traditional past participial contexts) to show that perfect meaning cannot arise compositionally

PPP, the lack of a passive variant of the IPP furthermore suggests that, unlike perfect information, passive information is stored in the participial form and not in the auxiliary. Therefore, a passive auxiliary is not able to give rise to a passive interpretation without being accompanied by a properly marked past participial form. In Haider's (2003: 125en10) words: "IPP would destroy the effect of the participle, namely the blocking of the external argument [and hence] passive must be spared by IPP in German and Dutch."

Additional support for the importance of the perfect auxiliary HAVE for the composition of perfect meaning comes from the unexpected displacement of the perfect auxiliary to cluster-initial position in German. While German is usually quite strict in terms of imposing OV order, contexts featuring the IPP mark an exception by virtue of moving the auxiliary past the verbal cluster. In other words, "the auxiliary has to invert with the cluster comprised of the dependent and the IPP-infinitive" (Hinterhölzl 1998: 62) at least in the case of modals, as we could see in the example in (77b) above (*hat schreiben wollen*, lit. has write want. INF) (cf. Bader & Schmid 2009: 176). This movement may be accounted for by the assumption that this position allows it to provide indications about the tense information of the clause as soon as possible (cf. Bærentzen 2004: 137f.).[92] This thus prevents misinterpretations of the various infinitival forms that are involved, reminiscent of garden path structures and assumedly reduces computational load. In other words, preposing might in fact be semantically motivated by the fact that the perfect auxiliary in IPP-constructions is the only element in the clause that overtly expresses tense information (cf. Bærentzen 2004: 137f.).[93]

---

from the computation of the expression. Instead, what he suggests is that the perfect is an inseparable construction (in the sense of Construction Grammar) that occurs in two allomorphic variants (cf. Vogel 2009: 315).

92 This finds support in the fact that a similar movement operation is also employed in verbal clusters headed by the future auxiliary *werden* ('will') (cf. Haider 2003: 110; Bader & Schmid 2009: 178): *dass sie das Buch wird lesen wollen* ('that she will want to read the book', lit. that she the book will read want). Note that the cluster-initial position is the standard position for the perfect auxiliary in Dutch anyway (cf. Hinterhölzl 1998: 62).

93 HAVE-preposing is not always a necessity, i.e first of all there are restructuring elements that do not force (but optionally permit) the non-canonical placement of the auxiliary even in German (e.g. perception verbs like *sehen* 'see' and *hören* 'hear') and additionally there are IPP-languages that do not trigger differences in word order at all (see Schmid 2002; IJbema 1997). Nevertheless, the fact that there are languages in which it occasionally is a necessity (e.g. with modal auxiliaries in German, cf. Bader 2014: 36) and even cases in which it is optionally permitted indicate that it may well be semantically motivated, yet contingent on structural considerations like whether the position is generally available and, if it is, which kinds of elements it may house.

These assumptions are also supported by Ørsnes' (2008: 125) observation that the IPP is not available whenever the perfect auxiliary is elided.

In addition to impoverishment, there may also be alternative 'repair strategies' employed in the context of verb cluster formation. Höhle (2006) for instance points to Middle German dialects which derive alternative forms including a weak participial suffix on a bare stem, as in *darfd* (stemming from *gedorfd* 'allowed'), *he:sd* (*gehe:san* 'told'), and *waisd* (*gewisan* 'taught') (cf. Hinterhölzl 2009: 205). Furthermore, another strategy may be found – though quite rarely – in earlier stages of German, as observable in *Hand wir unser eigen insigel geton henket?* ('Have we hanged our own seal?', lit. have we our own seal do.PTCP hang.PTCP) (cf. Hinterhölzl 2009: 206). Here, a single auxiliary is apparently able to license two past participles, which is why Hinterhölzl (2009: 206) refers to these as 'double participle constructions'.[94] As we will see in the next section, this phenomenon may regularly be found in Frisian, Swedish and Norwegian and is commonly referred to as 'Participium pro Infinitivo' (cf. den Dikken & Hoekstra 1997; Wiklund 2001).

2.5.3 Participium pro Infinitivo

The characteristic property of the 'Participium pro Infinitivo' (PPI) boils down to constituting a 'mirror image' of the IPP (cf. Schmid 2002: 112), as can be seen in the Frisian example in (81), adopted from den Dikken & Hoekstra (1997: 1058).

(81) Hy soe it dien/ dwaan wollen ha.
 he would it do.PTCP/ do.INF want.PTCP have.INF
 'He would have liked to do it.'

As we can see here, Frisian optionally allows for the realisation of two past participial forms in a verb cluster governed by a single perfect auxiliary. In contrast to the IPP's characteristic habit of erasing past participial morphology, the PPI is therefore special by virtue of realising an additional instance of the past participial marker on a second verbal form in the cluster. This is unexpected given that a single exponent of the perfect auxiliary *ha* ('have') typically only takes a single verbal complement (in the present case *wollen* 'want'), as we have

---

[94] This stands in contrast to something like the German double-perfect, observable in *hat gesehen gehabt* ('has had seen', lit. has see.PTCP have.PTCP). Here, there are two past participial forms as well, but each of them is licensed by a designated auxiliary (as in *has been seen*), one of which shows up in participial form itself.

seen in each and every participial construction so far. Accordingly, den Dikken & Hoekstra (1997: 1058) assume that the unexpected second participle is "not directly selected by a token of the auxiliary of the perfect [but rather] parasitise[s] on the presence of the 'real' (i.e. *ha*-complemented) participle". Hence, this form is referred to as a 'parasitic participle' (cf. den Dikken & Hoekstra 1997: 1058). This basically entails that the improperly inflected 'parasitic' form is analysed as the photographic negative of the IPP's 'hidden participle'. The context in which the two phenomena surface is also identical, namely a verb cluster consisting of an auxiliary, a modal, and a verb,[95] where the modal, and only the modal, should occur in participial form, contrary to fact in IPP and PPI contexts. This particular context thus "seems to act as a trigger for the change in the verb form" (Schmid 2002: 113).

Crucially being absent in all the *ge*-languages that allow for the IPP, the occurrence of the PPI is not restricted to Frisian. In fact, one may also find instances of this phenomenon in other North Germanic languages (see Lindqvist 1944; Ljunggren 1934).[96] This is observable in the Faroese, Norwegian and Swedish examples in (82a-c), respectively, adopted from Wiklund (2001: 201).

(82) a. Han hevði viljað lisið/lesa bókina
       He   had   want.PTCP read.PTCP/read.INF the.book
       'He had wanted to read the book.'
    b. Jeg hadde villet lest/lese boka
       I   had   want.PTCP read.PTCP/read.INF the.book
       'I had wanted to read the book.'
    c. Jag hade velat läst/läsa boken
       I   had want.PTCP read.PTCP/read.INF the.book
       'I had wanted to read the book.'

While the occurrence of the PPI is restricted to certain variants of Norwegian and Swedish, it is broadly available in Faroese and Frisian, although it appears to be

---

[95] Note that there is no restriction limiting the number of parasitic participles in a given verb cluster to one (consider *Hy soe it dien kinnen wollen ha* 'He would have liked to be able to do it.', lit. he would it do.PTCP can.PTCP want.PTCP have.INF) (cf. den Dikken & Hoekstra 1997: 1068–1070).
[96] The applicability of the term PPI hinges on the question of whether Swedish supines are past participles. Otherwise, the term *dubbelsupinum* 'double supine' (or 'Supinum pro Infinitivo') is more appropriate and hence frequently used in the literature on Swedish (cf. Wiklund 2001: 201; den Dikken & Hoekstra 1997: 1086fn28).

optional in all of these languages (cf. Schmid 2002: 112).[97] In the other Germanic languages, e.g. Danish, and Icelandic, the PPI is consistently absent (cf. Wiklund 2001: 202; 2007: 190). The same holds true for English, where it naturally follows from the impossibility to embed modals, though (cf. Wurmbrand 2012a: 161).

The two most important properties of the PPI for our purposes in the present work are shared with the IPP as well as the PPP: its dependence on the presence of the perfect auxiliary HAVE and its lack of a divergent interpretation of the unexpected form. The former property relates to the fact that the PPI is barred in the context of the auxiliaries BE or WERDEN, i.e. the 'parasitic participle' may only occur in verbal clusters that are embedded under HAVE. Additionally, "the parasitic morphology is semantically vacuous[, i.e.] Par[asitic]Par[ticiple]s are not interpreted as a perfectives, [sic!] but rather the meaning is identical to the meaning of the infinitival construction" (Wurmbrand 2012a: 155). In other words, reminiscent of the plain form in the case of the IPP and the PPP, which is interpreted as a past participle and not as an infinitival form, the additional past participial form in a PPI-context is actually interpreted as an infinitival and not as a past participial form. Eventually, then, the semantic specifications in a given verb cluster remain the same regardless of what is suggested on the basis of their overt morphological ingredients. This ties in neatly with the observations we could make in the context of the PPP and the IPP, i.e. just like these phenomena the PPI suggests that perfect information is (at least partly) stored in the auxiliary HAVE. These are hence the only 'deviant' contexts in which perfect meaning may be derived and the periphrastic construction is thus not subject to ungrammaticality. The absence of a passive PPI, on the other hand, once more suggests that passive information is likely to be stored in the participial form alone and not – to a crucial extent at least – in the auxiliary.

Although we will once more not enter a principled theoretical discussion here, purely morphosyntactic accounts of the PPI usually raise many theoretical problems. In den Dikken & Hoekstra (1997: 1058f.), for instance, participles have to move into a licensing position in the domain of the auxiliary in order to be checked, where several elements may be licensed by one and the same auxiliary in the case of the PPI. This crucially rests upon the assumption that the participial semantics are not stored in the participial form but rather in the auxiliary that selects it (cf. den Dikken & Hoekstra 1997: 1068). This raises the question of why participial morphology is usually bound to be introduced in the context of a

---

97 The PPI is subject to dialectal as well as idiolectal variation in Norwegian and Swedish (cf. Schmid 2002: 112fn84). Here, just like in Frisian and Faroese, the PPI is optional although this, as Schmid (2002: 112f.) points out, may stem from the influence of the standard language in Norwegian and Swedish, which lack the PPI.

composite perfect, given that it is not semantically required for participial interpretations. Wurmbrand's (2012a) account tries to circumvent this problem by adopting Pesetsky & Torrego's (2007) dissociation of valuation and interpretability. This allows her to propose that an auxiliary may either value a participle or a participle value an auxiliary, which is subject to parametric variation (cf. Wurmbrand 2012a: 154). This variation is taken to stem from differences in morphological inventory, i.e. in *ge*-languages the latter direction is observed: the auxiliary contains unvalued (but interpretable) tense-features whereas the participial form is valued (cf. Wurmbrand 2012a: 160). In PPI-contexts, on the other hand, the perfect auxiliary contains an interpretable perfect (tense-)feature, which values the uninterpretable tense-features on the embedded modal as well as the main verb, both of which inflect as past participles (cf. Wurmbrand 2012a: 156f., 160). While struggling to provide an explanation for the IPP,[98] this assumption provides interesting theoretical insights and accounts for the PPI. However, even though the dissection of valuation and interpretability allows for an interesting approach to the PPI, its theoretical foundation cannot shake off the impression of being somewhat stipulative. Moreover, such an approach only technically accounts for the observable facts and attributes them to certain lexical items without ever accounting for why – conceptually speaking – the phenomenon only occurs in complex verb clusters headed by the perfect auxiliary HAVE.

Given the theoretical problems that such accounts raise, we will not assume that the PPI is primarily based on syntactic feature-valuation or checking, but rather suppose that the realisation of participial periphrases involving a verbal cluster is somewhat deviant and hence triggers morphological rescue strategies (cf. Hinterhölzl 2009: 209f.). These apparently impose a certain degree of cluster-internal conformity, which may be achieved in different ways, namely by employing impoverishment (IPP) or introducing ornamental morphology (PPI). Concerning the latter strategy employed in PPI-contexts, there principally is no reason to assume that the 'ornamental' piece of inflection is syntactically present (cf. Embick & Noyer 2007: 305f.), in analogy to impoverished items which still elicit the morphosyntactic characteristics of their participial counterparts. This ornamental material need not necessarily be new, but may in fact also be copied from another syntactic object: "Feature copying. A feature is present on a node *X* in the narrow syntax is copied [sic!] onto another node *Y* at PF" (Embick & Noyer 2007: 309). Thus, the featural reflex leading to the introduction of participial

---

[98] Wurmbrand (2012b: 130) considers the IPP, unlike the PPI, to be a PF-phenomenon (see also Zwart 2007).

morphology is copied from the participial form governed by the perfect auxiliary onto all other embedded verbs in the cluster, but only post-syntactically.[99] This leads to a clear demarcation of the participants of the verbal cluster, which may optionally be carried out in order to support interpretational clarity, but is not a necessity as there is no piece of morphology that is incompatible with the verbal cluster here. We will leave it at this highly tentative approach for now and briefly return to a technical account in 4.2.4 below.

Eventually, what the IPP and the PPI share is the fact that both of these phenomena arise in special contexts, namely verbal clusters featuring a participial form, a modal (or a different kind of restructuring element) and a perfect auxiliary, viz. an equivalent of the perfect auxiliary HAVE (or *zijn* 'be' in a highly restricted set of exceptions in Dutch). These similarities suggest that the IPP and the PPI are phenomena that allow for the formation of a complex verb cluster by different morphological means: impoverishment in the case of the IPP and the insertion of ornamental morphology in the case of the PPI. What is striking and particularly relevant for our present purposes is that all of these phenomena are restricted to the realisation of the perfect, (almost) exclusively demanding the designated perfect auxiliary HAVE to be around. This may be traced back to the feature-specification on the perfect auxiliary, which can thus be taken to include a sufficient amount of features to indicate a perfect interpretation (cf. Iatridou et al. 2001: 220f.). For the contexts exhibiting PPP and IPP, this accounts for why an impoverished ('hidden') participle may occur without endangering a proper perfect interpretation, which may thus be recovered regardless of the absence of participial morphology.[100] With respect to the PPI, the superfluous presence of a second participial form remains without interpretive effects because the participle alone cannot induce a perfect(ive) interpretation and passivisation may not be effected in the context of HAVE. Eventually, what is important to stress here is that even though the divergent realisations are ultimately analysed as PF-phenonema, focussing on semantic recoverability as a necessary condition for their application allows us to derive important insights for the distribution of properties in participial periphrases. In fact, the post-syntactic operations in question

---

99 In a similar vein, Hinterhölzl (2009: 210f.) assumes that the repair-operation deriving the IPP is also capable of deriving PPIs: instead of spelling out "the default morphology of an infinitive [,] one can also imagine that the entire feature matrix, including its formal feature is copied on to [sic!] the higher head." Given its morphosyntactic basis, this, however, requires deletion of the associated semantic features (cf. Hinterhölzl 2009: 211).

100 Note that there are, of course, numerous factors that play a crucial role with regard to whether impoverishment is applied, but the most important claim for our purposes is that recoverability is one of them.

may only be carried out if there remains a sufficient amount of material that unequivocally conveys the interpretation associated with the morphosyntactic properties of the construction at hand. Taking this seriously, we may conclude that all of the relevant information is stored in the past participles in eventive passive and BE-perfect contexts, whereas the auxiliary HAVE crucially contributes relevant perfect properties in the HAVE-perfect. We will return to the technical instantiations of these assumptions in Chapter 4.2.4 below, but may already conclude that rather than challenging the assumption of past participial (non-) identity, these contexts bear the potential of being particularly insightful in terms of determining the basic meaning of past participial forms.

2.5.4 Deponent verbs

While the major instances of divergent realisations of past participles, i.e. PPP, IPP, and PPI, have been introduced in the previous sections, we will now briefly turn to some minor insights provided by specialised participial forms, the so-called deponent verbs. These may most prominently be found in Latin and arguably shed light upon the allegedly compositional semantics of passive periphrases.

Quite generally, while not all past participles allow for usage in passive contexts based on their inherent properties (an unaccusative like *arrived* may for instance not be passivised), the formation of a past participle is generally possible for all verbs. Sometimes, the situation is reversed, though, i.e. there are past participles like *reputed* and *rumoured*, which "are wholly restricted to the passive – and are thus morphologically defective" (Ward et al. 2002: 1435). Although past participles that solely allow for the (active) perfect or the passive, respectively, are special in terms of involving certain restrictions on argument structure, they retain their basic properties and behave as expected. However, things do not always fall out as naturally, as a brief look at Latin deponent verbs shows. These are special in that the combination of a past participle with the auxiliary *esse* ('be') does not give rise to the usual combination of perfective and passive meaning, but instead elicits an active reading in a periphrastic construction like *secuta est* ('She has followed.', lit. follow.PTCP.F.SG is) (cf. Börjars et al. 1997: 171). In other words, the characteristic property of deponent verbs is that they exhibit a discrepancy of an active interpretation derived from a passive form (cf. Börjars et al. 1997: 172). Something quite similar may be observed in the context of so-called semi-deponent verbs. These employ imperfectives which occur as active forms, as in *gaudeo* ('I rejoice.', lit. rejoice.1.SG), whereas their perfectives have to appear in the passive form despite being interpreted as actives, as observable in *gavisus sum* ('I have rejoiced.', lit. rejoice.PASS.PFV is.1.SG) (cf. Börjars et al. 1997: 172). Items belonging to the latter kind of verbs thus "show different voice forms in different tenses" (Embick 2000: 190f.).

What is striking in the case of (semi-)deponent verbs is that "there is no common syntactic or semantic basis for uniting the deponent verbs" (Embick 2000: 192). Rather, it appears to be based on formal idiosyncracies, which either – according to Embick (2000: 190f.) – have to "be systematically correlated with the syntax of passivisation, [or] inherently possessed by certain Roots, for reasons that are not related to passive syntax". Embick (2000: 221f.), in an attempt to promote DM-ideas, assumes that only the latter possibility properly allows for passive morphology to come about without its associated passive semantics. As a matter of fact, Embick (2000: 221) claims that the lexicalist alternative is forced to resort to two distinct types of affixes, one that gives rise to passive sense and one that does not, only leading to a morphological passive. This is taken to "miss[] significant generalisations [in that p]assives and deponents are morphologically identical through all tenses, persons, and so on, and moreover behave the same way with respect to the formation of the perfect" (Embick 2000: 221). However, this flaw actually pertains to both approaches: in both cases a formal feature that does not impose any semantic consequences has to be associated with an unpredictable set of verbs. Thus, the DM-approach is no more insightful or persuasive than a lexicalist account, as it also has to stipulate the assignment of [pass] to certain roots, similar to the lexicalised assignment of a vacuous passive marker in the case of lexicalist approaches. In both analyses, the exceptional behaviour of deponent verbs is thus traced back to a conventional association of a semantically vacuous formal feature.

The most important conclusion that we may draw from the discussion of (semi-)deponents for the present purposes is that the participial form rather than the auxiliary apparently brings in passive information. This is primarily based on the observation that the special behaviour of deponents is restricted to a fairly small set of verbs, which are thus likely to contain diathesis information, rather than the passive auxiliaries (cf. Börjars et al. 1997: 171). This is underlined by the fact that Latin *esse* ('be') also occurs in the formation of the future active (*facturus esse* 'to be about to do') (cf. Börjars et al. 1997: 171), reminiscent of BE, which readily occurs with progressive elements in English (*Linnea is dancing*) and serves as a perfect auxiliary in German (*Er ist angekommen*, 'He has arrived.'). As Börjars et al. (1997: 171f.) point out, the auxiliary BE may also not be responsible for introducing perfect information given that it is impossible to use its perfective form *fuit/fuerit/fuerat* together with a past participial form, which hence also has to contain aspectual information in Latin. These findings are consistent with the conclusions drawn from the divergent realisations briefly investigated in the previous sections.

Eventually, then, there are several ways in which past participles may diverge from their canonical realisations. As we have just seen, one such exception concerns the morphologically defective (semi-)deponent forms of Latin, which (either consistently or only in the perfective paradigm) introduce passive morphology without inducing a passive interpretation. Given these peculiar idiosyncratic properties, these forms have arguably lexicalised their passive morphology, which remains syntactically (by virtue of motivating the insertion of an auxiliary) but not interpretationally (by virtue of not suppressing a semantic subject) active. This suggests that passive information is not stored in the auxiliary but rather in the participial form. This observation is supported by the other phenomena featuring divergent realisations that we have seen in the present chapter. The impoverishment-phenomena PPP and IPP suggest that passive information is solely introduced on the participial form, which is why its associated morphology may never be omitted. While the same arguably holds for BE-perfect contexts in which the participle apparently plays an essential role for perfect semantics, this is crucially different with HAVE-perfects, where the auxiliary thus contributes to the compositional interpretation of a composite perfect. The PPI, on the other hand, arguably involves ornamental morphology. This is also restricted to HAVE-perfects, as the additional participial element apparently does not interpretationally bring in any relevant information. In fact, it does not impose passive meaning by virtue of the presence of HAVE and may not in and of itself introduce a perfective interpretation, which is why the recovery of a proper (unaltered) interpretation is possible.

2.6 Implications from the historical development of past participles

Now that the most important empirical data have been laid out by focusing on synchronic occurrences of past participles, let us briefly take into consideration their diachronic development. As has been hinted at before, it is quite striking that passive and perfect(ive) participles may diachronically be traced back to one and the same source. What is very interesting with regard to the issue of past participial (non-)identity is what kind of a form this was and how it developed into the past participle that readily occurs in perfect and passive periphrases. As the grammaticalisation of these periphrases involves auxiliarisation, this discussion has to make recourse to the development of the particular auxiliaries involved. A potentially telling aspect of the nature of the periphrastic perfect and the analytic passive is that both constructions may be traced back to combinations of main verbs with deverbal adjectives that bear resultative as well as passive meaning. However, we have to be careful not to take such findings for granted as subsequent processes of grammaticalisation probably have altered a substantial amount of properties. This might either have induced non-identity or allowed past participles to retain their identity, in which case diachronic developments may well have the power to underline what is suggested by the synchronic data. The present section will start off with a brief consideration of what is known about the origin of participial forms and some basic properties of auxiliarisation, before turning to the grammaticalisation of the periphrastic passive and perfect.

Quite generally, only "[v]ery little is known about the origin of participial morphology" (Haspelmath 1990: 40), which forces us to keep our initial discussion of how participial elements come about quite superficial. Even though an obvious assumption may hold that participles stem from grammaticalisation of a free item "into a participle-forming affix [...], this type of development is rarely attested" (Haspelmath 1994: 167). In fact, what we rather find instead is that participles stem from (derivational) verbal adjectives (cf. Haspelmath 1994: 166). These are employed more and more regularly in distinct contexts until they may eventually be called participles (cf. Haspelmath 1994: 167). In other words, "[t]he process by which they most commonly arise is [...] not grammaticalisation, but analogy" (Haspelmath 1994: 167). Even though the amount of evidence on the origin of participial forms is quite scarce,[101] we may thus conclude that they stem from deverbal adjectives. In the case of past participles, these – as we will see in the discussion of the precursors of grammaticalised periphrases shortly – have an object-orientation. In fact, the main properties of past participial forms in their earliest instantiations are the following: their nature as deverbal adjectives which actually denote a resultative state, and their passive meaning in terms of being object-oriented, which comes along with the absence of a subject.[102] Therefore, resultative passive (or rather anticausative) meaning diachronically appears to be at the core of past participial elements (cf. Haspelmath 1990: 40).

Unlike what is occasionally claimed with respect to participial forms, grammaticalisation can clearly be observed to be at work in the context of auxiliaries. As briefly hinted at in Section 2.3, this process comprises semantic depletion (or

---

101 According to Haspelmath (1994: 168), a reason for this may probably be found in their longevity.
102 As Abraham (2006b: 484f.) points out, the passive meaning is likely to derive from the adjectival status of the past participial marker.

bleaching)[103] of a lexical verb, as for instance observable in Old High German (OHG) *habên* ('have'), which lost its lexical content of possession during that diachronic stage (cf. Şandor 2008: 32f.). Accordingly, what characterises auxiliaries most is their reduced amount of features (cf. Remberger 2006: 12). In fact, as their lack of a θ-grid shows,[104] they are often even regarded as semantically empty (cf. Remberger 2006: 12). On the other hand, all auxiliaries stem from an ancestor that is a lexical verb and they typically retain some of the properties of this element, e.g. certain selectional requirements, as we have seen in the context of HAVE and BE (cf. Remberger 2006: 11–13; see also Anderson 1989: 1). Remberger (2006: 13) eventually concludes that concrete meaning is bleached but gains new functional meaning.[105]

The precursors of properly grammaticalised periphrases often still remain functional (cf. Öhl 2009: 289f.), as observable in the German stative passive (formed with BE) and stative perfect (formed with HAVE) in (83).

(83) a. Er ist geschlagen.
       he is beat.PTCP
       'He is beaten.'
   b. Sie hat die Augen verbunden.
       She has the eyes bandage.PTCP
       'Her eyes are bandaged.'

These cases represent main verb combinations of the copula BE and the possessive verb HAVE with past participles that have a predicative function here, i.e. arguably are adjectival instances. The main verbs lose some of their semantic properties, i.e. the function of attributing a property to a referent and denoting possession in the present cases, when they develop into auxiliaries. This coincides with and constitutes an important ingredient for the grammaticalisation of the whole periphrasis. As auxiliarisation is thus tightly interwoven with grammaticalisation, we will now turn to the

---

103 This is anything but a novel concept, but has been introduced in von der Gabelentz (1891: 241f.) already.
104 Recall that this does not hold true for all elements that are taken to be auxiliaries, as we have briefly seen in the context of the dative passive in German, something that we will return to in Chapter 4.2.2.2.
105 Auxiliaries may also undergo decategorisation, i.e. lose their capacity of belonging to the category they stem from, and might even lose their standing as a designated word (cf. Remberger 2006: 14). Accordingly, Anderson (2006: 334) sees the grammaticalisation path of auxiliaries as follows: lexical verb > auxiliary verb > affix > ∅.

specific instantiation of grammaticalisation in the context of the historical development of the analytic perfect and the passive.

With respect to passive periphrases, the participial form starts out as a predicative deverbal adjective which already brings in passive (or anticausative) meaning via its inherent object-orientation, but also includes resultative semantics (cf. Haspelmath 1994: 169).[106] Accordingly, this form is initially tied to these semantic ingredients and may hence only derive perfective predicates that are bound to remain passive (cf. Abraham 2006a: 7; 2006b: 484). Prior to the grammaticalisation of proper passive periphrases, these properties are retained in combinations with main verbs. In OHG, for instance, *wërdan* ('become') could not yet be combined with non-terminative verbs (cf. Abraham 1992: 3f.). This arguably stems from the inherent lexical properties of WERDEN that were (largely) to be dropped in their development towards auxiliaryhood (cf. Abraham 1992: 3f.). As Musan (1998: 124) points out, the German eventive passive stems from an ingressive construction, i.e. one in which the main verb semantics of WERDEN are still clearly observable. According to Eckardt (2011: 391), this is observable in Behaghel's (1924: 200) example from OHG in (84), which crucially does not (yet) denote a proper eventive passive, but rather WERDEN conveys a transition by virtue of attributing a change of state to a referent.

(84) arslagan   uuirdit   Christ
     slaughter.PTCP *become* Christ
     'Christ will become (a) slaughtered (one).'

This construction is thus strongly reminiscent of what is assumed with respect to stative passives and stative perfects. While Abraham (2006a: 5f.; 2006b: 489)[107] claims that the general mechanism of deriving passive sense from an underlying aspectual meaning remains the same, this shifts off a crucial amount of work to implication. This is why we will rather tentatively

---

106 Josep M. Fontana (p.c.) points out that the claim that (eventive) passive participles are diachronically derived from deverbal adjectives is misguided at least with respect to Latin (and Romance), but probably also beyond. The participles could apparently always give rise to eventive passives, which might be taken to suggest that they were verbal all along. This does not necessarily challenge the broad conclusions drawn in the present chapter and it also need not question the claim of a common source of passive and perfect participles, though: even if the initial forms gave rise to eventive passive interpretations, inserting them into stative contexts rendered them anticausative, which marked the source of resultative participles. These in turn regained their verbal properties upon the grammaticalisation of perfect periphrases. We will leave such more fine-grained diachronic questions to future research and acknowledge that there is much more to be said about the historical development.

107 Note that this point is already made in Abraham (1992: 3f.; 1998: 163).

assume that the grammaticalisation of the periphrastic passive[108] does not only involve the auxiliarisation of WERDEN, but also involves changes to the effect of allowing for a verbal past participle, i.e. depriving the participle of its adjectival and hence resultative characteristics. This appears to carry over to English BE, which has been employed as the passive auxiliary due to the absence of a proper alternative, as we will see below. As pointed out by Lightfoot (1979), the English passive was increasingly extended to a large number of syntactic environments from Old English (OE) and Middle English (ME) to Modern English (ModE) (cf. Haspelmath 1990: 40).

In German, viz. OHG, the copula *wesan/sîn* ('be') could also be combined with deverbal adjectives that were to develop into past participles, although this was also dependent on particular aspectual properties (cf. Abraham 1992: 3f.). This entails that the combination of BE and a participial element was restricted to resultative predicates with an object (transitives and unaccusatives), similar to what we may still observe in the stative passive, e.g. in German. Unlike in English, where BE was eventually employed in periphrastic passives due to the absence of WERDEN, the BE-perfect "was the result of a reanalysis of the adjectival passive, with copula BE, as a periphrastic verbal perfect passive, replacing a synthetic form" (Ackema 1999: 137f.).[109] In other words, the BE-perfect stems from the resultative stative passive, which raises the question of what changes this development diachronically brought with it. Some approaches deny that there is grammaticalisation involved here (cf. Gillmann 2011: 203f.), arguing that the BE-perfect still is a copular construction with a predicative adjective (see Teuber 2005: 10f.) or still marks a resultative construction (see Leiss 1992: 164). Two observations that immediately shed doubt upon such assumptions are the following. First, the stative passive, unlike the BE-perfect, still combines with transitive predicates (which are then rendered anticausative) as long as these allow for a resultative reading, as observable in (83a). Second, there is a clear difference in interpretation between a proper BE-perfect and a stative passive, as we have seen on the basis of cases that are ambiguous between an eventive perfect and a stative passive reading before. Thus, we will follow Gillmann (2011: 203f.) in assuming that grammaticalisation – though potentially only

---

108 Abraham (2006a: 7f.; 2006b: 469) refers to the question of how a proper verbal passive arose between Early Modern German and Modern Standard German as the Diachronic Passive Riddle.
109 Traditional proponents of this view are Wilmanns (1906: 134f.) and Zieglschmid (1929). See also Öhl (2009: 298–300) for a discussion of what might have changed in the auxiliarisation of the copula *sein* ('be').

weakly so – is involved here as well.[110] This boils down to auxiliarisation of BE to the effect that it is not restricted to attribute a property to a referent anymore, on the one hand, and a loss of the adjectival characteristics of the deverbal form, on the other. Eventually, one of the sources for the periphrastic perfect is the copula construction with BE and a deverbal adjective (cf. Bybee & Dahl 1989: 67f.). As briefly hinted at before, the existence of such a copular construction – though crucially not of a proper BE-perfect (cf. Larsson 2009: 433) – even appears to be a prerequisite for the development of a HAVE-perfect (cf. Leiss 1992: 166f.; see Benveniste 1960/1966).[111] While the BE-perfect has often been treated novercally, we will now see that the grammaticalisation of the HAVE-perfect is quite well-studied (cf. Gillmann 2011: 203).

As mentioned before, the HAVE-perfect stems from a stative perfect construction (cf. Migdalski 2006: 148; Larsson 2009: 1).[112] In fact, the HAVE-perfect "originated from a possessive construction formed with 'have' as the main verb, which was followed by a DP complement and a passive participle" (Migdalski 2006: 148).[113] This is observable in (83b), which shows that this 'passive participle' is the resultative deverbal adjective that marks the origin of all past participial forms. Even though this is not observable in its German remnant anymore, the predicative participial element involved in these constructions typically agrees with the nominal element it modifies (cf. Migdalski 2006: 148).[114] These stative perfect

---

[110] Note that Gillmann (2011: 203f., 209f.) additionally points to an extension of the applicability of the BE-perfect with respect to (manner of) motion verbs. This leads her to claim that "[t]he reanalysis of *sein* + second participle is reflected by the distribution of the auxiliaries which is not strictly conditioned by *aktionsart* anymore" (Gillmann 2011: 203). We will abstract away from this as these changes may well be based on the lexicalisation of particular classes of verbs rather than the auxiliaries involved, as briefly seen in Chapter 2.3.

[111] Therefore, it is typically not the case that a BE-perfect arises and then is lost in HAVE-only languages like English and Swedish (cf. Larsson 2009: 429–433). In fact, the BE-perfect need not predate the HAVE-perfect, as observable in Danish, where the BE-perfect developed later than the HAVE-perfect (cf. Larsson 2009: 429–433).

[112] The stative perfect remnants may but need not (consider **Jan has the manuscript written*) still be functional. German, as we have seen, may still make use of a stative construction featuring HAVE and the same also holds for Dutch, as Ackema (1999: 167–169) points out with the help of the following example: *Jan heeft het manuscript geschreven* ('Jan has written the manuscript.' vs. 'Jan has the manuscript that is in a written state.').

[113] Note that this idea is already present in Behaghel (1928).

[114] Such a construction may for instance be found in Latin: *Habeo cibum coctum* (have.1.SG food.ACC.SG.M cooked.ACC.SG.M) (cf. Pinkster 1987: 210). According to Öhl (2009: 273f.), this construction did not develop into a periphrastic HAVE-perfect until Late Latin, when it finally dropped its agreement morphology.

2.6 Implications from the historical development of past participles

constructions have been grammaticalised in Germanic as well as Romance, though arguably at different stages in time (cf. Öhl 2009: 266). The two language families share, however, that the diachronic reanalysis (and thus auxiliarisation) of the possessive lexical verb corresponding to HAVE was accompanied by a structural reanalysis of predicative constructions involving HAVE and a past participle (cf. Öhl 2009: 284). In other words, the HAVE-perfect results from reanalysing "a (passive) participle with adjectival properties [...] as a perfect participle which is employed to form a complex tense" (Larsson 2009: 10). In German, this process may be traced back to OHG (cf. Öhl 2009: 284). Here, the lexical verbs *habên* and *eigan* ('have') take participles that agree with their objects and initially express a present result, but increasingly lose their lexical meaning and undergo auxiliarisation (cf. Şandor 2008: 32f.). This process – first applying to transitives, then also to intransitives – is accompanied by a loss of agreement morphology (case inflection) on the participial element, forms a complex predicate with the auxiliary and brings with it that the passive meaning increasingly vanishes (cf. Şandor 2008: 34). In English, the situation is not entirely clear and "it is a matter of debate whether 'have'-perfects reached grammaticalisation already in Old English, or only in Middle English" (Migdalski 2006: 151). Accordingly, there is uncertainty as to whether the combination of *habban* ('have') and a past participle still gave rise to a resultative perfect or already exhibited the former as a fully-fledged perfect auxiliary in OE, in which case the possessive perfect construction would already have been grammaticalised (cf. Łęcki 2010: 164). Abstracting away from the intricate discussion of the precise temporal placement of the development (see Łęcki 2010: 204f.; Migdalski 2006: 151f.; Larsson 2009: 140), what is clear is that this development was completed in ME (cf. Łęcki 2010: 146).

Given that the development of a stative perfect into a proper HAVE-perfect apparently proceeds along similar lines in Germanic and Romance, let us briefly regard its grammaticalisation path, which may be found in (85), as sketched by Łęcki (2010: 149).

(85) Stage I   He   has   meat
              (possessor) (poss. verb) (possessee)

Stage II He   has   meat   cooked
              (possessor) (poss. verb) (possessee) (modifier)
              (reanalysis)

Stage III He   has   meat   cooked
              (agent)   (auxiliary) (direct object) (main verb)

Stage IV He   has   cooked   meat
              (agent)   (auxiliary) (main verb)   (direct object)
              (analogy)

Stage V   He   has   cooked/died
          (agent)   (auxiliary) (main verb)

As Łęcki (2010: 149f.) argues, this grammaticalisation path – though investigated primarily for English here – may be taken to hold universally in those languages in which a perfect auxiliary corresponding to HAVE is available.[115] Accordingly, what we can see at Stage I and II is the main verb heritage of HAVE, which is first regularly found in canonical constructions denoting possession at Stage I. The possessees may then be modified by deverbal adjectives, i.e. 'resultative passive participles', at Stage II. The most crucial development then applies between Stage II and III, where the resultatively interpreted predicate complexes need to be reanalysed and the formerly possessive main verb needs to be recategorised as an inflectional element, a perfect auxiliary (cf. Öhl 2009: 290).[116] This entails that "[t]hrough subsequent reanalysis, the participle came to be construed as predicating an action of the individual to whom the subject refers" (Michaelis 2006: 223). Upon completion of this reanalysis, grammatical consequences like the loss of agreement morphology (cf. Łęcki 2010: 150) and changes in word order come about (Stages III and IV). Especially the former thus overtly marks the transition of an object-oriented deverbal adjective to a verbal past participle that may realise its subject with the help of HAVE. Subsequently, the HAVE-perfect is analogically extended to contexts that are not properly grasped by competing constructions yet (e.g. unergative predicates in German).

A further question that may be raised in this context is why certain languages (like English, Spanish and Icelandic) have developed a periphrastic perfect in which all contexts are formed with the help of HAVE, while others (e.g. German, French and Danish) still distinguish between HAVE and BE. This primarily concerns the question of whether unaccusative predicates may form a perfect with HAVE or BE, as transitives and unergatives are generally selected by HAVE in both kinds of languages. The development of a HAVE-only pattern may be seen in English, where earlier stages (OE and ME) arguably allowed

---

[115] Note that this intuition is also present in Bybee & Dahl's (1989: 68f.) universal grammaticalisation path of the past tense, which states the following order: resultative > present perfect > past (cf. Gillmann 2011: 204–207).

[116] Many approaches (see, for instance, Abraham 1986; 1991: 129, 1992: 5; Salvi 1987; Hoekstra 1986a; Migdalski 2006: 157f.) suggest that the grammaticalisation of stative perfects to fully-fledged periphrastic perfects proceeded in terms of a single process of reanalysis of a main verb towards an auxiliary on the basis of a small clause headed by an adjective and reanalysed as a VP. Öhl (2009: 286–288) argues against this by claiming that prior to the recategorisation of HAVE, there must have been a reanalysis of the combination of past participle and HAVE to a complex predicate. We will not be concerned with such specific concerns here.

both HAVE and BE to form a periphrastic perfect with unaccusative predicates at the same time (cf. Ackema 1999: 124). As Łęcki (2010: 157) points out, "[a]s early as in Old English the dividing line between BEON and HABBAN followed by past participles of intransitive verbs was beginning to blur." This interchangeability is also observable in Middle Dutch (MidD), which – rather than granting HAVE the formation of perfects of all kinds at the expense of a BE-perfect (cf. Anderson 2000: 813) – took a different route than English by virtue of developing a fully-fledged auxiliary alternation in Modern Dutch (ModD) (cf. Ackema 1999: 124f.). This difference may (somewhat trivially) be tied to whether or not BE is perfect forming in the languages in question (cf. Ackema 1999: 134).

In English, HAVE is generalised to unaccusative contexts (and usually not even the copula BE may be combined with such predicates in stative passives anymore), whereas the auxiliary BE increasingly lost ground. According to Łęcki (2010: 163), this "is most often attributed to the heavy functional load of the auxiliary, which was already employed in other constructions like passive and, accordingly, it was confusingly ambiguous". This is crucially different in German and Dutch, where there is a passive auxiliary that is distinct from BE, namely WERDEN. In fact, a cognate of the latter also existed in OE, but here it was lost (cf. Klein 2010: 1240), which is why BE ended up as being the only element that could show up in periphrastic passive constructions. As Ackema (1999: 137) points out, "in ModE the construction with BE is not an alternative to the one with HAVE for forming perfects [due to] BE [having] lost its perfectivity in the course of ME changing to ModE". This is thus crucially tied to the loss of English *weorþan* ('become'), something that did not happen in Dutch or German, where *worden* or *werden* ('become') are still employed (cf. Ackema 1999: 137–140).

Eventually, then, once HAVE and BE are reanalysed in the context of adjectival participles in order to form perfect active and passive periphrases, one of two routes is taken (cf. Ackema 1999: 138). One possibility is that the auxiliaries remain perfect-forming (giving rise to auxiliary alternation), which presupposes the availability of a non-perfect passive auxiliary like WERDEN, present in both MidD and OE but only retained in ModD (cf. Ackema 1999: 138f.). Alternatively, if the designated non-perfect passive auxiliary is dropped, as in the case of OE *weorþan* ('become'), its passive function is taken over by BE, which is henceforth used in non-perfect passives (cf. Ackema 1999: 138f.). In the latter variant, HAVE is bound to be generalised to all kinds of predicates (HAVE-only), as BE is not allowed to form perfect periphrases by virtue of its burden of forming the eventive passive (cf. Ackema 1999: 138f.).[117] This concludes our brief excursus to the historical development of auxiliary alternation[118] as opposed to the HAVE-only pattern, which shall suffice for the present purposes, although many issues remain. These for instance concern the characteristics of languages that have a somewhat larger system of auxiliaries: both Italian as well as Icelandic make use of BE in periphrastic eventive passives, but also have a designated passive auxiliary, which raises the question of why the former shows auxiliary alternation in the composite perfect, whereas the latter is a HAVE-only language. These observations indicate that there either is more to the determination of perfect-forming auxiliaries or the timing of the availability of an auxiliary to be used exclusively for passives is the decisive factor here.

This leaves the question of why none of the Germanic and Romance languages just generalised BE to all perfect contexts (cf. Öhl 2009: 296). This may be tied to the participial heritage as deverbal adjectives with an object-orientation, i.e. passive semantics, which require the help of their auxiliaries in order to introduce a subject. In fact, prior to the grammaticalisation of the HAVE-perfect and its analogical extension to intransitive cases, past participles of unergative predicates could not be formed at all (cf. Öhl 2009: 296; see also Behaghel 1899: 69). The reason for this is that there simply was no context of use for such cases yet. In adjectival distributions, they are ungrammatical as they cannot modify a nominal referent due to the past participial object-orientation. In the context of the perfect auxiliary BE, on the other hand, it is also impossible for them to realise their external argument, based on the properties that the auxiliary retains from its (unaccusative) main verb counterpart. The perfect auxiliary HAVE, however, stems from a transitive main verb and may hence introduce an external argument as well as trigger accusative case assignment by virtue of the argument structural properties that it has retained (cf. Öhl 2009: 297f.). Eventually, then, BE simply is not compatible with predicates that bear an external argument, which is why it may only ever give rise to passives (in English) or unaccusative perfects (in German).[119]

---

117 A similar extension is also observable in Romance, e.g. in Old Spanish, where unaccusatives were formed with *ser* ('be') but increasingly lost their ability to form a perfect, which is nowadays formed with *haber* ('have'), while the former is restricted to expressing a passive reading (cf. Lois 1990: 234).

118 See Larsson (2009: 142f., 184f.) for a discussion of the development of auxiliary alternation in Scandinavian.

119 This is crucially different in languages like Slavic, which bear substantially distinct past participial elements. Here, the perfect participle retains the capability of introducing an external argument and assigning accusative case all by itself, which is why these may readily be combined with BE.

2.6 Implications from the historical development of past participles — 131

While some of the specific characteristics laid bare in the present section will be of importance in the theoretical discussion in Chapter 4, most important for the discussion of past participial (non-)identity is that perfect(ive) and passive participles indeed have the same source (see Dal 2014 [1952]: 128–130; Schrodt 2004: 9–11; Mitchell 1985: 12, 280f.; Robinson 1992: 169–171). This common source is a deverbal adjective that bears resultative meaning and has an object-orientation by virtue of which it is interpreted as being passive.[120] As Migdalski (2006: 142) puts it, "past participles historically originate from passive participles". This item may initially be found in contexts in which it modifies a nominal referent, i.e. in copular constructions with WERDEN and BE (stative passives) or in possessive constructions with HAVE (stative perfects). In these constructions it is restricted to denoting a resultative property and object-oriented in the sense of treating the element that it modifies like its internal argument. These constructions may then be grammaticalised in order to replace older synthetic forms by virtue of denoting the perfect and the passive (cf. Ackema 1999: 145). This grammaticalisation certainly features auxiliarisation, but arguably also has an effect on the deverbal adjective. According to Ackema (1999: 146), it includes "a syntactic restructuring of the adjectival participle as a verbal form [...] happen[ing] earlier in the passive perfect than in either the active perfect or the passive imperfect". What is striking here, then, is that in the novel periphrastic constructions "the same past participle is used in both the passive and the perfect, while in the[ir synthetic counterparts] distinct passive and perfect morphology can be distinguished" (Ackema 1999: 145). Eventually, "due to the process of verbalisation, the paradigm of the past participle is extended to all verbs, and it also covers verbs which disallow passivisation" (Migdalski 2006: 151). Accordingly, Migdalski (2006: 150f.) concludes that "the passive participle is the same element, whether it occurs in a passive construction or as a past participle in a compound tense formed with the auxiliary 'have'". This marks the identity view that we will also endorse in the present work given that none of the empirical data discussed in the present chapter substantially challenge it.

*

The present second chapter presented a wide range of empirical data in order to work out the main characteristics of past participles in periphrases and – occasionally at least – beyond against the backdrop of past participial (non-) identity. While this laid bare the fact that there are languages featuring substantially distinct passive and perfect(ive) participles, Germanic and Romance

---

[120] According to Poitou (1994: 114), given their rather late development as deverbal adjectives, it is not surprising that the morphological change of the past participle historically is the last one a verb undergoes.

languages are apparently different in terms of consistently using one and the same piece of inflectional morphology in the periphrastic passive as well as the analytic perfect. Actually, Swedish is the odd man out here as it does not conform to this pattern and has developed a substantial distinction between passive participles and supines reminiscent of proper non-identity languages like Bulgarian. The latter, however, differ from Swedish in terms of solely employing the auxiliary BE in both contexts. In contrast to these substantial cases of participial polymorphy, i.e. those that have a proper grammatical basis, Romance and North Germanic languages exhibit shallow morphological differences in terms of past participial object-agreement. These may, however, convincingly be shown to follow from the particular properties of a given syntactic configuration rather than stemming from a grammatical distinction between a perfect(ive) and a passive participle.

The past participle could be shown to occur in periphrases as well as in bare uses. With respect to the former, what is striking is that auxiliary selection is based on argument structure but arguably also on event structure (or aktionsart), which probably has to do with the grammatical features that auxiliaries retain from their main verb ancestors. Therefore, BE and WERDEN are restricted to cases in which there syntactically is no external argument, i.e. unaccusatives and passives, whereas HAVE occurs in those cases in which an external argument has to be introduced, namely (di-)transitive and unergative predicates. With respect to event structure, which plays a role in terms of accounting for auxiliary alternation in the composite perfect, the relevant dimension of difference appears to relate primarily to the presence of a simple change of state, which triggers a BE-perfect. Some of these observations readily carry over to the intricate properties of bare occurrences. These share that they always show object-orientation towards an element that may typically be independently realised (pre- and postnominal cases) or might supposedly occasionally be introduced by the participial element itself (absolute clauses). Another shared characteristic is that they may never realise an external argument, which provides support for the assumption that HAVE plays an important role in this respect in periphrastic constructions. Additionally, they may either give rise to a resultative or an imperfective interpretation based on their aktionsart and the degree of a bias towards a stative interpretation, which may stem from adjectival morphology attached to the participial form or the particular structural embedding. In terms of category, it is assumed that upon attaching participial morphology to a verbal element, the latter loses some of its core verbal properties, but typically gains some adjectival properties in return.

In addition to these general empirical findings, insights could be adduced from divergent realisations of past participles, most importantly the PPP, IPP and

PPI. These morphological phenomena – abstracting away from some lexicalised exceptions in Dutch – are consistently restricted to contexts featuring the perfect auxiliary HAVE. Given that corresponding passive or BE-perfect versions of these divergent realisations are not available, it was proposed that HAVE includes relevant perfect meaning and may hence suffice for the recovery of a perfect interpretation. In the case of the passive and the BE-perfect, on the other hand, all the relevant information for a passive or perfect interpretation is stored in the participle, which is why a divergent realisation in terms of impoverishment or ornamental morphology on a second 'participial' form in a verbal cluster is barred. This entails that neither BE nor WERDEN comprises relevant perfect or passive information, quite unlike HAVE, which arguably includes the capability of introducing an external argument as well as a set of relevant perfect information.

Given that the distinct properties of the periphrastic passive and the analytic perfect always seem to stem from the different auxiliaries involved and their combination with participles derived from particular types of verbs, it is not far-fetched to assume that the passive and the perfect(ive) participle in Germanic and Romance are indeed one and the same, namely a past participle. A case for this may not only be made on the basis of synchronic data but receives additional support from observations regarding the diachronic development of past participles. Most importantly, these stem from one and the same form, namely a deverbal adjective that bears resultative meaning as well as an object-orientation. This 'passive perfective' element lost many of its adjectival properties upon being reanalysed in terms of playing a crucial role in the grammaticalisation of a periphrastic (imperfective) passive and an analytic (active) perfect. As part of this process, the participle regained some of its verbal properties, e.g. the ability to realise an internal argument in clausal functions, whereas its functional flexibility arguably stems from the auxiliarisation of one of several main verbs (HAVE, BE, or WERDEN). Thus, rather than hard-coding a difference into the participial forms, the diverse properties of past participial occurrences stem from the complex interaction of auxiliary, past participial morphology and verbal semantics, as will be explicated in detail in Section 4 below.

Prior to laying out a novel approach to past participial identity in Chapter 4, the next section will turn to previous approaches to past participial (non-)identity in order to discuss their flaws and merits. This raises awareness for potential problems but presumably also allows us to take over some of the concepts that appropriately account for the behaviour of past participles. Additionally, this discussion will put the general consequences of the assumption of (non-)identity into theoretical perspective.

3 Past participial (non-)identity in the literature

Now that the most relevant empirical data concerning the issue of the (non-)identity of passive and perfect(ive) participles have been laid out, it is time to take into consideration the theoretical dimension. Surprisingly, the amount of literature explicitly concerned with the question of past participial (non-)identity is relatively small and principled approaches are scarce. Nevertheless, due to the fact that both the perfect and the passive have received an extensive amount of attention, there is a bulk of literature tentatively addressing the issue and bringing forth some interesting insights. The present chapter will provide a discussion of previous approaches to past participial (non-)identity, considering both principled approaches as well as those that only discuss the issue in passing.

The two major strands of approaches directly accrue from the underlying question of past participial (non-)identity: either past participles are ambiguous between a passive and a perfect(ive) interpretation and hence there are two substantially distinct items or one and the same element is employed in both cases (cf. Wunderlich 1997: 2). Accordingly, the major approaches to be lined up shortly are those that advocate past participial non-identity, on the one hand, and those that propose that the past participial shallow identity in form is mirrored by an identity in terms of their syntacticosemantic properties. Instances of the former kind, to be addressed in chapter 3.1, are usually fairly straightforward in terms of assuming that passive and perfect(ive) participles are just accidentally homophonous and crucially bear distinct sets of syntacticosemantic features. Approaches based on identity, discussed in chapter 3.2, on the other hand, come in distinct kinds based on which (if any) relevant information they attribute to the past participle. While these approaches share the assumption that the identity of past participial forms reaches down to syntactic as well as semantic properties, they differ in whether the past participle is held responsible for introducing (aspects of) passive and/or perfect(ive) meaning or taken to be semantically vacuous.

Following the discussion of the distinct kinds of approaches to past participial (non-)identity,[1] the present chapter will briefly put their major flaws and merits into perspective in section 3.3. Coupled with the empirical findings of the previous

---

[1] While there already have been attempts to provide an overview of the distinct kinds of approaches to past participial identity, most prominently in Vater (2002), Wunderlich (1997), Wanner (2009), Ackema (1999), and Müller (2007), none of these succeeds in providing an exhaustive overview of the different possibilities.

section, this will eventually guide us towards a proper answer to the issue at hand and occasionally anticipate ingredients of its theoretical implementation.

3.1 The ambiguity of past participles

The basic assumption of what may be referred to as ambiguity (or non-identity) approaches is that exponents of passive participles are just coincidentally realised by morphological markers that are homophonous with those used to realise perfect(ive) participles. Taken seriously, this reasoning suggests that the present participle's morphological marker *-ing* in English is just as much of a designated item as the passive participle or the perfect(ive) participle. In fact, the former is just as closely related to the two distinct forms of the past participle as those are to one another. Accordingly, these are realised by affixes that differ in terms of their feature sets despite exhibiting shallow identity with respect to morphologically being spelled out by, say, *-en*. This puts perfect(ive) and passive participles on a par with other homophonous morphological realisations like the regular plural inflectional suffix and the 3rd person agreement morphology, both of which are realised by the morphological marker *-s* in English (cf. Embick 2003: 146). Even without resorting to the empirical findings laid out in the previous section, this is an intuitively peculiar consequence given the vast amount of similarities that the two past participial forms exhibit. Nevertheless, there are approaches that explicitly argue for past participial non-identity.

Traditional grammar extensively makes use of the distinction of past participles into two designated subcategories (cf. Haider 1984: 23). Even though this suggests that participial homonymy is the prevalent view in traditional works (cf. Abraham 1986: 110f.), given that these are typically not explicitly concerned with past participial ambiguity there usually remain doubts about whether this is taken seriously or solely a terminological distinction.[2] While it remained implicit in traditional approaches, the issue of past participial (non-)identity has explicitly been discussed in the literature ever since the 1980s. In fact, the ambiguity approach to past participles is most strongly advocated in Drijkoningen (1989), Bierwisch (1990), Aronoff (1994), and – though less clearly so – in Lois (1990),

---

2 Gunkel (2003: 69f.) supports the view that the distinction was merely a terminological issue lacking theoretical substance, which entails that traditional grammar remains agnostic about the matter at hand.

but also finds followers in more recent works (e.g. in exponents of Head-Driven Phrase-Structure Grammar).[3]

Drijkoningen's (1989) work on verbal affixation resolutely speaks out against more recent trends pursued in works such as Hoekstra (1984), Fabb (1984), and Roberts (1985). Whereas these earlier approaches strongly rely on the auxiliaries that are involved in participial constructions, Drijkoningen (1989: 80) focusses on affixes and suggests "that the affixes are relevant rather than the auxiliaries". This foreshadows the (somewhat trivial) consequence that identity approaches instead have to attribute the distinctions to stem from ingredients other than the morphological marker involved in past participle formation. Drijkoningen (1989: 71), on the other hand, explicitly suggests that there is both a designated passive participial affix as well as a designated perfective participial affix, which crucially differ in terms of the features they introduce. Accordingly, as Drijkoningen (1989: 71) puts it, there is a "past participle with a passive value (PASS) and [a] past participle with a perfective value (PERF)". These two syntacticosemantically distinct affixes, PASS and PERF, are taken "to generalise in morphology rather than in syntax" (Drijkoningen 1989: 72). This bears the inevitable "consequence, however, that it must be assumed that in all the relevant languages the passive morphology and the perfect morphology are accidentally homophonous" (Ackema 1999: 87) – quite a conspicuous coincidence, to say the least.

The ambiguity of past participles is argued to be empirically supported by evidence from synthetic languages, which are claimed to "show that [the] affixes PERF and PASS have exactly the same function in languages and constructions without auxiliaries" (Drijkoningen 1989: 80). Therefore, in an attempt to provide a general theory capturing the facts of both analytic as well as synthetic languages, Drijkoningen (1989: 92) claims that an explanation based on the auxiliaries is problematic and ought to be abolished in favour of one that focusses on the affixes involved. However, some caution is in order concerning the correlation of the passive and the perfect in analytic and synthetic languages. First, as pointed out before, homophony may never be observed in languages that express the perfect and the passive synthetically (cf. Ackema 1999: 87f.). Second, while it seems to hold true that the passive is similar in synthetic and analytic languages, this supposedly does not carry over to the perfect. In fact, there are at least interpretational differences in that the universal perfect apparently demands an analytic construction,

---

[3] In addition to the rather clear-cut ambiguity approaches that we will be concerned with here, ambiguity is often also assumed without detailed discussion (see, amongst others, Jacobs 1994: 312; Warner 1993: 74f.).

which is somewhat surprising if the affixes have exactly the same function in analytic as well as synthetic cases. Furthermore, the logical question that the ambiguity approach has to face is what the auxiliaries are needed for in analytic languages if everything there is to perfect and passive is in the affixes involved. This objection pertains not only to Drijkoningen (1989) but, in fact, to each and every ambiguity approach to past participles. These *per definitionem* strip away the necessity for auxiliaries in terms of their lack of introducing relevant passive or perfect information and instead attribute those entirely to the two distinct (yet homophonous) affixes. In order to cope with the lack of a proper justification for the introduction of auxiliaries, Drijkoningen (1989: 87) reduces the function of auxiliaries to the requirement for a correlation between auxiliaries and affixes. Accordingly, auxiliaries are merely required "in order to get a one-to-one correspondence between affixes and verbs [where] [t]he number of auxiliaries is the number of affixes minus one" (Drijkoningen 1989: 86f.). This is a highly dubious formal justification.

The idea of semantically vacuous auxiliaries is also prominently featured in Bierwisch's (1990: 189) closely related ambiguity approach, which attributes passivisation and perfectivisation to distinct inflectional affixes. While the participial marker's identity is once more restricted to its shallow morphophonological nature, the German perfect auxiliaries *hab* ('have') and *sei* ('be') are claimed to be identical to the passive auxiliary *werd* ('become') (cf. Bierwisch 1990: 189). The only differences are taken to concern their phonological form and the feature [±Pass], which determines selection of either the active (i.e. perfect) or passive participle, but does not introduce any relevant information (cf. Bierwisch 1990: 189).

Lois (1990: 241) – though primarily concerned with auxiliary alternation and agreement – also defends the non-identity of participial affixes and hence "dissociat[es] the two participles (active and passive), in spite of their morphological 'identity'". The salient distinction between the passive and the perfect(ive) participial suffix is assumed to boil down to whether or not it is an argument (cf. Lois 1990: 240–242). Argument-status – as ascribed to the past participial affix in many identity approaches, as we will see below – is attributed to the passive participial suffix, which allows it to receive (or 'absorb') the subject θ-role as well as object case and (in some languages, at least) triggers agreement (cf. Lois 1990: 240–242). The perfect(ive) participial affix, on the other hand, cannot function as an argument and hence also cannot receive the subject θ-role or exhibit agreement (cf. Lois 1990: 240–242). This is formalised in terms of θ-absorption, a notion that will be explicated more precisely in the context of identity approaches, viz. those that suggest that the underlying meaning of the past participle is 'passive' in chapter 3.2.2 below. The crucial difference between identity approaches assuming θ-absorption and Lois' (1990) ambiguity approach is that the former attribute 'argument-like' properties to perfect periphrases as well. While these approaches have to resort to independent mechanisms for the introduction of the θ-role in question in perfect cases, Lois (1990: 251) restricts θ-absorption to those participial lexical entries that are passive.[4] Eventually, then, the two kinds of participles differ in exactly this property, i.e. in whether or not absorption is at work, whereas additional differences in terms of carrying perfect semantics are not explicitly discussed, but probably called for.

An elaborate formal implementation of the non-identity of passive and perfect(ive) participles is put forth by Aronoff (1994). In order to capture the shallow identity of passive and perfect(ive) participles, Aronoff (1994: 23–25) suggests that both kinds of past participles are derived by the same morphophonological function F_{en}. An argument for the assumption that it is indeed one and the same morphological marker as instantiated by F_{en} comes from verbs like *kneeled/knelt* that show a certain amount of variation, which crucially never leads to distinct exponents for passive and perfect participles (cf. Aronoff 1994: 24). This function, however, may be assigned distinct morphosyntactic values, mirroring its two syntactic uses: "to form the passive verb and to form the perfect verb (always in company with the verb HAVE)" (Aronoff 1994: 24f.). Although Aronoff (1994: 24f.) acknowledges that diachronic considerations suggest that the two past participles are substantially identical (see Benveniste 1960/1966 and chapter 2.6), it is assumed that the two are in fact entirely independent from each other syntactically. Support for this view is claimed to come "[f]rom a universal perspective, [where] it would be odd for passive and perfect constructions to be identical at some deep syntactic level, since the two only rarely coincide morphologically" (Aronoff 1994: 24f.). This argument, however, once more does not take into consideration the potential contribution of the auxiliaries. In order to reconcile the identity of the morphophonological function F_{en} in passive and perfect cases with the syntacticosemantic non-identity of passive and perfect(ive) participles, Aronoff (1994: 25) proposes a purely morphological level, the *morphomic* level, for functions like F_{en}, so-called *morphomes*. This level is taken to be responsible for operations that are completely independent from syntax and phonology and thus constitutes an indirect "mapping from morphosyntax to phonological realization"

---

[4] For Gunkel (2003: 69), the possibility of case absorption, which is closely related to θ-absorption in terms of attributing argument-like properties to the participial affix, necessarily requires a lexical distinction of passive and perfect(ive) participle in that only the former may impose case absorption. However, this view neglects the possibility of reinstating the absorbed properties via an auxiliary, as regularly proposed in identity approaches.

(Aronoff 1994: 25). The morphomic level often remains invisible, as "a singleton morphosyntactic set [is] mapped onto a singleton morphomic set, which itself is mapped onto a singleton morphophonogical set" (Aronoff 1994: 25). In contexts like the shallow identity of past participles, on the other hand, the merits of a distinct level of designated morphological processing are claimed to come to the fore (cf. Aronoff 1994: 25).

Quite generally, Aronoff (1994: 176fn35) acknowledges that "complex morphological identity is a good heuristic for syntactic identity [but argues that] this heuristic [may not simply be elevated] to a theoretical claim". This leaves enough room for his approach to past participial ambiguity, although he also points to the lack of a detailed account of the (non-)identity of past participles (cf. Aronoff 1994: 176fn35). As he puts it, "[i]t might very well turn out in the end that the two constructions are synchronically related in their syntax in such a way that the identity of the participles is explained" (Aronoff 1994: 176fn35). Even though Aronoff (1994) thus provides a technical apparatus to deal with syntactically unrelated forms that are principally realised by the same morphological means, the need for a proper clarification and explanation with respect to past participial (non-)identity remains.

Briefly turning to other grammatical theories, the ambiguity assumption is also prevalent in a number of Construction Grammar (CxG), Lexical Functional Grammar (LFG) and Head-Driven Phrase-Structure Grammar (HPSG) approaches.[5] The latter for instance usually assume two designated lexical entries for passive and perfect(ive) participial forms (cf. Müller 2007: 307f.). An exponent of this kind is put forth by Pollard & Sag (1987: 213f.), who explicitly assume that the lexical rule for passive formation just uses the same morphological operation as the one used to form perfect(ive) participles.[6] Closely related to Pollard & Sag (1987) in spirit, Bresnan's (1978: 21; 1982: 18–21) LFG approach acknowledges the identity of form through the application of the same morphological operation in both the rule of perfect formation as well as passive formation. Likewise, Michaelis & Ruppenhofer's (2001) CxG-approach entertains distinct linking constructions for the perfect and the passive.

---

5 See Müller (2007: 342f.) for a concise list of LFG- as well as HPSG-approaches that entertain ambiguity and those that assume identity as well as his chapter on the passive (Müller 2007: 287–343) for discussion.
6 See also Kunze (1996: 655f.), Vierhuff, Hildebrandt & Eickmeyer (2003: 231), Kiss (1992: 276), Hinrichs & Nakazawa (1998), Kathol (1998: 255), and Müller (2001).

While it is tempting to simply attribute the distinct properties of passive and perfect(ive) participles to syntacticosemantically different yet homophonous affixes, what all of the ambiguity approaches share is that they cannot properly explain this homophony (cf. Ackema 1999: 87). In other words, "the ambiguity assumption [...] is confronted with the question why perfect and passive are systematically encoded by the same verb form" (Wunderlich 1997: 2). As Wanner (2009: 71) points out, it is quite a stretch to assume "that the two forms just happen to look identical [...] considering all the allomorphs of the morpheme in question". Although this may be technically grasped in an approach like the one by Aronoff (1994), a conceptual motivation is missing. Additionally, what the ambiguity assumption leaves without an answer is why this formal identity cross-linguistically holds between the distinct kinds of past participles but never between, say, the passive participle and the present participle (cf. Ackema 1999: 87f.). Furthermore, the non-identity view fails to account for the lack of morphophonological identity in languages forming passive and perfect synthetically (cf. Ackema 1999: 87f.). Actually, proponents of ambiguity approaches (see Drijkoningen 1989; Aronoff 1994) have taken this lack of morphological identity in languages that use synthetic forms to build the passive and the perfect to argue against the identity of past participial constructions. These cases only show, however, that passive and perfective may be encoded by means of designated morphological markers, which does not impose any necessity for the impossibility of substantial identity in languages that form the two periphrastically (cf. Ackema 1999: 88). According to Ackema (1999: 88), this "only shows even more strikingly that the consistent identity of the past participles in periphrastic passives and perfects is unexpected and in need of an explanation".

The most important argument against the non-identity of past participles is that none of the empirical data discussed in chapter 2 provide evidence to this effect. In fact, neither the diachronic development nor the synchronic properties of past participles support the assumption of past participial non-identity in Germanic (with the exception of Swedish) and Romance. Rather, what these data suggest is that it is not a general difference in terms of perfect as opposed to passive but the specific structural configuration (e.g. in terms of object-displacement) and its ingredients (e.g. in terms of event structure) that decisively contributes to the behaviour as well as the interpretation of a past participial construction. Eventually, then, our interim conclusion has to hold that it is highly unlikely that there is substantial non-identity involved in the case of passive and perfect(ive) participles (cf. Ackema 1999: 87).

In conclusion, we may put on record that the ambiguity assumption is intuitively appealing due to the distinct properties of perfect and passive participial exponents and raises some important questions, but at the same time leaves many problems unsolved. Relevant questions range from "Why, if the two forms are only accidentally homophonous, does consistent morphological identity pertain to all of their uses in a given language?" to "Why is past participial ambiguity restricted to languages in which these are formed with periphrastic constructions and never arises in those that make use of synthetic constructions?". Although the slight extension of the lexicon that is required in ambiguity approaches probably does not constitute a major issue, assuming that a single past participial marker gives rise to two unrelated sets of syntacticosemantic information should be quite well-founded. This, however, is not the case, since the observable differences between particular realisations of past participles do not divide into perfect and passive, but rather correspond to the presence or absence of the auxiliary HAVE. This, in turn, arguably is a consequence of the particular properties of the verb that the past participial marker combines with rather than a substantial grammatical distinction in terms of different types of participial formation being involved.

3.2 Identity in form equals identity in meaning

At the crossroads of approaches to the ambiguity as opposed to the identity of past participles, we find exponents that obscure the notion of identity to a certain extent and will hence informally be referred to as 'faint identity' approaches. These approaches are identity approaches in the sense that the participial marker is taken to be one and the same in passive and perfect contexts. However, this identity is obscured by the fact that it is often not the participial marker but the specific configuration in which it occurs that determines the syntacticosemantic properties of the past participle. While approaches that crucially rest upon the contribution of auxiliaries are remotely similar, these allow us to clearly tell apart the contribution of the participial element and its auxiliaries, quite unlike what is the case in DM-approaches (see Embick & Noyer 2007; Embick 2003; 2004). These approaches rely on numerous kinds and combinations of functional heads that conspire to embed roots. Accordingly, the structural domain that is eventually spelled out as a past participle allows for a large degree of flexibility in terms of the functional projections that are or are not involved. This is for instance observable in Embick's (2003: 149) structural analysis of the eventive passive *The door was opened* in (86).

(86)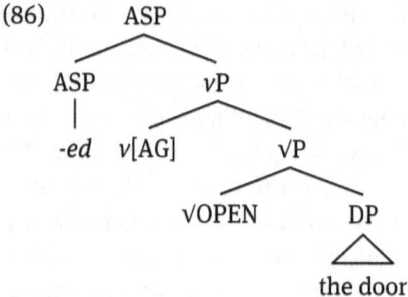

While the participial affix is introduced in the functional head ASP, it arguably does not contribute to the passivisation of the predicate, which in turn hinges on the properties of the verbalising head v. Thus, the distinct structural ingredients conspire to compositionally give rise to the eventive passive interpretation, although it is left open how the passive participle may receive an imperfective reading, unlike its perfect counterpart. As the past participial affix appears in perfect and passive contexts, it is argued that "the signals are not specified for voice [and] not uniform aspectually" (Embick 1997: 147).[7] Eventually, then, the explicitly assumed identity of past participles in DM-approaches like Embick (1997; 2003: 147f., 2004), Abraham (2006b: 491–494) and Helland & Pitz (2012) needs to be handled with care. In fact, what is not clear at all in these cases is whether the distinctions between passive and perfect(ive) participles follow from properties crucially related to the participial morphology or rather stem from independent properties of the immediate structural context.[8] Doubts about the latter option may be raised based on the observation that participial morphology certainly plays a role in participial constructions, as we could see in chapter 2. On the other hand, these approaches provide important insights when it comes to the more fine-grained properties of bare instances of past participles (see Embick 2003; 2004) and also

---

[7] Embick (1997: 148) opts for the past participle to include the feature [Anterior], which does not necessarily bring with it the introduction of the feature [Perfective]. This still fails to account for passive cases, though.
[8] The same objection may be raised against Struckmeier (2007: 44f.), where past participles and their auxiliaries are claimed to be mutual exponents of a single feature set in T, but the passive characteristics of a participial construction merely stem from the requirements of T regarding the selection of vP or VP.

bear the merit of raising awareness for the many pitfalls of proper identity approaches.

Eventually, as it is the specific structural configuration rather than the participial marker that eventually determines the behaviour (and hence type) of past participles, 'faint identity' approaches are found on the verge of identity and ambiguity. Given their aforementioned drawbacks in terms of the discussion of past participial (non-)identity, we will not be concerned with such approaches any more. The main idea of attributing the observable differences to components other than the participial marker is shared by proper identity approaches, though. These, however, hold an ingredient responsible that is clearly distinct from the past participial element, viz. typically the auxiliary. As a matter of fact, there are 'biased identity' approaches that assume that the underlying meaning of the past participle is either passive or perfect(ive), where the opposed contribution is attributed to the auxiliary. Additionally, there are approaches that attribute aspects of both the passive as well as the perfect to the participial element, where the auxiliaries are still relevant in terms of contributing to the expression of an active perfect and an imperfective passive. Lastly, there are also approaches to the identity of past participles that assume that the past participle is semantically vacuous and hence take all ingredients in the periphrastic perfect and passive to stem from the auxiliaries involved. Unlike the biased assumption of either passive or perfect(ive) information on the participial form, the presumption of abstract meaning or semantic vacuity may be termed 'neutral identity'. Quite generally, identity approaches thus crucially differ in terms of how much (if any) relevant information they contribute to the past participle and how much of it is induced by the auxiliaries. The four conceivable strands of research that have just been outlined are summarised in (87) and (88), which briefly sketch the 'biased identity' as opposed to 'neutral identity' approaches, respectively.[9]

(87) **Biased identity**
   a. the basic meaning of past participial morphology is temporal or aspectual (i.e. something along the lines of 'perfect(ive)' meaning) – **the 'tense/aspect' hypothesis**
   b. the underlying meaning of the past participial marker is 'passive' (i.e. forming a participle induces changes to the argument structure affecting

---

[9] Abraham (2006a, b), primarily being concerned with how passive meaning is derived from participial forms, refers to the kinds of 'biased identity' in (87) as follows: the Passive Aspect hypothesis and the Passive Argument hypothesis. As we will see shortly, the former designation should be extended by 'tense', as not all of the approaches speaking out for a temporal contribution of the past participle focus on aspect.

the diathetic properties of a given verb) – **the 'argument structure' hypothesis**

(88) **Neutral identity**
 a. the past participial marker includes both passive as well as perfect(ive) meaning, one or both of which may be abstract (or 'underspecified') – **the 'amalgamation' hypothesis**
 b. the formation of a past participle does not introduce any syntacticosemantic specifications of a passive or perfect(ive) kind (i.e. the participial marker is 'semantically vacuous') – **the 'semantic vacuity' hypothesis**

The biased identity approaches in (87) are straightforward in their central ideas yet come in quite a variety of different shapes. Those that are in line with neutral identity in (88), on the other hand, differ considerably in terms of their main assumptions, most importantly in terms of whether or not they attribute relevant information to the past participle. Approaches of the kind in (88a) presume that past participle formation adds relevant properties and are 'neutral' in the sense that both perfect(ive) as well as passive information is taken to be involved. The importance of the auxiliaries may not be neglected here, though, in terms of their contribution to the expression of an active perfect and/or an imperfective passive. Accounts of the kind in (88b), on the other hand, crucially deny this and take the participial marker to be entirely irrelevant for interpretation. Accordingly, the latter either take the participial marker to be a formal element stripped of any semantic content yet introducing special formal requirements, or they assume it to be a formal reflex of the participial construction as such. We will now turn to each of the options in (87) and (88) in turn.

3.2.1 The tense/aspect hypothesis

The first type of the biased identity approach to be considered assumes that the basic meaning of the past participle boils down to tense or aspect and either neglects or denies argument structural effects of participle formation. This entails that the passive has to be induced by other means, i.e. by contextual factors or the auxiliary (cf. Vater 2002: 357). Prominent proponents of this kind, often mainly concerned with the structure and meaning of the perfect, are Grewendorf (1995), Soare (2007: 190), Giorgi & Pianesi (1997: 39), Lübbe & Rapp (2011: 272), Zeller (1994), Savova (1989), Musan (1998: 121f.), and Vennemann (1987).

Grewendorf (1995) proposes that past participles inherently bear a perfective interpretation. This assumption is based on an adaptation of Zagona's (1991) claim that the auxiliary assigns an aspectual feature [+completed] to the participial form, thus rendering the past participle 'perfective' (cf. Grewendorf 1995: 83). Whereas Zagona's (1991) auxiliary-driven account crucially does not attribute inherent aspectuality to the participle itself, this is exactly what is advocated in Grewendorf (1995). According to Grewendorf (1995: 83), the past participle contains the aspectual specification of 'completion', which induces anteriority as a 'logical consequence'. In other words, the perfectivity of an event implicates its temporal precedence (cf. Grewendorf 1995: 83). The assumption of a perfective past participle is also advocated, amongst others, by Giorgi & Pianesi (1997: 39), Remberger (2006: 124) (following Coseriu 1976: 126) and Soare (2007: 190). A major problem of these approaches is that they neglect the imperfectivity of past participles in passive contexts like *Peter wird geschlagen* ('Peter is (being) hit.'). As a matter of fact, Grewendorf (1995: 83fn9) brings the lack of anteriority on passive participles in as an argument against the inherent anteriority of past participles, but does not take a stand on this with respect to perfectivity, which is not exempt from this fundamental issue. Lübbe & Rapp (2011: 281f.), to name one final example, focus on attributive occurrences and argue that perfective aspect is an inherent property of the past participle that may not be deleted. In fact, what is proposed here is that this inherent perfective aspect induces weak or strong perfective aspect depending on whether the event is telic or atelic: telic events are completely included in the time that is considered, whereas atelic ones do not necessarily exhibit the same quality (cf. Lübbe & Rapp 2011: 269–272). Accordingly, achievements like *freilassen* ('release') and accomplishments like *schreiben* ('write') are necessarily brought to an end in cases like *der freigelassene Gefangene* ('the released prisoner') and *die geschriebene Dissertation* ('the written dissertation') (cf. Lübbe & Rapp 2011: 270). Activities like *tragen* ('carry') and states like *bewundern* ('admire') in cases like *das getragene Kind* ('the carried child') and *der bewunderte Schauspieler* ('the admired actor'), on the other hand, are only weakly perfective in the sense that they just bring one of several subevents to an end, which need not entail that the overall event ceases as well (cf. Lübbe & Rapp 2011: 270). This aktionsart-based account, however, is too strict to properly account for periphrastic instances of past participles, which are not addressed by Lübbe & Rapp (2011). This is observable on the basis of the imperfectivity of periphrastic passives of achievements such as *Der Gefangene wird freigelassen* ('The prisoner is (being) released.') and accomplishments like *Die Dissertation wird geschrieben* ('The dissertation is (being) written.'). Although assuming that past participles include aspectual information that is contingent on the aktionsart or event structure of the verb they are derived from is thus intuitively appealing, just resorting to a distinction in telicity apparently is not enough.

In addition to approaches advocating the inherent perfectivity of past participles, there are those that attribute tense- rather than aspect-specifications to participial forms. Zeller (1994: 81, 89–91), for instance, explicitly argues that past participles comprise temporal specifications, namely the basic meaning 'perfect'. Accordingly, the past participle is held responsible for attributing the time interval of the event entirely to a point that is prior to the time interval of the reference time (cf. Zeller 1994: 89–91). Crucially, although the participle is taken to be specified for the decisive feature [PAST] in analogy to proper past tense, this feature is different from the anteriority specifications of its preterite counterpart (cf. Zeller 1994: 90). This becomes obvious with the help of Reichenbach's (1947) traditional terminology, i.e. Speech time (S), Reference time (R), Event time (E).[10] Zeller (1994: 89–91) assumes that the temporal specification of the past participle expresses that E precedes R, whereas the simple past conveys that R precedes S (cf. Iatridou et al. 2001: 190). The same is observable in the approaches put forth by Savova (1989: 68f.), arguing for [+PRECEDENCE], as well as Musan (1998: 121–123), Ballweg (1988) and Belitschenko (1980: 376). Eventually, in finite clauses like *He had hit him*, both relations are expressed at once: while the participle establishes precedence between E and R, the auxiliary induces a relation – in this simple past case also precedence – between R and S (cf. Savova 1989: 73; Zeller 1994: 90). However, even with this distinction in place, the objection raised before with respect to passive cases comes to the fore again: these simply do not exhibit any inherent anteriority (cf. Grewendorf 1995: 83fn9). In other words, it is quite hard to justify the presence of the feature [PAST] or [+PRECEDENCE] in a case like the aforementioned *Peter wird geschlagen* ('Peter is (being) hit.'). Therefore, although Savova (1989: 76f.) points out that the basic meaning of past participles cannot be perfective or passive as these are not universally present on all groups of verbs, her conclusion that it has to be a more general tense specification arguably evokes precisely the same problems.[11] Musan (1998: 123)

---

10 As Iatridou et al. (2001: 190) puts it, "E is the point (or interval, depending on the framework) at which the eventuality holds, S is the utterance time, and R is a reference point/interval." We will mainly resort to Klein's (1994) adaptation of Reichenbach's (1947) ideas below, but stick to the traditional terminology for now.

11 Savova's (1989: 68–73) [+PRECEDENCE] is actually more flexible than the past tense specifications of other tense-based approaches since it only establishes temporal precedence for the

acknowledges this and points out that passives constitute "the standard argument against the assumption that the past participle triggers the anteriority in perfect constructions". Nevertheless, a proper reconciliation is sought in vain. In fact, Musan (1998: 123f.) just claims that "passive constructions are highly grammaticalised [and] the intuitive non-anteriority of participles in this one construction is not a good argument against the anteriority of past participles in general." This, however, is nothing more than a desperate attempt to justify an untenable position, which even implicitly makes recourse to the assumption that past participles may not be identical after all. Eventually, then, even though proponents of tense-driven accounts often accuse aspect-driven ones of their lack of flexibility, these are apparently not flexible enough either.

A supposed reconciliation of these problems may be found in Breul & Wegner's (2017) neutral identity approach that will be discussed in more detail in section 3.2.3, but may briefly be sketched in the present context already. Breul & Wegner (2017: 44) claim that – beside passive information – the formation of a past participle converts a situation (or eventuality) into its post-time state, an idea which is loosely based on proposals by Vennemann (1987) and Klein (1994; 2000), amongst others. Such a post-time state is defined as "the time after the time at which there was a situation denoted by the verb" (Breul & Wegner 2017: 45). Reminiscent of Lübbe & Rapp's (2011) aktionsart-based approach to attributive past participles, this post-time state may be the last instantiation of a situation, in which case the situation comes to an end, or it may just be a post-time state of a subsituation, in which case the overall situation may still be ongoing (cf. Breul & Wegner 2017: 45). Accordingly, as Breul & Wegner (2017: 45) point out, homogeneous situations like *live*, *boil*, or *walk* allow for the denotation of a post-time state of a subsituation and may hence induce imperfectivity. Heterogeneous situations like *explode*, *graduate*, or *drink*, on the other hand, do not allow for post-time states of subsituations given that these are not of the same kind (cf. Breul & Wegner 2017: 45). This leaves the question of how to account for the imperfectivity of 'heterogeneous' situations like *Der Gefangene wird freigelassen* ('The prisoner is (being) released.'). These are assumed to be contingent on the contribution of the auxiliary *werden* ('become'), which adds dynamic semantics to the post-time state denoted by the past participle (cf. Breul & Wegner 2017: 47f.). In analogy to the future auxiliary *werden* ('become'), the semantic contribution of the passive auxiliary

---

beginning of the event and holds the aktionsart properties responsible for whether or not the event comes to an end. It is thus flexible enough to account for universal perfect readings (*Jack has loved Kate ever since he laid eyes on her*), unlike the strict perfectivity approaches, which predict the situation to have ceased regardless of aktionsart.

foreshadows the existence of a post-time state and the situation which leads to it holds at the present (cf. Breul & Wegner 2017: 48). In English, this is different in that the passive auxiliary *be* does not introduce any relevant semantic information and the presence of a dynamic semantic aspect in a case like *Cars are built by robots these days* stems from semantic entailment (cf. Breul & Wegner 2017: 49). Accordingly, the main assumption here is that the existence of a post-time state of a situation entails the existence of the situation itself (cf. Breul & Wegner 2017: 49). While this is intuitively appealing and flexible enough to account for passives as well, unlike the other approaches identifying tense/aspect as the basic meaning of past participles, it may be a little bit too weak to be sufficiently insightful. In fact, as explicitly pointed out, "a past participle as such does not specify whether [the situation continues to last during the post-time of some of its subphases] or whether the situation has ended" (cf. Breul & Wegner 2017: 45). Therefore, it often turns out to be difficult to make reliable predictions and the responsibility is regularly shifted off to implication. Although we will briefly return to this approach in the context of neutral identity approaches, viz. those following the amalgamation hypothesis, let us conclude for now that this approach, though certainly appealing, still leaves some aspects to be desired.

The approaches explicitly discussed as exponents of the tense/aspect hypothesis thus far neglect that the perfect auxiliaries introduce any relevant perfect(ive) information. Accordingly, Giorgi & Pianesi (1997: 39) suggest that their presence is required only by syntax and Grewendorf (1995) similarly holds the auxiliaries to be semantically empty. This, of course, does not neglect their contribution in terms of overtly expressing the relation between R and S, which stems from T rather than the auxiliary itself, though. However, as the empirical data introduced in chapter 2 clearly indicate, there has to be relevant perfect information – beyond its expression of finiteness – on the auxiliaries at least in the case of HAVE. This marks a major drawback of the approaches considered thus far, regardless of whether they are flexible enough to account for the imperfectivity of passive periphrases.

In addition to the biased approaches considered so far, there are also some that only attribute somewhat abstract meaning components of the perfect to the past participle, though. These properties do not suffice to denote a proper perfect, which is why these approaches resort to the importance of auxiliaries in terms of contributing relevant perfect semantics (see Ehrich & Vater 1989; Ehrich 1992; Ballweg 1988; 1989; Iatridou et al. 2001: 211f., 220f.). Ballweg (1989), for instance, claims that the combination of participial marker and auxiliary is responsible for denoting anteriority in terms of the perfect (cf. Musan 1998: 114). In a similar vein, in Iatridou et al.'s (2001: 211f., 220f.) compositional approach, past participles bear the feature [bounded], yet this feature alone is potentially not sufficient to express perfect meaning, which may only be brought about with the help of a perfect auxiliary. This, however, need not hold for all past participles based on the properties of their underlying verbs, as we will see below. In other words, as underlined by the data considered in chapter 2, it may well be that HAVE has to contribute relevant perfect information, whereas BE does not do so. Accordingly, while approaches of this kind share that none of the components of a past participial construction is *per se* sufficient to induce perfect meaning, this may either hold for verbs of all kinds or just for certain subsets. Hence, whenever the past participle is not sufficient, perfect information may only come about through the combination of a perfect auxiliary and the past participle. This reasoning is also pursued – at least tentatively while overall remaining agnostic as to past participial (non-)identity – in Breul (2014: 459f.). Here, the possibility is offered that the feature content of perfect and passive participles is identical, where the perfect auxiliary comprises a perfect feature "that provides the perfect tense interpretation, possibly in combination with the semantics of the participle" (Breul 2014: 459). In addition to such compositional approaches, those that take past participles to be underlyingly passive as well as a subset of those assuming semantic vacuity are usually bound to assume that the auxiliaries are solely responsible for adding perfect meaning.

Most of the approaches considered in the present section – with the notable exception of Breul & Wegner (2017) as a neutral identity approach – are not principally concerned with and thus regularly remain agnostic about the derivation of the periphrastic passive.[12] An exception to this pattern may be found in the work of Abraham (1998; 2000; 2006a; b), who assumes that past participles carry aspectual information but is still explicitly concerned with the derivation of the passive.[13] Abraham (1998: 154) argues for German that the resultative state is an inherent part of the past participle, whereas the event that led to this state is eventually implied (cf. Abraham 1998: 154).[14] The resultative state is taken to

---

12 This is denounced by Aronoff (1994: 24): "The most recent detailed analysis of [perfect] semantics (Klein 1992) makes no connection to the passive [n]or is there any currently popular analysis of its syntax that attempts to accommodate the perfect to recent accounts of the passive (which pretend to universality)".
13 Note that Abraham (1998) and Abraham (2000), the latter a slightly revised work, are virtually identical.
14 Abraham (2006a: 6; 2006b: 465f.) claims that this is subject to parameterisation: whereas German follows the 'passive aspect hypothesis', English is an exponent of the 'passive argument hypothesis'. This is claimed to be observable by the possibility of evoking a perfect interpretation together with the semantically vacuous copula BE in German, while this is not possible with the respective equivalent in English (cf. Abraham 2006b: 465f.).

account for the analytic perfect, somewhat reminiscent of what is proposed in Breul & Wegner (2017). The passive interpretation, on the other hand, is assumed to come about as a last resort mechanism in that the stative phase requires an eventive phase, which in turn is brought in via implication if there is no other way (cf. Abraham 1998: 157; Abraham 2000: 152f.). In other words, forcing an eventive interpretation in the case of the periphrastic passive adds an implicit (or existentially bound) causer. Consequently, the distinct functions of the past participle come about via implication on the basis of a resultative state. The passive is thus taken to be aspectually derived (cf. Abraham 1998: 162; Abraham 2006a: 10; 2006b: 484). The specific kind of passive (stative vs. eventive) and perfect meaning is eventually compositionally determined with the help of the auxiliaries, which are specified for subcategorisation and aspect/aktionsart, but crucially not for θ-roles (cf. Abraham 2000: 142). Although this approach bears insightful ideas, its major proposal of deriving the passive from a resultative state cannot shake off the impression of being highly contrived in that implication is held responsible for imposing passivisation. In spite of the fact that this is an interesting take and certainly bears a certain appeal with respect to the diachronic development of past participles and their object-orientation, it shifts way too much of its burden off to implication. Additionally, implication is probably also called for in the derivation of active perfect cases since the subject somehow needs to be related to the implied cause of the resultative state in a case like *Chandra hat Naz geküsst* ('Chandra has kissed Naz.'). Moreover, it is also not entirely clear why implication should render the overall interpretation imperfective in the case of the periphrastic passive, especially since the resultative state is still present.

This concludes the discussion of biased identity approaches of the tense/aspect kind. As we could see, the most prominent objection to the assumption that the past participle inherently comprises perfective aspect or perfect tense is its lack thereof in passive contexts (cf. Vater 2002: 357). This may only be reconciled by a more abstract and hence more flexible contribution. Abraham (1998; 2000; 2006a; b) tries to accommodate for the issues of perfectivity, i.e. a resultative state, by a large degree of implication. In Lübbe & Rapp's (2011) account of attributive past participles and Breul & Wegner's (2017) post-time state, perfectivity is rather closely tied to verbal properties, although implication still plays an important role. Eventually, what these approaches share – though to different degrees – is their reliance on implication as well as the inherent properties of the predicates that form the basis of past participial formation. While the former should ideally be minimised, the latter will also play a major role in the approach to be laid out below.

Whereas the imperfectivity of past participles in passive contexts constitutes a main problem for proponents of the tense/aspect hypothesis, the type of approaches that we will turn to next takes this observation as its starting point. These approaches assume that the basic meaning of past participles is 'passive'.

3.2.2 The argument structure hypothesis

The main claim of approaches assuming the basic meaning of past participles to be 'passive' is that the formation of a participle involves some kind of change to the argument structure of the underlying verb. The trailblazer for this kind of approach is to be found in Rouveret & Vergnaud's (1980: 192–194) highly influential assumption that the case assignment properties of past participles are determined by the auxiliaries with which they occur. This entails that past participial morphology disposes the lexical verb of its capacity to assign objective (accusative) case, which may or may not then be assigned by the auxiliary in question "via the past participle" (Rouveret & Vergnaud 1980: 193). Therefore, the past participle may only govern a direct object when it is introduced in the context of a case-assigning auxiliary (cf. Rouveret & Vergnaud 1980: 194).[15] Accordingly, the interaction of auxiliary and past participle eventually elicits distinctions in terms of the ability for accusative case assignment. In fact, the respective auxiliary's (in-)ability to reinstate the possibility of case-assignment is taken to follow from its main verb progenitor, i.e. "*have* assigns Case when it is a main verb (it takes a direct object), but not *be*" (Rouveret & Vergnaud 1980: 193).[16]

Strongly related to Rouveret & Vergnaud's (1980) insights, Roberts (1984: 216f.) traces the characteristics of the past participial marker back to its "property of 'absorbing' Accusative Case, thereby preventing the Verb from assigning this Case to the object NP". This renders past participial morphology an argument-changing exponent of verbal inflection in that the participle is incapable of autonomously licensing a direct object (cf. Roberts 1984: 216f.). In other words, the past participial morpheme is assigned (or 'absorbs') the case properties of the

---

15 This is in line with Chomsky's (1981: 54f., 117f.) case theory that sees the basic property of the passive construction in the participle's lack of accusative case, yet apparently does not extend this assumption to perfect contexts, which renders this an implicit non-identity approach.
16 This entails that copular constructions like *Mary is an actress* and *Marie ist eine Schauspielerin* ('Mary is an actress.', Mary is a.NOM actress.NOM) do not feature structural case-assignment to the internal argument governed by copula BE but instead resort to default case assignment (cf. Schütze 2001: 224; Breul 2008: 240f.).

verb it combines with (cf. Roberts 1984: 217). This is commonly referred to as 'case absorption' and applies internally to the participial phrase. Accordingly, the capacity of accusative case assignment to an internal argument eventually hinges on the auxiliary involved, where it is once again the transitive main verb heritage of HAVE in contrast to the unaccusative BE that evokes differences in argument structural realisation (cf. Roberts 1984: 218f.). While the presence of HAVE in active periphrastic perfects assures that the effect on argument structure is forestalled, this is clearly an identity approach in the sense that the predicate's argument structure is affected by case-absorption, regardless of whether this may be made up for by an auxiliary or not (cf. Roberts 1984: 217).

These ideas are deepened by Roberts (1985; 1987: 40f.) and also prominently featured in quite a large number of distinct approaches. According to Aronoff (1994: 24), assumptions along these lines make up the "the most widely accepted treatment of the passive" in Chomskyan syntax. They may for instance be found in a large number of (biased) identity approaches such as Hoekstra (1984; 1986b; 2003 [1986]), Fabb (1984), Baker (1988), van den Wyngaerd (1988), Jaeggli (1986), Baker, Johnson & Roberts (1989) as well as Broekhuis & van Dijk (1995: 43f.), Shibatani (1985: 841), Friedemann & Siloni (1997: 88f.), Broekhuis & Migdalski (2003: 3), Migdalski (2006: 128f., 2010: 131f.), and Wanner (2009: 15f.).

While case-absorption also marks the core of Hoekstra (1984; 1986b; 2003 [1986]) and van den Wyngaerd (1988), these additionally highlight an effect that past participial formation induces regarding the assignment of the external θ-role. According to van den Wyngaerd (1988: 161), the participial marker absorbs the external θ-role and, as a consequence, demands accusative case, which may only come from the verb in passive cases, given the unaccusative characteristics of passive auxiliaries. This entails that the internal argument may not be case-marked by the verb, as its accusative case has to be assigned to the participial element, which is why movement (to a position in which structural case is assigned) is triggered in passive contexts (cf. van den Wyngaerd 1988: 161; Jaeggli 1986: 590). This is observable in the (highly) sketchy structural representation underlying *Rustin was bitten* in (89a), which illustrates the basic mechanisms at work in approximation to those approaches attributing θ- and case-absorption to the participial marker.

(89) a.

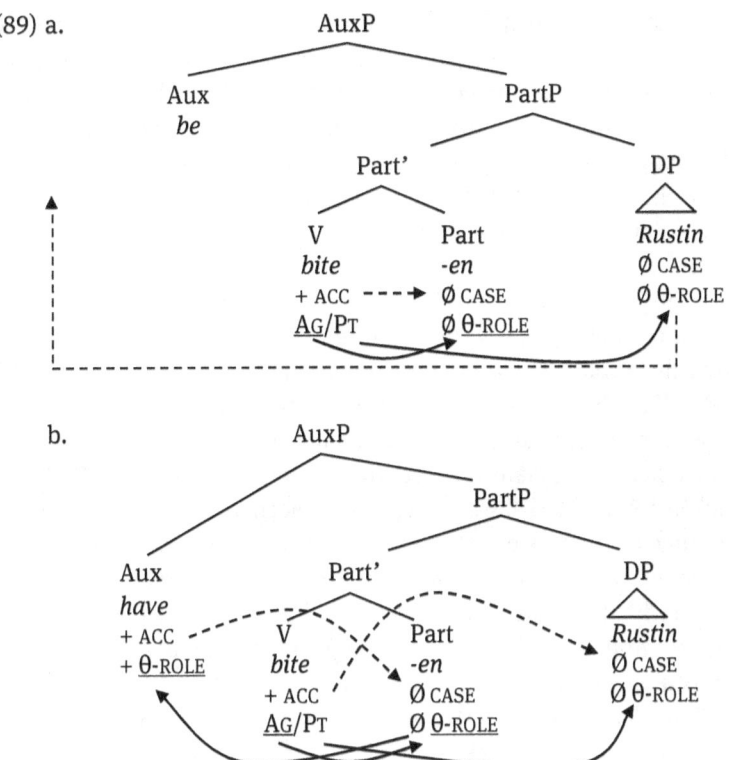

b.

The active perfect *The dog has bitten Rustin* in (89b) differs only with respect to the properties introduced by HAVE. As Cowper (1989a: 92) points out, "in passive constructions, -en receives case from the verb it is attached to, while in perfective constructions, it receives case from have" (emphases in original). This is typically assumed to be a consequence of the transitive auxiliary's "property of 'transmitting' to the subject the external θ-role 'absorbed' by the past participle" (Lois 1990: 250f.).[17] Eventually, in accord with Burzio's Generalization (cf. Burzio 1986), it is assumed that lack of case-assignment properties entails lack of an external θ-role, which may only be reinstated with the help of a suitable (transitive) auxiliary (i.e. HAVE). Further proponents of these ideas are Åfarli

---

17 Note that the representation in (89b) at first sight appears to suggest non-identity given the differences in the participial domain. However, the observable differences are a reflex of HAVE's capability of taking up the external θ-role and rely on the modular nature of Government and Binding Theory in the sense that θ-role assignment (at deep structure) precedes structural case-assignment (at surface structure).

(1989), Jaeggli (1986) and Baker (1988), who focus on the θ-role and share the assumption that "the addition of passive morphology to a verb entails the addition of a verb-internal argument to that verb [and] [t]his argument must receive the external role inherently assigned by the verb" (Åfarli 1989: 102). Crucially, this shows that approaches arguing for case- and θ-absorption attribute argument-like properties to the participial marker and therefore often even suggest that the participial marker is, in fact, an argument.[18]

Θ-absorption is also the essential concept in more recent approaches like Ackema (1995; 1999) and Ackema & Marelj (2012). These share the assumption that "participial morphology rather than the syntactic subject is assigned the verb's external theta-role [which] holds in perfects just as well as in passives" (Ackema & Marelj 2012: 228). This, however, is formally instantiated in a novel and interesting way here, namely the proposal that complex predicate formation between an auxiliary and a main verb features 'θ-merger' (cf. Ackema & Marelj 2012: 229). Ackema & Marelj (2012: 229) define this mechanism as "the formation of a single argument structure out of the argument structures of the component predicative elements of the complex predicate, in which theta-roles of one part can be collapsed with theta-roles of the other part".[19] This is where the auxiliaries gain centre stage: while BE is thematically empty and thus cannot assign any θ-roles when it combines with a participle, HAVE "has a subject θ-role to assign" (Ackema 1999: 96). This θ-role crucially is semantically vacuous, though, which is why θ-merger is required (cf. Ackema 1999: 108).[20] Given its lack of a θ-role, applying this mechanism in the case of BE remains without any effect and the complex predicate does not differ thematically from the non-finite predicate that it comprises (cf. Ackema 1999: 108). With HAVE, on the other hand, the semantically empty θ-role of the auxiliary is "merged with one of the θ-roles of the main verb" (Ackema 1999: 108). As the internal argument receives its internal θ-role from the main verb predicate, the θ-merged role is bound to be the external one, which has been absorbed by the participial morphology (cf. Ackema & Marelj 2012: 235). As Ackema (1999: 107f.) points out, this renders the two θ-roles

---

18 This is not shared by all of these approaches, though. While Roberts (1985) and Jaeggli (1986), amongst others, argue that the participial marker functions as an argument, Baker, Johnson & Roberts (1989) "analyze passive syntax as resulting universally from an abstract subject pronoun of sorts in Infl" (Aronoff 1994: 24).

19 As Ackema & Marelj (2012: 229) point out, this process can also be found in Rosen (1990), Neeleman (1994), and Neeleman & van de Koot (2002). In fact, something similar is also employed in Cowper (1989a, b).

20 The concept of θ-merger is formalised (in a rather flexible fashion) as follows: "If two predicative categories are s-dominated by a single X°, the Θ-roles they assign may be considered nondistinct" (Ackema 1999: 107).

nondistinct and thus allows us "to derive that the subject is interpreted as being associated with the main verb's subject θ-role" (Ackema 1999: 107). These workings of θ-merger are represented in (90) for the simple perfect sentence *John has read a book*, taken from Ackema & Marelj (2012: 235), where the indices indicate θ-assignment.

(90)
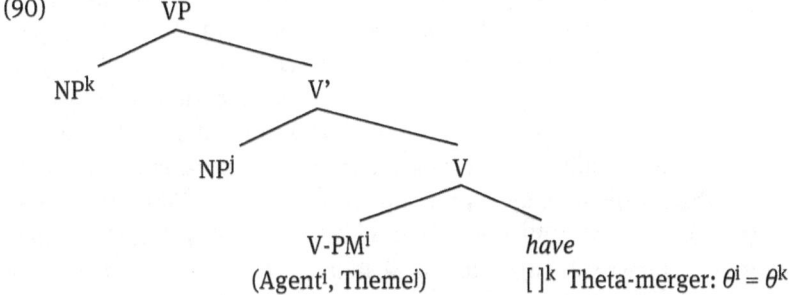

As we can see here, the concept of θ-merger is based on the assumption of θ-absorption and provides a proper formalisation of the intuition that HAVE retrieves the external θ-role, which – once absorbed – could not be assigned to an argument without independent help. Whenever it is retrieved by HAVE, the external argument may properly be licensed in terms of θ-assignment. While this comes at the expense of having to assume an additional mechanism, it allows us to account for the diathetic properties of passive and perfect periphrases on the basis of a single past participle, where differences solely arise due to θ-merger of the main verb with the θ-role of the auxiliary HAVE (cf. Ackema & Marelj 2012: 229). What the case-/θ-absorption approaches generally do not account for, though, is perfect semantics, which is either entirely neglected or shifted off to the contribution of the auxiliaries.

Cowper (1989a, b) contests that the past participial marker is an argument of the verb and instead follows di Sciullo & Williams (1987) (see also Wanner 2009: 16) by taking the past participial affix to be attached to the verb in the lexicon. Other than in syntactic approaches to case-/θ-absorption, where the participial affix typically is analysed as an argument, Cowper (1989a: 87) thus holds a lexical operation responsible for "the discharge of one thematic position and one structural case feature". As this is once more assumed to hold for past participles in passive and perfect contexts alike, the auxiliaries take centre stage again. In fact, the relevant properties for case assignment to the object as well as the θ-role assigned to the subject are attributed to, i.e. originate in, the auxiliary HAVE (cf. Cowper 1989a: 88). Under the assumption that HAVE is identical in all of its various uses, i.e. in all of its manifestations as a main verb as well as an auxiliary, it is claimed that HAVE is special in terms of being "thematically underspecified; in other words, it has thematic positions which are devoid of thematic content" (Cowper 1989a: 88; cf. Cowper 1989b: 86).[21] Hence, Cowper's (1989a, b) argument is quite similar to Ackema & Marelj (2012: 232f.) in that "[t]he roles assigned to the arguments of *have* seem to be determined almost completely by the arguments themselves" (Cowper 1989b: 86). While the thematic content is often specified pragmatically in different (main verb) contexts, in the case of perfect(ive) HAVE this is claimed to be different (cf. Cowper 1989a: 88). As Cowper (1989a: 89) claims, "the free thematic content [of the past participle] is transmitted to have and linked to have's external thematic position [whenever] the thematically underspecified element [...] properly govern[s] the element with the free thematic content" (emphases in original). This, then, marks an alternative to Ackema's (1995; 1999) and Ackema & Marelj's (2012) formalisation in terms of θ-merger. This alternative is taken to do without any extra machinery but remains fairly unspecific with respect to the precise technical instantiation of the transmission of the external semantic role, which is just assumed to "take place under conditions similar to those described by the head movement constraint" (Cowper 1989a: 89).

Eventually, regardless of the precise technical incorporation of the transmission of the external θ-role, the underspecification of the perfect auxiliary HAVE is intuitively appealing, yet may have to be restricted to the thematic side of things. As we have seen in chapter 2, there is evidence that suggests that HAVE is likely to carry perfect information. Since approaches subscribing to the argument structure hypothesis are usually only concerned with the diathetic properties of passive and perfect periphrases, the possibility of relevant perfect information on HAVE is, however, usually not denied but merely neglected.

An attempt to provide a proper approach to past participial identity with an inherently passive participial marker that does not resort to either θ-/case-absorption (or thematic underspecification) is put forth by Haider (1984; 1986). Haider (1984: 23) argues for past participial identity in terms of the lexical operation of 'argument blocking', which renders the underlying participial marker passive by virtue of imposing a reduction in argument structure.[22] This

---

[21] See also Migdalski (2006: 150), who assumes "that 'have' has the same properties related to case and theta role assignment whether it is a lexical verb or an auxiliary".
[22] Note that similar ideas are also present in Sternefeld (1984), Grewendorf (1989: 21), and Zifonun, Hoffmann & Strecker (1997: 1790f.). Additionally, whereas Heinz & Matiasek (1994) assume (de-)blocking in the spirit of Haider (1984; 1986), many HPSG-approaches, impose blocking via the influence of a suitable auxiliary (cf. Müller 2007: 307f.). These exponents – see Kathol

reduction may, however, be undone by an auxiliary if it is capable of 'deblocking' the argument in question (cf. Haider 1986: 3). Haider (1986: 22f.) calls the argument that is blocked the 'designated argument' (henceforth DA), an argument that is thus specifically marked (cf. Müller 2007: 308). This argument typically corresponds to what would be expected to be (or is) realised as the external argument, the argument bearing 'subject properties', of a given verb (cf. Müller 2007: 308). The blocking of this argument is accompanied by a lack of case assignment, which may – just like for Rouveret & Vergnaud (1980) – be made up for by a transitive auxiliary. Accordingly, argument (de-)blocking is closely related to case assignment, i.e. "case alternations [are] concomitant with argument reduction" (Haider 1986: 3). Once more, it is the perfect auxiliary HAVE which affects how the verb's argument structure is syntactically realised in perfect periphrases, whereas the effects of participial formation remain visible in passive cases (cf. Haider 1986: 7).

Haider's (1984; 1986) assumptions, despite having been quite influential, are subject to ongoing criticism. Gunkel (2003: 73), while following the conception of (de-)blocking (cf. Gunkel 1999: 142, 2003: 120f.), for instance criticises the concept of DA. What is taken to be problematic is that verbs which are expected to give rise to a DA do not form a consistent class, i.e. do not possess significant grammatical similarities, e.g. in terms of allowing for passivisation (cf. Gunkel 2003: 73f.). This becomes observable with verbs like *function*, which allow for an active perfect, but do not occur in periphrastic passives. The most frequent point of criticism, however, concerns the mechanism of blocking. This is for instance observable in von Stechow (1990: 183–185), where it is argued that "'[d]eblocking' makes even less sense than blocking" and that it cannot account for the facts of auxiliary selection properly. In the same vein, Abraham (1986: 103) claims that (de-)blocking does not yield any explanations. It is, according to Abraham (1986: 108f.), "an unnecessary technical assumption [that does not, in unison with case-assignment,] cover the whole story of passive and the past participle". Eventually, the notion of (de-)blocking indeed appears to be cumbersome in that it raises the question of why to block it in the first place if there is a mechanism to undo the change. Especially in the light of the MP's leading principle of economy this is anything but desirable and seems more like an extremely artificial stipulation than a natural principle.

As we have seen, what most of these 'argument structure' approaches inherently share by virtue of assuming that the external argument is in some

---

(1991; 1994), Lebeth (1994), Pollard (1994), Ryu (1997), Müller (1999; 2002), Gunkel (2003) – are hence not bound to assume an underlying passive participle.

way affected by past participial formation is the underlying necessity to delegate much of the observable differences to the auxiliaries. These eventually are responsible for the traditional distinction between passive and perfect(ive) participles based on whether or not they are able to introduce an argument that may not properly be realised by the past participle. This follows naturally since the change may not be imposed by the participial element itself in an identity approach and the auxiliary is a logical candidate in that passive and perfect auxiliaries are typically in complementary opposition. The technical instantiation of these ideas, however, remains problematic in that many approaches have to resort to designated mechanisms in order to account for the observable behaviour.

Primarily being concerned with the derivation of the passive, these 'argument structure' approaches to biased identity do not provide an explanation for why an active clause elicits perfect interpretation whereas its passive counterpart does not. Similar to what we have seen in the context of 'tense/aspect' approaches to biased identity, this stems from a neglect of those grammatical aspects that do not constitute the primary focus, i.e. passive imperfectivity in 'tense/aspects' approaches and perfect semantics in 'argument structure' ones. While those aspects could simply be shifted off to the auxiliaries, this is problematic in the perfect case, as it would render the participial marker ornamental for the analytic perfect (cf. Breul 2014: 465fn19). Additionally, this is also quite unexpected for the passive case given the passive readings of attributive past participles, for instance. It is, in fact, quite seldom that one finds an approach that considers both sides of the coin in sufficient detail. Besides Abraham's (2006a, b) attempt of deriving passive semantics from aspectual properties, approaches of this kind may be found with regard to the explicit conflation of passive and perfect information on a single form in the next section.

3.2.3 The amalgamation hypothesis

In addition to biased identity approaches with a perfect(ive) or passive focus, there is room for impartial identity approaches assuming the past participial marker to be neutral between a passive and a perfect(ive) reading. This may be instantiated in one of two ways: either the past participial marker unites passive and perfect(ive) information, aspects of which may remain abstract, or it does not comprise any relevant information at all. While the latter option will be regarded in the next section on the semantic vacuity hypothesis, we will now turn to the variant arguing for abstract meaning to be stored in the participial form. Accounts of this kind are expected to fall together with 'tense/aspect' or 'argument structure' approaches by virtue of the participle's ability to express at least one of the two functions autonomously. However, even if both ingredients are autonomously expressed by the participial element, this does not neglect the importance of the auxiliaries at least with respect to the expression of active voice.

As we have seen, the biased identity approaches that assume passive meaning to be at the core of the past participle have to attribute the expression of active voice to the auxiliaries. On the other hand, these usually neglect the imperfectivity of passive occurrences of past participles as opposed to the perfectivity of those in perfect contexts. Approaches that assume the past participle to carry perfect(ive) information typically run into similar problems with respect to this objection in that they cannot properly account for the temporal semantics of passive cases. However, with respect to the latter kind, not all approaches assuming the past participle to carry tense/aspect information deny the auxiliary's contribution of relevant perfect semantics. In fact, whereas most of the approaches discussed in chapter 3.2.1 claim that the auxiliaries only establish a relation to the time of utterance (or S, in Reichenbach's 1947 terms), we have also briefly seen some that attribute relevant perfect semantics to the auxiliaries. This possibility is for instance offered in Breul (2014: 459), which qualifies as an exponent of the amalgamation hypothesis in that it acknowledges the possibility of a past participle that unites passive and perfect information. In fact, Breul (2014: 465) assumes that the past participle comprises all the relevant passive features, whereas a perfect interpretation is either derived from "the perfect auxiliary alone or [...] the perfect auxiliary in combination with the feature equipment of the participle". Quite generally, the relevant perfect contribution may either be taken to hold for all perfect auxiliaries or only a subset, i.e. typically only HAVE, in line with the data discussed in chapter 2. Both of these subkinds, however, do not neglect that the participle also contributes relevant perfect information, which may then be described as being somewhat abstract in the sense that it does not suffice to induce a perfect reading without independent help. While this compositional take is most commonly pursued in the context of the tense/aspect hypothesis (see Ehrich & Vater 1989; Ehrich 1992; Ballweg 1988; 1989; Iatridou et al. 2001: 211f., 220f.), it is also occasionally assumed in the context of neutral identity, as just mentioned for Breul (2014). Another fairly implicit approach to neutral identity that follows this intuition may be found in Klein (1999: 73f.; 2010: 1238f.).

Primarily being concerned with German, Klein (1999: 73f.) claims that the participial marker assigns posteriority properties to the entity it refers to, i.e. the argument that ends up participating in the participial event. On the basis of this posteriority-inducing non-finite element, the auxiliaries may contribute in different ways to the event denominated by the participle, for instance in the sense of providing an argument and associating it with a temporal specification (cf.

Klein 1999: 73–77). While *sein* ('be') does not change anything, the passive auxiliary *werden* ('become') adds a temporal specification of precedence to the internal argument, whose properties thus differ from those it is attributed by the posterior event instantiated by the past participle (cf. Klein 1999: 75). Finally, *hab-* ('have') adds a temporal specification for an argument to the effect that it is located at a posterior point with respect to the action denominated by the participle (cf. Klein 1999: 76f.; see also Klein 2010: 1242). These ideas are elaborated and extended to other languages in Klein's (2010) attempt at converging argument structure and temporal characteristics subsumed under 'event structure' into a single 'argument-time structure'. Primarily being concerned with temporal characteristics, Klein's (1999; 2010) approaches, however, remain implicit with respect to the passive and apparently just attribute the suppression of the external argument to the non-finiteness of the past participle. Nevertheless, given that this property may clearly not stem from the auxiliary here, this is an approach that (implicitly) follows the amalgamation hypothesis. In fact, it attributes both passive as well as perfect characteristics to the past participle, although the denotation of a proper perfect as well as the expression of active voice hinge on the choice of a particular auxiliary.

A more explicit approach to the amalgamation of passive and perfect information in a single past participial element may be found in Breul & Wegner (2017), which is explicitly concerned with the question of past participial (non-)identity. In this work, it is proposed that the lexical operation forming past participles evokes the 'deletion of a non-primary argument position' (cf. Breul & Wegner 2017: 17). In fact, what is predicted to be deleted is "the argument position for the highest-ranking non-primary argument" (Breul & Wegner 2017: 17). Given the deletion of an argument position but not the argument itself, this operation is taken to elicit an unlinked θ-role whenever past participial formation applies to a predicate carrying a non-primary argument position (cf. Breul & Wegner 2017: 18f.).[23] The ranking of the arguments in terms of their mapping as primary or non-primary arguments (of different kinds) is governed by Proto-Agent and Proto-Patient properties in the sense of Dowty (1991) (cf. Breul & Wegner 2017: 14). In

---

[23] Note that this operation is eventually extended in order to exclude passives of verbs that assign lexical case to their non-primary argument: "the argument position for the highest-ranking non-primary argument is de-leted, [sic!] unless case is assigned lexically to it" (Breul & Wegner 2017: 38). This is necessary with verbs like *auffallen* ('strike'), *gelingen* ('succeed'), and *unterlaufen* ('occur'), e.g. in **Ein Fehler wurde (ihm) unterlaufen* (lit. A mistake became (him) occur.PTCP).

order to assure that a passive may be formed, however, there are also more fine-grained semantic restrictions, i.e. the presence of an unlinked θ-role is a necessary but not a sufficient condition for the denotation of passive meaning (cf. Breul & Wegner 2017: 33f.). Eventually, the distribution of the auxiliaries is fully governed by three argument structural parameters: 1) the presence or absence of an unlinked θ-role and whether the auxiliary is sensitive to it, 2) whether the auxiliary opens up an argument position, and 3) how this position may be satisfied, i.e. whether it has to be satisfied by an explicit primary argument or an implicit argument associated with the unlinked θ-role (cf. Breul & Wegner 2017: 26–28). This is supposed to take care of the expression of active voice in that HAVE may contribute an argument position in which the argument associated with the participle's unlinked θ-role may be realised (cf. Breul & Wegner 2017: 28–30). Besides this argument structural effect, as discussed in section 3.2.1, past participle formation converts a situation into its post-time state (cf. Breul & Wegner 2017: 44). This, as mentioned before, is sufficiently flexible to account for imperfective passive cases as well as the denotation associated with the analytic perfect, but arguably leaves too much to implication by leaving open whether a homogeneous event continues to last during the post-time of some of its sub-phases or not. Additionally, the passive auxiliary WERDEN is ascribed dynamic as well as future semantics, whereas HAVE is deprived of any perfect contribution in contrast to the data introduced in chapter 2. Futhermore, this approach rests upon some non-standard assumption concerning the distribution of verbs into several classes with respect to the primary and non-primary arguments they project, which is just claimed to be governed by Dowty's (1991) proto roles. This is conceptually odd with verbs like *lack*, *resemble*, and *suit*, which are suggested to comprise two non-primary arguments, although it is not quite clear why they lack a primary argument. Eventually, this exponent constitutes the most elaborate approach of the amalgamation hypothesis and is descriptively adequate in terms of being able to account for a wide range of English and German data. However, it lacks in explanatory adequacy, some of its technical specificities and presuppositions are questionable, and some of its major assumptions, most importantly neglecting the semantic contribution of HAVE, do not match the empirical data discussed before.

As to be expected given the problems just identified as well as the distinctions in scope and framework, the account to be laid out in the present work differs considerably from Breul & Wegner's (2017) approach to past participial identity, though certainly being inspired by considerations that stem from its descriptive investigations. The most important conclusion gained from the discussion of the drawbacks of biased identity and their reconciliation in the context of the amalgamation hypothesis is that it is indeed possible and desirable to conflate passive and perfect information in a single form. As this hypothesis is in line with the insights offered in chapter 2, this is the route to be pursued in the novel approach laid out below. This novel account will strongly rely on verbal event structure on the basis of which perfectivity is or is not induced, which may or may not in turn impose a requirement for the perfect contribution of HAVE. Before we go there, however, let us briefly regard approaches that deny that past participles introduce relevant passive or perfect information at all and briefly summarise the challenges and opportunities of (non-)identity in general.

3.2.4 The semantic vacuity hypothesis

The final type of approaches to consider in the present chapter comes in two kinds that share the intuition that the past participle does not introduce relevant passive or perfect information. On the one hand, there are those that attribute all of the relevant information to the auxiliaries and hence leave the past participle unspecified or make explicit that it is semantically vacuous. On the other hand, there are also non-compositional constructional approaches which hold that neither the auxiliary nor the past participle brings in relevant information for eliciting passive or perfect meaning and instead attribute this to the construction as a whole.

A moderate instantiation of the former kind may be found in Toman (1986: 368f.), where the flexibility in past participial behaviour is delegated to distinctions in the main verb heritage of the respective auxiliary involved. Whereas BE and WERDEN cannot assign structural case, HAVE is able to govern an internal argument by virtue of comprising accusative case (cf. Toman 1986: 368f.). The interaction of auxiliary and participle is formalised in terms of θ-inheritance (cf. Toman 1986: 370–373). This process allows the auxiliary to "affect the mode in which the argument structure of the [past participle] is realised [by virtue of] form[ing] a single inheritance domain with the [past participle]" (Toman 1986: 376). The percolation of the relevant features of the individual elements in a given inheritance domain is illustrated (rather informally) for *angekommen sein* ('have arrived', lit. arrive.PTCP be) in (91), taken from Toman (1986: 373).

(91)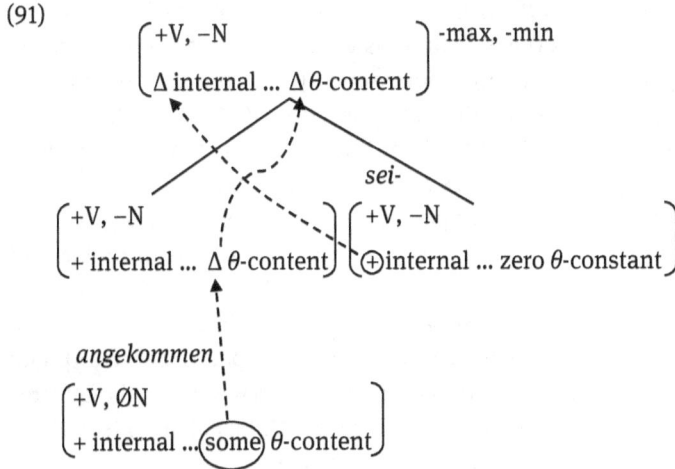

The central assumption here is that – in contrast to biased identity approaches following the argument structure hypothesis – no changes to the θ-grid are evoked in the formation of a past participle (cf. Toman 1986: 373). These just follow from the interaction with a given auxiliary with which the participle forms an inheritance domain. Hence, the distinction between active and passive stems solely from the auxiliaries. Wunderlich (1997: 2) and Vater (2002: 357) consider this to be sufficient to render this approach an instance in which the basic meaning is 'perfect'. However, since Toman (1986) does not address perfect meaning, this rather boils down to an implicit semantic vacuity approach. Accordingly, moderate instances of this kind typically deny either a passive or perfect(ive) contribution, but remain agnostic as to whether the other kind of information is stored in the past participle. Similar to Toman (1986), Rapp (1997: 128f.), for instance, argues against past participles being inherently passive but still remains rather agnostic about what their basic meaning is then.

More explicit approaches to semantic vacuity are provided by Kathol (1991; 1994) and Pollard (1994), who argue against a participial contribution of the temporal/aspectual kind but nevertheless do not attribute passive meaning to the past participles. Kathol (1991: 126), for instance, claims that "all of the particular aspectual and tense properties of perfect tense are a result of the auxiliary, not of the participle". Additonally, changes to the underlying argument structure are imposed by the auxiliary *werden*, i.e. the auxiliary evokes the observable difference without any prior changes to argument structure imposed by participial formation (cf. Kathol 1991: 118f.; Pollard 1994: 283). Something similar can also be seen in von Stechow (1990: 171f., 178), who calls *werden* ('become') a passiviser which blocks accusative government and thus governs case absorption. Further proponents of these ideas – though not explicitly denying the tense/aspect hypothesis – are Abraham (1986: 110f.) and Fanselow (1987: 165), who assume that *werden* ('become') and *sein* ('be') 'filter out' certain (external) arguments, whereas *haben* ('have') does not impose argument reduction.

Whereas the semantic vacuity of past participial morphology is just a by-product in many approaches relying on the auxiliaries, a general problem of these approaches is that they cannot account for bare instances of past participles. In fact, if there is no relevant passive or perfect(ive) information stored in the participial form, there is no way to account for a past participle's interpretation in its bare use, which clearly differs from its verbal stem. Although this problem is often acknowledged (see Toman 1986: 378f.; Pollard 1994: 280f.; Kathol 1994: 265f.), a proper solution is not to be found.

Taking the properties of attributive past participles seriously, Wunderlich (1997: 2–4) provides another fairly implicit approach to semantic vacuity that attributes perfect information to the auxiliaries, but claims that a passive interpretation does not solely stem from the auxiliary. However, the latter is also not inherently stored in the past participle, which retains the verbal θ-grid, but rather stems from the optional application of existentially binding the external argument (cf. Wunderlich 1997: 4). Accordingly, Wunderlich (1997: 2) points out the following: "since the passive participles form a proper subset of participles it is more likely that passive is an additional rather than an alternative piece of information". The presence of an existentially bound external argument is a necessary requirement, although an analytic passive still demands the insertion of a passive auxiliary (cf. Wunderlich 1997: 4). Eventually, then, neither passive nor perfect information is inherently stored in the past participle, but – unlike in the other approaches to semantic vacuity considered thus far – it is not necessarily the case that the relevant contribution is entirely attributed to the auxiliaries. This serves to account for the passive characteristics of bare occurrences, but is not very insightful by virtue of shifting passive semantics off to the application of a designated mechanism that serves to existentially bind the external argument.

The arguably most radical and explicit instantiation of the semantic vacuity of past participial morphology is pursued by von Stechow & Sternefeld (1988) and von Stechow (1990; 1998). This is for instance observable in von Stechow's (1998: 1) explicit claim that "participle morphology as such doesn't [...] have any meaning at all in isolation". In other words, the main assumption here is that "[t]here is no such thing as a core meaning of the participle II morphology" (von Stechow 1998: 3). Similar to other approaches solely based on the contribution of the auxiliaries, all of the differences between the periphrastic passive and the analytic perfect are thus traced back to the auxiliaries (cf. von Stechow 1998: 1; von Stechow & Sternefeld 1988). Hence, the passive auxiliary acts as a passiviser and blocks accusative government, whereas the temporal auxiliary adds tense-aspect information (cf. von Stechow 1990: 171f.). This is claimed to find support in the observation that the reading of the past participle may not be reduced to either passive or perfect, as is for instance observable in the fact that perfect meaning is not present in passive contexts (cf. von Stechow 1998: 7). In fact, it is claimed that uses like the analytic perfect, the eventive passive, the stative passive and the attributive participle "are so different both syntactically and semantically that it is very doubtful that there is a uniform meaning associated with the Participle II morphology" (von Stechow 1998: 4). According to von Stechow (1998: 4), there are only two ways to resolve this, namely assuming four semantically unrelated meanings or accepting that "the participle morphology has no meaning at all: there is no morphological ambiguity; we rather have different auxiliaries and different constructions".

This approach shares the drawbacks briefly brought forth in the context of other approaches that solely rely on the contribution of the auxiliaries. In fact, such approaches generally have a hard time accounting for the properties of bare past participles, where just resorting to the constructional embedding often simply will not do. Additionally, semantic vacuity entails that past participial morphology generally constitutes ornamental morphology, which just coincidentally shares the same form in passive and perfect contexts. Most importantly, however, the assumption of semantic vacuity neglects the large amount of shared characterics, e.g. the fact that the external argument may never be realised unless HAVE is around and its semantic role cannot even be associated with the element it modifies in adnominal contexts. Furthermore, it cannot account for many of the observations, for instance regarding divergent realisations of past participles, laid bare in chapter 2.

Unlike the exponents considered so far, there are also some approaches of the semantic vacuity kind that take a constructional stance and thus disregard the meaning components of the individual parts. Accordingly, these non-compositional approaches do not consider the potential contribution of a past participle and an auxiliary, but rather claim that meaning is assigned to the construction as a whole, i.e. the overall interpretation simply stems from the construction in question (cf. Spencer 2001: 281f.). Blevins (2003: 763), for instance, instantiates this via the properties [PERFECT] and [PASSIVE], which are realised by the combination of HAVE + past participle and BE + past participle, respectively. This intuition is also adhered to in Spencer (2001: 281f.) and Ackerman & Webelhuth (1998). According to Ackerman & Webelhuth (1998:

139fn2), 'past participle' is just a morphological category exponents of which "enter into the expression of predicates with various meanings and functions, e. g., the active predicative participle of the perfect, passives, etc.". Reminiscent of (but more radical than) Aronoff's (1994) introduction of the morphomic level, at the core of these conjectures is the assumption that there is no need for one-to-one correspondences between form and meaning. Rather, meaning is assigned to functional units, e.g. the passive participial construction, and does not have to be assigned to individual forms. Hence, these approaches do without any need to identify which of the ingredients contributes aspectual information in a perfect construction (cf. Spencer 2001: 281f.) or passive semantics in a passive construction (cf. Ackerman & Webelhuth 1998: 139f.fn2).

One of the major flaws of constructional approaches is that they shift a lot of work off to the lexicon, which is where the relevant constructions are built and stored (cf. Ackerman & Webelhuth 1998: 25–29). Although this might not be an inherent problem in terms of storage capacity, it refuses the explanatory insights we strive for. Furthermore, a constructional stance strongly neglects the large amount of characteristics shared between the individual elements within constructions like the analytic perfect and the periphrastic passive. This, unfortunately, bars insightful conclusions as to the properties of past participles.

3.3 Challenges and opportunities of (non-)identity

This concludes our overview of approaches to past participial (non-)identity and the possible routes they pursue. We will now briefly recapitulate their main problems and merits in order to determine the orientation of the novel approach to be laid out below. The distinct kinds of approaches to the (non-)identity of past participles that we have seen are summarised in (92), where the assumption of non-identity in (92a) is lined up against the various types of identity approaches in (92b-d).

(92) the (non-)identitypast participial (non-)identity spectrum of past participles

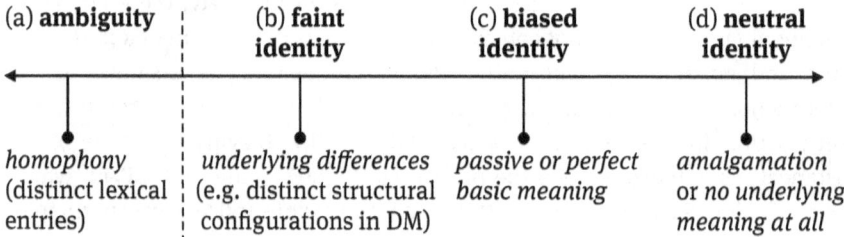

(a) **ambiguity**	(b) **faint identity**	(c) **biased identity**	(d) **neutral identity**
homophony (distinct lexical entries)	*underlying differences* (e.g. distinct structural configurations in DM)	*passive or perfect basic meaning*	*amalgamation* or *no underlying meaning at all*

3.3 Challenges and opportunities of (non-)identity — 167

The assumption of non-identity in (92a), though providing an easy way out, cannot explain the accidental morphological identity of the two distinct affixes and is actually not in any way supported by the data introduced in chapter 2. In fact, these do not provide evidence for a substantial split between passive and perfect(ive) participles, but rather show that certain auxiliaries as well as the properties of the underlying verb play an important role with respect to the properties of a participial construction. As we have seen, this does not only hold for synchronic considerations, but may also be derived from a diachronic perspective, where a substantial split is not to be attributed to the participial form but differences in behaviour coincide with auxiliarisation. Eventually the ambiguity approach is neither empirically supported nor particularly insightful, which is why the existence of two syntacticosemantically distinct participial forms is rejected in the present work.

The alternative of assuming past participial identity in (92b-d), on the other hand, has to account for the nature of the past participle's basic meaning, which is anything but a trivial undertaking. In fact, none of the possible kinds of approaches to identity intuitively provides an easy answer to the issue at hand. The assumption of faint identity in (92b), for instance, is problematic in the sense that it leaves open whether relevant contributions stem from the participial marker or are just effects of the structural configuration into which it is inserted. Accordingly, this approach to the identity of past participles makes it difficult to properly account for the issue of past participial (non-)identity.

The assumption of biased identity in (92c) is no less problematic since settling for either an inherent passive or perfect(ive) contribution usually neglects the importance of its respective counterpart. The relevant contribution of this counterpart, i.e. passive in tense/aspect approaches and perfect(ive) in argument structure approaches, is typically just shifted off to the auxiliaries. However, this is highly problematic in both variants. The presence of passive meaning in bare instances suggests that the verbal argument structure is affected by past participial formation and hence speaks out for a passive bias. While this may be accounted for by resorting to the properties of HAVE in an identity approach, the suppression of an argument cannot be a necessary requirement for the formation of a past participle, as the existence of unaccusative past participles like *arrived* makes clear. These would end up being semantically vacuous if the argument structural effect is all there is to past participle formation. On the other hand, the tense/aspect bias has to face similar challenges. A past participle cannot possess fully-fledged perfect(ive) information or else passive auxiliaries would not only have to block argument realisation but somehow also have to be held responsible for annulling a perfect(ive) interpretation in periphrastic passives. While certainly allowing for important insights, biased identity approaches are thus theoretically problematic. Moreover, the empirical considerations laid out in chapter 2 do not provide evidence for the assumption that either only passive or only perfect(ive) aspects are stored in the participial marker, whereas all else stems from the auxiliaries.

The remaining option is the assumption of neutral identity in (92d), which comes in two kinds. One of these boils down to taking the past participial marker to be semantically vacuous. This deprives past participial morphology of any meaning whatsoever and hence usually attributes all the relevant passive and perfect(ive) information to the auxiliaries involved. This has to face challenges similar to those of biased identity approaches, though to a more radical extent given that distinct properties may never be accounted for by resorting to the past participial morpheme at hand. Alternatively, the assumption of semantic vacuity may also be found in constructional approaches, where meaning is assigned to the construction rather than one or both of the constituents in a periphrastic configuration. These, however, do not provide any relevant insights with respect to the issue at hand, which is why they are neglected. Quite generally, approaches to the semantic vacuity of past participles share that they cannot account for why a single form is used in the distinct contexts, if these are not related in some way in terms of their grammatical properties. This is reminiscent of how non-identity approaches cannot account for the accidental homophony of the distinct forms and, just like these, suffers from a lack of substantial insights. Additionally, the distinctions in behaviour observed in chapter 2 do not point towards semantically unrelated exponents. Rather, they suggest that the past participle introduces some relevant information contingent on the properties of the verb that it is derived from, which may in turn be influenced by the structural environment, most importantly the particular auxiliary employed.

The second kind of neutral identity approach is one that amalgamates passive and perfect(ive) information in a single form. Given the apparent incompatibility of these two ingredients, such approaches are usually forced to assume that some of the relevant properties in question remain fairly abstract. With respect to the denotation of perfect meaning and the imperfective periphrastic passive, for instance, relevant properties are either shifted off to implication or the contribution of the passive auxiliary in the very few exponents of approaches following the amalgamation hypothesis. Simply relying on implication, however, lacks in explanatory adequacy and the assumption of relevant temporal information on WERDEN effecting an imperfective interpretation is quite dubious. Less problematic is the derivation of an active perfect from a past participle that bears passive properties, which may be attributed to the contribution of a perfect auxiliary. Eventually, though some problems remain with respect to the perfect(ive) ingredient, the amalgamation view appears to be most capable of accounting for the empirical data reviewed so far. In fact, an approach along these lines bears the potential to account for the wide range of synchronic data and also takes seriously the historical development of the past participle out of a deverbal adjective that bears passive as well as resultative properties.

Although we have seen that virtually every conceivable option to past participial basic meaning has been pursued, none of the existing approaches comes without theoretical burden, i.e. all of the approaches considered so far are subject to substantial theoretical criticism. Additionally, none of the aforementioned approaches is able to properly account for all of the empirical data discussed in chapter 2. However, coupling these theoretical considerations with the empirical findings laid bare in the previous chapter suggests that an identity approach along the lines of the amalgamation hypothesis is what is called for. Accordingly, the novel approach to be laid out shortly will follow the main intuitions of uniting passive and perfect(ive) information in a single form. On the other hand, it will differ from previous approaches by virtue of taking seriously the perfect semantic contribution of HAVE as well as the fine-grained event structural properties of the underlying verb. The latter will crucially be held responsible for determining whether a past participle is perfect(ive) or not.

*

Now that the most important empirical data as well as problems and merits of previous approaches to past participial (non-)identity have been taken into consideration, we are finally in a position to intertwine all of our findings into a proper novel approach. As none of the synchronic and diachronic empirical data discussed in chapter 2 point towards substantial non-identity and its assumption is actually also theoretically flawed, this approach will subscribe to the substantial identity of passive and perfect(ive) participles. In fact, we will assume that past participle formation has an effect on the expression of the external argument, yet also contributes aspectual information in the sense that perfectivity may be induced if the event structure of the underlying verb allows for it. Accordingly, the approach to be laid out conflates relevant passive and perfect information and thus marks an exponent of what was termed the amalgamation hypothesis.

The decision for laying out an approach along these lines is based on the observation that past participles generally lack the capability of realising an external argument, unless governed by HAVE. Similar to what is proposed in many of the biased identity approaches following the argument structure hypothesis, we may thus conclude that HAVE contributes in crucial ways to the expression of the external argument. With respect to the contribution of aspectual information, past participles cannot generally be claimed to be perfective, but rather only consistently denote that an event is ended if formed on the basis of a simple change of state (e.g. *arrive, disappear*). In all other cases, crucially whenever the event is atelic or a causer is semantically present, the participle cannot properly denote perfectivity, which is why the periphrastic passive is inherently imperfective. Transitive and unergative predicates as well as atelic two-place unaccusatives accordingly require independent support in order to denote a perfective situation. This support may come from the auxiliary HAVE, which, as we have seen, can be shown to contribute relevant perfect information to the effect that it allows a participial event to be brought to an end. These assumptions eventually allow us to conclude that – rather than a substantial distinction between passive and perfect(ive) participles – there is just one past participle that conflates syntacticosemantic aspects of both the passive and the perfect. This conclusion is also supported by diachronic considerations, since the past participle stems from a deverbal adjective that used to bear both resultative and passive characteristics.

Though many of the approaches we have just seen provide important ingredients that will be adapted below (e.g. the intuition behind θ-merger and the importance of verbal aktionsart or event structure for the contribution of perfectivity), none of these does justice to the intricate cross-linguistic properties of past participles. Therefore, the novel approach – though borrowing many intuitions and occasionally also adapting their incorporation – will crucially differ from what has been proposed before. Accordingly, the next chapter will carve out and technically instantiate the aforementioned assumptions in a compositional approach to the amalgamation of passive and perfective information in a single past participle.

4 A compositional approach to the identity of past participles

The most central conclusion to be drawn from the previous chapters is that there is no principled reason to subscribe to the non-identity of past participles. While there are languages that make a substantial distinction and provide the morphological means to mark it (e.g. Bulgarian, Russian and Latin), Romance and Germanic languages – with the exception of Swedish – do not possess substantially distinct passive and perfect(ive) participles. In other words, morphophonological identity mirrors substantial syntacticosemantic identity in all of those languages under investigation that do not make a morphological distinction between a perfect(ive) participle and a passive participle. As a matter of fact, empirical data as well as theoretical considerations suggest that distinctions in the grammatical behaviour as well as the interpretation of past participles stem from other sources. The most important factors determining whether a participial construction is perfect or passive are the properties of the verbs that past participles are derived from as well as the immediate structural context, most prominently in terms of which auxiliary is employed. Hence, the present chapter will present a compositional approach to the identity of past participles, which in crucial ways relies on the grammatical contributions of certain auxiliaries as well as the underlying properties of the verbs that participate in past participle formation. Despite the importance of these factors, however, the contribution of past participial morphology is imperative.

As we have seen, previous approaches proclaiming the identity of past participles struggle to provide a satisfactory answer to the question of what is contributed by past participial morphology. The approach to be laid out shortly attempts to account for the basic meaning of past participles by attributing both argument structural as well as aspectual information to the participial form. In fact, what the past participial marker inherently comprises is an effect on the expression of an external argument as well as aspectual specifications that are sufficient to render certain types of predicates perfective. In other words, past participles conflate essential ingredients of a passive as well as a perfect kind. These contributions are decisive and in crucial ways interact with the aforementioned compositional ingredients of past participial constructions, which is why such constructions are flexible enough to denote an imperfective passive as well as an active perfect.

In an attempt to incorporate these assumptions into a proper theory,[1] the present chapter will be structured as follows. Chapter 4.1 is devoted to the (pre-theoretical) discussion of the relevant ingredients of past participial constructions in terms of identifying their individual contributions. To be precise, subsection 4.1.1 is devoted to the argument structural effect of past participles, 4.1.2 focusses on its aspectual contribution, and 4.1.3 discusses the role of the auxiliaries. As it is largely based on the empirical findings introduced in chapter 2, this discussion will crucially rely on both periphrastic as well as bare instantiations of past participles, although special care is in order as none of these occurrences may straightforwardly be said to allow for an unmediated view.[2] Once the contributions of the compositional ingredients have been identified, section 4.2 will focus on the syntax and semantics of past participles. Accordingly, it will first present a technical incorporation of how past participles are derived from verbs and then turn to how they are combined with auxiliaries in order to form participial periphrases in chapter 4.2.1. This theoretical investigation of the combinatorial properties is extended in sections 4.2.2 and 4.2.3, which will provide a theoretical investigation of the syntactic as well as semantic properties of past participial forms in their two major uses, the periphrastic passive and the analytic perfect, respectively. This discussion raises the question of whether these technical considerations are sufficient to grasp the shallow polymorphy in terms of participial agreement and the divergent realisations of past participles, both of which we encountered in chapter 2. These issues will thus briefly be revisited in section 4.2.4. While chapter 4.2 attempts to account for the intricate properties of periphrastic constructions, section 4.3 (tentatively) extends the present theory to bare instantiations of past participles, which automatically takes us back to categorial concerns.

---

[1] As mentioned before, this theory will focus on English and German, as these languages draw the distinctions most important for the current issue (auxiliary alternation, a passive auxiliary that is not BE, and lexical dative case). Nevertheless, the null hypothesis is that it accounts for the properties of other identity languages as well.
[2] This is trivially true for periphrastic constructions, but also holds for bare instances, which are more or less strongly contingent on (and potentially influenced by) their structural environment, as is for instance observable in the case of stative adnominals (*the disappeared girl*) and absolute clauses (*The lawn mowed, he went home*).

4.1 The basic meaning of past participles and what the auxiliaries contribute

The range of empirical data considered in the present work has exposed some characteristics that are highly likely to be shared by all past participles. These are basically of a three-fold nature, namely the trivial observation that past participles are non-finite, the finding that past participial morphology imposes a restriction on the expression of an external argument, and the observation that there has to be some kind of aspectual information stored within past participial forms. We will now briefly recapitulate what justifies the inherent presence of these properties in past participles and then move on to scrutinise which compositional ingredients are provided by the auxiliaries. This discussion will be based on data from English and German and resort to periphrastic uses as well as bare instances of past participles. In both of these cases, the past participle is syntactically and semantically anchored in a construction that is likely to impose its own distributional requirements. However, abstracting away from the 'static noise' of the particular structural context may provide us with fairly clear indications of what needs to be assumed as the inherent meaning of past participles. This, in turn, allows us to specify which aspects are contributed by external factors like the auxiliaries or an adjectival morpheme.

Quite trivially, one of the basic ingredients of past participle formation is that it renders a verbal base non-finite. In fact, past participles can only ever give rise to finite constructions in collaboration with finite auxiliaries. This entails that finiteness is contributed by the auxiliaries and cannot be expressed by the participial forms themselves. In other words, a past participle may only ever occur without an auxiliary when a given construction does not require a finite verb, i.e. in its bare (auxiliaryless) occurrence as a non-finite adjunct. Accordingly, we never find the bare instantiation of a past participle in a context in which it marks an integral part of a finite clause (cf. Wanner 2009: 15). Thus, one of the constitutive properties of past participles is that they are non-finite, i.e. they are never inflected for tense. In addition to non-finiteness, the participial form comprises relevant information of two kinds, namely an argument structural effect and aspectual information which will be discussed in 4.1.1 and 4.1.2 in turn.

4.1.1 The argument structural effect

The argument structural effect of past participial morphology is clearly observable in bare instances of past participles. In fact, both the adnominal instances in

(93) as well as the adverbial uses in (94) are subject to the suppression of an external argument.

(93) a. das dem   Mann   gegebene Buch
       the the.DAT man.DAT given   book
       'the book given to the man'
    b. the man given the book (by John)

(94) a. Carried (by his mother), the baby felt safe.
    b. The dragon slain, the knight took his rest.

These cases of (di-)transitive predicates show that bare instances of past participles are not capable of realising their external arguments without independent help. While this may often be traced back to considerations of case assignment (viz. the lack of nominative case in non-finite constructions), it is striking that the argument modified by the participle in adnominal adjuncts like those in (93) may also not be interpreted as the participle's external argument. Likewise, the adverbial cases in (94) do not straightforwardly allow for the semantic association of the past participle's external semantic role with an argument of the main clause. In fact, the latter may only instantiate the past participle's internal argument in (94a). However, the absolute clause in (94b) shows that the association of an argument of the main clause with the participle's external argument may occasionally loosely come about pragmatically. Here, the event of slaying the dragon need not have been carried out by the knight, although this is inferred. Eventually, the only possibility to instantiate an argument that is supposed to be interpreted as the past participle's external argument in bare cases is by means of resorting to an adjunct BY-phrase. Accordingly, past participles virtually bear passive characteristics in terms of their argument structure in contexts in which they are introduced without the aid of an auxiliary (cf. Gunkel 1999: 142). This argument structural effect crucially only affects the expression of the external argument. Internal arguments of a given past participle may, on the other hand, either readily be realised, as in (93) and (94b), or semantically be associated with the element that the participle modifies, as in (93) and (94a), depending on the particular structural configuration.

The suppression of an external argument may also be observed in predicative constructions. The one that comes closest to bare instantiations is the stative passive, which arguably consists of a copula that takes an adjectival past participle, as in (95).

(95) a. Das Haus ist gebaut.
     the house is   build.PTCP
     'The house is (in the resultative state of having been) built.'
  b. Das Mädchen ist immer noch verschwunden.
     the girl   is ever   still   disappear.PTCP
     'The girl is still (in the resultative state of having been) disappeared.'

Emphasising a resultative state, the argument of a stative passive may not be interpreted as the external argument of the past participle, as becomes clear with the passive interpretation of (95a). Rather, like with the unaccusative in (95b), the sole argument is interpreted as the participle's internal argument. This observation carries over to the periphrastic passive formed with BE or WERDEN as well as the analytic BE-perfect in languages that resort to auxiliary alternation, as shown in (96). In fact, the proper syntactic realisation of an external argument is only licit in a single context, the periphrastic perfect formed with HAVE.

(96) a. Ross was kissed by Rachel.
  b. Ross wurde   von Rachel geküsst.
     Ross became by   Rachel kiss.PTCP
     'Ross was kissed by Rachel.'
  c. Der Zug ist angekommen.
     the train is arrive.PTCP
     'The train has arrived.'

The consistent behaviour of past participles in terms of their argument structure in all but one structural configuration provides ample evidence for the assumption that the suppression of an external argument (if present) is part of the grammatical information introduced by past participial morphology. The exceptional behaviour of past participles realised in the context of HAVE may, in turn, safely be attributed to the contribution of this perfect auxiliary.

Additional support for the argument structural contribution of past participial morphology comes from the divergent realisations we encountered in chapter 2.5 and the historical development of past participles briefly discussed in chapter 2.6. Divergent realisations of past participles show that past participial morphology is instrumental for the interpretation of a periphrastic passive and may thus never undergo impoverishment (unlike in HAVE-perfect contexts). The diachronic development of past participles provides support for the argument structural effect of past participle formation by virtue of their origin as deverbal adjectives that bear passive characteristics. In fact, the grammaticalisation of an active periphrastic perfect may be traced back to a resultative construction, the stative perfect. This construction is made up out of a deverbal adjective that is associated with a nominal expression whose resultative state it expresses in the context of the possessive main verb HAVE. The deverbal adjective in a stative perfect semantically relates to the nominal element it modifies by taking it as its internal argument, crucially bound to leave the external one syntactically unrealised and thus exhibiting passive characteristics (cf. Migdalski 2006: 142). The proper grammaticalisation of an active perfect is eventually contingent on the auxiliarisation of HAVE, which subsequently introduces an argument that is not conceptualised as the subject of an event of possession anymore, but rather marks the external argument of the past participle. Given this development, it is not surprising that the HAVE-perfect is initially restricted to transitive predicates, whereas unergative instances – lacking an internal argument and thus exempt from occurrences as object-oriented deverbal adjectives – of the analytic perfect come about only much later via analogical extension of the periphrastic HAVE-perfect. If the auxiliary BE is reserved for passive use, analogical extension also applies to unaccusative past participles, although these do not demand an argument structural contribution.

The argument structural effect of past participle formation is occasionally challenged by bare instances of supposedly unergative predicates. These should be exempt from adnominal and adverbial instantiations of past participles. However, cases like those in (97) are grammatical (see also Breul & Wegner 2017: 6).

(97) a. the showered girl
 b. Showered and changed, she went back into the gym and found Frulein Silber standing modestly in the background [...]. (retrieved from the BNC)

Given that the sole argument of an unergative predicate is expected to be suppressed in past participle formation, it should be downright impossible to derive bare past participles from unergative verbs. This holds true in ungrammatical attributive cases like *the slept girl and adverbial ones like *Slept for an hour, the boy was still extremely tired. As a matter of fact, however, the predicates in (97) do not belong to this type of verbs. Rather, they are examples of inherently transitive predicates that have unergative homonyms. This can be seen in that we do not have the capability to force a reading in which the associated nominal expression unequivocally provides the external argument of the participial event. In fact, the nominal element associated with the past participle is interpreted as its internal argument. While it is strongly inferred that the reduced external argument equals the referent of the nominal expression modified by the past participle with predicates like *shower* and *change* (as well as *wash, shave, hide,* etc.), this is by no means a grammatical necessity. In other words, these cases do not exhibit the disjoint reference effect that is characteristic of eventive passives (see Baker, Johnson & Roberts 1989).[3] This becomes observable once we add a BY-phrase in the corresponding structures to introduce an overt causer for the obtained result of being showered and changed, e.g. in the German attributive counterpart to (97b), *das von seiner Mutter geduschte und umgezogene Kind* ('the child showered and changed by his mother', lit. the by its mother shower.PTCP and change.PTCP child). Eventually, it is unlikely that a designated agent (not equal to the referent of the internal argument) is responsible for carrying out the action in question in cases like (97). This is why such predicates at first sight appear to be unergative but actually are transitive instances regularly used in a reflexive fashion. Proper unergatives, which *per definitionem* only bring in an external argument, are ungrammatical.

Potentially more substantial exceptions may be found in the context of prenominal cases like the German examples in (98) and (99) (cf. Lübbe & Rapp 2011: 284f.).

(98) a. ein geschworener / erfahrener Richter
      a   sworn.A   / *experienced*.A *judge*
      'a sworn/experienced judge'
 b. der abgedankte Chef
      the resigned.A   *boss*
      'the resigned boss'

(99) a. die stattgefundene Reformation
      the take.place.PTCP *reformation*
      'the reformation that has taken place'
 b. das abgenommene Interesse
      the decrease.PTCP   *interest*
      'the decreased interest'

The predicates in (98a) are lexicalised as adjectives whose meanings are not transparent in terms of going back to a base verb anymore (cf. Lübbe & Rapp

---

[3] We will briefly return to this effect in terms of delineating verbal and adjectival participles in 4.3.1 below.

2011: 285).⁴ In a similar vein, the predicate in (98b) is a lexicalised adjective that co-exists alongside a productive past participle (cf. Lübbe & Rapp 2011: 287). Given their adjectival nature, the predicates in these cases attribute a property to a referent and do not make recourse to a proper event in doing so. Therefore, these cases do not pose exceptions to the suppression of the external argument in past participles, simply because they are not past participial. In addition to these cases of proper adjectives, some more substantial exceptions come forth with predicates like those in (99). The Theme-unergatives in (99) arguably are not lexicalised as adjectives, but nevertheless occasionally allow for occurrences in which the sole external argument is semantically associated with the element that is modified. This, however, is not restricted to unergative predicates that are expected to be ungrammatical, but also carries over to transitive verbs licensing dative objects in German: *der gehuldigte König* ('the king that is paid homage', lit. the pay.homage.PTCP king) (cf. Lübbe & Rapp 2011: 263). Lübbe & Rapp (2011: 263, 284) treat such unexpected cases as ungrammatical yet acceptable attributive past participles that are licensed by the mechanism of 'argument adaptation'.⁵ This pragmatic rescue mechanism may occasionally set aside argument structural irregularities and make up for them pragmatically (cf. Lübbe & Rapp 2011: 284). Thus, the exceptional behaviour of such cases does not shed substantial doubt upon the suppression of an external argument.

The second and arguably most substantial kind of exceptions comes from the unexpected behaviour of (manner of) motion predicates that was briefly discussed in chapter 2.3. As we have seen above, predicates of this kind exhibit special characteristics in numerous languages. These do not only show in periphrastic constructions but actually carry over to bare past participial instances, as the small set of examples in (100) shows.

(100) a. Das Mädchen ist zum Ausgang gerannt/ getanzt/ geschwommen.
   the girl   is to.the exit   run.PTCP/*dance*.PTCP/*swim*.PTCP
   'The girl has run/danced/swum to the exit.'

---

4 The famous German football player Günter Netzer once provided a neat contrast between a productive verbal past participle (*gestanden*, 'stood') and a lexicalised adjective (*gestanden*, 'seasoned') carrying a different meaning: *Da haben Spieler auf dem Spielfeld gestanden, gestandene Spieler* ('Players stood on the pitch, seasoned players.', lit. there have players on the pitch stand.PTCP, seasoned.A players).
5 Due to their mixed behaviour and their assumed ungrammaticality, these exponents are taken to make up a twilight zone ('Grauzone') between grammar and lexicon (cf. Lübbe & Rapp 2011: 285).

b. Das Mädchen hat (leidenschaftlich) *gerannt/ getanzt/ geschwommen.
   *the girl   has passionately   run.*PTCP/*dance*.PTCP/*swim*.PTCP
   'The girl has run/danced/swum passionately.'
c. das *(zum Ausgang) gerannte/getanzte/ geschwommene Mädchen
   *the   to.the exit   run.*PTCP/*dance*.PTCP/ swim*.PTCP   girl
   'the girl that has run/danced/swum to the exit'

Although we expect predicates like *run, dance,* and *swim* to exhibit unergative characteristics, the cases in (100) challenge this assumption by virtue of their ability to occur with BE as well as allowing for attributive uses. Leaving the intricate differences of (manner of) motion predicates in periphrastic perfects like those in (100a) and (100b) aside for the time being, the general tendency that we could see was that a verb is either lexicalised with respect to comprising an endpoint or marks a result in the context of a directional modifier. This shift towards a resultative reading is arguably contingent on the mapping of the predicate's sole argument as an internal rather than an external argument. This becomes clear with predicates like *tanzen* ('dance') and *schwimmen* ('swim'), which – although they differ with respect to whether they require a directional modifier when they occur with BE – allow for both BE and HAVE when forming a perfect. These two auxiliaries trigger interpretive distinctions, though: the former emphasises the result that follows from the motion, i.e. a change of location, which the sole argument undergoes, whereas the latter ascribes an action to an argument that actively carries it out.[6] In other words, when occurring in a BE-perfect, the argument bears a considerable amount of Proto-Patient properties, whereas it bears Proto-Agent properties in the HAVE-perfect (cf. Breul & Wegner 2017: 40).[7] Therefore, these cases, though certainly demanding a more elaborate discussion, do not come with an external argument and are hence exempt from the argument structural effect of past participial morphology. This is underlined by the consistent acceptability of such instances in attributive contexts. However, as we can see in (100c), these are only grammatical if the

---

[6] Something similar may be observed in the case of telic particles (Sybesma & Vanden Wyngaerd 1996 call these 'perfective particles') in German, where intransitive *brennen* (burn) is unergative, but its telic counterparts *abbrennen* ('burn down') and *verbrennen* ('burn to ashes') are unaccusative. In English, similar examples may not easily be found, as there are no telic particles. Instead, the telicity is generally hard-coded in the verbs, which leads to a high degree of homonymy, as observable with *burned*. Whenever there is no homonymy, the distinction is expressed by non-homonymic lexemes (consider *wither* and *bloom* vs. *verblühen* and *blühen*).

[7] According to Gunkel (2003: 111), the argument of a (manner of) motion verb is associated with Proto-Agent and Proto-Patient properties since it governs a motion in which it is moved by itself and thus also controls itself.

participle is complemented by a directional modifier.[8] Most importantly, though, these only ever allow for the BE-perfect interpretation of ascribing Proto-Patient properties to the argument in question, which renders it an internal argument. Eventually, then, these cases can also be excluded from posing proper exceptions to the suppression of the external argument by past participial morphology.

Based on the findings that have just been recapitulated, we can safely conclude that the past participle bears the basic properties in (101).

(101) the basic properties of past participial morphology (preliminary version)
    a. non-finiteness
    b. restriction on the expression of argument structure to the effect that an external argument (if present) is suppressed (i.e. it may not syntactically be realised other than in the form of an adjunct and its semantic role may not be associated with the nominal element modified by the past participle)

In contrast to proponents of the view that either passive or perfect(ive) participles bear additional information in comparison to the other (see, for instance, Bresnan 1982: 18–21 and Wunderlich 1997: 7), we will take seriously the amalgamation hypothesis and thus assume that the reduction in argument structure is inherently shared by all past participial forms. In fact, the properties in (101) are taken to follow from a lexical operation that adds non-finiteness and marks the external argument for existential binding. The latter, however, is only a necessary, but not a sufficient condition for the denotation of a proper passive (cf. Wanner 2009: 52). As we will see in more detail in chapter 4.2.2, sometimes the reduction is applied to verbs that are semantically not suited to give rise to a passive reading, e.g. those that have an external argument that does not comprise a sufficient amount of Proto-Agent properties (*The letter was contained). Additionally, the suppression of an external argument may be resolved by the contribution of HAVE (cf. Ackema 1999; Ackema & Marelj 2012) in order to denote an active perfect.

There are also cases in which the contribution in (101b) remains without an effect, namely verbs that inherently lack an external argument, i.e. unaccusative

---

8 This shows that the class of (manner of) motion verbs consistently allows for taking an internal argument, although the items of this class differ with respect to whether or not the additional introduction of a directional modifier is required depending on the particular structural embedding (attributive vs. periphrastic) as well as the individual amount of lexicalisation.

predicates. In addition to the periphrastic BE-perfect in (96c), bare instantiations of past participles derived from such predicates may be found in (102).

(102) a. der angekommene Zug[9]
 the arrived   train
 'the train that has arrived'
 b. The train arrived at platform 9 3/4 quickly came to a halt.[10]
 c. Arrived at the station, the train quickly came to a halt.

Crucially, these unaccusative past participles do not behave 'actively' but actually also possess a 'passive' argument structure in terms of inherently lacking an external argument. Accordingly, bare unaccusative occurrences cannot be drawn from to argue that the basic meaning of a past participle (occasionally) is the denotation of an active perfect. Hence, all kinds of predicates are subject to the restriction in (101b), but whenever there inherently is no external argument, this simply remains without an effect. This has important repercussions for the basic meaning of past participles in that the properties in (101) may not be all there is to past participle formation. In fact, since forms like *arrived* remain without an argument structural effect, these would remain semantically vacuous and virtually identical to proper infinitival forms like (*to*) *arrive*. Hence, the argument structural effect of past participial morphology may not be its sole purpose.

4.1.2 The aspectual contribution

In addition to the argument structural effect, the formation of a past participle introduces aspectual information. These properties, however, cannot generally be the conveyor of fully-fledged perfectivity. In fact, the reading is trivially bound to be perfective in cases like those in (103), whereas the examples in (104) mark cases in which the reading that pertains may be imperfective.

---

9 As mentioned before, English is generally reluctant with respect to unaccusatives in prenominal (and stative passive) contexts. Accordingly, Ramchand (2008: 78fn6) judges *the arrived train* to be ungrammatical, whereas *the recently arrived train* is taken to be perfectly fine.
10 A similar example is attested in Radford (1997: 213): *The train arrived at platform 4 is the 8.28 for London Euston*. A factor potentially rendering postnominal occurrences of unaccusatives somewhat marked is the high risk of inducing a garden path situation, which may not immediately be resolved by an agentive *by*-phrase.

(103) a. Der Zug ist gerade angekommen.
    the train is just arrive.PTCP
    'The train has just arrived.'
  b. The train has just arrived.

(104) a. Der Mann wird gesehen.
    the man becomes see.PTCP
    'The man is (being) seen.'
  b. The man is (being) seen.

The past participles derived from unaccusative predicates in (103) are perfective regardless of whether they occur with BE (in auxiliary alternating languages) or HAVE (in HAVE-only languages). The transitive ones in (104), on the other hand, cannot be inherently perfective, or else the simultaneity that they convey is unexpected. This is underlined by examples of the periphrastic perfect in cases like those in (105).

(105) a. Ich habe dich schon immer geliebt.
    I have you PARTICLE *always love*.PTCP
    'I have always loved you.'
  b. Jack has loved Kate ever since he first laid eyes on her.

These instances force a universal perfect reading due to the presence of an adverbial modifier that opens up an interval that holds up to the present, given that it is not closed (cf. Iatridou et al. 2001: 191). Hence, the reading that ensues is one in which the participial event is not ended. This shows that the past participle cannot inherently be perfective, which is underlined by a comparison of bare instances like those in (107) as opposed to those in (106).

(106) a. das verschwundene Mädchen
    the disappear.PTCP *girl*
    'the disappeared girl'
  b. the (recently) disappeared girl
  c. Disappeared in the forest, the girl was returned to her parents shortly.

(107) a. die (von drei Pferden) gezogene Kutsche
    die (by three horses) pull.PTCP *carriage*
  b. the pulled carriage
  c. Pulled by three horses, the carriage quickly gained speed.

Whereas the examples in (106) do not allow for an imperfective reading in their bare instantiations, the participles in (107) at least cannot be excluded from denoting imperfectivity. In fact, while a resultative interpretation is also possible for reasons that we will turn to in chapter 4.3, we cannot deny the possibility of an ongoing event. This raises the question of the precise nature of the aspectual information stored in the past participle. This will largely be left for the discussion in chapter 4.2.3, but may briefly be sketched as follows. The aspectual information contributed by past participles is of a perfective kind, which is, however, strongly contingent on the event structure of the underlying predicate. In fact, on the basis of predicates that denote a simple change of state (*disappeared, arrived; unterlaufen* 'occurred to') crucially lacking a cause, the past participial morpheme gives rise to perfectivity. With other kinds of predicates, i.e. inherently atelic ones (e.g. *pulled, carried; gefallen* 'appealed to') as well as telic ones that feature the overt expression of a cause (e.g. *searched, built; bought*), on the other hand, proper perfectivity does not come about.[11] Accordingly, the third crucial ingredient of past participle formation is perfective information that is deficient in the sense that it is contingent on the aktionsart or event structure of the verbal base (unlike proper perfectivity in aspectual languages like those of Slavic).[12] In a nutshell, then, this gives us the basic properties of the past participial marker in our enhanced version of (101) in (108).

(108) the basic properties of past participial morphology (revised version)
    a. non-finiteness
    b. restriction on the expression of argument structure to the effect that an external argument (if present) is suppressed (i.e. it may not syntactically be realised other than in the form of an adjunct and its semantic role may not be associated with the nominal element modified by the past participle)
    c. aspectual information that is contingent on the aktionsart or event structure of the verbal base, i.e. defective (or deficient) perfectivity

---

[11] It is tempting to tie the instantiation of perfectivity to telicity, but this is challenged by telic achievements like *finden* ('find'), which give rise to a periphrastic perfect (*Er hat den Schlüssel gefunden*, 'He has found the key.'), but also occur in (imperfective) eventive passives (*Der Schlüssel wird gefunden*, 'The key is (being) found.').

[12] In a similar vein, Wunderlich (1997: 1–3) claims that verbs selected by BE bear the feature [+perf], "a lexical feature, which in some cases is predicted on the basis of the verb's meaning". What is particularly interesting about Slavic is that languages like Bulgarian also employ neutral aspectual markers in addition to perfective and imperfective ones and these only combine with processes and accomplishments, on the basis of which they convey imperfective properties (cf. Iatridou et al. 2001: 210). These are thus also event-structure sensitive.

The existence of aspectual information that only induces perfectivity on the basis of a simple change of state is supported by the historical development of past participles. As we have seen, the deverbal adjective that the participle started out as was initially delimited to transitive verbs, where it was strictly limited to denoting a resultative state. Crucially, this resultative situation was not allowed to introduce an agentive modifier, reminiscent of what we can typically still observe in the stative perfect and the stative passive.[13] Accordingly, the proper denotation of completion as induced by participial morphology was long delimited to a particular kind of predicates and it does not appear to be far-fetched that it still is.

Eventually, the deficient perfectivity constitutes the rather abstract aspectual contribution of past participial morphology. As a matter of fact, the possibility that this set of features is deficient (and hence sensitive to aktionsart or event structure) is usually overlooked in approaches to past participial (non-)identity, which explains why former attempts proclaiming perfectivity to be at the core of past participial morphology raised problems. In contrast to the problematic approaches resorting to fully-fledged perfectivity, defective perfectivity only forces simple change of states (which are *per definitionem* telic) to come to an end. Atelic situations as well as all of those featuring the expression of a cause, on the other hand, may not properly be ended by the contribution of the past participial marker. In other words, the aspectual information stored in past participles is only sufficient to give rise to a perfective situation when aided by the verb's inherent aktionsart or event structure.[14]

4.1.3 The contribution of the auxiliaries

The presence of an insufficient set of perfectivity on the past participial morpheme raises the question of what triggers a perfect interpretation in periphrastic

---

13 Accordingly, the stative passive *Tywin ist von seinen Feinden geschlagen* (lit. Tywin is by his enemies beat.PTCP) is ungrammatical and so is the stative perfect *Sie hat die Augen von Maria verbunden* (lit. she has the eyes by Mary bandage.PTCP, not 'She has bandaged Mary's eyes.').
14 The properties identified in (108) thus explain why past participles are considerably more complex than present participles. Present participles comprise a proper set of aspectual specifications that are largely insensitive to the properties of the verbal base (other than barring states) and are not restricted in terms of argument structure, as observable in *der ankommende/ angekommene Zug* ('the arriving/the arrived train') (cf. Lübbe & Rapp 2011: 283). Past participles, on the other hand, are sensitive to the event structure of the verbal base with respect to the expression of perfectivity and are subject to the suppression of the external argument.

4.1 The basic meaning of past participles and what the auxiliaries contribute — 185

perfects based on past participles that do not manage to denote completion. This is where the auxiliaries come in. As we have seen in the context of divergent realisations of past participles in chapter 2.5, there is ample evidence for the assumption that unlike BE and WERDEN, HAVE contributes relevant information to the perfect interpretation of a clause.[15] Examples like those exhibiting the PPP and the IPP in (109) show that the impoverishment of participial morphology is only possible in the context of HAVE.[16]

(109) a. Then, on a more serious note, she adds, "I need humor to connect with people." And *connect she has*, with readers and critics.
b. dass Rick ihn hat sehen   wollen
that Rick him has see.INF *want*.INF
'that Rick has wanted to see him'

The absence of corresponding passive as well as BE-perfect counterparts of these phenomena strongly supports the basic ingredients identified in (108). As a matter of fact, while a perfect interpretation may be retrieved on the basis of the presence of HAVE, such an interpretation may not be derived from BE in the periphrastic perfect of a language exhibiting auxiliary alternation.[17] Instead, the past participle comprises all the relevant perfect information in the case of a BE-perfect, which follows naturally from the assumption that BE-perfects are based on unaccusative predicates which denote a simple change of state and may hence elicit perfectivity. In a similar vein, the past participle in an eventive passive is instrumental because it comprises the suppression of the external argument and is hence not dispensable. This is underlined by the Norwegian PPI in (110) (cf. Wiklund 2001: 201), which spells participial morphology out twice without any interpretive effect.

---

15 While this is explicitly denied by Chomsky (1993: 30f.), who suggests that HAVE and BE are semantically vacuous, we will side with Hornstein (1990), Broekhuis & van Dijk (1995: 48) and others who attribute relevant information at least to the former, as this is strongly supported by the data discussed in chapter 2. This suggests that the auxiliaries are the driving force in the grammaticalisation of periphrastic constructions.
16 As we have seen, impoverishment does not have an effect on interpretation (LF) *per se*, but is only possible if the associated semantics are recoverable from an element that contributes to the semantics in question.
17 The highly restricted occurrences of the IPP in BE-perfects that we could identify in chapter 2.5.2 actually do not challenge this, as these are crucially restricted to aspectual verbs (*gaan, komen, blijven*). The verbal semantics of these kinds of predicates are likely to be lexically associated with a sense of completion, which is why perfectivity may be recovered despite the absence of both participial morphology as well as HAVE.

(110) Jeg hadde villet   lest/   lese   boka
      I   had   want.PTCP read.PTCP/ read.INF the.book
      'I had wanted to read the book.'

The superfluously marked form in these contexts does not induce argument suppression nor does it trigger perfectivity. The former may be accounted for by the presence of HAVE, which is able to introduce the shared external argument of the verbal cluster. The lack of perfectivity, however, is contingent on the presence of a set of aspectual information that is not sufficient to give rise to perfectivity given the properties of the base verb.

The importance of HAVE cannot be reduced to its argument structural contribution in these contexts, as the unaccusative cases of the PPP in (111) show.

(111) a. This dessert was made out of the desire for the warm weather to just arrive. And *arrive it has*. (retrieved from http://www.langijo.com/langijo/category/in-the-kitchen-x-the-first-bundle-of-rhubarb/, accessed on October 20, 2015)
 b. Until a month ago, the dehydrator had been sitting unused, waiting, like us, for the snow to melt. And *melt it has*, at least enough to start getting outside in our tent again. (retrieved from http://becominganomad.wordpress.com/tag/dehydrating/, accessed on October 20, 2015)

The grammaticality of the PPP in unaccusative contexts emphasises that the auxiliary's capability to realise an otherwise non-realisable external argument cannot be the sole contribution of HAVE besides finiteness. Rather, impoverishment of the past participial form is possible in spite of the fact that the auxiliary is not necessary in order to realise (or signal the realisation of) a suppressed argument. Even though an operation on the argument structure of *arrive* or – though not as clearly – *melt* is not necessary, as there is no external argument that could be realised by HAVE, impoverishment of the past participial form is allowed for. Of course, this is not unexpected since HAVE is generalised to all verbs in English, but the fact that PPP, IPP and PPI split up into HAVE vs. BE and WERDEN regardless of the unergative and transitive vs. unaccusative distinction is telling here. This suggests that in addition to expressing finiteness and argument structural properties, HAVE also contains relevant perfect information (cf. Iatridou et al. 2001: 220), which cannot be derived from (or signalled by) the past participial form in these contexts.[18] In the context of

---

[18] This is not the only possible conclusion that may be drawn from the divergent realisations of past participles. In fact, the perfect auxiliary might merely serve as a signal for a perfect

the IPP in Standard German, this assumption gains additional support from the observation that the perfect auxiliary often moves to an otherwise illicit position left-adjacent to the verbal cluster in order to signal the presence of a periphrastic perfect construction (cf. Bader 2014: 8; Hinterhölzl 1998: 62), as observable in (112).

(112) a. dass Charlie sie hat küssen *gewollt/ wollen
       that Charlie her has kiss want.PTCP/ *want*.INF
       'that Charlie has wanted to kiss her'
    b. *dass Charlie sie küssen gewollt / wollen hat
       that Charlie her kiss want.PTCP/ *want*.INF has

In analogy to the observation that the arguably contentful future-auxiliary *werden* ('will') is also preposed in the context of verbal clusters (cf. Haider 2003: 110; Bader & Schmid 2009: 180), this operation may be semantically motivated (cf. Bærentzen 2004: 137f.),[19] which presupposes that there is relevant perfect information in HAVE.

Additional evidence for the perfect contribution of HAVE comes from a class of verbs that internally shows differences in auxiliary selection. In fact, telic instances of two-place unaccusatives in German occur with BE, whereas atelic cases have to be introduced by HAVE. Examples of these may be found in (113) and (114), respectively.

(113) a. Die Lösung ist ihm entfallen.
       the solution is him.DAT *escape*.PTCP
       'The solution has escaped him.' (or 'He has forgotten the solution.')
    b. Ihm ist ein Fehler unterlaufen.
       him.DAT *is a mistake occur.to*.PTCP
       'A mistake has occurred to him.'

(114) a. Der Frau hat das Kleid gefallen.
       the.DAT *woman has the dress appeal.to*.PTCP
       'The dress has appealed to the woman'

---

interpretation. However, the assumption that such a signalling function comes about by convention alone is questionable, i.e. there rather needs to be a substantial contribution in order for an element to be a proper 'signal' for a construction of a certain kind.

19 Although there are languages that resort to the IPP but do not trigger HAVE-preposing, this does not necessarily challenge its semantic motivation, since the auxiliary may either canonically be placed in the cluster-initial position (as in Dutch) or end up in another non-canonical position (e.g. in cluster-final position in Afrikaans) (cf. IJbema 1997: 148f.; see also Schmid 2002).

b. Das Geld hat ihm zugestanden.
the money has him.DAT *concede*.PTCP
'The money was due to him.'

These predicates show that the contribution of HAVE cannot solely be of an argument structural nature. In fact, the cases in (113) and (114) share that they inherently lack an external argument. Hence, HAVE is not necessary with respect to the introduction of an external argument, but nevertheless employed in atelic cases like those in (114).

Eventually, these findings indicate that in the case of the HAVE-perfect (unlike with BE), the auxiliary to a crucial extent contributes perfect information. Occasionally, such data are taken to argue against a compositional interpretation of the HAVE-perfect, where all the relevant perfect information is stored in HAVE, as for instance observable in Vogel's (2009: 315) discussion of the IPP. However, this conclusion is challenged by the consequence that it would generally render past participial morphology ornamental in HAVE-perfects (cf. Breul 2014: 465fn19). Instead, we will assume that HAVE contributes essentially to the expression of a periphrastic perfect,[20] yet there is still some relevant perfect information stored in the participial form (cf. Breul 2014: 465), the omission of which may interpretively be made up for in the context of HAVE (though crucially not with BE). This perfect information on the past participle does not induce proper perfectivity with predicates other than simple changes of state (unaccusatives), but arguably still contributes to a perfect interpretation in a way to be outlined in chapter 4.2.3.

This leaves the question concerning the nature of the relevant perfect contribution of the perfect auxiliary HAVE. What is likely given that HAVE cannot be the conveyor of fully-fledged perfectivity (considering the availability of a universal perfect) is that it establishes the relation of a past event to a present one, a posterior time (see, for instance, Wunderlich 1997: 4, where this is also attributed to BE, though). This contribution suffices to shift the participial event into the past, which usually – but not always – allows us to derive perfectivity by implication, the default reading. The perfect contribution of HAVE is crucially not called for in the case of past participles that properly express perfectivity by themselves. Accordingly, such cases (i.e. past participles of unaccusative predicates that express a simple change of state) are not introduced by HAVE in

---

20 This accounts for the impossibility to substantially omit the auxiliary in languages comprising identical past participles. The non-identity language Swedish (unlike its close relatives Danish and Norwegian), on the other hand, readily allows for this in certain contexts, most regularly in subordinate clauses (cf. Kjellmer 2003: 16).

4.1 The basic meaning of past participles and what the auxiliaries contribute — 189

languages exhibiting auxiliary alternation in the analytic perfect. Rather, they are introduced by the perfect auxiliary BE (as in *John ist angekommen*, 'John has arrived.', lit. John is arrive.PTCP), which does not contribute any relevant perfect semantics (nor contribute to the expression of argument structure). The past participles in such cases introduce an event that has been completed, which in turn suffices to derive the posteriority of the Reference (or Topic) time by implication. The same holds true for the somewhat unexpected cases of intransitive predicates briefly revisited before, i.e. (manner of) motion verbs. These are special in terms of selecting BE, e.g. in German, where some goal either still has to be overtly realised (as with *getanzt*, 'danced') or has been lexically associated with the verbal semantics (as with *gerannt*, 'run'). As briefly discussed before, these predicates are not construed as agentive activities, but rather as simple changes of location that feature an argument that bears a certain amount of Proto-Patient properties. Based on these properties, the past participial marker may successfully induce perfectivity. Hence, just like in the context of proto-typical unaccusatives, HAVE is not required to introduce a post-time, as this may readily be derived from the perfective past participial form by implication. All that is left to be established in BE-selecting contexts then is the relation of the completed event to a point of utterance, which is exactly what BE supplies in terms of taking up finiteness. While HAVE also does so, the difference is the crucial addition of denoting a post-time to the past participial event, which is not terminated by participial morphology. These ingredients and their interaction will be discussed in detail in chapter 4.2.3 below.

Besides its perfect contribution, the perfect auxiliary HAVE is special with regard to its ability to retrieve a suppressed external argument. As we have seen, this appears to be quite a solid finding, given that any occurrence of a past participle occurring without HAVE lacks an external argument. While technical discussions will be postponed to the next chapter, the main assumption here is that the perfect auxiliary HAVE retrieves the external semantic role suppressed by the past participle and provides a configuration in which it may be instantiated by virtue of the proper realisation of an external argument (cf. Ackema & Marelj 2012: 227f.). In fact, the argument structural suppression will be taken to boil down to lexically marking the external semantic role for existential binding. This renders it illicit for syntactic assignment, which may, however, be made up for by HAVE, which is capable of retrieving and assigning the external semantic role. Accordingly, "whereas BE is genuinely without any argument structure, HAVE assigns an external theta-role" (Ackema & Marelj 2012: 228f.). The essential properties associated with the perfect auxiliary HAVE may thus be found in (115a). Given the contribution to the expression of argument structure as well as perfect semantics, HAVE is considerably more elaborate than the designated passive auxiliary WERDEN in (115b) and the auxiliary BE in (115c), which serves as a passive auxiliary in English and a perfect auxiliary in German.

(115) a. HAVE: expressing tense (and hence making up for the past participle's non-finiteness), retrieving the external θ-role (i.e. reintroducing the semantic role lexically marked for existential binding, if present) and assigning it to an argument not specified for a thematic role in Spec-Aux or raising the closest argument already bearing a thematic role, denoting posterior time
b. WERDEN: expressing tense (and hence making up for the past participle's non-finiteness)
c. BE (passive in HAVE-only languages; perfect in auxiliary alternating languages): expressing tense (and hence making up for the past participle's non-finiteness), syntactic effect of raising an internal argument

The auxiliaries quite generally are responsible for allowing a past participle to fulfill the function of the main predicate of a complete clause, which stems from their ability to take up finiteness. In addition, while an argument structural and perfect semantic contribution is restricted to HAVE, WERDEN and BE are virtually 'elsewhere auxiliaries' in that they do not semantically contribute anything substantial (cf. Bjorkman 2011: 125). These semantically vacuous auxiliaries, however, differ in terms of whether they are contingent on raising an internal argument (WERDEN is not, whereas BE is) (cf. Breul & Wegner 2017: 30f.).[21]

These findings allow us to account for the combinatorial properties of past participles and auxiliaries in periphrastic constructions. In fact, BE may either combine with an imperfective participle in order to denote a periphrastic passive (as in English) or it may take an unaccusative participle, in which case the past participle bears perfective specifications and thus marks a BE-perfect (as in German). In other words, the cross-linguistic instantiations of BE are parameterised in terms of their combination with past participles bearing an imperfective or a perfective value. Given the semantic vacuity of BE, the meaning of the passive is bound to be stored in the past participle (cf. Wanner 2009: 18) and the same holds for the perfectivity of past participles derived from unaccusative

---

[21] This accounts for the fact that impersonal passives formed with *werden* in German are grammatical (*Es wurde gesungen*, 'People sang.', lit. it became sing.PTCP), whereas those formed with *be* in English are not (**It was sung*). On the other hand, an impersonal passive with WERDEN is marginal in Swedish, whereas the Icelandic BE-passive allows for an impersonal passive (cf. Abraham 2006a: 13; Zaenen, Maling & Thráinsson 1985: 98), which shows that this syntactic effect is either parameterised or hinges on external factors.

predicates, which eventually allows for a perfect reading. The perfect auxiliary HAVE, on the other hand, is a fairly more complex auxiliary in that it combines with participles that are not inherently perfective and contributes relevant perfect semantics. Additionally, it may have an argument structural effect, which is, however, not a requirement for its realisation. In fact, as we have seen in the context of atelic two-place unaccusatives in (114), there are contexts in which it merely raises an internal argument (rather than licensing an external one). This is also clearly observable in HAVE-only languages, where HAVE combines with an unaccusative past participle (*The train has arrived*), given that BE is reserved for passives and a licit alternative is thus absent. Accordingly, a clear and insightful picture of the properties of HAVE may first and foremost be derived from its unadulterated use in languages resorting to auxiliary alternation. This leaves the question of whether HAVE-only languages raise problems with respect to the assumption that both HAVE as well as the past participle contribute relevant perfect semantics in periphrastic perfects based on unaccusative predicates. As we will see in chapter 4.2.3 on the properties of the analytic perfect, this does not pose a substantial problem given that the two ingredients are not in complementary distribution: HAVE expresses posteriority (i.e. a relation between E and R or Klein's 1994 Time of the Situation and Topic Time), whereas the past participle of an unaccusative denotes perfectivity (i.e. the completion of E or Klein's 1994 Time of the Situation). Eventually, then, while having one of these ingredients allows us to derive the other via implication, this is not a necessity, i.e. it may well be the case that both of these are overtly expressed.

While we have seen a bulk of evidence highlighting the substantial contribution of HAVE, there are actually also examples challenging the assumption that WERDEN is semantically vacuous. This may for instance be seen in (116) and (117).

(116) a. The song is sung.
  b. Das Lied ist gesungen.
     the song is   sing.PTCP
     'The song is sung.'

(117) a. The song is passionately (being) sung by Sigur Rós.
  b. Das Lied wird   leidenschaftlich von Sigur Rós gesungen.
     the song becomes passionately   by Sigur Rós sing.PTCP
     'The song is passionately being sung by Sigur Rós.'

While the English examples in (116a) and (117a) feature a structural ambiguity and thus need to be handled with care, the German examples in (116b) and (117b) clearly mark an interpretive contrast by employing different lexemes for the stative passive (copular *sein*) and the eventive passive (the auxiliary *werden*). The stative passive instantiated in (116b) and – alongside a less readily retrievable alternative reading – in (116a) interpretively focusses on the resultative state of the event of singing. This is achieved by attributing the resultative state of the participial event to a nominal referent (to be addressed in section 4.3), which is in turn semantically treated like the participle's internal argument. Hence, we can assume with Klein (1999: 74f.) that all BE does here is add finiteness and indicate that the properties denoted by the participle are attributed to the referent at the relevant time. This attribution crucially forces a stative reading, which is why eventive modifiers (e.g. BY-phrases and manner adverbs) are usually illicit, something we will return to in chapter 4.3.[22] The alternative reading of (116a) – 'the song is *being* sung' rather than 'the song is attributed the *resultative state of having been sung*' – is typically referred to as an eventive passive, but only hardly retrievable in a present tense context. However, an eventive interpretation clearly becomes more readily accessible once we add eventive modifiers, as observable in (117a), which may not be interpreted as a resultative state. Rather, it is interpreted either as a proper event or a reiterated situation (in terms of a general statement about the song being sung repeatedly), where the former may more strongly be instantiated by the addition of present participial *being*. The fact that this reading is forced by *werden* ('become') in German, as in (117b), may be taken to suggest that this passive auxiliary lexically brings in a processual character. This is supported by the fact that its main verb counterpart (and ancestor) expresses a transition (cf. Klein 1999: 75f.).[23] Toman (1986: 375), in a similar vein, claims that *werden* ('become') bears the feature [-stative]. The passive auxiliary BE, on the other hand, is generally accepted to be semantically vacuous and should thus be unable to occur in the context of proper processes, if those are introduced by WERDEN.

Rather than attributing a semantic contribution to WERDEN, however, we will assume that the differences in interpretation stem from the need to disambiguate and a preferred reading in English rather than a substantial semantic contribution of the auxiliary in German. This is supported by the fact that both languages behave similarly with respect to bare instantiations

---

[22] A similar stative structure, as we have seen, comes forth in the guise of the stative perfect (e.g. in German).

[23] In fact, main verb *werden* ('become'), behaves like a copula with the additional ingredient of introducing a transition, as can be seen in the example *John wird Koch* ('John becomes a cook.', lit. John becomes cook).

4.1 The basic meaning of past participles and what the auxiliaries contribute — 193

and their dynamic readings (e.g. in bare participial clauses of atelic verbs like *carry*). Additionally, the reluctance of an eventive BE-passive interpretation without additional help by progressive morphology or eventive modifiers in the present tense is apparently not shared cross-linguistically (as observable in Icelandic, amongst others). Hence, it is somewhat dubious to conclude that WERDEN is special in terms of providing progressivity. Instead, the observable difference between German and English in the examples in (116) is attributed to the disambiguation of the eventive and the stative reading. This is not an issue in German, as clearly different lexemes are involved, but poses problems in English due to the homonymy of copular and auxiliary BE. In fact, as we have seen, the standard reading of an unmodified case like the one in (116a) is a stative passive interpretation. This apparently is only the case in present tense contexts, as these focus on the result of a prior event that is relevant at time of utterance. In a past tense case like *The song was sung*, on the other hand, we rather favour an interpretation in which the process that led to the result is focused on. The reason for this preference may be that we already know that we are in a post-situation of the process in question and hence need not (primarily, at least) express its result. Although a progressive form may still be realised for the sake of disambiguation, it need not necessarily be in order to induce an eventive passive reading, as becomes observable in *The song was being sung*. In a nutshell, present tense cases need to be accompanied either by progressive *being*, eventive modifiers, or agentive BY-phrases in order to unequivocally give rise to an eventive interpretation, as the default reading is a stative passive, unlike in the past tense.

There is one strongly related context in terms of ambiguity, namely perfect formation with BE in languages exhibiting auxiliary alternation alongside a homonymous copula. Similar to the homonymy of BE in stative passive and eventive passive contexts in English, there is a bulk of evidence pointing towards a perfect auxiliary *sein* ('be') in addition to the copula *sein* ('be') (used to form stative passives) in German. Similar to *be* in English, this occasionally leads to ambiguity as the past participles selected by the auxiliary *sein* ('be') are not mutually exclusive to those featured in stative passive, i.e. copular *sein* ('be'), cases. This is observable on the basis of the ambiguity in (118).

(118) Das Mädchen ist verschwunden.
     the girl   is disappear.PTCP
     stative passive: 'The girl is disappeared.'
     BE-perfect: 'The girl has disappeared.'

Similar to what we have just seen with the stative passive and the eventive passive in English, a disambiguation is possible with the help of adverbial modification. As Wunderlich (1997: 24f.) and Thieroff (1994: 104f.) point out, the periphrastic perfect reading may be forced by adverbial modification of iterative *schon oft* ('often', lit. already often), whereas the stative passive arises once we insert *immer noch* ('still', lit. ever still) (or *noch immer*, cf. Vater 2002: 359–361). Crucially, in the latter case we do not derive an eventive perfect situation, but once again clearly only attribute a result to the argument in question. The periphrastic BE-perfect, on the other hand, gives rise to a proper present perfect interpretation in which there clearly is an event that is eventually terminated. Given that BE only ever combines with predicates that do not introduce a causer, an external argument is not realised here. However, with respect to the exponent of BE in German and English, there is one vital difference, namely that *sein* ('be') is contingent on the perfectivity of the past participle, whereas *be* may only be realised in the context of an imperfective past participle. Other than this difference in terms of subcategorisation, the properties of the two auxiliaries are identical.[24] The interpretive differences between the BE-perfect and the BE-passive thus boil down to the perfectivity of the past participle in question and the availability of an external argument that is not realised but existentially bound.

Based on the basic properties of past participial forms as well as the auxiliaries they occur with, as identified in (108) and (115) respectively, what may now be turned to is how these ingredients interact to give rise to the various kinds of past participial constructions. As a starting point, we will turn to the formation of past participles from verbal bases in 'word syntax', i.e. how the properties identified in (108) are technically induced. Subsequently, the focus will be on the most prototypical instantiations of past participial constructions and how they are compositionally derived from the combination of past participles and auxiliaries. Accordingly, section 4.2.1 will lay out the technical means of how auxiliaries interact with past participles in order to form periphrastic past participial constructions. While this already takes us down the rabbit hole of a syntactic account, the chapters 4.2.2 and 4.2.3 will supplement these theoretical considerations with analyses of the syntactic as well as semantic properties of the periphrastic passive and the analytic perfect, respectively. Section 4.2.4 will then briefly revisit the most important

---

24 Metaphorically speaking, then, the major difference between languages exhibiting auxiliary alternation and their HAVE-only counterparts is that the auxiliary BE in the former acts like the photographic negative of its counterpart in the latter.

phenomena identified in chapter 2 in order to incorporate them technically. Finally, section 4.3 will extend the theory to bare instances and turn to the categorial questions this raises.

4.2 The syntax and semantics of past participles

Now that the basic properties of past participles and the auxiliaries they form periphrases with have roughly been sketched out, what remains to be accounted for are the technical specifics of a proper analysis of past participial identity. Accordingly, the main aim of the present chapter is to provide a theoretically sound approach to the compositional make-up of past participial constructions against the backdrop of the identity of past participles in passive and perfect periphrases. Tackling this issue from bottom to top first brings us to the question of how the morphological process of forming a past participle may be modelled in the context of a (moderate) lexicalist framework. The outcome of this process is a dependent syntactic object that may more or less strongly be interwoven into a given clausal structure, depending on its functional superstructure. Based on the precise properties of this functional environment and the verbal properties retained by the past participle, the participial construction eventually elicits different interpretations. Once the morphosyntactic process of past participial formation has been introduced, the present chapter will thus discuss the syntactic and semantic properties of the prototypical past participial constructions, i.e. the periphrastic passive and the analytic perfect.

In unison with the framework laid out in chapter 1.2 and based on the assumption that their formation is lexical in nature, past participles are taken to be derived from verbal items in word syntax. Unlike in DM as well as lexicalist approaches treating past participial morphology as constituting an argument that absorbs accusative case and/or the external semantic role (see, amongst others, Roberts 1984, Jaeggli 1986, and Åfarli 1989), this entails that past participles are not formed in (phrasal) syntax. Rather, they are derived in a lexical workspace based on syntactic machinery, i.e. word syntax. This allows us to take seriously the intuition that past participle formation boils down to a (morpheme-based) lexical operation (cf. Wanner 2009: 21), yet allows us to largely circumvent the stipulation of designated morphological processes or lexical rules.[25]

---

[25] See Breul (2014: 460f.) for a brief overview of the distinct possibilities of deriving a past participle in DM, a word-based morphology and a lexicalist system structurally accounting for past participle formation.

Given the basic properties of past participles identified in the previous section, i. e. non-finiteness, the suppression of the external argument, and defective perfectivity, their formation may thus be conceived as the merging of a verbal element and a functional head, as in (119).[26]

(119) a.
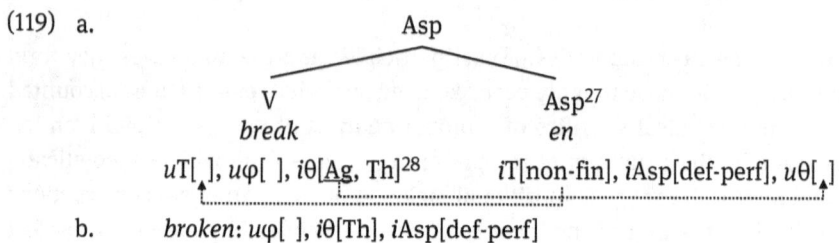

b.   *broken*: $u\varphi[\ ]$, $i\theta[\text{Th}]$, $i\text{Asp}[\text{def-perf}]$

Merging the lexical items in (119a) elicits the past participle in (119b) by virtue of the application of feature valuation processes. To be precise, the uninterpretable tense-feature on the verb (uT) is valued with the help of the past participial morphology's non-finite information (eliciting $\cancel{u\text{T}}$[non-fin]), i.e. the verbal form is supplemented with (interpretable) non-finite tense information

---

[26] The approach to be laid out is lexicalist in so far as it assumes (functional and lexical) items to be stored in the lexicon, yet attributes word-formation to a morphological level that works with syntactic machinery, rather than an active lexicon comprising its own rules. For simplicity's sake, we will largely remain agnostic about the internal structure of the elements supplied by the lexicon. While a (radical) root-based system appears to be problematic, many of the inherent properties encoded by certain features here may just as well be encoded by functional projections and hence introduced in word syntax rather than stored in the lexicon. This is implicitly assumed for event structure in the present approach anyway, as the explanation of why only simple changes of state are rendered perfective by the participial head hinges on the claim that it only affects its immediate complement, which is thus bound to be a functional head denoting BECOME rather than CAUSE (or DO).

[27] Categorial labels are only included for representational clarity. In fact, labels are taken to be identified rather than created (cf. Chomsky 2008: 145) and the syntactic category of an element is determined on the basis of its morphosyntactic properties in a given context (cf. Rauh 2016: 38). While we assume a bare phrase structure (cf. Chomsky 1995a), this is not represented for the sake of clarity and representational adequacy.

[28] In terms of Reinhart's (2002) Theta System the traditional Agent role dissolves into a +c (cause change) and a +m (mental state) feature (hence the feature cluster [+c+m]), whereas a Theme boils down to [−c−m].

(iT[non-fin]).²⁹ Additionally, the non-finite past participial morpheme bears aspectual information, which arguably marks its most salient contribution (hence the informal label Asp, although the clumsy alternative Asp-Pass would be more appropriate). This aspectual information, as we have seen, is quite unlike its fully-fledged counterparts in aspectual languages and may only elicit perfectivity on the basis of a simple change of state, i.e. if its verbal complement is a BECOME-operator (crucially lacking a CAUSE). As this is not the case with the transitive verb *break* due to the presence of an Agent, the semantic value that *i*Asp[def-perf] elicits is of an imperfective rather than a perfective nature. This should suffice to account for the basic properties of non-finiteness and the aspectual contribution of (im)perfectivity.

In addition to aspectual features, predicates that take an internal argument introduce interpretable semantic roles in terms of θ-features (iθ) and a selectional reflex governing their requirement to be associated with a nominal referent. The latter is grasped in terms of the presence of an uninterpretable φ-feature (uφ),³⁰ which eventually instantiates (object-)agreement morphology under certain conditions in those languages overtly expressing it (e.g. Icelandic, French, and Italian). As past participial morphology combines with verbal predicates and may even affect the expression of argument structure, it is bound to be sensitive to the presence of θ-features by virtue of comprising an uninterpretable θ-feature (uθ). This feature is valued word-internally and lexically takes care of the Agent-role by marking it for existential binding, which has as its consequence that this role becomes syntactically inactive.³¹ This formally accounts for why the participle *broken* in (119b) to be introduced in phrasal syntax syntactically bears a θ-feature that is only valued for a Theme-role (iθ[Th]). Nevertheless, the external argument remains semantically active (as a CAUSE-operator), either as an implicit argument in passives (potentially associated with a BY-phrase) or to be associated with the argument introduced by HAVE. The latter gives rise to

---

29 Note that iT[non-fin] may remain syntactically active but is not relevant for the further computation.
30 It is usually the disposal of thematic roles rather than the presence of designated formal features (in this case uφ) that is taken to be responsible for the need to syntactically realise arguments. In order to dissociate semantic roles and the syntactic positions in which they are assigned, we will assume both φ- and θ-features to play a role. The advantages of this view will also come to the fore in the context of bare past participles in chapter 4.3.
31 Note that uθ does not necessarily select for an external semantic role, but may also be valued by the neo-Davidsonian event variable (see Higginbotham 1985) if there is no external semantic role in the verbal θ-grid.

an active perfect, which thus demands additional support by an auxiliary. These two possible routes crucially have syntactic consequences: while passive cases may not feature v, the argument structural realisation of a causer in active clauses demands the presence of the functional projection v in phrasal syntax.[32] In the latter case, the argument introduced in Spec, v cannot retrieve the external semantic role, as this role has been lexically marked for existential binding and is hence syntactically unavailable. Rather, it is formally introduced in v, but has to move to Spec, Aux in order to retrieve a semantic role. This only works out in the case of HAVE, as this auxiliary is able to assign a role that has been marked for existential binding (similar to BY but with the crucial distinction that BY forms an adjunct, whereas HAVE contributes to the realisation of argument structure, i.e. $i\theta[\underline{Ag}]$ in the present case).[33]

While the basic properties of past participles in chapter 4.1 are anything but incompatible with other theoretical frameworks (e.g. fully-fledged anti-lexicalist ones or lexicalist ones assuming participial morphology to be syntactic in nature), the present theory will be based on the formal properties of past participle formation just laid out. Based on these formal characteristics, the subsequent section will provide the (technical) basics of a proper analysis in its shallow discussion of the derivation of the two prototypical periphrastic uses, before we venture into a more detailed discussion also taking into consideration semantic factors in chapters 4.2.2 and 4.2.3.

4.2.1 The basics: the formation of past participial periphrases

Based on the formal features that past participles come equipped with when entering the syntactic derivation, i.e. phrasal syntax, the properties of clauses that include a periphrastic passive or an analytic perfect may technically be accounted for. To this effect, we need to take into consideration the formal features that are introduced by the auxiliaries and examine how these technically interact with their participial complements in order to form past

---

32 Thus, the expression of diathesis is first and foremost based on lexical properties rather than solely being based on the presence of a (Voice- or) v-head, which is just a consequence of this lexical predisposition.

33 Accordingly, v is contingent on HAVE in past participial contexts, as it is bound to introduce an argument that eventually serves as a causer and the external argument introduced in Spec, v otherwise cannot retrieve a θ-role. Note that this may alternatively also be grasped by distinct functional heads (e.g. Chomsky's 2001 v* and v).

participial periphrases. Once we have provided an approach to how this may be carried out for the two prototypical past participial constructions within the theoretical confines previously set up in subsections 4.2.1.1 and 4.2.1.2, the present chapter will briefly extend its view to clauses featuring multiple auxiliaries in subsection 4.2.1.3 and then turn to necessary theoretical extensions in subsection 4.2.1.4.

4.2.1.1 Derivations including the semantically vacuous auxiliaries BE and WERDEN

First turning to the syntactic derivation of the periphrastic passive, we will see that its essential characteristics follow from the formal properties attributed to the past participle and their syntactic consequences. One of the major formal effects of past participle formation is that the external semantic role of the underlying verb is rendered syntactically inactive by virtue of being lexically marked for existential binding. This marking acquits the predicate of its desire to realise the external argument syntactically, since it assures that the latter may be taken care of semantically. Hence, unless this semantic role is introduced independently, the functional projection standardly held responsible for syntactically realising an external argument cannot be licensed. Accordingly, causative v remains absent in passive constructions and the same holds for unaccusative configurations, which inherently lack an external argument (cf. Chomsky 1995b; 2000: 107). Given that v is also responsible for structural case assignment, the internal argument has to be displaced to a position in which it may retrieve structural case after all. To be precise, the displacement of the internal argument follows from the fact that this argument cannot value its uninterpretable and unvalued case-feature (uC) *in situ*. Rather, it has to move to Spec, T, where it may receive a case-value from T.[34] This movement, however, may not proceed in one fell swoop, since successive-cyclic movement through Spec, Aux is triggered by the auxiliary's $u\varphi$ for reasons that we will return to shortly. The derivation of the eventive passive *The girl was kissed* is represented in (120).

---

[34] We will not discuss whether feature-valuation is restricted to pairs of unvalued uninterpretable and valued interpretable features (see Pesetsky & Torrego 2002; 2006; 2007), but acknowledge that case assignment is one of the contexts in which the existence of a valued uninterpretable feature might be called for. Accordingly, we simply follow Adger (2003) in assuming an uninterpretable but valued case-feature, as it otherwise remains unclear what the interpretational contribution of (structural) case is supposed to be. Furthermore, we will not be concerned with the question of whether case is a designated feature (see Adger 2003) or just part of a complex set of φ-features (see Chomsky 2000; 2001; 2004; 2007; 2008), but simply side with the former view.

(120)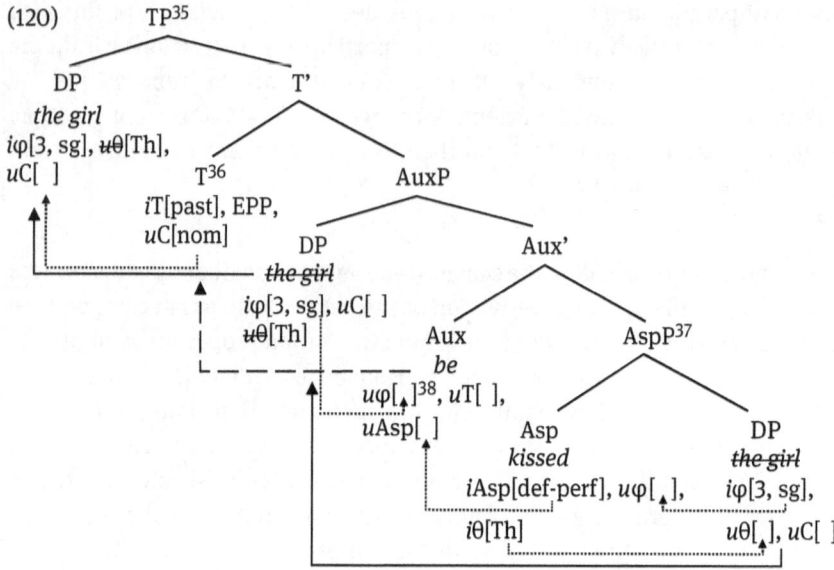

In addition to the argument structural effect and the syntactic consequences it imposes, the past participle is a non-finite form that introduces aspectual

---

35 A CP-layer consisting of an empty C-head is introduced on top of the TP in order to type-specify the clause as declarative. We will abstract away from such technical issues not directly pertaining to the current discussion.

36 The question of what motivates Aux-to-T movement (and head movement in general) is far from settled. As we cannot appropriately enter this discussion here, we will simply follow Adger (2003: 180): "when [the uninterpretable tense-feature] on an auxiliary is checked by the tense feature of T, the auxiliary needs to get into a local relationship with T". This holds for uT on Aux by virtue of being strong, whereas uT on V (or v) is weak, hence not motivating movement (at least in present-day English) (cf. Adger 2003: 180f.). This accounts for why finite lexical verbs, in contrast to auxiliaries, remain *in situ*. Note that in both cases the uT in question have to probe up, marking a case of upward (or reverse) agree (see, e.g., Haegeman and Lohndal 2010; Merchant 2011; Wurmbrand 2012a). In fact, "[a]n increasing number of authors have identified cases like this one in which syntactic features seem to be interpreted 'higher' than they are morphologically realized" (Bjorkman 2011: 41).

37 Not being concerned with labelling here, we may assume that it is always the probe that provides the label (cf. Cecchetto & Donati 2010: 247). When there is more than one probe (as with *kissed* and *the girl*), either the element provided by the lexicon (or word syntax) becomes the label (if the number of probes is equal) or "a double Probe wins over a single Probe" (Cecchetto & Donati 2010: 247; see also Cecchetto & Donati 2015: 40).

38 Note that the auxiliary raises an argument via its uφ although the argument's iφ has already been checked by the participle before. Accordingly, we assume that iφ-features remain active

information (*i*Asp[def-perf]). In order to form the predicational core of a clause, the past participle has to be accompanied by an auxiliary that mediates between the clause's tense-head (T) and the (non-finite) aspectual form (Asp).[39] On the one hand, the auxiliary includes an uninterpretable tense-feature (*u*T), which needs to be valued (past, present or infinitival) on the basis of the interpretable tense-feature (*i*T) on T. Thus, the auxiliary morphologically expresses tense, i.e. the relation between R and S (or Klein's 1994 Topic Time and Utterance Time). On the other hand, the auxiliaries employed in participial constructions are sensitive to the presence of aspectual information on the past participle, i.e. the auxiliary bears an uninterpretable aspectual feature (*u*Asp) and thus has to be introduced in the local domain of a participial form. In fact, passive auxiliaries like BE and WERDEN are only compatible with imperfective past participles, which is why the semantic value that *i*Asp[def-perf] elicits in passive cases like (120) is bound to be imperfective or else the derivation crashes (as in *The man was arrived*).

The contribution to the morphological expression of temporal specifications (*u*T) and the sensitivity to the presence of an aspectual form (*u*Asp) are properties that are shared by all auxiliaries. Hence, a given auxiliary substantially contributes to anchoring a participial event in time by virtue of providing a temporal context for the aspectual information introduced by the participial form. In addition, all of the auxiliaries comprise uninterpretable φ-features (*u*φ). In the present case in (120), such a *u*φ-feature on passive BE necessitates raising the closest available element bearing an interpretable counterpart (here the internal argument *the girl*) to Spec, Aux. This valued *u*φ (specified for 3rd person singular in the present case) may overtly be spelled out if *u*T gets a (finite) value. However, auxiliaries are cross-linguistically parameterised in terms of whether their *u*φ may receive a default spell-out, as we may see in the context of impersonal passives in German.

---

after valuing *u*φ. This view (see, for instance, Chomsky 1995b: 282 and Richards 2015: 825) is empirically supported by cases in which agreement morphology is realised on both the auxiliary and its auxiliate, e.g. the Latin perfect passive *Feminae captae sunt* ('The women have been seized.'). In fact, the alternative (an interpretable feature is only active until it undergoes checking) is problematic in that it has to incorporate look-ahead (the interpretable feature is active before the introduction of its uninterpretable counterpart) or tucking in (once we postpone movement to phasal transfer).

39 This also holds for present participles, where BE needs to step in to allow the aspectual non-finite form to be realised as the main predicate of a complete clause. Whenever a participial form occurs as an adjunct or in an incomplete clause, the aspectual information may pragmatically be tied to the external clausal context, though, which might have important consequences for its interpretation, as we will briefly see in chapter 4.3.

While the formal features identified for the passive auxiliary BE (e.g. in English) may also be attributed to the designated passive auxiliary WERDEN (e.g. in German), i.e. both comprise uT, uAsp, and $u\varphi$, the latter is more flexible in German in terms of allowing for default valuation. This results in the possibility of an impersonal passive and accounts for its ungrammaticality in English, as observable in (121) and (122), respectively.

(121) a. Es   wurde   getanzt.
         there /it became   dance.PTCP
         'People danced.'
     b. Jetzt   wird   geschlafen!
         now   becomes   sleep.PTCP
         'Now it is time to sleep.'

(122) a. *There/*It is danced.
     b. *Now is slept!

The German eventive passive in (121) allows for passive constructions that do without the realisation of a single argument and may optionally introduce an expletive, whereas this is strictly barred in English, regardless of whether an expletive is involved. While the distinction between (121b) and (122b) may be traced back to the presence of an EPP-feature on T in English but not in German, this does not suffice to account for (121a) and (122a), given that expletives are sufficient to satisfy the EPP (*There is a man in the garden*). Rather, these examples point to parametric variation in the availability of default φ-feature valuation (cf. Ruys 2010; Schäfer 2013: 354). Accordingly, languages which allow for impersonal passives (e.g. German, Icelandic, Dutch, Norwegian) allow for a situation in which, "[i]n the absence of any appropriate nominal category, the φ-features on an unvalued probe undergo default valuation [typically 3rd person, singular]" (Schäfer 2013: 354).[40] This possibility is crucially absent in languages which do not allow for impersonal passives (e.g. English). In other words, the English passive auxiliary *be* includes $u\varphi$ that always need to be valued by an interpretable counterpart. This triggers displacement of an argument out of the participial domain, as in (120). German *werden*, on the other hand, grants default φ-feature valuation (unlike the perfect auxiliaries *sein* and *haben*) and may thus do without raising, hence permitting impersonal passives. These differences are not distributed neatly

---

[40] See Breul & Wegner (2017: 30f.) for an approach based more neutrally on the absence of a deficient argument position.

along the lines of instances of WERDEN and BE, though. Rather, the possibility of default φ-feature valuation and thus the possibility to give rise to an impersonal passive is parameterised regardless of the particular lexeme.⁴¹ Apart from this distinction and general cross-linguistic differences, the structure of the designated WERDEN-passive is taken to be formally identical to that of an eventive BE-passive.

Eventually, the formal properties attributed to the passive auxiliary and the past participle account for the syntactic absence (as opposed to semantic presence) of an external argument, the realisation and displacement of an internal argument (if present), the temporal role of the auxiliary as well as the aspectual contribution of the participle. Focussing on the properties that lead to a passive interpretation, we may conclude that the implicit presence of a causer stems from the presence of an existentially bound external θ-role. This role may in fact also be overtly expressed, though crucially not as part of the clause's argument structure. Rather, it may only be introduced by an adjunct headed by a preposition like BY, which is capable of associating an argument with an existentially bound semantic role. This $u\varphi$-bearing preposition is thus bound to be able to value the argument's $u\theta$- and uC-features.

With respect to the formal properties relevant for the present discussion of past participial identity, the German periphrastic perfect formed with *sein* ('be') is quite similar to the BE-passive in (120). Most importantly, the German perfect auxiliary also bears $u\varphi$, uT, and uAsp, although it crucially differs from passive BE with regard to being compatible only with perfective past participles. In other words, the semantic value that iAsp[def-perf] elicits has to be perfective or else the derivation crashes (*Leslie ist unterstützt*, lit. Leslie is support.PTCP). An additional distinction, of course, concerns the fact that the passive auxiliary BE (as well as WERDEN) is introduced in contexts in which an external argument is existentially bound, whereas the perfect auxiliary BE may only be introduced in case an external argument is inherently absent. This, however, correlates with the auxiliaries' sensitivity to imperfective as opposed to perfective iAsp and thus need not be hard-coded.⁴² Consequently, the two variants of BE may be traced

---

41 Abraham (2006a: 13) claims for Swedish that it does not allow for an impersonal passive with the designated passive auxiliary *blir* (cf.), as observable in *Det blir sjunget* ('People sang.', lit. there became sing.PTCP). However, as we have seen in the context of the Swedish supine (e.g. in (66)), such cases seem to be possible, but crucially in competition with (and thus dispreferred over) the synthetic passive (cf. Larsson 2009: 36fn25). Moreover, Icelandic can also give rise to an impersonal passive with *vera* ('be') as in *Það var dansað í gær* ('People danced yesterday.', lit. there was dance.PTCP yesterday) (cf. Zaenen, Maling & Thráinsson 1985: 98).

42 This leaves cases like *The car was cost/*Das Auto wurde gekostet* and *Die Lösung wurde eingeleuchtet* (lit. The solution became be.understandable.PTCP). In both cases, existential binding may not apply: the external argument of the former bears an insufficient amount of Proto-Agent

back to equivalent lexemes, cross-linguistically associated with different contexts of application. We may thus assume that both variants of BE as well as WERDEN are semantically empty. Given the amount of shared properties, it is not surprising that the relevant aspects of the structure for the German BE-perfect in (123) largely correlate with those of the eventive BE-passive in (120).

(123)

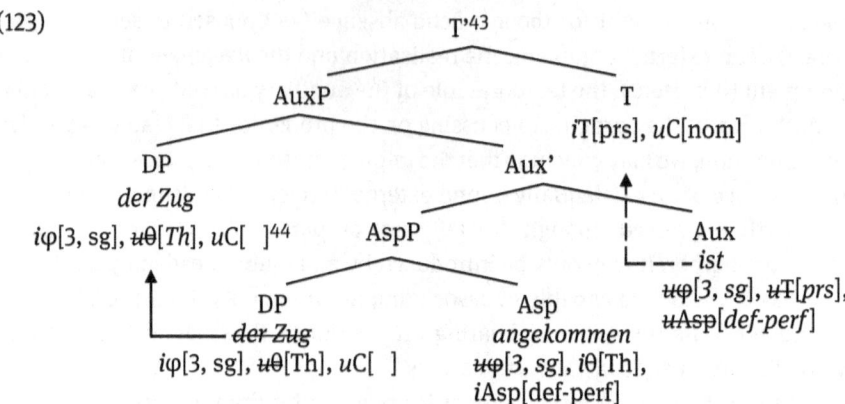

The most important distinction between (120) and (123) concerns the properties of the verb from which the past participle is derived in word syntax. The eventive passive is based on a deverbal past participle whose external semantic role is existentially bound and which remains imperfective. The BE-perfect, on the other hand, features a deverbal past participle whose underlying verb inherently lacks an external semantic role and which is rendered perfective by the aspectual information on the past participial marker (since the predicate denotes a simple change of

---

properties, while the latter lacks an external argument altogether. Crucially, the participle in question is neither perfective nor does it give rise to a passive interpretation (and the semantically vacuous BE and WERDEN cannot do anything about this), which is why the derivation crashes by virtue of violating the Principle of Full Interpretability (cf. Chomsky 1995b: 194).

43 We will follow the standard assumption that German finite verbs move from V (through v, whenever present) to T and from there to C, whereas finite auxiliaries move from Aux to T to C. Additionally, a constituent is bound to fill Spec, C in main clauses due to an EPP-feature on C. Together with the PF-claim that the German TP as well as vP/VP is head-final, this accounts for the German word order and 'verb second' characteristics.

44 Note that the feature-valuation processes represented in a detailed fashion for expository purposes above are now simplified: the strikethrough notation on uninterpretable features (*uT*) indicates that valuation has applied whereas a given value in italics (*prs*) indicates that this value has been supplied during the derivation.

state). While the past participles in question thus formally look identical (*u*φ[ ], *i*θ [Th], *i*Asp[def-perf]), their semantic properties are substantially different (presence vs. absence of an existentially bound external argument; imperfectivity vs. perfectivity). All other relevant formal properties – most importantly head-movement of Aux to T and the lack of accusative case triggering displacement of the internal argument – are identical. Crucially, the ungrammaticality of (di-)transitive and atelic predicates as part of a BE-perfect stems from the auxiliary's sensitivity to a past participle denoting perfectivity.[45] This, in turn, conceptually follows from the observation that all of the relevant perfect information in a BE-perfect is found on the past participle. This raises the question of how configurations featuring the perfect auxiliary HAVE differ from the straightforward properties of the compositional derivation of the BE-passive, the WERDEN-passive and the BE-perfect.

4.2.1.2 Configurations headed by the perfect auxiliary HAVE

While the differences between the auxiliaries BE (both in its passive as well as perfect variant) and WERDEN are shallow, the formal properties of the perfect auxiliary HAVE are substantially different. Given the properties identified in chapter 4.1, HAVE is special by virtue of substantially contributing to the expression of argument structure as well as bearing relevant perfect semantics. The latter boil down to an aspectual feature that denotes the posteriority of a situation, which is formally instantiated in that HAVE inherently bears *i*Asp[posterior] (in addition to the formal characteristics shared with the other auxiliaries: *u*φ, *u*T, and *u*Asp). To be precise, this feature leads to the denotation of a post-time with respect to the event introduced by the past participle (with which it has to combine via *u*Asp). Furthermore, the auxiliary – like all others – sets up the relation to the temporal frame (Topic Time, cf. Klein 1992: 538) supplied by the tense information in T (via the presence of *u*T). These formal properties are represented in the syntactic configuration of a prototypical HAVE-perfect in (124).

---

[45] This accounts for why English, but not German, may employ BE in the context of present participles. Present participles possess a non-defective set of aspectual features (*i*Asp[progressive]), although they are also sensitive to certain verbal properties, namely the presence of an event (rather than a state), as observable with the ungrammaticality of *John is knowing the lyrics*. If the *u*Asp on BE is sensitive to imperfectivity, it may also combine with present participles (cf. *The train is arriving at platform 9 3/4*). This leaves several questions, e.g. concerning the valuation of *u*φ in examples like *There was sleeping* and *It was raining*, which have to be left to future research. Furthermore, there are also languages like Danish, in which BE is apparently not sensitive to a particular value and may hence be combined with past participles in order to denote a perfect as well with present participles (*Jeg er ventende på bussen*, 'I am waiting for the bus.', lit. I am waiting for bus.the).

(124)

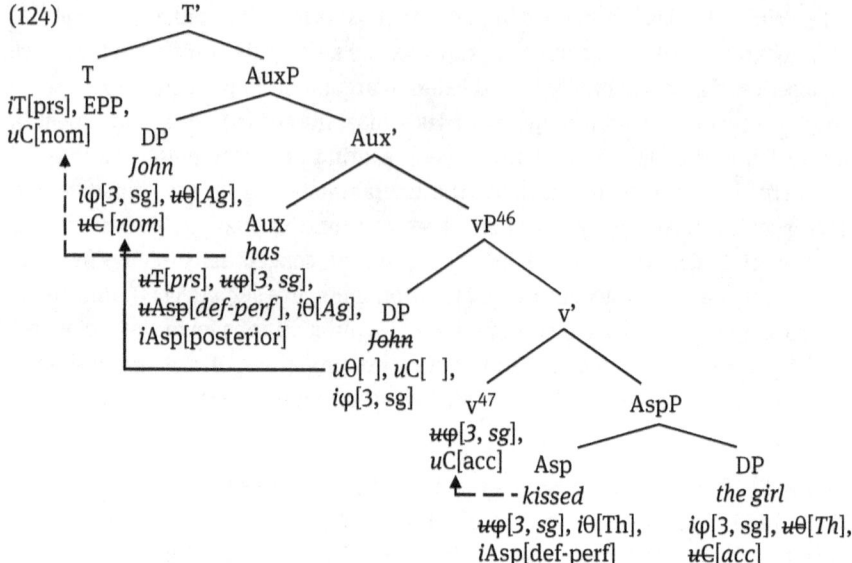

Just like in the context of the BE-passive in (120), the past participle *kissed* bears an external semantic role that is lexically marked for existential binding and hence not available for the syntactic licensing of an external argument without independent help. However, in contrast to eventive passive and BE-perfect configurations, the functional projection v – standardly taken to be responsible for accusative case assignment, the realisation of the external argument and semantically associated with expressing a causer – may nonetheless be introduced. This is granted by the fact that the argument which v formally has to introduce by virtue of bearing *uφ* may receive a θ-value at a later stage for reasons that we will return to shortly. Accordingly, the past participle values its *uφ* on the basis of the internal argument, which in turn

---

46 The phase status of v does not pose any problems here as an argument realised in the AspP is only raised in case v is not introduced. If v is present and triggers phasal transfer of its complement, the formal properties of the past participle nonetheless remain available through the head-movement of Asp-to-v (or V-to-v).

47 Whenever v is present, it triggers head movement of V/Asp. Just like the properties of head movement in general (cf. Bauke 2014: 252–254 for a brief overview of the various possibilities), the precise motivation for this is still mysterious and typically neglected (cf. Radford 2009: 294, where v is just a strong affix that attracts V to adjoin to it, and the common habit of treating this as a PF-movement operation without semantic effects). We will not submit to this discussion and hence abstract away from the potential cause(s) of head movement.

values its $u\theta$ and may – in contrast to what we have seen in passive and BE-perfect contexts – be valued for accusative case (uC), since v comes equipped with the structural case value [acc]. This leaves the question of how the argument introduced in Spec, v in order to value the latter's $u\varphi$ comes into possession of a θ-value.[48]

In addition to introducing relevant perfect semantics (iAsp[posterior]), the perfect auxiliary HAVE differs from BE and WERDEN by virtue of having an effect on the expression of the external argument. In fact, HAVE, in the spirit of Ackema & Marelj's (2012: 229) θ-merger,[49] bears an empty θ-role and may hence retrieve a semantic role that would otherwise be left unassigned. While we will return to the technical specifics of this process below, the basic assumption in the present approach is that HAVE is able to supply a semantic role that has been lexically marked for existential binding in its complement vP to an argument in its own local domain (Spec, Aux). This argument has to be a causer (and hence an external argument) by virtue of having been introduced in Spec, v, but cannot be specified for a particular θ-role in the absence of v. Hence, in the present case in (124), HAVE retrieves the external semantic role and supplies it to an argument as $i\theta[Ag]$, on the basis of which the argument's $u\theta$ may be checked and valued.[50] Given this belated assignment of the semantic role in AuxP, v's semantic predisposition is observed in that there is no semantic mismatch between the thematic role and the causative denotation of v.

In a nutshell, then, the syntactic realisation of an external argument is contingent on the introduction of the perfect auxiliary HAVE, which may retrieve the external semantic role and eventually makes it formally accessible for the argument introduced in Spec, v. Without the help of HAVE, on the other hand, the realisation of an external argument in the context of a past participle is not possible in any identity language. Additionally, the perfect semantic contribution of HAVE is

---

48 Note that raising the internal argument to Spec, v (in order to value v's $u\varphi$) leads the derivation to crash for two reasons: first, raising an internal argument through Spec, v is illicit since it is not interpreted as a causer while v syntactically imposes causation, and second, the internal argument is valued for accusative case and may hence not end up in Spec, T, where nominative case is assigned.
49 See also, amongst others, Toman (1986), Roberts (1987), Cowper (1989a, b), Ackema (1999) and Ackema & Marelj (2012) for various technical instantiations of what may be referred to as 'θ-inheritance'.
50 This capability of HAVE might call for a technical extension. Either we take Ackema & Marelj's (2012: 229) idea of θ-merger seriously and assume a designated process to be at work or we attribute the property of retrieving a θ-role lexically marked for existential binding to HAVE. Given that the latter option is reminiscent of what may be claimed for BY-phrases and does without designated mechanisms, this is what we opt for.

imperative for the denotation of a proper perfect interpretation whenever the past participle in question does not denote a perfective situation by itself (i.e. whenever the underlying verbal event structure is not a simple change of state). Given these contributions, we may conclude that the introduction of HAVE is a necessary condition for the realisation of an external argument as well as the denotation of the perfect in case the aspectual information on the past participle elicits imperfectivity. However, there are also contexts in which HAVE is called for despite contributing neither to the expression of argument structure (e.g. atelic two-place unaccusatives in German and unaccusatives in English) nor being called for in order to denote a perfect reading (e.g. unaccusatives in English). We will now briefly turn to one such unexpected case, namely the introduction of HAVE in the context of unaccusative predicates in the HAVE-only language English (and return to another shortly).

In HAVE-only languages, the absence of a perfect-forming variant of BE (which is reserved for passive cases by virtue of only combining with past participles denoting imperfectivity) leads to the use of HAVE in cases in which it is neither bound to introduce an external argument nor required to add posteriority. Postponing the role of HAVE's aspectual contribution for a second, this immediately raises the question of whether the formal properties of HAVE may also account for cases in which there is no external argument. This issue will be addressed on the basis of the structural configuration for the unaccusative HAVE-perfect *The train has arrived* in (125).

(125)
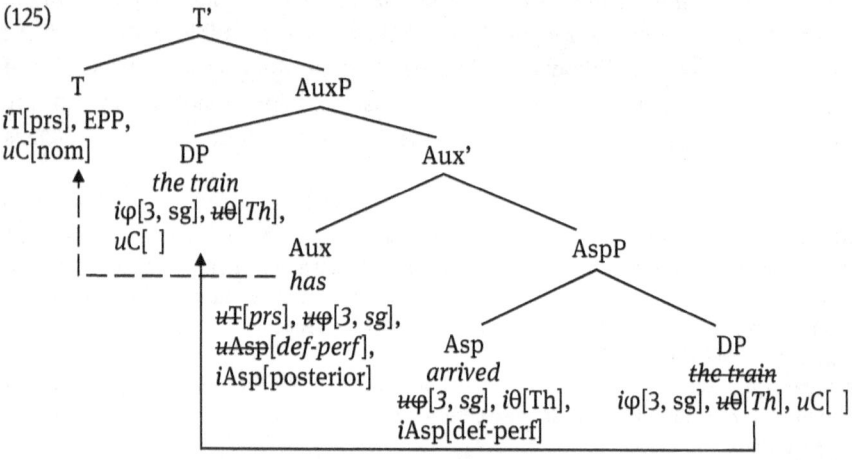

The present derivation strongly resembles the unaccusative BE-perfect in (123) by virtue of the lack of a v-layer and the displacement of the internal argument to

Spec, Aux. The introduction of HAVE, however, is unexpected given that we have seen that this perfect auxiliary may license an external argument (i.e. reinstate a θ-role) and comes equipped with *i*Asp[posterior]. Crucially, though, the introduction of an external semantic role (e.g. *i*θ[*Ag*]) is contingent on the previous application of lexically marking this role for existential binding. This, in turn, is not a necessary condition for the use of HAVE. Rather, whenever no such lexically-marked role is around, HAVE simply does not have anything to contribute to the expression of argument structure (and hence closely resembles the other auxiliaries). Hence, in order to value its $u\varphi$, HAVE simply raises the closest internal argument. Accordingly, HAVE is generally quite flexible in terms of either providing a semantic role to an argument raised out of Spec, v or – in case there is no semantic role lexically marked for existential binding – only raising an argument (whose $u\theta$ have already been valued) out of AspP. In the latter case, HAVE strongly resembles the auxiliaries BE and WERDEN, yet it crucially differs by virtue of contributing aspectual information.

The presence of *i*Asp[posterior] on HAVE in (125) marks a major difference to the BE-perfect case, but apparently does not bear any interpretive consequences. In fact, as we can see in the context of the BE-perfect, the overt expression of posteriority is dispensable whenever the aspectual information on the past participle manages to induce a perfective situation. In these cases, posteriority is derived by implication from the completion of the participial event. Although this implication would also suffice in the case of the unaccusative HAVE-perfect, what we find here is that the posteriority is not derived from perfectivity, but rather overtly expressed. As we will see in more detail in chapter 4.2.3, this is unproblematic in that the two kinds of information are not in complementary distribution and may hence both be overtly spelled out. In a nutshell, then, HAVE has to contribute posteriority in case the past participle cannot properly denote the termination of the participial event, which is then typically derived from the posteriority via implication (more or less strongly, depending on the verbal aktionsart). Whenever the past participle does denote perfectivity, on the other hand, posteriority may either come about via implication or be overtly expressed. The latter option is only licit if there is no suitable alternative, though, as in English, where BE is reserved for (imperfective) passives. Eventually, then, HAVE in HAVE-only languages is underspecified in terms of its combination with past participles (governed by *u*Asp) whose aspectual properties give rise to a perfective as well as those that give rise to an imperfective value. This is different in languages making use of auxiliary alternation, where HAVE is only compatible with past participles that denote imperfectivity, although some flexibility is called for with respect to the argument structural contribution here as well.

In languages resorting to auxiliary alternation, the application of HAVE has to be restricted to those cases in which the perfect auxiliary BE cannot appear, i.e. we need to account for the fact that the two are mutually exclusive. Other than that, however, the properties of a HAVE-perfect are essentially similar, as we can see in the structural representation of the prototypical German instance in (126).

(126)
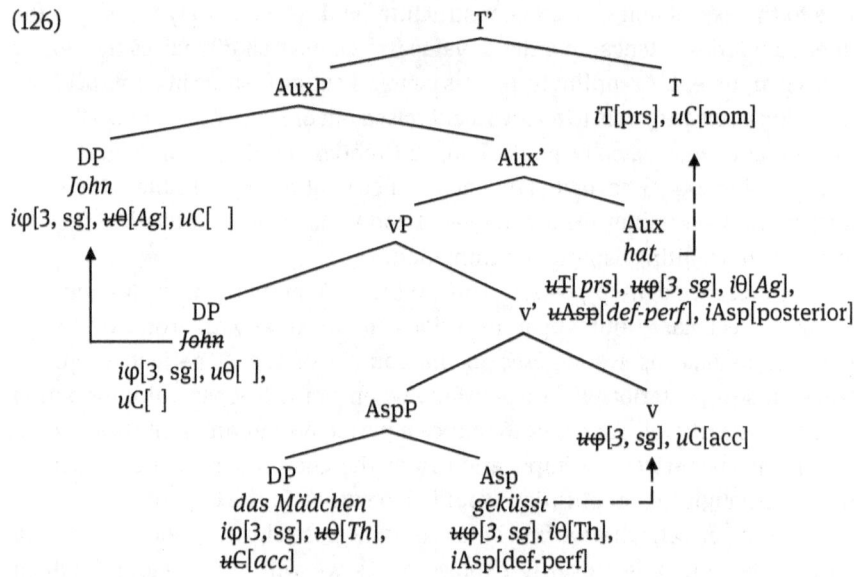

Just like in HAVE-only languages like English, the perfect auxiliary HAVE syntactically supplies the lexically-marked semantic role (*i*θ[*Ag*]) and thus allows the external argument introduced in the causative projection v to value its *u*θ-feature by virtue of moving to Spec, Aux. Reminiscent of what we could see in the case of the English HAVE-perfect of unaccusatives in (125), however, this is not a necessity, i.e. the presence of HAVE does not necessarily entail the realisation of an external argument. Although languages making use of auxiliary alternation do not exhibit such cases in a wide variety of contexts, given that BE often steps in instead, they do exist. This is observable in the case of periphrastic perfects formed on the basis of atelic two-place unaccusatives in languages resorting to auxiliary alternation like German. Predicates of this type, e.g. *gefallen* ('appeal to'), *einleuchten* ('make sense'), *schmeicheln* ('flatter'), and *missfallen* ('displease') in German, do without an external argument. Accordingly, there is no vP in the structural representation of the atelic two-place unaccusative *Das*

Kleid hat dem Mann gefallen ('The dress has appealed to the man', lit. the dress has the.DAT man appeal.to.PTCP) in (127).

(127)
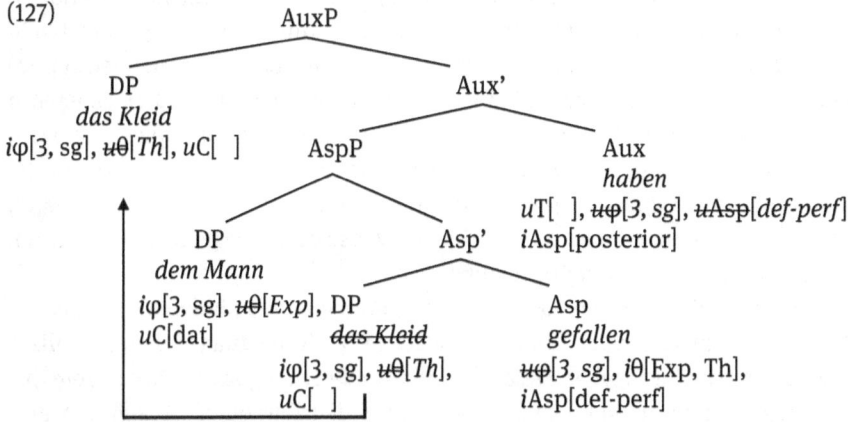

While a structural difference concerns the presence of an argument that bears inherent (dative) case, the role of HAVE is fundamentally similar to what we could observe in (125). In other words, due to the absence of an external semantic role lexically marked for existential binding, HAVE does not contribute to the expression of argument structure. Rather, the perfect auxiliary merely raises an argument (whose $u\theta$-feature has successfully been valued in AspP already) to Spec, Aux in order to value its $u\varphi$-feature. Once more, the inherent absence of an external semantic role bars the introduction of v, as there is no causer around. This raises the question of what motivates the introduction of HAVE, then, which automatically brings us to accounting for the mutual exclusivity of HAVE and BE in languages resorting to auxiliary alternation.

The motivation for the insertion of HAVE (rather than BE) in such cases is that its aspectual contribution of posteriority is essential for the denotation of a proper perfect interpretation. This is clearly observable on the basis of a different kind of two-place unaccusative predicates: telic two-place unaccusatives like *entgehen* ('elude'), *gelingen* ('succeed'), *unterlaufen* ('occur'), *entfallen* ('escape'), *widerfahren* ('befall'), *geschehen* ('happen'). These predicates are semantically unlike their unbounded counterparts in that they introduce a simple change of state rather than an atelic situation. As this entails that the aspectual information on the past participle succeeds in denoting perfectivity, a proper perfect interpretation (where posteriority is derived via implication) is possible without independent help. Hence, the perfect auxiliary BE – contingent on a perfective past participle – is employed. The perfect auxiliary HAVE, on the other hand, is sensitive to the imperfectivity of its past participial complement, which is why it is introduced in the context of *gefallen* ('appeal to') in (127), where it substantially contributes to the denotation of a perfect by virtue of introducing posteriority. Accordingly, we may conclude that the perfect auxiliary HAVE is also flexible in languages resorting to auxiliary alternation in terms of its argument structural contribution, but more restricted in terms of its subcategorisation. In fact, HAVE in HAVE-only languages like English is compatible with past participles that eventually elicit an imperfective value as well as those that elicit a perfective value. Its counterpart in auxiliary alternation languages like German, on the other hand, may only be combined with past participles whose defective perfectivity does not manage to induce a perfective reading.

This formally accounts for why HAVE is not generally able to also appear in those periphrastic perfect cases that select for BE in languages using auxiliary alternation (similar to what we can find in HAVE-only languages). Apart from this sensitivity to a particular aspectual value, the distribution of HAVE and BE also follows naturally from economy considerations. Since the featural interaction of HAVE is costly (in terms of trying to recover a lexically-marked θ-role and the presence of aspectual information), it is only licit in cases in which it is absolutely necessary. This is the case if there is an external semantic role marked for existential binding (and an argument lacking a semantic role is introduced in Spec, v) or a lack of perfectivity in both HAVE-only languages as well as those making use of auxiliary alternation. If neither of these factors motivates the introduction of HAVE, the alternative auxiliary BE, if available, needs to step in, since it is considerably cheaper in that it only comprises the ability to inflect for finiteness, a sensitivity to aspectual features and φ-features triggering a raising operation. On the other hand, this auxiliary may well be illicit for application in perfect contexts, as in English, where BE is reserved for passive contexts and thus sensitive to the presence of an imperfective participle. This suffices to formally account for the distribution of auxiliaries in the two kinds of languages.[51]

4.2.1.3 The interaction of multiple auxiliaries

Now that we have seen how the prototypical periphrastic passive and the analytic perfect may syntactically be formed, let us briefly turn to the combination of

---

[51] Lexical idiosyncrasies may, of course, considerably diffuse this picture, as we have seen in the context of (manner of) motion as well as (maintenance of) position predicates. These are, to different degrees, semantically associated with an endpoint and hence conceptualised as simple changes of state rather than atelic events.

the two by employing multiple auxiliaries.⁵² A typical instance of such a construction consists of the combination of a past participle derived from a lexical verb with a passive auxiliary, which occurs in a past participial form itself and hence needs to be licensed by a designated auxiliary. Such a configuration may for instance be found in the English example *The girl has been kissed* in (129a) and its German counterpart *Das Mädchen ist geküsst worden* (lit. the girl is kiss. PTCP become.PREFIXLESS-PTCP) in (129b) further below. Before we turn to the formal properties of these (phrasal syntactic) structures, let us briefly take a look at the formation of a past participle on the basis of an auxiliary in word syntax (BE and WERDEN in the present case). This is represented for *been* in (128).

(128) a.

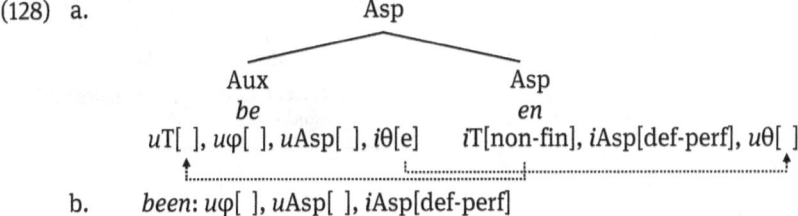

b.   *been*: *u*φ[ ], *u*Asp[ ], *i*Asp[def-perf]

The possibility to derive a past participle from an auxiliary shows that auxiliaries need to retain some basic θ-properties or else the participial marker could not value its *u*θ. These properties may be semantically bleached and do not suffice to supply semantic roles to arguments, but nevertheless serve to provide a value to a participial marker. A candidate for this more abstract value is the neo-Davidsonian event variable (e) (see Higginbotham 1985). The feature interaction in (128a) thus provides not only u̶T̶[*non-fin*] but also u̶θ̶[*e*], both of which are irrelevant for purposes of phrasal syntax (just like their checked counterparts). This leaves the question of why there is no word-internal valuation of *u*Asp given the presence of *i*Asp[def-perf] on the participial marker, i.e. how the former can remain unvalued and hence active in phrasal syntax. The central reason for this is that *i*Asp[def-perf] cannot provide a value prior to being combined with a verbal element since its value is contingent on event structural properties.⁵³ Thus, the valuation of *u*Asp needs to be postponed to phrasal syntax, where the auxiliaries in participial form are hence still contingent on the presence of a past participle.

---

52 In order to keep this discussion brief, we will not be concerned with modal auxiliaries here, although these may arguably also be grasped by the present theory in a straightforward fashion.
53 Note that even if it was possible to value *u*Asp in word syntax on the basis of the participial marker's *i*Asp, this would not go through in the case of *been* and *worden*, since both auxiliaries are sensitive to an imperfective value that may not be supplied on the basis of their own verbal (change of state) properties.

(129) a.

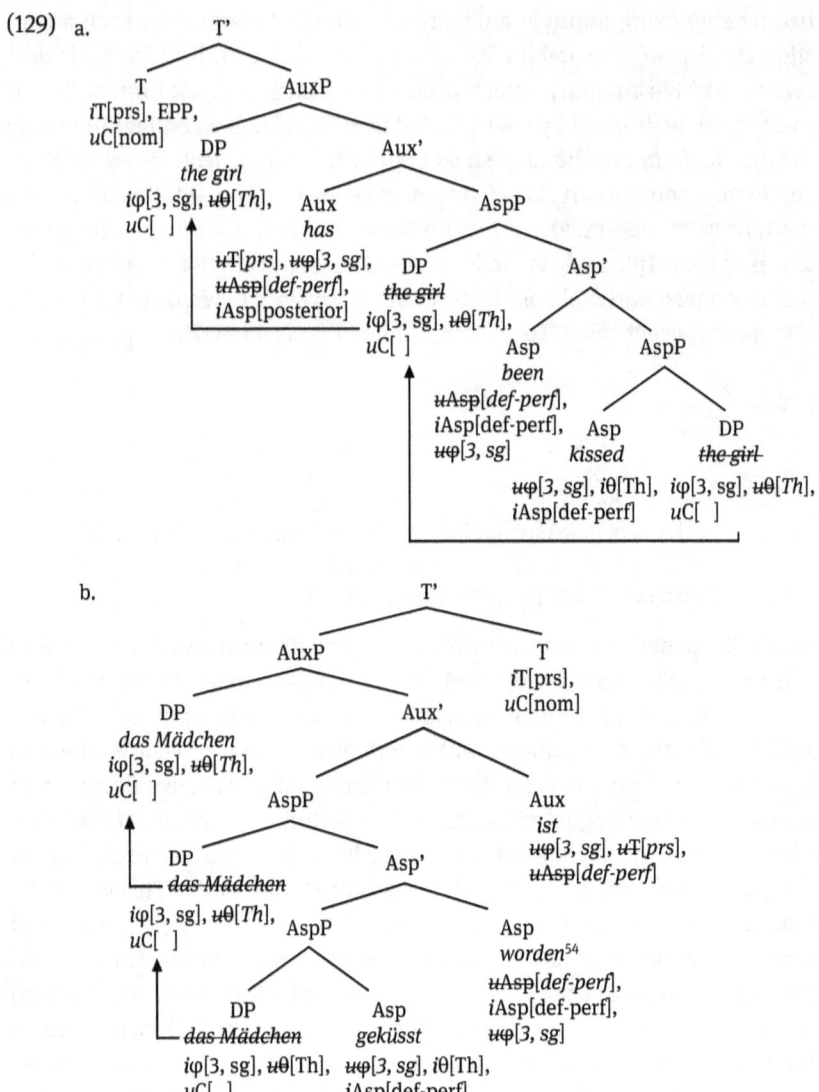

b.

---

54 The auxiliary comes in the prefixless participial form *worden* rather than *geworden*, which is still employed for the main verb of WERDEN, as observable in the difference between *Er ist krank geworden* ('He became ill.', lit. he is ill become.PTCP) and *Er ist geehrt worden* ('He was honored.', lit. he is honored become.PREFIXLESS-PTCP). According to Hinterhölzl (2009: 199f.), *worden* ('been') is a "remnant[] of the prefixless participle", from which it historically stems. We may thus treat it as the lexicalisation of an IPP-realisation.

As we can see in the structural representations in (129), the perfect auxiliaries HAVE in English and BE in German value their *u*Asp on the basis of the aspectual information introduced by the auxiliaries that have taken up participial morphology in word syntax. While it is once again irrelevant for HAVE (which is always employed as a perfect auxiliary given that there is no licit alternative), the perfect auxiliary BE in (129b) is sensitive to a perfective value.[55] This value is readily supplied by the participial form of the passive auxiliary WERDEN due to its remnant change-of-state semantics.[56] This leaves the interaction of the passive auxiliaries BE and WERDEN with their participial complements derived from main verbs. Due to their sensitivity to past participles whose aspectual properties elicit an imperfective value, the auxiliaries *been* and *worden* may properly value their *u*Asp-features on the basis of the *i*Asp-counterparts of their participial complements *kissed* and *geküsst*. These formal properties account for why a perfect interpretation comes about (even without the presence of posteriority), although the participial event need not necessarily be terminated (as in a universal perfect like *She has not been loved since her boyfriend left her*).[57]

With respect to argument structure, the past participles *kissed* and *geküsst* syntactically only bear an internal semantic role, which is supplied locally to an argument that has to be displaced by virtue of lacking structural

---

[55] Evidence for the (somewhat trivial) claim that the auxiliary is sensitive to the past participial auxiliary rather than the main verb comes from present participial cases like *The house is being built*. Here, the lower instance of BE takes up present participial morphology while selecting a past participle. In both instances, the auxiliary BE is sensitive to the imperfectivity of its participial complement (progressivity on *being* and imperfectivity on *built*).

[56] The auxiliary lexically retains these properties from its main verb counterpart: *Jack ist Arzt geworden* ('Jack became a doctor.', lit. Jack is doctor become.PTCP). Note that this does not contradict the semantic vacuity assigned to this auxiliary: the auxiliary does not convey any semantic properties, but its lexical heritage still has it elicit the value 'perfective' when brought together with the participial morpheme.

[57] These properties also account for the ungrammaticality of examples like **He has had seen him* and **Der Mann ist angekommen gewesen* (lit. the man is arrive.PTCP be.PTCP) in contrast to *He has had a new car* and *Der Mann ist Autor gewesen* ('The man was an author.', lit. the man is author be.PTCP). While the latter instances featuring main verbs are fine, the former include two auxiliaries of the same kind and are ungrammatical since one auxiliary then does not provide any new information. In fact, *had* need not provide posteriority nor license an external argument (as this is already achieved by *has*). Likewise, *gewesen* need not provide perfectivity, as this is supplied by *angekommen*. Based on this line of reasoning, it is not surprising that both English and German entertain a future perfect, as observable in *The boy will have seen the man* and *Der Junge wird den Mann gesehen haben* ('The boy will have seen the man.', lit. the boy become the man see.PTCP have).

case. Once more, the passive interpretation stems from the fact that the external semantic role is marked for existential binding. Crucially, HAVE in (129a), though generally able to reintroduce a lexically-marked role, cannot do so in the present case, because *kissed* is not its complement. In other words, the role that HAVE is supposed to realise is bound to reside in the element it is syntactically sensitive to via *u*Asp, i.e. the locally closest participle. In the present example, this does not hold true as HAVE is sensitive to *been*, which – given its origin as an auxiliary – does not bear any thematic role. Thus, despite not contributing semantically, the presence of *been* technically contributes to the expression of a passive in that it prevents HAVE from licensing an external argument.

4.2.1.4 Theoretical implications: some necessary technical extensions

Now that a formal approach to the main characteristics of the prototypical past participial periphrases has been introduced, let us briefly touch upon some implications as well as necessary theoretical extensions. One of the implications brought to light in the present section concerns the direction of auxiliary selection, i.e. the question of whether the auxiliary selects the past participle or vice versa. While the traditional assumption is that the auxiliary governs the participial form (see Bech 1983 [1955]: 15f., 25), this situation is often reversed (see Remberger 2006: 121fn48) or even parameterised (see Wurmbrand 2012a, where languages may either possess a lexically valued past participle or auxiliary) in more recent accounts. Given that past participles may also occur in bare realisations, it appears to be safe to conclude that there is no designated formal requirement for auxiliaries on past participles. Rather, past participles derived from main verbs may only come equipped with a *u*φ-feature (there may be several instances of these or none at all depending on the number of internal arguments) longing for valuation on the basis of a nominal expression. Relevant auxiliaries, on the other hand, are sensitive to the past participle's aspectual information due to the presence of a *u*Asp-feature. By virtue of possessing this unvalued feature, the auxiliaries act as probes (or governors) selecting the past participial forms and not vice versa. Besides this formal requirement, however, the auxiliaries are generally called for in order for past participles to be able to appear in complete clauses. In other words, the auxiliaries make up for their auxiliates' deficiencies in terms of morphologically inflecting for finiteness and hence providing a temporal frame for the participial situation. Hence, there rather is a mutual craving in proper clauses: auxiliaries need past participles in order to value their features, whereas past participles need auxiliaries in order to be able to occur in proper clauses, but not elsewhere. Quite generally, selection is based on abstract formal features rather than s- (or c-)selection in the present approach.[58] While these assumptions are in line with standard minimalist frameworks, there are two necessary extensions that need to be addressed.

The present approach is strongly based on the interaction between formal features as governed by the mechanism of feature valuation (typically referred to simply as Agree). With respect to this mechanism, the present analysis pointed to two fairly non-standard extensions to core minimalist proposals in passing (namely in footnotes 34 and 36 above). The first one of these concerns the question of whether Agree is restricted to pairs of uninterpretable and unvalued features (uF[ ]) that need to be valued and checked by interpretable and valued features (iF[val]). Chomsky's (2000; 2001) traditional definition suggests that feature valuation only holds between a uF probe and its iF counterpart. In the structures proposed thus far, this neat distribution was suspended in one case: inherently valued uC (uC[acc] on v and uC[nom] on T) that have been taken to be able to value and check uC[ ] on a given nominal expression. Accordingly, two uninterpretable instances need to be able to undergo Agree, which is necessary in order to assure that structural case does not receive an interpretation. An extension along these lines is anything but novel. Its necessity has actually repeatedly been proposed in recent papers on the possible patterns of feature-valuation (see Pesetsky & Torrego 2002; 2006; 2007). The main assumption in these approaches is that the canonical analogy between uninterpretable and unvalued is unfounded and may be abolished in favour of allowing for interpretable unvalued (iF[ ]) and uninterpretable (inherently) valued (uF[val]) features. While assuming that this is generally possible is problematic in that it renders the system too unrestrictive by virtue of making room for extensive overgeneration, restricting its application to the highly restricted (and lexically motivated) context of structural case assignment considerably weakens these objections.

The second necessary extension that was mentioned concerns the directional flexibility of Agree. While its standard definition holds that a uF[ ]-feature may only be valued (and checked) by an iF[val]-counterpart when c-commanding it, this was not obliged in the case of uT on Aux. In this context (as well as uT on V) this process needs to allow for Reverse (or Upwards) Agree, as defined in (130), taken from Wurmbrand (2016: 263).

---

[58] In other words, s- and c-selection are epiphenomena of the interaction of formal features and anything else would mean "an unwelcome deviation from core minimalist assumptions" (Bauke 2014: 8).

(130) A feature F: __ on α is valued by a feature F: val on β, iff
　　i.　β c-commands α AND
　　ii.　α is *accessible* to β. [*accessible*: not spelled-out]
　　iii.　α does not value a feature of β.

This extension is necessary whenever a tense-value is provided by T (say *i*T[past]) and morphologically instantiated on the basis of an auxiliary that bears *u*T[ ] (cf. Adger 2003: 180). Given that T c-commands Aux, the two are part of the same phasal domain, and there is no additional formal interaction between Aux and T, the conditions in (130) are obliged. Additionally, as we will see in section 4.2.4, Reverse Agree also provides some interesting insights in the context of participial object-agreement (cf. Bjorkman 2011: 154f.). Based on the rather strict definition in (130), this mechanism typically does not run into problems of overgeneration and is often more or less implicitly employed already (see Adger 2003; Haegeman and Lohndal 2010; Merchant 2011; and Wurmbrand 2012a).

In addition to these extensions, another implication of the present theory is that auxiliaries and their main verb counterparts are not identical, i.e. the auxiliaries HAVE, BE and WERDEN do not introduce the same formal features as their homonymous main verbs. In this respect, the present account thus differs for instance from those that speak out for the identity of main verb and auxiliary HAVE (see, amongst others, Cowper 1989a: 88, Ackema & Marelj 2012: 233, Belvin 1993; 1996; and Ritter & Rosen 1997). While the auxiliaries are like their main verb counterparts in terms of comprising *u*T and share with many verbs that they bear *u*φ, they differ in terms of containing *u*Asp (and the occasional ability of valuing *u*φ by default in the case of WERDEN). The most salient distinction in the case of HAVE is that the auxiliary is inherently valued for aspectual properties (*i*Asp [posterior]), whereas lexical verbs never bring with them any aspectual information (unless aided by participial morphology). On the other hand, HAVE is slightly more like its verbal counterpart than any other auxiliary in terms of supplying a semantic role, which needs to stem from its participial complement, though. Thus, HAVE is semantically specified for aspectual information and contributes to the expression of argument structure, whereas BE and WERDEN never do so. Quite generally, the auxiliaries share that they do not bring in any semantic roles themselves, which goes hand in hand with a lack of proper lexical meaning, i.e. auxiliaries undergo semantic bleaching (cf. Remberger 2006: 13; Salvi 1987: 232f.). Lexical verbs, in turn, are always fully equipped with *i*θ-features (e.g. *i*θ [Ag, Th]), although word-formation processes might have an effect on the expression of these. While argument structural characteristics are not retained by auxiliaries, the verbal aktionsart, as we have seen in the context of structures featuring more than one auxiliary, apparently is, at least on an abstract level.

Additionally, auxiliaries and their main verb counterparts have often been taken to resemble one another in terms of case assignment. Accordingly, the auxiliary HAVE is often taken to be able to assign accusative case due to retaining case properties from its main verb ancestor, whereas BE is often taken to lack this ability since main verb (or copula) BE cannot assign accusative case either (cf. Roberts 1984: 218f.). In the present approach, HAVE's occurrence in accusative structures rather follows from its ability to license the external argument introduced in Spec, v and is thus epiphenomenal for the use of v bearing accusative case. The auxiliaries BE and WERDEN, by contrast, cannot co-occur with an external argument and thus do not show up in structures in which v assigns accusative case.

Eventually, given that some (fairly abstract) verbal properties are retained while auxiliaries also involve novel formal characteristics, it is not surprising that their syntactic category is hotly debated. There are for instance approaches claiming that they head the designated category Aux (see Chomsky 1957; Steele 1999: 51f., Akmajian & Wasow 1975) as opposed to those claiming that they are fully-fledged verbs (see Huddleston 1984: 6) or those that claim that they are directly introduced in T (see Reuland 1983). We will not elaborate on this discussion here, as we assume that explicit labels are redundant since syntactic categories are derivative of their (formal) feature clusters in the sense of Rauh (2000a; 2000b; 2010: 144). Consequently, it is the presence or absence of certain formal features that may lead to a more or less verbal behaviour.

Now that the basic formal properties of the periphrastic passive and the analytic perfect have been laid out by virtue of modelling their syntactic derivation, we may turn to the detailed discussion of the two configurations. Accordingly, the subsequent chapter 4.2.2 will extend the empirical domain of the periphrastic passive by virtue of considering the impersonal and the dative passive and turn to its semantic properties. Section 4.2.3 will then underpin the formal analysis of the analytic perfect by virtue of accounting for its semantics. Finally, chapter 4.2.4 will round things off by considering how the present approach may account for divergent realisations of past participles and polymorphy.

4.2.2 The periphrastic passive

While the previous section was restricted to the basic properties of the compositional ingredients of the prototypical past participial periphrases and their syntactic interaction, we may now zoom in on the semantics of the two major functions they express. Starting with the periphrastic passive, the present chapter will focus on passivisation as well as its semantic effects and extend the empirical scope to further kinds of periphrastic instantiations of the passive. Accordingly, chapter 4.2.2.1 is devoted to semantic and syntactic restrictions on passivisation. Section 4.2.2.2 then extends the scope of the analysis by turning to passives of ditransitive predicates and chapter 4.2.2.3 focusses on the main semantic consequence of passivisation, namely existentially binding the external semantic role.

Despite its unrivalled status in syntactic research, the passive still lacks a generally agreed upon analysis. In fact, its major properties have properly been identified in the second half of the 20th century, yet the precise theoretical incorporation of these – as to be expected as the phenomenon from which an unequalled amount of theoretical assumptions have been derived – is still subject to substantial debate. What is typically agreed upon is that the passive induces some kind of a reduction (or demotion) of the external argument. This process might be taken to boil down to a loss of the ability to assign an external θ-role that goes along with a lack of accusative case (see Burzio's 1986 Generalization). Based on these properties, more recent minimalist proposals held a single functional projection accountable for the introduction of an external argument as well as the assignment of accusative case: Kratzer's (1996) VoiceP, often referred to simply as (little) vP (cf. Chomsky 1995).[59] While those approaches often do not provide an explanation for why vP is not available in passive periphrases, there are also those that explicitly tie this to the properties of the passive auxiliary, which is assumed to select VP rather than vP (cf. Struckmeier 2007: 45). Something remotely similar is observable in Sternefeld's (1995: 76) syntactic approach to passives, which suggests that the auxiliary is primarily responsible for inducing passivisation by virtue of requiring an empty specifier. In this analysis, passive auxiliaries are taken to introduce a voice phrase, as a part of which they license a pro that is bound to comprise an external semantic role (cf. Sternefeld 1995: 76). Supposing that a perfect auxiliary should then be introduced by a distinct kind of voice phrase (namely one that does not require pro) renders this approach reminiscent of more recent trends arguing for distinct kinds of voice heads. This is for instance observable in Chomsky's (2001: 9) distinction between the transitive functional head v* and its defective counterpart v, which is employed in passive and unaccusative cases. As pointed out in the previous section, the present approach acknowledges the

---

[59] Note that a strict correlation of the presence of an external argument and the assignment of accusative case demands that unergatives be analysed as hidden transitives, e.g. in the sense of Hale & Keyser (1993: 54f.; 2002: 15), where unergatives are generally taken to comprise an object, albeit one that is incorporated into the verb. The alternative view holds that accusative case is present, but not syntactically assigned in unergative cases.

importance of the functional projection v, but crucially does not solely rely upon this syntactic ingredient in order to grasp the properties of passives. Rather, given that this would diffuse the participial contribution by virtue of simply tracing argument structural differences back to distinct functional heads in syntax, we assume that passivisation is primarily triggered by the properties of the past participial form, which has syntactic effects.[60]

As laid out in the previous section, the major properties of passivisation (in terms of a suppression of the external argument and a loss of accusative case) syntactically follow from the external argument's inability to retrieve a thematic role when introduced in Spec, v in the present approach.[61] This inability is traced back to the lexical contribution of past participial formation, as defined by the operation in (131) (see also Rothstein 2001: 142 and Reinhart 2002).

(131) Marking the external argument for existential binding
When a past participial affix attaches to a verbal element in word syntax, it marks the verb's external semantic role (if there is one), i.e. the θ-role to be assigned to an argument in Spec, v in an active counterpart, for existential binding. This marking renders the external θ-role inactive for syntactic purposes by means of rendering the associated feature-value unavailable.

This operation is based on the wide-spread idea that passive formation involves existential binding (cf. Wunderlich 2012: 2231), which semantically takes care of an argument so that it need not be realised syntactically anymore. In order for an external argument to participate in existential binding, it has to be lexically marked.[62] In other words, the lexical marking that past participles impose on the verbal bases they attach to allows the external semantic role to be dealt with semantically rather than having to be assigned in syntax as part of the predicate's argument structure. Accordingly, the formal value of the external θ-role is not available for purposes of regular syntactic processing, thus vanishing from the formerly complex $i\theta$-cluster upon the formation of a past participle on the basis of

---

[60] This is supported by the fact that passives are cross-linguistically accompanied by specific morphology (cf. Haspelmath 1990: 27). As pointed out by Dryer (1982), forming the passive with the help of an auxiliary is rather uncommon cross-linguistically, the usual case being passive morphology on a finite verb (cf. Wanner 2009: 15f.). This is for instance observable in the Danish, Swedish and Norwegian synthetic passive.
[61] See also Lois (1990: 254), where a past participle is taken not to be able to assign "the external θ-role to its own subject position".
[62] This is assumed in analogy to Meltzer-Asscher's (2011; 2012) mechanism of lexically marking an internal argument for λ-abstraction, which we will return to in the discussion of adjectival instances in chapter 4.3.

the verbal stem. This explicitly excludes Spec, v from being the locus of the assignment of an external θ-role, i.e. the external argument cannot retrieve an external semantic role from the verbal host in this position.

This lexically-driven approach to the passive differs from strongly syntactic accounts that rely on the presence of an empty category (say pro) that is regularly assigned the external semantic role (see, for instance, von Stechow 1990: 145; Sternefeld 1984: 245, 1995: 76; Rapp 1997: 158–160). The latter kind of approaches is based on the assumption that in passives "the theta role of the subject should still be available in syntactic structure, although it cannot overtly be realised as a subject NP" (Sternefeld 1995: 68). However, such an approach raises problems with respect to the licensing of BY-phrases.[63] These are for instance taken to bind pro and then undergo covert movement to the verbal domain in order to bind the instance of pro that is introduced by the passive auxiliary (cf. Sternefeld 1995: 71). An alternative attempt to deal with this is Leiss' (1992: 86f.) proposal that rather than the adjunct expressing it, the external semantic role is just doubled whenever a BY-phrase occurs. These attempts show that purely syntactic approaches struggle to account for the properties of long passives[64] and the same is observable in those accounts that attribute argument-like properties to the participial morpheme (see, amongst others, Fabb 1984; Baker 1988; Roberts 1985; 1987; Jaeggli 1986). Such approaches suggest that the participial element absorbs the external semantic role and hence raise the same problems as the view based on the presence of an empty category. The present take based on the lexical marking of an external role, on the other hand, straightforwardly accounts for BY-phrases in that these – similar to HAVE – bear the capability to syntactically introduce an external role that has been lexically marked on the past participle it attaches to. In fact, the preposition BY introduces an adjunct and bears a uAsp-feature that governs the association with a past participle bearing the lexically-marked external role, as represented in (132).

---

[63] Note that while Gunkel (2003: 65fn8) points out that BY-phrases are uncontroversially treated as adjuncts (see, amongst many others, Höhle 1978: 161; von Stechow 1990: 174; Leiss 1992: 86f.), the arguments they introduce nevertheless need to be associated with a semantic role.

[64] Peter Svenonius (p.c.) points out that a challenge an identity approach along these lines has to face is that even quirky (dative) subjects in languages like Icelandic are subject to passivisation. This calls for the stipulation that such arguments are also properly introduced by the auxiliary HAVE and then control pro. In the present approach, on the other hand, this follows naturally since even arguments marked for dative case are introduced in Spec, v and then get their θ-role from the auxiliary once they move into Spec, Aux.

(132)

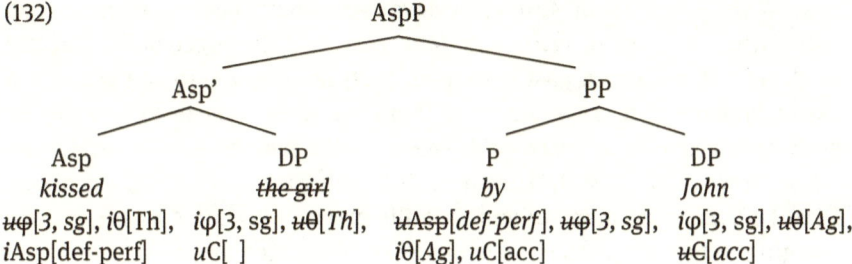

In addition to uAsp, BY houses a uφ-feature that demands the introduction of a DP, which may in turn value its unvalued uC-feature on the basis of the value provided by the preposition. The most crucial contribution of BY for the present purposes is its introduction of a valued iθ-feature, which renders the lexically-marked role available for purposes of syntactic valuation.

A syntactic consequence of the operation in (131) is that the functional projection v may not occur (without leading the derivation to crash) unless the argument that it introduces is supplied with a θ-value at a later stage of the derivation (i.e. unless HAVE is introduced). In fact, v is syntactically bound to introduce causation (which is supposedly directly expressed semantically in case an external argument is existentially bound), but this does not suffice for a proper thematic licensing. Hence, HAVE has to introduce a specific θ-role. Thus, the main purpose of the functional projection v is its contribution of causation and the association of this contribution with an argument that acts as a causer. Beside this contribution, v also introduces structural case, which hence has to be absent in unaccusative and passive cases in which there is no v. The effect that passivisation has on case assignment is therefore only an epiphenomenon. This is quite unlike what we find in traditional approaches like Rouveret & Vergnaud (1980) and Chomsky (1981), where the main property of the passive is taken to be its absorption of accusative case. This view, however, was soon challenged by approaches focusing on the suppression of the external argument instead (cf. Åfarli 1989: 102). Åfarli (1989: 105), for instance, points out that passive morphology "need not receive abstract Case in Norwegian". The same point may be made in German, where impersonal passives (*Es wird getanzt*, 'There is dancing.', lit. it becomes dance.PTCP) feature verbs that do not involve a reduction of accusative case. Accordingly, closely tying passive formation to the reduction of accusative case does not suffice to uncover the main properties of the passive. Rather than relying on case, a stronger focus was imposed on the role of the external semantic role in more recent works. This – unlike in strongly case-driven approaches – allows us to predict which classes of verbs may form passives. Quite generally, the fact that "every verb forms a past participle, [but] not every verb can occur in a passive construction [suggests that] there are grammatical constraints on passivisation that not every verb meets" (Wanner 2009: 52). In Haider (1984), Grewendorf (1989), Toman (1986), von Stechow (1990), Grimshaw (1990: 113), amongst many others, it is the external semantic role – the one belonging to the 'deep structure subject' or 'designated argument' nowadays associated with v – that is blocked (cf. Rapp 1997: 125f.). This is acknowledged in the operation in (131), where it is the external θ-role that is lexically marked for existential binding. Given that this is the element that is usually (i.e. in active clauses) introduced in the causative projection v, this role is semantically predicted to mark the cause of the event. Thus, a necessary (but not a sufficient) condition for the proper denotation of a passive is the presence of an external semantic role, i.e. the presence of a CAUSE-operator in the verbal semantics.

4.2.2.1 Semantic and syntactic restrictions on passivisation

The requirement for the presence of an external semantic role that is then suppressed for the denotation of a passive interpretation rules out the formation of passives from predicates that inherently lack a cause. Accordingly, unaccusatives should generally not be able to occur in passive constructions. This holds true consistently for English and typically also in German, as we can see in (133).

(133) a. *The girl was disappeared.
     b. *Das Mädchen/ *Hier wurde verschwunden.
         the girl/   here became disappear.PTCP
     c. *He was resembled (by his mother).
     d. *Ihm/ *Es wurde (von seiner Mutter) geähnelt.
         he.DAT/it became (by his   mother) resemble.PTCP

Besides the lack of a passive interpretation, these examples are also generally ungrammatical. This follows naturally from the incompatibility of the passive auxiliaries BE and WERDEN with past participles that encode perfectivity in (133a) and (133b). The examples in (133c) and (133d) similarly do not include an external argument and hence cannot give rise to a passive interpretation. Ungrammaticality ensues here, though, primarily because the past participle eventually neither imposes an argument structural effect nor may it denote perfectivity, which marks a violation of the Principle of Full Interpretability (cf. Chomsky 1995: 194).[65] However, the clear-cut ungrammaticality of unaccusatives is diffused by German impersonal cases like those in (134), adopted from Rapp (1997: 134).

(134) a. In Bosnien wird (*von Zivilisten) weiter gestorben.
   in Bosnia becomes by civilians still die.PTCP
   'People keep dying in Bosnia.'
   b. In seinen Vorlesungen wird (*von Studenten) immer eingeschlafen.
   in his lectures becomes by students always fall.to.sleep.PTCP
   'People always fall to sleep in his lectures.'

These examples show that unaccusatives are clearly "not as easily compatible with the passive voice, but by no means totally excluded" (cf. König & Gast 2009: 132). They should thus not *per se* be taken to be impossible. Taking this seriously, Rapp (1997: 134f.) even claims that the syntactic criterion of taking the presence of an external argument as a necessary requirement for passive formation is not a licit assumption. Indeed, these cases violate both of the conditions set up earlier, namely the formal incompatibility of a passive auxiliary with a past participle that denotes perfectivity and the assumption that passivisation affects the realisation of an external argument. However, their low frequency as well as additional restrictions like the inability to realise the sole argument in an agentive BY-phrase suggest that rather than a grammatical structure we are dealing with a construction that is ungrammatical but acceptable here.[66] What is striking on the basis of the examples of (134) is that the marginal occurrence of 'unaccusative passives' is apparently only possible if an unbounded reading is enforced (emphasised by adverbial modification of *still* and *always* in the present cases, which reiterate the event) (cf. Primus 2011: 83f.).[67] This indicates that the

---

65 Note that this is different in HAVE-perfect cases of these predicates, as the aspectual contribution of HAVE supplies the past participle with a right to exist by virtue of adding to a proper perfect denotation.
66 See Lübbe & Rapp's (2011: 284f.) argument adaptation that we briefly saw in the context of unexpected attributive instantiations above as well as Haider (2011) for additional instances of such constructions.
67 Similar cases that are also interpreted in an atelic fashion are found in Dutch (cf. Zaenen 1993; Primus 2011; Ackema 1999: 105). See also Primus (2010) and Kiparsky (2013) for problems of ruling out unaccusatives.

perfectivity expected to be denoted by the past participle needs to be suspended in order for a passive structure to be acceptable at least. The existential binding of the sole argument may then come about by a pragmatic rescue mechanism (in analogy to Lübbe & Rapp's 2011 argument adaption), which allows the internal argument to be interpreted as if it is an external one, although this is not grammatically instantiated (as we can see on the basis of the ungrammaticality of BY-phrases).

While we may thus stick to the initial assumption that the presence of an external semantic role is a requirement for the denotation of a passive, not all predicates possessing an external argument may give rise to a proper periphrastic passive. This observation, which strongly highlights the importance of (more fine-grained) semantic factors, may be derived from examples like those in (135) and (136), the latter of which are adopted from Rapp (1997: 134).

(135) a. *Es/ *Hier wurde geblüht.
　　　　 it/　 here　 became　bloom.PTCP
　　b. *Es/ *Hier wurde geglüht.
　　　　 it/　 here　 became　glow.PTCP

(136) a. *Die Antwort wurde　 von ihm　gewusst.
　　　　 the answer　becomes　by him　 know.PTCP
　　b. *Die Stadt wurde　von Bergen　 umgeben.
　　　　 the city　became by　 mountains surround.PTCP
　　c. *The ring was possessed.
　　d. *Two hours were lasted.
　　e. *Er wurde　von der Tatsache　erstaunt.
　　　　 he became　by　 the fact　　　amaze.PTCP

Given that all of these cases are expected to introduce an external semantic role by virtue of being unergative or transitive, these examples show that the presence of such a role is not sufficient for the grammaticality of a passive. In other words, while this semantic role is always marked for existential binding in the formation of a past participle, this marking does not guarantee that existential binding may properly be carried out at LF. Rather than being solely based on syntactic criteria (as assumed in Grimshaw 1990), there needs to be room for semantic restrictions blocking certain verbs from undergoing passive formation, which are often left pending in approaches solely relying on external arguments (cf. Rapp 1997: 130–134). In fact, as existential binding is carried out at the semantic component, it is contingent on the specific semantic properties of the external semantic role rather than just its mere presence. Therefore, existential binding on the basis of a lexically-marked semantic role only works out if the argument in question bears a sufficient set of Proto-Agent properties (cf. Dowty 1991). This rules out the Theme-unergatives in (135), which simply do not meet this requirement.[68] The same may be claimed for the psych verb in (136a), which – unlike its counterpart *sehen* ('see') – does not comprise a substantial amount of Proto-Agent properties and hence cannot give rise to a grammatical passive. This also holds for the locative in (136b), which is particularly interesting in that resorting to the BY-phrase *von einer Mauer* ('by a wall') renders this example grammatical. This follows from the additional Proto-Agent properties attributed to the external argument by virtue of a wall supposedly being actively placed around a city in order to surround it, unlike mountains. The semantic insufficiency of the external argument may also be attested for verbs of possession (*haben* 'have', *bekommen* 'receive', *besitzen* 'possess') and measurement (*wiegen* 'weigh', *kosten* 'cost', *dauern* 'last') (cf. Eisenberg 1999: 127; König & Gast 2009: 130) like those in (136c) and (136d), respectively.[69] Additionally, the verb of emotion in (136e) is reminiscent of the locative case in that using *von Maria* ('by Mary') instead elicits a grammatical passive by virtue of attributing a larger amount of Proto-Agentive properties to the external semantic role in question.[70] Eventually, then, only a

---

[68] Note that such cases are independently ruled out in English anyway, since English does not allow for impersonal passives, i.e. passives derived from intransitive predicates. Note further that the class of Theme-unergatives supposedly also houses so-called weather-verbs. These – though bearing special characteristics in solely realising an expletive – thus similarly do not give rise to passive structures. Accordingly, cases like *regnen* ('rain') and *schneien* ('snow') are excluded from existential binding by virtue of lacking a sufficient amount of Proto-Agent properties: **Hier wird geregnet/geschneit* (lit. here became rain.PTCP/snow.PTCP).

[69] Rapp (1997: 124f.), following Engel (1988: 453), identifies the following verbal categories as being illicit for passivisation in German: verbs of possession (*bekommen* 'receive', *besitzen* 'possess', *enthalten* 'contain', *erhalten* 'obtain', *haben* 'have', *kriegen* 'get'), including verbs of 'mental possession' (*kennen* 'know', *wissen* 'know'), and verbs like *gelten* ('obtain'), *kosten* ('cost'), *umfassen* ('include'), *wiegen* ('weigh').

[70] Note that in English the ungrammaticality of eventive passives is often veiled behind the grammaticality of a stative reading, as observable in #/**The answer was known*, which may be interpreted as featuring the adjective *known* (reminiscent of German *bekannt*, 'known', as opposed to the verbal *gekannt* 'known').

subset of the external semantic roles properly marked by (131) gives rise to a fully-fledged passive interpretation.

As pointed out before, the passivisation of intransitive predicates in languages like German (as well as Dutch, Danish, Norwegian, Italian, and Spanish) emphasises that the loss of case assignment cannot be the defining property of passivisation. In fact, this entails that "subjectivization, or promotion of an internal argument, is just an epiphenomenon" (Abraham 2006a: 3; see also Wanner 2009: 16). This becomes clear in the German and Danish unergative examples in (137a) and (137b), the latter of which is adopted from Müller & Ørsnes (2013: 143).

(137) a. Es   wird   gearbeitet.
       here becomes work.PTCP
       'There is working.'
   b. Der   bliver   arbejdet.
       there become work.PTCP
       'There is working.'

Similar examples may not be found in English (and only marginally in Swedish), for instance, as not every language entertaining a personal passive also has an impersonal one. In fact, while "[i]mpersonal passives also are found in many languages [...] they occur more rarely and usually if a language has a construction of this kind, then it will also have the direct object [i.e. the personal] passive" (Ackerman & Webelhuth 1998: 131). While the possibility of an impersonal passive was occasionally taken to question that movement is involved in passivisation (see Sternefeld 1984), we have seen that passivisation may but need not involve the displacement of an internal argument (cf. Fanselow 1987: 176f., 179). In fact, the cross-linguistic difference in terms of whether movement is a requirement for a grammatical passive hinges on the specific properties of the passive auxiliary involved, viz. there is parametric variation with respect to whether it allows for default φ-feature valuation (cf. Ruys 2010; Schäfer 2013: 354). In other words, languages employing impersonal passives allow for the passive auxiliary's the φ-features to be valued by default, typically receiving 3rd person singular specifications (cf Schäfer 2013: 354). This is sketchily represented in (138).

(138)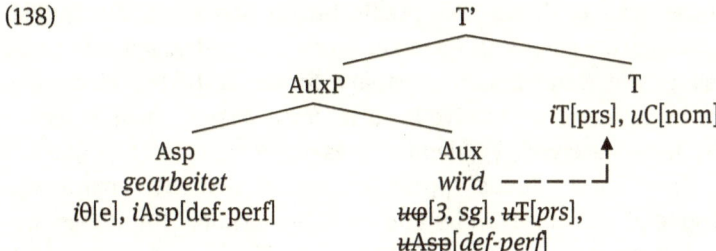

The crucial point here is that the uφ in *werden* receive the default 3rd person singular value, as there is no argument around that could provide a value (cf. Schäfer 2013: 354). In English, on the other hand, there is no default valuation of φ-features and hence the derivation crashes in a configuration like (138), i.e. whenever there is no argument that may be raised through Spec, Aux.[71] The expletives in (137) are not able to value φ-features (by virtue of lacking φ-feature specifications) but only serve structural requirements in that they satisfy EPP-features. This is underlined by parametric differences with respect to the presence of an EPP-feature in embedded clauses, as in (139) (cf. Müller & Ørsnes 2013: 143).

(139) a. weil (*es) noch gearbeitet wird
   because there still work.PTCP *becomes*
   'because there still is working'
   b. fordi *(der) bliver arbejdet
   because there become work.PTCP
   'because there is working'

While the Danish example in (139b) demands the presence of an expletive, its German counterpart in (139a) does without one. Rather than the properties of the impersonal passive, such differences arguably stem from more general distinctions in word order according to Müller & Ørsnes (2013: 143), i.e. while the two languages share relevant V2-properties in main clauses, they exhibit intricate differences in embedded clauses.

4.2.2.2 The passives of ditransitive predicates

In addition to the observable differences with respect to impersonal passives, interesting distinctions may also be found in the context of passive

---

[71] As hinted at above, this difference in terms of whether φ-features may be valued by default is not neatly distributed along the lines of distinct auxiliaries. There are also exponents of BE that allow for it, for instance.

formation on the basis of ditransitive predicates. At first sight, the English *get*-passive of a ditransitive, as in *Jesse got given a calendar*, appears to be closely related to the German dative passive formed with the auxiliaries *kriegen* ('get') or *bekommen* ('receive'), as in *Jesse bekam einen Kalender geschenkt* (lit. Jesse received a calendar present.PTCP). In fact, what the auxiliaries in these constructions appear to share is that they comprise a fairly large degree of verbal semantics and arguably have not (or at least not fully) been auxiliarised (cf. Haegeman 1985: 55). This is observable with alternations like *Was he beaten up?* and *Did he get beaten up?*, which show that only the fully-fledged auxiliary *be* may undergo head-movement, whereas instances with *get* have to resort to *do*-support (since lexical verbs may not undergo head-movement to T in English). A certain degree of substantial verbal semantics is also observable in the German dative passive auxiliaries *kriegen* ('get') or *bekommen* ('receive'), which – unlike *get* – are only combinable with predicates that realise an indirect object that instantiates the semantic role of Recipient, Bene- or Malefactive. This shows that the semantic bleaching that is typical for the grammaticalisation of auxiliaries is only weakly imposed in the case of *get*, *kriegen* ('get') and *bekommen* ('receive'). Crucially, despite its verbal semantics, the English passive *get* is not that interesting in the context of ditransitive passives in that it combines with (di-)transitives and intransitive predicates alike and – although König & Gast (2009: 125f.) also point to some semantic differences – virtually boils down to a stylistic variant of the BE-passive (cf. Wanner 2009: 85f.). The dative passive auxiliaries *kriegen* ('get') and *bekommen* ('receive'), on the other hand, affect the expression of arguments, viz. case assignment, in crucial ways and hence deserve special attention, as can be seen in (140).

(140) a. Der   Junge   bekam   einen Kalender geschenkt.
         the.NOM boy   received   a.ACC calendar present.PTCP
         'The boy was given a calendar.'
     b. Der   Junge   kriegte   seinen Ball weggenommen.
         the.NOM boy   got   his.ACC ball take.away.PTCP
         'The boy got his ball taken away from him.'

The eponymous property of dative passives is that a dative object is raised to become the clause's subject, which marks a "construction [that] belong[s more] to informal, spoken German than to the written language, especially with *kriegen* as auxiliary" (König & Gast 2009: 130). Accordingly, the argument that is expected to bear dative case in the context of an active predicate moves into or through the subject position Spec, T and may end up in the sentence-initial position Spec, C in main clauses like those in (140). Postponing the discussion of how the raised argument acquires structural nominative (instead of inherent dative) case, a general characteristic of the dative passive in German is that it is typically only possible with ditransitive predicates. As a matter of fact, while the dative passive is consistently ruled out for intransitive predicates in German (cf. Gunkel 2003: 103), it is usually also not possible to derive a dative passive on the basis of a transitive predicate that comprises a semantic role to be associated with an argument that bears dative case. However, the latter cases, e.g. *Er bekam geholfen ('He was helped.', lit. he became help.PTCP), are occasionally possible in some dialects of German (cf. König & Gast 2009: 130; see also Gunkel 2003: 103). Such observations actually have consequences for the discussion of whether the dative passive is a real passive featuring a proper passive auxiliary (see Alexiadou, Anagnostopoulou & Sevdali 2014: 14f.; Zifonun et al. 1997; Bader & Häussler 2013). As we can see on the basis of the differences in the grammaticality of transitive cases, "[d]epending on the dialect, some traces of [the auxiliary's] lexical history are still active and prevent unlimited combinations" (Alexiadou, Anagnostopoulou & Sevdali 2014: 17).[72] Regardless of whether *kriegen* ('get') and *bekommen* ('receive') are restricted to ditransitive predicates, what substantially supports the passive nature of the dative passive construction is that it demands the presence of an agentive external semantic role (cf. Gunkel 2003: 103; Rapp 1997: 129f.). Accordingly, the proper existential binding of an external argument is a prerequisite for the grammaticality of a dative passive, which is why two-place unaccusatives (*schmeicheln* 'flatter', *einleuchten* 'make sense'; *gelingen* 'succeed', *unterlaufen* 'occur') do not elicit dative passives despite including a suitable indirect object. Given these observations, we may conclude that only a subset of the verbs conforming with the passivisation operation in (131) give rise to a dative passive by virtue of the restrictions imposed by *kriegen* ('get') and *bekommen* ('receive').

Before we turn to the syntactic instantiation of the restrictions imposed by the auxiliaries in dative passives, let us briefly compare the characteristics of the dative passive to those of the regular WERDEN-passive on the basis of the examples in (141).

---

[72] Note that the same uncertainty with respect to whether *bekommen* ('get') is an auxiliary or a lexical verb pertains to instances of *få* ('get') in Norwegian, Danish and Swedish (cf. Lødrup 1996; Klingvall 2011).

(141) a. Dem   Jungen   wurde   ein   Kalender geschenkt.
         the.DAT boy.DAT became   a.NOM   calendar give.PTCP
         'The boy was given a calendar.'
     b. Dem   Jungen   wurde   sein   Ball   weggenommen.
         the.DAT boy.DAT became   his.NOM ball   take.away.PTCP
         'His ball was taken away from him.'

These examples show that the WERDEN-passive of ditransitive verbs in German raises the indirect object, crucially leaving its lexically-assigned dative case intact. The dative passive cases in (140), on the other hand, displace the same argument (i.e. the one bearing a Recipient/Malefactive role in the present case), but do not realise it as a dative argument. This first and foremost raises the essential question of what happens to the dative case, which has frequently been analysed as being 'filtered out' in the dative passive, unlike in the WERDEN-passive (cf. Fanselow 1987: 164f.; Rapp 1997: 126–128). In addition to the alternation of nominative and dative case on the Recipient/Malefactive (*der Junge* vs. dative *dem Jungen*), the dative passive and WERDEN-passive differ in marking the Theme as either accusative or nominative (*einen Kalender* vs. *ein Kalender*). Metaphorically speaking, there is a domino effect between the assignment of dative case and the realisation of nominative or accusative case (i.e. NOM-ACC vs. DAT-NOM).[73] We will now briefly turn to the formal properties of the WERDEN-passive and the dative passive in an attempt to provide a proper analysis of dative passives in the present framework.

The analysis of the WERDEN-passive is rather unproblematic and follows from the properties of the past participle derived from a ditransitive verb and the passive auxiliary in a straightforward fashion. What is different from the analyses laid out so far is the realisation of a second argument, which is what makes the representation in (142) interesting after all.

---

[73] Müller (2015: 19) traces this back to the properties of a passive variant of the functional projection v, which licenses both dative as well as accusative case, but only one of the two in a given instance. The choice of ACC vs. DAT is traced back to the point of DP-insertion, which thus determines auxiliary selection: *bekommen* ('receive') selects a vP licensing ACC, whereas *werden* ('become') licenses DAT (cf. Müller 2015: 19). This is incompatible with the present approach in so far as it relies on the presence of a special variant of v in eventive passives.

(142)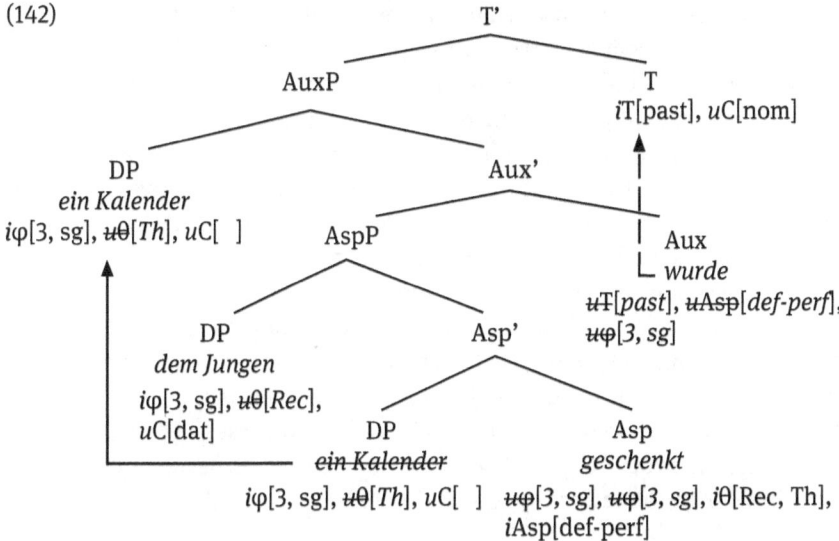

This structure serves to derive the canonical order *Dem Jungen wurde ein Kalender geschenkt*, as introduced in (141a). Additionally, it is the underlying structure of the word order alternation *Ein Kalender wurde dem Jungen geschenkt* (lit. a.NOM calendar became the.DAT boy.DAT present.PTCP), where C's EPP-feature raises an argument in order to satisfy its requirement for some constituent to fill Spec, C.[74] Most interesting about the structure in (142) is how the two arguments, which are eventually spelled out as dative (Recipient) and nominative (Theme), receive their case values. The assignment of the dative case, an 'inherent case', is restricted to arguments with specific thematic roles in those languages which exhibit it (cf. Chomsky 1986; 1995; Wanner 2009: 53). Accordingly, in German the assignment of dative case is restricted to arguments comprising the semantic role of Recipients, Goals, Beneficiaries (cf. Wanner 2009: 61) and Maleficiaries. Consequently, the morphological expression of dative case appears to allow for the proper realisation of an argument that is valued for a particular semantic role in-between the two extremes Proto-Agent and Proto-Patient, which are in turn dealt with by structural case. Thus, we will take the traditional definition of inherent (or lexical) case (see Chomsky 1981; Haider 2010: 251) seriously and assume that the DP *dem Jungen* ('the boy') comes equipped with a valued

---

[74] This may also be achieved by another constituent: *Heute wurde dem Jungen ein Kalender geschenkt* ('Today, a calendar was given to the boy as a present.', lit. today became the.DAT boy. DAT a.NOM calendar present.PTCP).

case-feature *u*C[dat] when inserted into phrasal syntax.[75] Therefore, dative arguments are self-sufficient at least in terms of their case-licensing, but nevertheless need to be associated with a constituent that provides them with a θ-value. This leaves the assignment of nominative case to the Theme-argument *ein Kalender* ('a calendar'). Just like in the regular eventive passive, the internal argument that comes with an unvalued case-feature may not be assigned accusative case due to the absence of v, which is why it has to be displaced to Spec, T.[76] The potential alternative of raising the dative argument leads the derivation to crash, since the unvalued case-feature on the Theme-argument may not be valued in Spec, T.

Given that English has lost its inherent dative case, the formation of a passive derived from a ditransitive predicate has to resort to an alternative strategy. In fact, English is bound to raise the indirect object (Recipient in the present case) to Spec, T in order for it to receive structural (nominative) case.[77] Thus, the lack of inherent case is structurally made up for by movement, as becomes observable on the basis of the structural representation in (143).

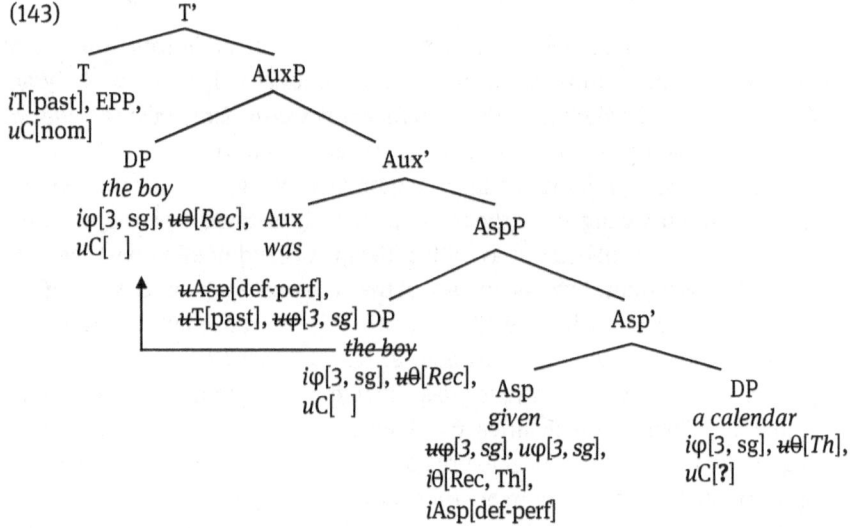

---

[75] The dative value nevertheless is introduced by an uninterpretable case-feature, as it is associated with the expression of a certain semantic role yet the argument in question still needs to be valued for that θ-role.

[76] Hence, the auxiliary agrees with the Theme (rather than the Recipient): *Dem Jungen wurden zehn Kalender geschenkt* ('The boy was presented ten calendars.', lit. the.DAT boy.DAT became.PL ten calendars present.PTCP).

[77] Locality considerations are responsible for raising the Recipient rather than the Theme in the present case.

While the indirect object thus properly receives structural case, the Theme-argument – unlike in German – remains without structural case due to the absence of v (as well as the fact that the Recipient occupies Spec, T). A way to deal with this deficiency may be found in the concept of default case assignment (cf. Schütze 2001; McFadden 2007).[78] A default case may occasionally be assigned, if the structural context sufficiently distinguishes the different arguments (as in the present case). In other words, one of the arguments may remain without a properly assigned (inherent or structural) case and instead retrieve a case value by default. As observable in copular constructions like *It is him* and *Er ist ein Student* ('He is a student', he is a.NOM student.NOM), this case is the accusative in English, whereas it is the nominative in German (cf. Schütze 2001: 208, 224; McFadden 2007: 229; Breul 2008: 240f.). Though making use of a different value, the two languages thus generally share the applicability of a last resort mechanism[79] which occasionally allows arguments to value their uC by default. This is at work in the English ditransitive passive in (143), where *a calendar* carries default accusative case (i.e. $uC[?]$ boils down to $uC[acc]$).[80] In German, on the other hand, T properly assigns nominative case to the direct object, given that the indirect one is self-sufficient in terms of carrying inherent case, as in (142).

This puts us in a position to deal with dative passive cases, which crucially differ from the WERDEN-passive (NOM and DAT) as well as BE-passive (NOM and default ACC) of ditransitive predicates in terms of case-assignment. In fact, the dative passive with *bekommen* ('receive') and *kriegen* ('receive') instantiates a nominative argument (*der Junge* 'the boy', lit. the.NOM boy.NOM) as well as an accusative one (*einen Kalender* 'a calendar', lit. a.ACC calendar.ACC), as we could see in (140). Given the absence of v and the fact that default case is nominative in German, the presence of accusative case on the Theme-argument is quite surprising. Additionally, the fact that the Recipient-argument carries nominative rather than dative case raises the question of how inherent specifications can be abrogated. This takes us back to the initial observation that *bekommen* ('receive')

---

78 Schütze (2001: 206) provides the following definition: "The default case forms of a language are those that are used to spell out nominal expressions (e.g., DPs) that are not associated with any case feature assigned or otherwise determined by syntactic mechanisms."
79 Note that McFadden (2007: 231) points out that "[d]efault case is not the case that is assigned when other cases fail, but the actual lack of case." This holds for the present cases, where there simply is no case value left.
80 The Recipient may also be licensed by a preposition, in which case the Theme is raised and properly retrieves nominative case from T (as this position is not occupied by the Recipient): *A calendar was given to the boy.*

and *kriegen* ('receive') retain verbal semantics, i.e. they are not fully grammaticalised as auxiliaries. While these forms have started to take up the life of an auxiliary by becoming sensitive to past participial forms (via uAsp), their thematic properties remain intact at least in so far as they retain their verbal association with a set of θ-roles, in the present case *i*θ[Rec, Th]. This allows them to occur as verbal forms that may properly project a v-layer since the Recipient is their external argument, as shown in (144).

(144)

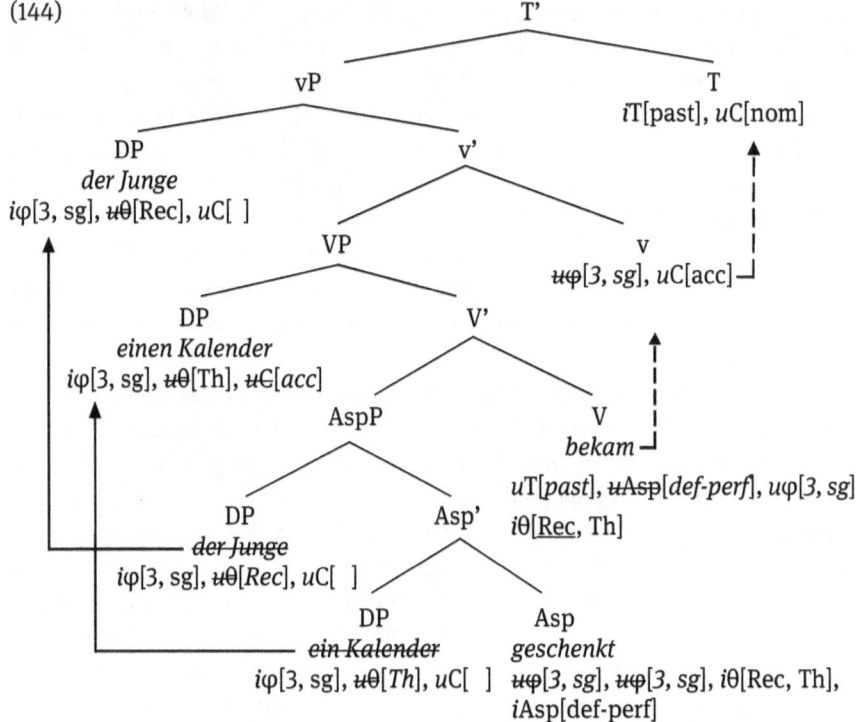

Unlike fully grammaticalised auxiliaries, the forms *bekommen* ('receive') and *kriegen* ('receive') by virtue of retaining a fully-functional θ-grid[81] are only compatible with verbal complements that bear similar thematic properties.

---

81 As we have seen, there is dialectal variation as to how much of this θ-grid is left. In fact, some dialects already allow transitive predicates that realise dative case in their active (and WERDEN-passive) instantiations to form a dative passive, as in *weil sie widersprochen bekam* ('because someone answered back to her', lit. because she answer.back.PTCP received) (cf. Gunkel 2003:103). In a similar vein, Bader & Häussler (2013) show that *bekommen* ('receive') is often not bound to be combined with verbs sharing the same semantic structure.

Accordingly, Haider (2010: 257) – referring to these as 'quasi-auxiliaries' or 'semi-lexical verbs' – claims that such elements "impose a format restriction for the thematic content they inherit from the selected participle". Whenever this is not obliged, the derivation crashes (at LF). The essential consequence of the strongly verbal nature of the dative passive 'auxiliaries' is that they have to be accompanied by the functional projection v, just like their transitive main verb counterparts. Accordingly, *bekommen* ('receive') and *kriegen* ('receive') introduce external arguments, unlike the embedded participial form, whose external argument (an Agent in the present case) is bound existentially and may only be introduced with the help of a BY-phrase. The derivation of the dative passive in (144) thus resembles the structures we encountered before with respect to what happens within AspP, but exhibits some salient distinctions with regard to the presence of a proper verbal domain (vP and VP) on top of it. Hence, the realisation of the two internal arguments of the participle *geschenkt* ('given as a present') is straightforward, but what happens to these in the domain of *bekommen/kriegen* deserves some special attention. In fact, the quasi-auxiliary – sensitive to the presence of a past participle due to its unvalued uAsp-feature – raises the internal argument, which has already been valued for a Theme-role, in order to value its $u\varphi$-feature. Given that a direct association with the predicate is reserved for internal arguments, the Theme-argument has to be raised to Spec, V, rather than the Recipient, which is bound to be associated with v. Thus, v raises the argument that bears a sufficient amount of Proto-Agent properties to semantically be compatible with the causative semantics of v. This, in turn, allows v to value its $u\varphi$-feature. After the successful application of V-to-v head-movement, the Theme-argument may receive accusative case in Spec, V, whereas the Recipient-argument has to move to Spec, T in order to value its uC on the basis of T's uC[nom].

This brings us back to the arguably most intricate property of this structural configuration, namely the question of why the Recipient does not bear dative case. In other words, why is the Recipient not inherently valued for dative case, but instead inflects for nominative case in Spec, T? This arguably has to do with the properties of inherent case, which are similar to default case in terms of being inserted at the point of spell-out, but quite unlike it in stemming from a lexical predisposition. However, this association of an inherent case with a given argument only succeeds, i.e. the uC-value may only be inserted at the point of spell-out, if the valued $u\theta$ (in this case $u\theta$[Rec]) bear the respective association in all their θ-positions. In the present example, this is crucially not the case, as the argument moves through Spec, v, a position in which the $i\theta$ of *bekommen* ('receive') are matched with those of *der Junge* ('the boy') to assure identity (see Haider 2010: 257 for an analysis in which this is described in terms of 'the pooling of the argument structure'). As the thematic roles of the dative-passive 'auxiliary' are not lexically associated with an inherent case, this case may not be morphologically instated at spell-out and hence the derivation crashes unless the argument moves into a position in which it can get structural (nominative) case. In the WERDEN-passive case in (142), the situation is fundamentally different as WERDEN does not bring in its own $i\theta$-features and hence does not affect the distribution and realisation of inherent case. Accordingly, as the clear association of the (Recipient) θ-role with the indirect object (in Spec, Asp) remains intact in this case, only the derivation in which the recipient instantiates dative case converges.

4.2.2.3 Semantic consequences of passivisation: existential binding

Now that the empirical domain of the present approach to the passive has been extended to impersonal and ditransitive passives, let us briefly address the semantic consequences of passivisation as imposed by (131). What needs to be clear up front in this context is that passivisation – despite having "effects on word order and the realization of arguments [–] does not change the propositional content of the clause" (Wanner 2009: 47; cf. also Siewierska 1984: 3).[82] In fact, the passive – traditionally defined as the marked alternative to active structures (cf. Siewierska 1984: 2f.)[83]– while suppressing an argument syntactically, does not do so semantically. In other words, "all arguments are still represented, [even] if not necessarily overtly" (Wanner 2009: 47). The implicit subject hence remains a salient part of the passive clause (cf. Siewierska 1988: 245). The present approach acknowledges these observations by tracing the difference between an active and a passive configuration back to the question of whether the external argument is expressed syntactically or solely semantically: in an active clause the argument is realised as part of the syntactic argument structure, and in a passive clause it is existentially bound. However, although active and passive are thus equivalent in terms of their truth conditions, some (non-propositional) difference in meaning may be attested (cf. Siewierska 1988: 245fn3).

The existential binding of the external argument has the effect of changing the 'relative prominence' of the arguments involved (cf. Blevins 2006: 236).

---

[82] Brinker (1971: 109) claims that active and passive show the highest degree of equivalence in meaning and are usually interchangeable, which is why he assumes that passivisation is almost completely of a stylistic nature.
[83] According to König & Gast (2009: 122) "[t]here is general agreement on the fact that the **active voice** is the basic voice in English and German" (emphasis in original).

Typically, this is claimed to 'promote' the object, whereas the subject is 'demoted' (cf. Siewierska 1988: 243f.; Abraham 2006a: 2, 8f., König & Gast 2009: 122). However, as we have seen in the context of impersonal passives, the former is apparently just an epiphenomenon rather than a central property of passivisation. This is underlined by the observation that the thematic range of potentially promoted objects, if present, is quite broad, whereas the demotion of a subject may be tied to a specific set of agentive properties (cf. Siewierska 1988: 243f.). Accordingly, Shibatani (1985: 830) claims that "the primary function [of passivisation] is that of 'agent defocusing'" (see also Haider's 1986: 15f. blocking of a designated argument). While we have come across some (marginal) exceptions to this in the context of unaccusatives in German, we could attribute these to ungrammatical but – for specific reasons – acceptable structures which hence do not substantially question the importance of an Agent-like argument for the denotation of a passive.[84] Hence, the present approach sticks to the importance of an external argument for passivisation. In fact, as we have seen, given that the choice of what is mapped as an external argument, i.e. to Spec, v, hinges on causativity rather than agentivity, not every external argument is automatically sufficient to give rise to a proper passive. Thus, while the presence of an external argument is a necessary condition for passivisation, it is the amount of Proto-Agent properties (cf. Dowty 1991) that eventually determines whether a given (external) argument may be existentially bound and hence give rise to passive semantics.

The lack of an (overtly expressed) agent in an A-position in passives follows from the existential binding of the associated thematic role. In the present approach, the operation in (175) lexically marks an external argument for existential binding and it is this lexical marking that leads to the syntactic suppression of the external argument (unless a θ-position is provided by HAVE). A successful lexical marking does not guarantee proper passive semantics, as it is determined as late as at LF whether this marking really leads to a proper existential binding on the basis of the argument's Proto-Agent properties. Assuming existential binding to be at the core of the passive suffices to account for the observation that an external argument is syntactically suppressed, while its semantic content is retained in terms of an open variable that may, but need not, explicitly be filled. It thus crucially accounts for the fact that "[t]he 'passive reading' is an interpretation of the clause in which none of the arguments of the

---

84 Note that these exceptions are occasionally also taken more seriously to the effect of questioning the importance of Agent-demotion. Accordingly, Abraham (2000: 146) claims that the passive's main function is not to allow Agent-less sentences, but this is just an epiphenomenon. The same point is made in Blevins (2006: 236).

verbs is missing" (Wanner 2009: 28). Eventually, passivisation via existential binding does not effect any changes on the semantic level other than the consequence that the external argument is not locally bound via functional application (λ-conversion), but rather remains a variable "to be determined contextually (or by an adjunct)" (Bierwisch 1990: 182).

This leaves the question of how to formally implement existential binding. Bierwisch (1990: 182f.) simply claims that there is an "open variable [which] replaces [the variable] originally bound by the subject θ-role". In a similar vein, Bresnan (1978: 20f.) represents the blocked argument in *The cake was eaten* as x and hence derives ∃xEAT(x,ιyCAKE(y)) (or, in her formalisation, simply (∃x) x EAT NP1 for *be eaten*). In the present approach, the past participial morpheme is responsible for picking out an external semantic role (if available) to be bound existentially by means of lexically marking it. This change affects the saturation of the external argument. As this is the only effect, the semantic structure of the participial predicate *geschlagen* ('hit'), as in *geschlagen wird* ('is (being) hit'), is propositionally identical to *schlägt* ('hit'), as represented in (145) (see also Rothstein 2001: 142).

(145) λyλxλe[HIT(e) & AG(e)=y & PAT(e)=x]
 a. HIT(e) & AG(e)=john & PAT(e)=bill *John schlägt Bill.*
             ('John hits Bill.')
 b. ∃y{HIT(e) & AG(e)=y & PAT(e)=bill]} *Bill wird geschlagen*
             ('Bill is (being) hit.')

Disambiguation between an active and a passive interpretation ensues as soon as λ-conversion either binds the variable with (the denotational meaning of) an argument realised in its local domain, as in (145a), or with a variable to be bound existentially (and possibly associated with an element in the co- or context), as in (145b). While the propositional readings of the two variants are thus equivalent, the passive evokes changes in terms of information structure. With respect to the latter, Wanner (2009: 110) points out that "[i]n English, the subject position is usually linked to the topic of a clause, and the passive is a way of making an argument that is not the agent the topic." Haspelmath (1990: 60f.) sees 'inactivisation' as the main function of the passive, from which "[t]he two functions of agent backgrounding and patient foregrounding follow automatically". This main (pragmatic or information structural) purpose of the passive is acknowledged in the present approach in terms of the argument structural detour over existentially binding the external argument.

Eventually, the contribution of passivisation is quite weak and essentially affects information structure, where its consequences may often also be expressed by other means (e.g. topicalisation in German). Hence, it is actually not surprising that the forms that are used to impose a passive reading are also employed for other purposes, e.g. encoding aspectual information (cf. Abraham 2006b: 463). In fact, the passive cross-linguistically is quite an aspect-sensitive phenomenon (cf. Leiss 1992: 71). This is for instance observable in Russian (and Latin), where a periphrastic passive may only be formed on the basis of a perfective predicate. In a similar vein, the Germanic prefix *ge-* was first and foremost an aspectual marker in earlier stages before being employed in participial contexts, where a passive sense was initially restricted to perfective instances (cf. Abraham 2006a: 7f.). Such observations led Beedham (1981; 1998) and Abraham (2006b: 484f.) to assume that the passive is even synchronically an aspectual category (or at least derived from one). Shibatani (1985: 841) also suggests that passive voice and perfectivity are semantically akin, but takes the passive as his starting point. To be precise, what is claimed here is that the passive's main function of inactivising the subject "has the effect of shifting the perspective from the agent's side to the patient's, and accordingly from the beginning to the end of the event" (Shibatani 1985: 841). Such correlations suggest that the relation between aktionsart (or event structure), aspectual marking and argument structure is an extremely fruitful field of work (see Klein 2010 for a groundbreaking attempt to have the event and argument structure converge into a single 'argument-time structure').

In the present approach, the strong relation between aspectual information and passive voice is acknowledged in the basic properties of past participles, which virtually unify passive and perfective ingredients rather than deriving one from the other. Accordingly, past participles introduce defective perfectivity, the consequences of which will be investigated in a more detailed fashion in the next section, i.e. chapter 4.2.3 on the analytic perfect. Additionally, they bring with them the lexical marking of an external argument for existential binding, which serves to suppress the syntactic realisation of an external argument (if there is one), but does not have any substantial semantic consequences apart from affecting information structure, as pointed out in the present section. Regardless of the specific technical incorporation, the close relation between passivity and perfectivity may arguably be traced back to the deverbal resultative adjectives that past participial forms historically originate from, as briefly discussed in chapter 2.6. The synchronic properties of past participles in the modern instantiations of the identity languages discussed in the present work may thus be assumed to stem from the inherent resultativity as well as object-orientation of their deverbal adjectival ancestors. With respect to the latter, what is particularly interesting is that the resultative adjective is a stative category that does not allow for an agentive reading, i.e. crucially disposes of the external argument in its entirety. Upon the grammaticalisation of a periphrastic passive, the participial element is arguably relieved of (some of) its adjectival restrictions, but still not capable of properly licensing an external argument, which is why a causative phase is bound to be introduced by means of existential binding.[85]

We will now turn to the aspectual contribution of past participial morphology, where it is striking that the past participle does not induce any substantial changes with respect to the aspectual reading in the periphrastic passive. In fact, as we have just seen, a periphrastic passive expresses the same propositional meaning as its active counterpart, where the only difference concerns how the external argument is dealt with. While the formation of a periphrastic passive thus bears certain information structural consequences, it leaves the temporal and aspectual properties unchanged, i.e. finiteness is provided by the auxiliary and the aspectual reading remains 'imperfective'. This raises the question of what the precise nature of the past participial aspectual contribution is and how it manages not to effect changes to the aspectual interpretation of periphrastic passives, whereas it arguably is a crucial component of the denotation of a periphrastic perfect.

4.2.3 The analytic perfect

Given that the occurrence of a past participle in a periphrastic passive arguably does not elicit any substantial aspectual consequences, the central problem of previous approaches to past participial identity was that they struggled to account for how a past participle in a periphrastic perfect may denote a perfect interpretation. The present approach accounts for this by means of taking into consideration the verbal semantics of the predicate on the basis of which past participle is based, on the one hand, as well as the relevant semantic contribution of the perfect auxiliary HAVE, on the other. In fact, past participles comprise a set of aspectual properties which only elicit proper perfectivity on the basis of a simple change of state, while HAVE introduces posteriority. The reason for this may be taken to be one of scope: whenever a CAUSE (which is necessarily atelic) is present in the event structure of the underlying predicate, the aspectual

---

[85] Abraham (1998: 157; 2000: 152f.) takes this to be at the core of the synchronic derivation of passive semantics, whereas we will acknowledge that it potentially plays a role diachronically, but is not the way in which a passive is derived in Modern Standard German or Present Day English.

properties of the past participle may not impose perfectivity on the more deeply embedded BECOME-predicate. The present chapter will explicate these aspectual properties in a more detailed fashion in order to provide an account of the compositional semantics of the periphrastic perfect.[86]

The discussion of the basic properties of past participles and the auxiliaries they occur with brought forth some formal features that may safely be assumed to play a crucial role in the denotation of a periphrastic perfect. The syntactically relevant formal features involved in the derivation of the periphrastic perfect are summarised in (146) and (147), where those properties that contribute to the temporal-aspectual denotation are given in bold.

(146) a. [$_{Asp}$ ARRIVED]: $u\varphi$[ ], $i\theta$[Th], ***i*Asp[def-perf]**
      b. [$_{Aux}$ HAVE]: uT[ ], $u\varphi$[ ], uAsp[ ], ***i*Asp[posterior]** (optional: $i\theta$[*val*])
      c. [$_T$ ∅]:   ***i*T [prs]**, EPP, uC[nom]

(147) a. [$_{Asp}$ CARRIED]: $u\varphi$[ ], $i\theta$[(∃Ag,) Th], ***i*Asp[def-perf]**
      b. [$_{Aux}$ BE]: uT[ ], $u\varphi$[ ], uAsp[ ]
      c. [$_T$ ∅]:   ***i*T [prs]**, EPP, uC[nom]

With respect to past participles like those in (146a) and (147a), we have seen that these are non-finite verb forms (i.e. verbs that value their uT[ ] on the basis of iT[non-fin] in word syntax)[87] which include aspectual information, namely defective perfectivity. On the basis of the unaccusative predicate in (146a), *i*Asp[def-perf] elicits a perfective denotation due to the presence of a simple change of state, whereas it is not sufficient to induce the termination of the atelic event in (147a). When this set of aspectual information induces perfectivity, as in the former case, the semantically vacuous auxiliary BE in (147b) may be used for the formation of an analytic perfect, as observable in languages resorting to auxiliary alternation. With respect to the temporal frame that BE inflects for on the basis of T as in (146c), the proper termination of the participial event suffices to induce T's posteriority via implication. The alternative employed in HAVE-only

---

[86] Note that the compositionality of the perfect is by no means uncontested (see e.g. Wunderlich 1970; Comrie 1985; Nerbonne 1985) and those approaches that adopt it exhibit fundamental differences with regard to which ingredients (past participle, auxiliary or both) contribute perfect semantics (cf. Musan 1998: 113–115, 121).

[87] Klingvall (2011: 56), following Larsson (2009: 61f.), claims that past participles are non-finite forms that lack a tense-specification altogether, whereas the Swedish supine is also non-finite but comes equipped with a past tense value. See Wegner (2017) for a discussion of the special status of the supine in Germanic.

languages is to overtly express the posteriority of T with respect to the participial event with the auxiliary HAVE in (146b). While this is not a vital necessity with past participles eliciting the value 'perfective', as in (146a), given that posteriority may be induced by implication, it marks a crucial ingredient in the case of past participles that are not properly ended by defective perfectivity, as the one in (147a). This atelic past participle does not include features that sufficiently allow for a perfective interpretation, which is why the combination of BE and the past participle CARRIED is insufficient to form a periphrastic perfect. Rather, the relevant perfect information on HAVE in (146b) is what allows for a perfect interpretation. In fact, HAVE does not only allow for the proper syntactic licensing of the lexically-marked external argument (iθ[Ag]), but its introduction of posteriority may (yet need not) suffice to bring about the termination of the participial event via implication.[88] Hence, the present approach is based on the assumption that perfect information at least partially resides in the perfect auxiliary HAVE (cf. Iatridou et al. 2001: 220). Yet, past participial morphology is also "instrumental in determining the perfect aspect of the sentence" (Ackema 1999: 111fn13; see Hornstein 1990), although this only clearly shows in the case of change of state predicates.[89] Eventually, then, the compositional ingredients in (146) substantially contribute to a perfect interpretation, while those in (147) are strongly contingent on their structural environment, i.e. the event structure of the underlying verb, with respect to denoting a proper perfect.

Now that we have identified the most salient ingredients of the periphrastic perfect, namely aspectual information on the past participle, posteriority on HAVE, and tense information on T, we may turn more closely to these ingredients and their interaction. With respect to the aspectual contribution of the past participle, the denotation of fully-fledged perfectivity was often assumed to be at the heart of the past participial form (see, amongst others, Zagona 1991; Grewendorf 1995; Giorgi & Pianesi 1997; Weber 2002: 208, and Remberger 2006: 121). Some diachronic evidence for this view may actually be drawn from Germanic languages featuring the past participial prefix GE-, which bore

---

[88] Note that the concept of 'posteriority' comes quite close to what is commonly referred to as a perfect time span, i.e. a temporal interval that spans from some point in the past to utterance time (cf. Iatridou et al. 2001: 195), at least in the sense that the time of utterance follows some part of the eventuality. This does not necessarily say anything about whether the eventuality still holds, though.

[89] Iatridou et al. (2001: 220f.) put it as follows: "[i]t might be argued that separation [of past participles from the auxiliary HAVE] is impossible because in 'have'-perfects, the features of the perfect partly reside on 'have'; on this view, the particle by itself is simply not sufficient to 'bring about' the perfect."

aspectual information in earlier stages of its development (cf. Leiss 1992: 56; Sybesma & Vanden Wyngaerd 1997: 210).⁹⁰ However, as we have seen repeatedly, the common argument challenging the assumption of perfectivity in approaches assuming past participial identity is the fact that past participles in passive uses do not elicit a perfective interpretation (cf. Wunderlich 1997: 10). Additional counter-evidence against this aspectual view comes from within the periphrastic perfect, namely from universal perfect readings (*John has loved Mary ever since he first met her*), where a sense of completion is absent (cf. Embick 1997: 148). Rather than denoting fully-fledged perfectivity, the perfect contribution of the past participle thus has to be somewhat more flexible. Tense-based approaches assuming anteriority (see, amongst others, Zeller 1994: 81, 89f.; Ballweg 1988; Musan 1998: 121f.; Belitschenko 1980: 376) are no less problematic in this respect, though. These assume that the situation (or eventuality) in question occurred prior to the moment of utterance (cf. Iatridou et al. 2001: 189f.).⁹¹ While anteriority is often taken to shift the event in its entirety into the past, there are more flexible approaches based on precedence that principally leave open whether the participial event is terminated (cf. Savova 1989: 68, 73f.). This is potentially flexible enough to grasp the universal perfect, though at the expense of simply shifting off the question of how (im)perfectivity eventually comes about. Nevertheless, even these more flexible approaches are challenged by the fact that the periphrastic passive exhibits simultaneity rather than any substantial amount of anteriority (or precedence). This issue is tackled in Breul & Wegner (2017), where past participial formation is taken to convert a situation into its post-time state. This post-time state – depending on verbal semantics – may, but need not, be the last instantiation of a given situation (cf. Breul & Wegner 2017: 44f.). In fact, contingent on the presence of dynamic aspect (as introduced by WERDEN, but not by BE), subsequent sub-situations of homogeneous events may come about and simultaneity is thus possible (cf. Breul & Wegner 2017: 47f.). The occasional simultaneity of heterogeneous situations, on the other hand, follows from the semantic contribution of WERDEN, which foreshadows the existence of a post-time state, whose constitutive situation holds at the present (cf. Breul & Wegner 2017: 47f.). This approach is arguably more insightful than one based on precedence. However, it does not

---

90 Wurmbrand (2012a: 160) assumes that there is still some substance to this assumption today by proposing that past participial forms that are composed with the help of GE- are lexically valued for [T: perf].

91 As indicated above, this does not equal past tense specifications as it is – in Reichenbach's (1947) terms – not the precedence of Reference time with respect to Speech time, but rather the precedence of Event time with respect to Reference time that matters here (cf. Iatridou et al. 2001: 190).

acknowledge the relevant perfect semantic contribution of HAVE (rather than WERDEN) and arguably puts too much of an emphasis on stativity as a factor preventing simultaneity in eventive constructions, which is not cross-linguistically valid in the context of BE. Additionally, it shares with other flexible approaches that it relies to a crucial extent on implication with respect to whether a situation is brought to an end. The present approach to a certain extent also does so, but arguably takes things one step ahead in terms of acknowledging the relevant contribution of both the past participle and HAVE, which crucially diminishes the amount of implication.

Despite their shortcomings, the latter approaches based on precedence and a posterior state are arguably more appealing than the strict perfectivity- and anteriority-based ones by virtue of grasping both the imperfectivity of the periphrastic passive as well as the (common) perfectivity of the analytic perfect. The novel approach laid out in the present work is also based on a more flexible understanding in the sense that the event structure of the underlying predicate plays a salient role in terms of whether or not perfectivity grammatically comes about. This idea comes close to what Iatridou et al. (2001: 211f.) claim: (un)boundedness, i.e. the completion of a situation (or eventuality),[92] "is contributed by syntacticosemantic features of the verb that are retained when the verb becomes a participle" (Iatridou et al. 2001: 211f.). This approach to the semantic terminativity of a situation as strongly based on verbal properties is arguably flexible enough to account for the universal perfect under the assumption that telic predicates and activities encode boundedness in a periphrastic perfect, whereas statives need not do so (cf. Iatridou et al. 2001: 210f.).[93] Such an (un)bounded eventuality is then embedded within a perfect time span (cf. Iatridou et al. 2001: 211f.). This view based on boundedness also has repercussions for the denotation of anteriority, which is not taken to be expressed by an explicit feature, but rather assumed to follow from the boundedness of the participial situation and hence absent in the context of a universal perfect (cf. Iatridou et al. 2001: 213f.). While we will follow the latter intuition in terms of assuming that anteriority may be derived from the participial

---

92 Iatridou et al. (2001: 191) define boundedness as follows: "An eventuality is described as unbounded when it is ongoing at an interval (and is therefore not asserted to have reached an endpoint-achievement of the goal, in the case of telics; termination for atelics). An eventuality is described as bounded when it is contained in an interval (i.e., when it is asserted to have completed/terminated). The syntactico-semantic feature [unbounded] is realized by progressive or imperfective morphology, the feature [bounded] by the perfective."

93 Note that it is somewhat questionable – at least in the case of activities – that the syntacticosemantic features of the predicate contribute boundedness. The present approach rather traces the boundedness of such cases back to the contribution of HAVE, which is something we will return to in more detail shortly.

event if this is properly brought to an end (i.e. bounded or perfective), the present approach differs from Iatridou et al.'s (2001: 211f.) understanding of how boundedness is induced. In fact, Iatridou et al.'s (2001) approach is incompatible with the assumption of past participial identity since it predicts eventive passives of telic predicates and activities to denote boundedness and thus cannot explain the imperfectivity of passive instantiations. Hence, we will rather assume that the aspectual information stored on the past participial form is able to grammatically impose perfectivity if the underlying predicate is a simple change of state. This crucially differs from the assumption that it is all about the verbal properties, which are retained in past participle formation. Instead, while the verbal event structure is decisive for the denotation of perfectivity on the basis of unaccusative predicates, it is insufficient for encoding 'boundedness' on the basis of unergative and transitive ones. In those cases, we assume that external help is called for in order to induce the completion of the underlying event. This brings us back to the contribution of the auxiliary HAVE.

As we have seen, in addition to approaches which claim that perfect readings stem from temporal or aspectual information on the past participle, there are those that assume that perfect information resides only in the auxiliaries: Oku (1998: 34f.), for instance, associates perfectivity with the perfect auxiliary HAVE and Höhle (1992: 116) assumes that the auxiliary contributes anteriority. In a similar vein, Wunderlich (1997: 14f.) associates the function POST with perfect auxiliaries, which are hence taken to introduce posterior states (or processes). Wunderlich's (1997: 14) approach, however, also acknowledges a participial contribution by claiming that the auxiliaries differ in their sensitivity to a past participle with the specification [+perf] or [–perf] (Wunderlich 1997: 14). In fact, what is assumed here is that verbs selected by *sein* "are inherently perfective [and] do not really need an auxiliary that marks perfect" (Wunderlich 1997: 13). This at first sight seems to come quite close to what is assumed in the present approach, where HAVE is called for if the participle does not induce perfectivity. However, Wunderlich (1997: 13) does not consistently follow through with this route, but rather argues that the distinction between [+perf] and [–perf] does not necessarily bear semantic substance, as there are "verbs that are arbitrarily marked for *sein*-perfect". In other words, the verbs that have [+perf] need not necessarily give rise to a perfect reading (cf. Wunderlich 1997: 4).[94] This forces him to assume that BE is also able to contribute posteriority in order to denote a

---

94 Alternatively, see Lieber & Baayen (1997) for an approach to auxiliary selection in Dutch that is strongly based on verbal semantics: "When the eventual position or state of the verb's highest argument can be inferred from its meaning it takes BE, otherwise it takes HAVE." (Ackema 1999: 118)

perfect interpretation (cf. Wunderlich 1997: 4). This is crucially different in the present approach, where the auxiliaries differ with respect to whether they contribute to a perfect denotation: while BE is semantically vacuous, HAVE is bound to introduce posteriority.[95]

Even in approaches that do not attribute any relevant perfect information to the auxiliaries, their semantic role is typically not ignored, though. Rather, their temporal meaning is just restricted to establishing a relation between speech and reference time (cf. Zeller 1994: 91). This takes us back to the third essential ingredient of the periphrastic perfect, namely the presence of tense information, which is introduced on T, but may only overtly be expressed with the help of an auxiliary in periphrastic constructions. This is the source for the eponymous characteristic of the present perfect to encode the relation between a perfect situation, e.g. conceived as "a state that (in some sense or other) results from [...] the situation expressed by the verb itself" (Löbner 2002: 378f.), and present tense.[96] While the importance of tense information for the denotation of a proper perfect is not neglected in the present approach, the perfect is taken to be inherently complex in identity languages. It may either follow from a participial form that denotes a perfective situation or from the relevant perfect information (posteriority) on HAVE. This assumption takes seriously the compositional nature of the periphrastic perfect by correlating a complex meaning with a complex form (cf. Zeller 1994: 93). That this is a necessity becomes obvious once we take into consideration that the large majority of perfects is formed periphrastically (cf. Larsson 2009: 63) and that the universal perfect reading is in fact absent with synthetic perfects (cf. Iatridou et al. 2001: 216). Thus, we generally follow approaches like Ballweg (1988), Ehrich & Vater (1989) and Ehrich (1992), which claim "that the perfect reading results from the combination of the participle with an auxiliary" (Vater 2002: 357). However, this is rendered somewhat opaque by the fact that perfective past participles may be introduced by the semantically-vacuous BE, which nevertheless supplies a temporal frame by virtue of inflecting for finiteness. Additionally, given that HAVE may give rise to a periphrastic perfect

---

95 An appealing alternative to the perfect semantic contribution of HAVE comes from Klein's (1999: 73, 76) investigation of the relation between argument and event structure, where past participial morphology is taken to be insufficient to attribute posteriority to all of the arguments involved. In fact, the perfect auxiliary is assumed to attribute posteriority properties ('Nachzeiteigenschaften') to the external argument, whereas past participial morphology contributes such properties for arguments not introduced by *hab-* ('have') (cf. Klein 1999: 73).

96 Although the term 'present perfect' is occasionally carelessly used as a general term for the periphrastic perfect, it should of course be restricted to instances with auxiliaries inflected for present tense, while there also is the past perfect, future perfect, and tenseless perfect (cf. Portner 2011: 1218).

with an imperfective past participle, the question of what relevant perfect information such forms introduce is raised. Before we turn to this intricate issue, let us first focus on the general compositional make-up of the periphrastic perfect.

4.2.3.1 The compositional make-up of the periphrastic perfect

The three major ingredients of the periphrastic perfect, i.e. defective perfectivity, posteriority (if overtly expressed) and tense information, are structurally distributed over an equal number of functional projections. As we can see in the structural representation of the compositional derivation of the periphrastic perfect in (148), another essential ingredient is the event structure of the underlying verb from which a past participle derived.

(148)
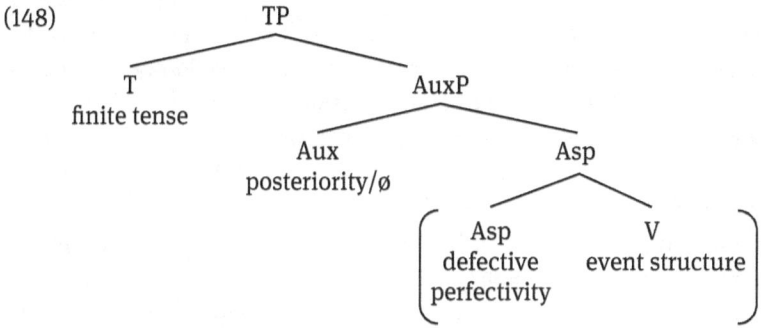

This decomposition of the components of the periphrastic perfect comes rather close to the fairly standard approach to the structure of the perfect as consisting of T, Asp and vP (cf. Pancheva 2003: 282) with the crucial addition of Aux as a potential carrier of relevant perfect information. Accordingly, while the traditional assumption is that the analytic perfect comes about by the interplay of tense (selecting aspect), aspect (selecting aktionsart) and aktionsart (cf. Pancheva 2003: 282), it is assumed here that aspectual information is 'scattered' (cf. Giorgi & Pianesi 1997: 39) whenever HAVE is around. In fact, aspectual information is an integral part of the past participial marker, which conflates with a verbal element in word syntax, as well as the perfect auxiliary HAVE. The former contains defective perfectivity and hence elicits (im)perfectivity on the basis of the properties of its verbal complement, whereas posteriority is expressed by HAVE regardless of the aspectual setting of its complement.

In line with the criticism levelled against a simple temporal or aspectual character of the perfect, it boils down to a complex combination of temporal and aspectual information contingent on event structure. In other words, the perfect is compositionally derived by the interplay of several aspects and hence "structurally more complex than other grammatical aspects such as the perfective or imperfective" (Pancheva 2003: 281).[97] This is grasped by a highly restricted set of functional heads and their interaction in terms of (formal) features. Accordingly, the present approach is strongly feature-based and hence does without a large number of additional functional projections. This is unlike what is assumed in recent (anti-lexicalist) approaches, which put emphasis on the cartographic nature of the verbal and temporal domain, for instance by holding a designated temporal (see Iatridou et al. 2001) or aspectual head (see Demirdache & Uribe-Etxebarria 2007) responsible for introducing the perfect (cf. Larsson 2009: 60).[98] While the cartographic perspective is by no means incompatible with what is proposed here,[99] the feature-based approach is opted for in order to retain transparency with respect to the underlying question of past participial (non-)identity. This allows us to stick to the traditional assumption of auxiliaries heading functional projections right above the (lexical) verbal domain (which may or may not feature the functional projection v) (cf. Larsson 2009: 60). Given that these basic structural considerations are sufficiently flexible for our purposes in the present work, we will now zoom in on the precise semantic contribution of each of the ingredients and their interaction in the periphrastic perfect.

Temporal and aspectual semantics are traditionally grasped on the basis of the system put forth by Reichenbach (1947). This system describes temporal relations by means of resorting to three basic coordinates: Speech time (S), Reference time (R), and Event time (E). S marks the time of utterance, R stands for the point (or interval) of reference and E expresses the point (or interval) at which a situation (or eventuality) holds (cf. Iatridou et al. 2001: 190).[100] Building on Reichenbach's (1947) system, Klein (1994) (see also Klein 1992: 532f., 535) distinguishes between the Time of the Situation (TSit), Topic Time

---

97 Ehrich & Vater (1989: 104) refer to this as the complexity-hypothesis to the perfect.
98 Larsson (2009: 60f.) even resorts to "a reduced biclausal structure with two separate TPs, one introducing a finite tense relating to the speech time, the other introducing a non-finite tense with the value [PAST]" (Larsson 2009: 61). See also Cowper (2005: 33) and Guéron (2007: 375f.) for biclausal approaches to the perfect.
99 See Guéron (2007: 369f.) for an alternative exploiting all of the functional projections constituting the clause, i.e. C associated with the Speech or Reference Time, T associated with Assertion time, and v+V predicated of Assertion time. We will not elaborate on these cartographic possibilities here.
100 Note that the terms 'situation' and 'eventuality' are taken to be on a par here with respect to serving as maximally neutral cover terms for states, events, processes, and activities. Crucially, the term 'situation' is not in any way intended to establish a connection to 'situation semantics' or the like.

(TT), and Utterance Time (TU). While TU is the time at which the utterance is made, TT is the time for which a given claim is made (cf. Klein 1992: 532f., 535). The relation between these two components is governed by tense information (cf. Klein 1992: 538). To be precise, TU is contained within TT in the present tense, whereas TT precedes TU in the past tense and TT follows TU in the future tense (cf. Klein 1992: 538). This leaves the aspectual component, which is particularly important, as we assume with Klein (1994) and Lübbe & Rapp (2011: 265f.) that finite verbs mark tense but not aspect, whereas participles mark aspect but are non-finite. At the centre of this component lies TSit, i.e. the time (or interval) at which the given eventuality holds. In fact, Klein (1992: 538) suggests that the aspectual component relates TSit to TT and claims that TT is in the posttime of TSit in the case of the present perfect (cf. Klein 1992: 538). As Klein (1992: 538) insists, "posttime is not defined by what is the case at TSit, nor by what is the case after TSit: it is just the time after TSit."[101] In a similar vein, Lübbe & Rapp (2011: 266) point out that the TT of a participle is not grammatically determined (pragmatics or temporal adverbials fulfil this role), whereas the relation between TT and TU (finite information) and the relation between TT and TSit (aspect) is. The latter aspectual relation is typically taken to entail that a situation is perceived in its entirety in the case of perfective aspect (cf. Haspelmath 2002: 65). This does justice to the traditional understanding of perfective aspect.[102] Equipped with these general considerations about (perfect) tense and aspect as well as the more detailed aspects of perfectivity (or boundedness) and posteriority, let us now turn to how the present approach handles perfect meaning.

What is fairly uncontroversial and can hence be taken over from Klein's (1992; 1994) account is that finite tense information relates TT to TU, which allows for the basic options past, present and future. In past participial periphrases, this information is introduced in T and overtly realised on the basis of an auxiliary, which gives rise to the past, present and future passive and the past, present and future perfect. This leaves the denotation of a 'posttime' and the perfectivity of the verbal event, both of which are more difficult to grasp. With respect to the former, the present approach suggests that the posteriority of a participial situation may either come about by implication if the participle elicits a perfective situation or it may be introduced by the perfect auxiliary

---

[101] The same intuition is still present in Klein (2010: 1241), where it is argued that expressions like *have slept* and *have fallen* "add a posttime, and they do not say anything about the descriptive properties which are assigned to any argument at this posttime."
[102] As Guéron (2007: 373) points out, "the speaker focuses on the boundaries of the event, ignoring its internal structure".

HAVE. In either case, TT is in the posttime of TSit, although this need not necessarily enforce boundedness (unless perfectivity is grammatically induced by participial morphology). This marks a deviation from approaches that hold that posteriority (or the denotation of a posttime) is a general capacity of past participial morphology, but is in line with those that take the perfect semantic contribution of HAVE seriously (see, e.g., Klein 1992: 538). The contribution of HAVE is a vital necessity for the formation of a periphrastic perfect whenever the past participle is unable to convey a perfective denotation. If it is, on the other hand, the perfective value makes up for the absence of posteriority when occurring with the auxiliary BE in auxiliary alternating languages, as this completion of the event allows posteriority to be implied (see also Grewendorf 1995: 83, where it is claimed that perfectivity entails anteriority).

Focussing on the (im)perfectivity of past participles, the present account generally follows approaches emphasising the importance of verbal properties (cf. Iatridou et al. 2001: 211f.).[103] However, it substantially differs from these in that more fine-grained event structural properties (see Dowty's 1979 decompositional approach) rather than merely aktionsart distinctions are considered. Actually, it is tempting and often sufficient to resort to differences in aktionsart in terms of telic and atelic predicates, a distinction based on "whether or not a situation is described as having an inherent or intended endpoint" (Depraetere 1996: 7). Simply claiming that perfectivity is determined based on telicity would properly account for the consistent (im)perfectivity of intransitive predicates (unaccusatives vs. unergatives). The imperfectivity of telic (di-)transitives, i.e. achievements and accomplishments, in passive constructions (*Der Schlüssel wird von Peter gefunden* 'The key is (being) found by Peter.'), on the other hand, raises problems against the backdrop of an identity approach. Under the assumption that perfectivity is grammatically enforced by the aspectual information on the past participle as a function of verbal properties, a more fine-grained picture is called for. In terms of the underlying event structure, what is striking is that only those past participles that denote simple changes of state (*arrive, disappear, arise, die, melt*$_{intransitive}$, *break*$_{intransitive}$) are consistently perfective. Since these are semantically reminiscent of the resultative deverbal adjectives of earlier stages that crucially do not introduce causative semantics (although they are derived from transitives), we may

---

103 While perfectivity and telicity arguably are unified in Iatridou et al.'s (2001) boundedness, see Binnick (1991: 191), Borik (2002), Depraetere (1995), and Verkuyl (1989) for approaches focusing on the importance of a distinction between the two concepts telicity and perfectivity. We will also take this distinction seriously here.

thus claim that perfectivity is only properly instated on the basis of the participial contribution if there is a simple change of state. To be precise, whenever there semantically is a CAUSE in the verbal semantics, perfectivity is not induced by the past participial morpheme and the same holds for inherently atelic phases (DO) (see Dowty 1979; for CAUSE, BECOME and DO and Filip 2011; for a brief overview of problems and merits of a decompositional approach).[104] If the verbal semantics only include a BECOME-predicate without a CAUSE (unaccusatives and telic two-place unaccusatives), on the other hand, perfectivity is successfully instated, i.e. TSit is properly terminated. Hence, the aspectual contribution of a given past participle is determined by its verbal event structure, although a perfective reading may also come about via implication on the basis of the posteriority introduced by HAVE. Eventually, then, the aspectual information stored on the past participial form is crucially different from the perfectivity in aspectual languages like Russian, Latin or Bulgarian. In Russian, for instance, perfectivity always induces a result state and hence imposes a telic reading regardless of the event structural properties of the underlying verb (cf. Basilico 2008: 1730). This insensitivity to verbal semantics is shared by other Slavic languages like Bulgarian, as we have seen, but not by the identity languages of Germanic and Romance. These differ in that perfectivity is not generally able to introduce a result, but rather is 'defective', i.e. the past participial marker may only successfully impose perfectivity or boundedness if the underlying event structure allows for this. Accordingly, we may refer to the aspectual contribution of past participles as 'defective perfectivity' or its clumsy (but less judgmental) alternative 'event-structure sensitive perfectivity'.

The compositional ingredients of the periphrastic perfect that we have identified in (148) may now be supplemented by the semantic properties of the individual components as in (149).

---

104 Assuming an atomic CAUSE as part of the decompositional semantics of transitive achievements (in addition to accomplishments) is fairly non-standard (i.e. not part of Dowty's 1979 aspect calculus), but may be justified by the following observations. First, the causative alternation that ensues with predicates like *melt* (*The ice melted*, *The sun melted the ice*) and *sink* (*The boat sank*, *The navy sank the boat*) shows that achievements may generally be associated with a CAUSE. Second, even predicates that do not partake in the causative alternation like *find* and *recognise* seem to involve a more abstract CAUSE (e.g. a mental predisposition of looking for or knowing something, respectively).

(149)

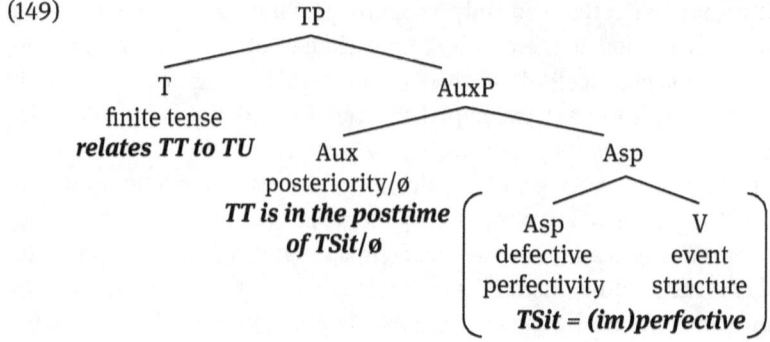

The explanatory force of this compositional approach to the periphrastic perfect becomes apparent once we turn to the properties of unaccusative and unergative predicates in a language that makes use of auxiliary alternation. Two such cases from German and a sketchy visualisation of their temporal semantics can be found in (150).

(150) a. Lena ist verschwunden.
    Lena is disappear.PTCP
    'Lena has disappeared.'

    TSit   TT   TU
    ←—————•|←——X→

  b. Die Kirche hat gebrannt.
    the church has burn.PTCP
    'The church has burned.'

    TSit   TT   TU
    ←————|→ ←——X→

On the basis of the unaccusative predicate in (150a), the defective perfectivity of the past participle elicits the value 'perfective' (or 'bounded'), which boils down to imposing an overt endpoint. This boundary may be perceived as a result state that properly brings TSit to an end, i.e. assures that there are no further instances of the participial event. In terms of establishing a relation to TT, the presence of this point of completion, i.e. the fact that TSit has ceased, implies that TSit precedes TT. Though not made explicit, TT is thus interpreted as posterior to the participial event (TSit < TT) and the event is viewed in its entirety. In other words, there is no overt expression of the relation of TSit to TT in such BE-perfect cases in languages using auxiliary alternation, but this is only derived from the boundedness that is imposed upon TSit.[105] This leaves relating TT to TU, which is managed by tense information on T. In the present case, this tense information conveys that TU is contained within TT and is overtly expressed on Aux. Eventually, while the situation resulting from the participial event (a result state) lasts, it is clear that the disappearing-event has reached completion. In a nutshell, perfectivity is fully instantiated and from this aspectual value, we can derive that the event that lead to the result state of disappearance lies in the past (with respect to TT). This is also assumed by Grewendorf (1995: 83), who claims that the completion of an event (perfectivity) entails anteriority of the participial event (not vice versa, as in Ballweg 1989; Klein 1994). The same point is made in Abraham (2000: 152), who suggests that perfectivity introduces a result state that implies the event that lead to it.

With atelic predicates like the Theme-unergative in (150b) essential differences ensue. These follow from the computation of the aspectual information and the verbal event structure, which elicits the value 'imperfective' (or 'unbounded') on the basis of an atelic predicate (e.g. DO). This has crucial consequences for the denotation of a periphrastic perfect, since there is no way to induce posteriority, thus relate TSit to TT, from an imperfective participial situation. In other words, there is no way to derive the precedence of TSit (with respect to TT) via implication if the event is still ongoing. This deficiency calls for external help, which is why HAVE is required to introduce relevant perfect information, namely posteriority.[106] Whereas the assumption of posteriority on the past participle is misguided in that it is both too weak to grasp perfective events and too strong in the context of the periphrastic passive, attributing this aspectual ingredient to HAVE does not face such problems. In fact, this contribution allows us to account for how the past participial deficiency of properly

---

105 As we have seen, the traditional way to grasp proper perfectivity is in terms of TSit in its entirety preceding TT. The present approach slightly deviates from this, although it is by no means incompatible with the traditional approach, where more fine-grained differences would then have to be held responsible for the difference between perfectivity (all instances of TSit precede TT) and posteriority (establishing a perfect time span in the sense that TT follows at least one sub-eventuality of TSit), as both mark relations between TSit and TT.

106 We have already seen plenty of evidence for the presence of perfect information on HAVE (most importantly with respect to the PPP, PPI and IPP, as well as predicates that select have although there is no argument structural reason for this, namely two-place unaccusatives like *einleuchten* 'resemble' and *fehlen* 'lack'). Evidence for the posteriority of HAVE may also be drawn from the behaviour of non-identity languages like Bulgarian (and Swedish), where the perfect participle autonomously establishes a perfect time span regardless of event structure in the absence of a perfect auxiliary, quite unlike in identity languages, where posteriority has to be brought in by the perfect auxiliary HAVE in order to establish a perfect time span (see Wegner 2017).

denoting perfectivity is made up for in the context of a periphrastic perfect. Eventually, posteriority makes sure that TSit precedes TT and via implication allows us to derive that TSit has come to an end, which marks the default (resultative or experiential) interpretation. This follows naturally since the main purpose of the perfect is to shift the eventuality to a point prior to TT and if there is no strong evidence to the contrary, this is taken to imply that no further instances of TSit hold. Accordingly, although the underlying participle does not introduce the value 'perfective', the event is viewed in its entirety due to the presence of posteriority and hence the situation is still considered to be ended. Depending on the precise nature of the aktionsart-properties of the underlying predicate, this default interpretation may, however, be overturned. This becomes clear in the context of atelic predicates. These regularly allow for an interpretation in which the participial event is ongoing in the context of an adverbial SINCE-phrase, the so-called universal perfect. While this shows most clearly in the context of stative cases like *John has been sick since July* and *Jack has loved Kate ever since he first saw her*, it occasionally also crops up in the case of activities like the English counterpart of (150b): *The church has burned since three hours*.[107] Such cases are less readily retrievable in German, where (150b) is reluctant to modification by *seit drei Stunden* ('since three hours') and the same carries over to stative counterparts. Even though König & Gast (2009: 89) explicitly deny this, what is striking is that the reading that obtains from interpreting such a structure apparently involves an ongoing eventuality.[108] Clearly, even if this use of the perfect is ruled out for German (and the availability of the universal perfect is thus properly parameterised), the general availability of a periphrastic perfect granting an ongoing situation provides evidence for the grammatical imperfectivity of past participles derived from predicates other than simple changes of state. A similar sense of an imperfective participial situation may be attested in the case of experiential readings, although these rely on the iteration of an event, where at least one (sub-)eventuality has to have

---

107 Cf.: *A fire in Sweetwater Creek State Park in Douglas County has burned since Saturday. About one acre of the hiking and walking trail burned. As of Sunday, it was 90 percent contained.* (https://www.ajc.com/news/local/latest-fire-breaks-out-georgia-gwinnett-college-campus/yQ9Xuepv01zvBbohlmF2xM/, accessed on January 4, 2017)

108 This might somewhat hesitantly be taken to suggest that such a construction is primarily degraded due to the availability of a morphological present tense that involves progressive properties (consider *Die Kirche brennt seit drei Stunden*, 'The church has been burning since three hours.', lit. the church burns since three hours). Note that there are cases of the universal perfect in German that are hardly degraded at all, e.g. Rothstein's (2008: 111) example in (153a) below. This puts König & Gast's (2009: 89) strict judgments into question.

come to an end.[109] Before we turn to the past participial contribution in 'imperfective' cases, i.e. the nature of the thin broken line in (150b), and the question of how the distinct perfect readings come about, let us briefly dwell on the derivation of a periphrastic perfect on the basis of a 'perfective' past participle in HAVE-only languages.

In HAVE-only languages like English, simple changes of state like *Lena has disappeared*, i.e. the English counterpart to (150a), also introduce HAVE, given that BE is incompatible with past participles that bear the value 'perfective'. Accordingly, posteriority is overtly introduced in cases in which this only comes about via implication in languages entertaining auxiliary alternation. This, however, turns out to be unproblematic given that the temporal semantic contribution of HAVE and Asp is not identical. In fact, while the former introduces posteriority, assuring that TSit precedes TT (and hence setting up a perfect time span), the latter denotes boundedness, thus inducing completion of TSit. Therefore, the two are not in complementary distribution and both ingredients may readily be spelled out. Accordingly, the temporal semantics of an unaccusative BE-perfect in a language like German is entirely analogous to that of an unaccusative HAVE-perfect in a language like English, as represented in (151).

(151) Lena has disappeared.

       TSit   TT   TU
    ◄────────►|◄────X──►

There is one crucial difference with respect to the determination of TT, though, namely whether an ingredient that relates TSit to TT is overtly introduced (posteriority on HAVE) or just derived by implication (from the perfectivity of TSit). However, this does not have any effect on the eventual perfect interpretation, i.e. in terms of their relevant perfect semantics the combinations of BE + *verschwunden* and HAVE + *disappeared* are identical.

Before we move on to the range of perfect uses, what remains to be discussed with respect to the aspectual information on the past participle is its contribution in cases in which it does not denote proper perfectivity. The general situation with respect to the specific aspectual value denoted by the past participle should be clear by now: those derived from simple changes of state (BECOME) are

---
[109] Note that these are always formed from imperfective participles in the non-identity language Bulgarian (cf. Pancheva 2003: 295f.). This underlines that the past participle in identity languages does not impose perfectivity unless derived from a simple change of state. Quite generally, such correlations emphasise the appeal of contrastive analyses between aspectual and non-aspectual languages.

perfective, whereas those derived from atelic processes (DO) or generally including a causative ingredient (CAUSE) do not sufficiently instantiate completion. As hinted at before, this may be justified by virtue of a hierarchical analysis of how events are composed: the aspectual head may only impose perfectivity on a telic complement, i.e. whenever a CAUSE intervenes (between Asp and BECOME) or the head combines with an atelic DO, the predicate is not rendered perfective by past participle formation. With respect to the types of verbs introduced in chapter 1.2, the former characterisation of a simple change of state only fits the classes of unaccusative (e.g. *disappear, arrive, break*) and telic two-place unaccusative predicates (e.g. *gelingen* 'succeed', *unterlaufen* 'occur'), where the latter differ in the presence of an argument that is affected by the change of state. On the basis of these kinds of verbs past participial morphology successfully conveys perfective semantics. Atelic cases (e.g. unergatives like *burn, cough, dance*, atelic transitives like *carry, pull, follow, love* and atelic two-place unaccusatives like *schmeicheln* 'flatter', *einleuchten* 'make sense'), on the other hand, fail to denote perfectivity. The same also pertains to telic transitives, i.e. achievements (e.g. *lose, start, recognise*) as well as accomplishments (e.g. *eat, built, mow*). These cannot be perfective or else their imperfective use in periphrastic passives like *Der Rasen wird gemäht* ('The lawn is (being) mowed', lit. the lawn becomes mow.PTCP) raises problems.[110] Although these comprise a change of state, namely an incremental one in the case of accomplishments and a punctual one in the case of achievements, the presence of a CAUSE prevents perfectivity from coming about. While the precise event structural characteristics of these types of verbs need not concern us here, what matters is that an atelic CAUSE-phase triggers the change of state in question in such cases. Eventually, then, the presence of an atelic period renders it impossible for defective perfectivity to impose completion upon the telic BECOME-predicate, as the CAUSE intervenes. This leaves the question of what it means for a past participle to be incapable of denoting perfectivity. What is fairly clear in this context is that it would be problematic to assume that the participial contribution of aspectual information turns out to be semantically vacuous in those cases in which perfectivity cannot be instated. Rather, the defective perfectivity also has a semantic consequence

---

110 We will return to supposedly exceptional cases of bare uses of these predicates that nevertheless seem to denote a result (e.g. the accomplishment *build* in *Entlang der Wupper gebaut, erstreckt sich die Schwebebahn über das ganze Tal*, 'Built alongside the Wupper, the suspension railway spans the whole valley.', lit. alongside the Wupper build.PTCP extends SELF the suspension.monorail across the whole valley) in chapter 4.3.1, where the basic claim is that the posteriority is contextually imposed, as imperfective readings are also available.

in case it cannot evoke a proper perfective reading by virtue of ending a sub-event of the DO- or CAUSE-phase. In fact, as already hinted at by the broken line in (150b), let us assume that a sub-event (of the DO- or CAUSE-phase) is brought to an end in such cases, yet this does not suffice for the whole situation to be brought to an end (nor the BECOME-phase – if there is one – to be evoke a change of state).

What remains to be addressed is the question of why defective perfectivity may only impose perfectivity upon simple changes of state. Lübbe & Rapp (2011: 271) – focussing on attributive constructions – find a reason for different readings in terms of whether a situation is brought to an end in the homogeneity as opposed to heterogeneity of the underlying past participial events. This is based on the traditional claim that atelic verbs possess sub-intervals that are identical to the overall event (homogeneous), whereas telic ones are inhomogeneous in that they possess sub-intervals that are not identical to the overall event (cf. Lübbe & Rapp 2011: 271; see also Dowty 1979). This leads Lübbe & Rapp (2011: 271) to define perfectivity in the sense that it effects that *one* event is included in TT in full: for telic verbs this is only the case if the overall event is completed (strong perfective aspect), whereas for atelic verbs it is also the case if the overall event is still ongoing (weak perfective aspect). This is supposed to provide an explanation for why the past participial perfectivity brings telic events to an end (i.e. TSit is fully included in TT), whereas completion is not necessarily evoked with atelic events (cf. Lübbe & Rapp 2011: 272). This is intuitively appealing for the realm of attributive past participles (with some drawbacks that we will return to in section 4.3), but cannot simply be adopted for periphrastic instances due to the existence of telic transitives (*find a nickle, lose a key, build a house, eat an apple*). These have to be imperfective in order to allow for periphrastic passives, as we have seen. Hence, it is rather assumed that past participles introduce defective perfectivity, a set of aspectual information that only suffices to induce a change of state with simple, i.e. non-causative, BECOME-predicates. This claim may, however, sensibly be conflated with homogeneity-considerations once we assume that past participial morphology cannot compromise the integrity of a predicate's event structure, but only has scope over (and hence may only have an effect on) the highest layer of a given event structure. Since telic transitive predicates feature a CAUSE-layer on top of their BECOME-layer, defective perfectivity may only bring an atomic ingredient of this atelic process to an end, which is crucially not enough to induce a change of state. If this layer does not intervene, defective perfectivity may still elicit an imperfective interpretation, e.g. because there is a DO-phase (processes), or properly induce the change of state in the BECOME-phase, hence imposing a perfective reading. Eventually, then, as indicated by the broken line in (150b), it is not the case that the atelic event is not affected at all. Rather, with an atelic predicate, the aspectual effect just does not prevent further instances of the same event to be reiterated and hence does not allow the BECOME-phase to give rise to a resultative reading. Thus, the past participle in question eventually remains imperfective or – in Lübbe & Rapp's (2011) terms – merely conveys 'weak perfectivity', which does not have an effect on the continuity of the underlying event. This is insufficient for the denotation of the analytic perfect (without independent help), but readily compatible with a periphrastic passive.[111] Hence, unlike approaches based on stronger concepts such as anteriority (tense) or (proper) perfectivity (aspect), the present account is sufficiently flexible to grasp the lack of a visible temporal semantic consequence in (eventive) passive cases. Now that the compositional semantics of the periphrastic perfect have been sketched and potential obstacles could be removed, let us turn to the distinct perfect interpretations (commonly termed perfect uses) this construction may elicit.

4.2.3.2 Accounting for distinct perfect uses

The instance of the periphrastic perfect that is typically treated as its default variant and hence most regularly discussed with respect to its main properties is the present perfect, which "serves to relate a past situation to a present state in some way" (Yao & Collins 2012: 387). This gave rise to the term 'current relevance', which entails that "a present perfect sentence says something both about the past, and about the present" (Portner 2011: 1225). However, the precise nature of the semantics of the present perfect are actually quite difficult to grasp (cf. Portner 2011: 1225). According to Yao & Collins (2012: 387), it "encompasses a range of interrelated notions such as recency, iterativity, experientiality, present possibility, and continuance of a state into the present". This is why the notions of 'extended now' (see, amongst others, McCoard 1978; Dowty 1979) and 'perfect time span' (see, amongst others, Iatridou et al. 2001; Rothstein 2008) have come to be used. The former characterises that the perfect locates a situation in an interval between TU and certain point in the

---

[111] Note that the presence of a sub-event that has been brought to an end may also be constitutive for the fact that some languages (like English to a certain extent) are somewhat reluctant to denote an eventive passive without supplementary dynamic properties: consider *John is (being) seen*. In order to grasp this parametric difference between German and English, Breul & Wegner (2017: 47f.) ascribe the auxiliary WERDEN dynamic properties. This is not taken over in the present approach, where the parametric differences are rather traced back to the homonymy between the auxiliary and the copula, as we have seen in chapter 4.1.3, but the role of stativity certainly demands a more detailed discussion regardless of which route one opts for.

past (cf. Yao & Collins 2012: 387). While this perspective entails that the interval ends at TU, approaches based on a 'perfect time span' are more flexible (cf. Portner 2011: 1232). In fact, these allow for a range of possibilities in that they do not force the interval to include TU, but also allow it to precede or abut TU (cf. Portner 2011: 1232). This intuition of a flexible nature of perfect semantics is shared in the present approach based on posteriority, where the fact that a participial (sub-)situation is located prior to TT does not necessarily rule out that TT is included within this interval.

Although we certainly cannot do justice to the elaborate discussion concerning the intricate properties of perfect readings, which are often crucially affected by additional factors like adverbial modification, let us briefly sketch how the present approach copes with the distinct uses of the perfect. Examples of the three main uses of the perfect, i.e. the universal, experiential and resultative perfect, may be found in (152) and (153) for German and English (see Rothstein 2008: 111).[112]

(152) a. Saul has lived in Albuquerque for 20 years / ever since 1996.
 b. Francis has played *Monument Valley*.
 c. Walt has arrived in New Hampshire.

(153) a. Ich habe dich schon immer geliebt.
   I have you PARTICLE always love.PTCP
   'I have always loved you.'
 b. Ich habe *500 Days of Summer* drei Mal gesehen.
   I have *500 Days of Summer* three times watch.PTCP
   'I have seen *500 Days of Summer* three times.'
 c. Ich habe meine Brille verloren.
   I have my glasses lose.PTCP
   'I have lost my glasses.'

These examples differ substantially in terms of their perfect semantics, which may analogously also be observed in the other identity languages of Romance and Germanic. The universal perfect in (152a) and (153a) that has repeatedly been addressed in the present work denotes a situation that holds from some point in the past, typically specified by an adverbial (e.g. *always, ever since*), to

---

[112] We will abstract away here from the perfect of recent past (or 'hot news' perfect), which arguably strongly hinges on the presence of an adverbial like *just*, as in *I have just passed the exam* (cf. Rothstein 2008: 111) and is often subsumed under the heading of the existential perfect (cf. Iatridou et al. 2001: 192)

the time of utterance, e.g. the present (cf. Pancheva 2003: 277; Iatridou et al. 2001: 191). Accordingly, the universal perfect is special in expressing a situation – in the present cases living somewhere and loving somebody – that is still ongoing. While this holds most clearly for statives, it is arguably (occasionally) also observable with processes, as we could see above. The experiential perfect in (152b) and (153b) is generally defined as assigning a certain experience to the subject (cf. Iatridou et al. 2001: 191). This use of the perfect characteristically allows for (re)iterative instantiations of a certain event. What is denoted here is basically only that stretching back from the present to a point in the past, there have been situations of a certain kind (cf. Pancheva 2003: 277). Crucially, as Rothstein (2008: 111) points out, this "does not say anything about whether the eventuality of the main verb still holds at the moment of speech". Accordingly, with respect to the examples at hand, ever since the point in time designated by TU, there was at least one interval during which the subject could be said to experience the event in question (cf. Iatridou et al. 2001: 191), i.e. playing *Monument Valley* and watching *500 Days of Summer*. Comparing the universal and the experiential perfect, we may conclude that these two differ in that the former denotes a single eventuality that holds throughout the whole interval up until the present, whereas the latter suggests that within a given interval, there is at least one sub-interval at which the situation in question holds true. Accordingly, while the universal perfect necessitates that the situation in question be ongoing, the experiential perfect suggests that the situation has ended at least once, but does not prevent further reiterations from coming about.

This leaves the resultative perfect in (152c) and (153c), which necessarily focuses on the result of a given situation. Hence, the situation in question – here arriving somewhere and losing something – may not be ongoing, but rather comes to an end so that a result comes into existence and this result holds at TU (cf. Pancheva 2003: 277). Given that the experiential and the resultative perfect share the proper completion of at least one sub-event (although they differ in terms of whether they allow for reiterations of the same event or are contingent on a result), it is not surprising that they are usually set apart from the universal perfect. In fact, the former readings are often subsumed under the same heading, e.g. as 'existential perfect' (see McCawley 1971; Mittwoch 1988) or 'experiential perfect' (see Rothstein 2008: 111), which points to terminological inconsistencies.

A general issue concerning these distinct readings of the perfect is whether they stem from grammatical distinctions (ambiguity) or rather are based on a uniform (monosemous) structure, where there may be differences as to which uses are uniform and which ones are not (see Iatridou et al. 2001:

192f. and Pancheva 2003: 280f. for overviews of the distinct approaches). According to Rothstein (2008: 111), the ideal outcome is a version of the latter view, where interpretational distinctions can be traced back to the properties of the underlying verb (aktionsart), adverbial modification and context. In line with this desire for a uniform picture, we will now briefly turn to how the compositional interaction between defective perfectivity and posteriority allows for the distinct uses in (152) and (153) on the basis of the underlying verbal semantics (event structure) and adverbial modification.[113] The importance of verbal event structure and adverbial modification, on the other hand, may quite clearly be shown to play a decisive role when it comes to the properties of the existential perfect, on the one hand, and the universal perfect, on the other.

With respect to the experiential perfect and the resultative perfect, the interpretational distinctions between the two kinds are fairly subtle and may be traced back to the underlying verbal event (regardless of adverbial modification). The experiential perfect is formed with processes (e.g. playing tennis, singing, dancing, building houses) and accomplishments (e.g. eating an apple, building a house), the latter of which are *per definitionem* concluded on the basis of the properties of their direct object, an Incremental Theme (see Dowty 1991). In the case of processes, it is sufficient to carry out a certain activity once for an experiential perfect to come about, whereas accomplishments are contingent on the reiteration of the causative process in question until the Incremental Theme is totally affected, which leads up to an endpoint. In the present approach, the denotation that this point of culmination is reached does not stem from perfectivity as denoted by a past participle, but rather comes about by virtue of the presence of posteriority, which shifts instantiations of the event in question into the past. This entails that the Incremental Theme has been affected and thus allows for a perfect interpretation. The affectedness of the Incremental Theme prevents further eventualities of the same kind to be carried out. This is crucially different with processes, which are not restricted by the delimiting properties of an Incremental Theme and thus allow for further iterations. Given that the past participle does not evoke proper perfectivity in either case, the experiential perfect is successfully grasped in both variants. Whenever an Incremental Theme is around, the event is telicised by virtue of the properties of the internal argument, which undergoes a change of state as

---

[113] This neglects the contribution of tense information, which does not play a decisive role with respect to the distinct perfect uses, as these may for instance readily occur in a past or future perfect as well (cf. Pancheva 2003: 277f.).

part of BECOME (cf. Pancheva 2003: 279; see also Parsons 1990; Kamp & Ryle 1993; and Giorgi & Pianesi 1997). With atelic processes (say *Peter has built houses* or *John has played tennis*), on the other hand, regarding the sub-event affected by defective perfectivity as lying in the past does not have any effect on the internal argument and hence there is nothing that could prevent further instantiations of the situation in question, i.e. reiterations are entirely unproblematic. Therefore, crucially depending on the nature of the internal argument (whether it allows for a change of state), nothing prevents the event in question from having been carried out repeatedly in the past and further instances from being carried out in the future as long as at least one instance lies in the past. As observable in (152b) and (153b), a reading in which there are several sub-intervals carrying out a given eventuality may, but need not, be forced via adverbial modification. Whenever this is not possible, there is an Incremental Theme that bars further instantiations of the triggering event in question, which is why this kind of experiential perfect seems to resemble a resultative perfect reading.

The resultative perfect in (152c) and (153c) differs from the experiential perfect by virtue of emphasising the presence of a result state that does not allow further instantiations of a given situation, but rather conveys that the result still holds at a given point in time. This may crucially be achieved in one of two ways. Either the past participle employed conveys perfectivity, in which case it may occur with BE in auxiliary alternating languages as it provides all that is necessary for a perfect interpretation, or it does not do so, in which case HAVE introduces posteriority. The former case overtly expresses a perfective situation and is observable in (152c), while the latter variant may be found in (153c). With respect to an imperfective past participle brought together with posteriority, a result comes about by virtue of the semantics of the underlying situation, namely a punctual change of state. In contrast to accomplishments, where a result state may only ensue if the internal argument bears specific properties (definite, affected), in the case of achievements, a punctual change of state is encoded in the verbal semantics regardless of the properties of the internal argument. If the posteriority on HAVE now denotes that TSit precedes TT, this suffices to denote a change of state, which thus triggers a result state. The fact that this necessarily induces a resultative reading may be traced back to the fact that the change of state in this case is punctual in nature. In both the context of proper perfectivity (in which case posteriority is implied) as well as posteriority (in which case resultativity is implied) a result state ensues and this result state is bound to hold up until the point in time explicitly pinpointed by the auxiliary, i.e. TU. This marks the crucial difference between the experiential and the resultative reading of the periphrastic perfect, i.e. the latter requires the result state to hold, whereas the former (by virtue of lacking an inherent result state) may do without this (cf. Pancheva 2003: 278f.). This fairly subtle distinction in interpretation may thus be explained on the basis of verbal semantics.

While the resultative and the experiential perfect are often taken to mark the core readings of the periphrastic perfect (the former more so than the latter), the universal perfect is somewhat distinct and arguably less prototypical (cf. Iatridou et al. 2001: 191; see Jespersen 1924; Comrie 1976). In fact, this reading – which conveys that a given eventuality holds up until TU – may only be found in those languages that exhibit past participles which are not inherently perfective (cf. Iatridou et al. 2001: 207f.). Assuming that past participles in identity languages introduce defective perfectivity, which does not manage to enforce perfectivity on the basis of predicates other than simple changes of state, it is thus not surprising that we regularly find a universal perfect in such languages. In fact, what also follows from this is that we may only ever find the universal perfect with those kinds of predicates that do not inherently give rise to a perfect result state. This naturally excludes past participles that are rendered perfective, i.e. simple changes of state, but actually also rules out incremental changes of state (accomplishments) as well as punctual changes of state (achievements) given that the posteriority on HAVE has to end the situation in question. Thus, the universal perfect is restricted to atelic verbs (cf. Pancheva 2003: 278).[114] The availability of universal perfects, however, is not only restricted to particular verbal properties but usually also taken to be contingent on adverbial modification (cf. Iatridou et al. 2001: 196–199; Pancheva 2003: 279f.).[115] Iatridou et al. (2001: 196), for instance, point out that "truly unmodified perfects are never U-perfects". The validity of this claim may be observed in (152a) and (153a), where omitting the adverbial modifiers *for 20 years, ever since 1996, schon immer* ('always') renders a universal perfect reading unavailable, as in the unmodified

---

114 In fact, Pancheva (2003: 278) claims that it is restricted to statives and progressives and Iatridou et al. (2001: 210f.) even suggest that it is restricted to statives. The latter is problematic in that it demands that periphrastic perfects derived from activities be regarded as hidden statives (cf. Iatridou et al. 2001: 233en43), while the former is also questionable, as we could see on the basis of a modified English counterpart to (150b). While such a case cannot be excluded from being an underlying progressive in German, its English counterpart does not necessarily need to exhibit progressive morphology to give rise to a universal perfect, which is unexpected given that English progressives are contingent on progressive morphology.

115 Pancheva (2003: 279f.) points out that the adverbials *always, ever since (2000), at least since 2000, for 10 days now* require a universal perfect, while *since 2000, for 10 days* allow it. The latter may trigger ambiguity between a universal and an experiential perfect, as in *I have been sick since 1990* (cf. Iatridou et al. 2001: 191).

(150b) and its English counterpart. In other words, *Saul has lived in Albuquerque*, *Ich habe dich geliebt* ('I have loved you') and *The church has burned* convey that the participial situation has ceased. In fact, what we get in these cases is an experiential perfect. This raises the question of what the adverbial modifiers capable of triggering (or forcing) a universal perfect contribute and how their absence leads to a perfective reading on the basis of the posteriority contributed by HAVE. Regarding the former issue, Iatridou et al. (2001: 196) point out that the adverbial modifier introduces a left boundary, i.e. a starting point for the perfect time span, which is not delimited by anything other than tense.[116] Hence, a sentence like **Saul has lived in Albuquerque at least/ever since 1996 but lives in Omaha now* is ungrammatical, because the lack of a right boundary makes it impossible to claim that the situation does not hold at TU anymore (cf. Iatridou et al. 2001: 194f.). Additionally, once we explicitly set the right boundary via adverbial modification as well, the universal perfect reading vanishes: *Saul has lived in Albuquerque from 1988 to 2010* (cf. Iatridou 2003: 149fn1). Now, given that the posteriority on HAVE shifts the participial eventuality into the past, it is not surprising that the default (non-universal) reading of a HAVE-perfect is that this concerns all participial sub-situations, conveying that the situation has come to an end at utterance time. If the beginning of a situation is emphasised by pinpointing a left boundary, but its end is not defined (neither by adverbial modification, the properties of the object nor the punctuality of the event), on the other hand, it is strongly implied that the eventuality persists. Hence, an imperfective interpretation is triggered. In this case, the time span is only delimited by TU, which is included by assertion (cf. Iatridou et al. 2001: 195).

As pointed out before, "the availability of the Universal reading depends on the availability of non-perfective participles" (Pancheva 2003: 278). Given the defective perfectivity of identity languages, these are expected to have a universal perfect. Languages that possess participles which carry proper perfectivity, on the other hand, are only expected to allow for a universal reading if they grant perfect formation with imperfective predicates. Indeed, this is exactly what we find. Greek, for instance, may only form perfects with a past participle bearing perfective morphology – while imperfective morphology exists, it is not perfect-forming – and hence cannot form a universal perfect (cf. Iatridou et al. 2001: 207f.). Bulgarian, also possessing a

---

[116] In fact, as Iatridou et al. (2001: 194f.) point out, "in the present perfect, RB is at (i.e., includes) the utterance time. In the past perfect, RB precedes the utterance time; in the future perfect, RB follows the utterance time."

morphological imperfective/perfective distinction, in turn, may form perfects with imperfective past participles and thus also has a universal perfect (cf. Iatridou et al. 2001: 208–210). In conclusion, the imperfectivity of a participle is a necessary condition for the formation of a universal perfect, which thus has a solid morphosyntactic basis rather than merely stemming from pragmatic considerations (cf. Iatridou et al. 2001: 216). In the identity languages at hand, the morphosyntactic composition on the basis of HAVE and an imperfective past participle, however, is not a sufficient condition, as adverbial modification is required in order to shift the default experiential reading to a universal one. While we cannot zoom in any more on any of these factors here, we have just found considerable evidence for the present compositional approach to the periphrastic perfect in that it accounts for the distinct perfect readings.[117] Additional evidence actually may be found in diachronic considerations, where the core use of the perfect, namely the resultative marks the starting point for the grammaticalisation of a fully-fledged periphrastic perfect. In fact, the perfect is always first restricted to resultatives formed on the basis of simple changes of state, before a proper perfect construction comes into existence, opening the perfect to other verb classes (cf. Gillmann 2011: 204).

4.2.3.3 Some cross-linguistic distinctions

Now that the compositional properties of the periphrastic perfect and the readings it elicits have been laid out against the backdrop of past participial identity, the remainder of the present discussion on perfect semantics will be devoted to a brief excursus to some major cross-linguistic differences supposedly challenging the present (unified) account. One of the most intriguing questions that may be posed with respect to the semantics of the English present perfect is what Klein (1992) calls 'the present perfect puzzle'.

(154) a. *The conference has begun yesterday.
     b. Die Konferenz hat gestern begonnen.
        the conference has yesterday begin.PTCP
        'The conference began yesterday.'

---

[117] Pancheva (2003: 277–279) also emphasises the role of aspect in giving rise to the different readings: "the Universal and the Resultative readings are derivable only by some, non-overlapping aspectual forms embedded in the perfect."

The ungrammaticality of the English example in (154a), as opposed to the grammaticality of its German counterpart in (154b), shows that the periphrastic perfect in the two languages differs with regard to its incompatibility of definite past time adverbials like *yesterday* or *last year* with the present perfect (cf. Thieroff 2000: 276). In fact, "only the latter can be modified by positional temporal adverbials expressing a definite position on the time axis" (Rothstein 2008: 55). The same incompatibility is observable in Icelandic, Swedish, Norwegian and Danish. French, on the other hand, patterns with German in allowing for adverbials like *hier* ('yesterday') (cf. Guéron 2007: 377). This raises the question of whether these differences stem from substantial variation between the periphrastic perfects in identity languages, an affirmative response to which would put into question the null hypothesis that the morphosyntactic properties of the periphrastic perfect in these languages are virtually identical.

A vital observation about the occurrence of this cross-linguistic difference is that it only concerns the present perfect, i.e. the temporal adverbials in question readily combine with other tenses in the past perfect, future perfect and the pluperfect even in those languages that exhibit the present perfect puzzle (cf. Thieroff 2000: 276; Rothstein 2008: 55). Accordingly, approaches to the present perfect puzzle typically focus on the characteristics of the present tense properties of the present perfect. Pancheva & von Stechow (2004), for instance, trace the observable distinctions back to a parameterisation in terms of whether or not the perfect time span includes TU. Pancheva & von Stechow (2004) correlate this with the question of whether or not a given language may flexibly use the present tense for future time reference, which holds for German, but not for English (cf. Larsson 2009: 83).[118] However, this correlation is problematic since Swedish, for example, patterns with German with respect to allowing for future time reference, but with English in terms of exhibiting the present perfect puzzle (cf. Rothstein 2008: 56). Accordingly, rather than present tense, Larsson (2009: 87) holds the properties of the temporal auxiliary responsible for the observable differences. In fact, she assumes that the distinctions arise since the perfect time span need not include TT in German, whereas it has to do so in English (cf. Larsson 2009: 95f.). To be precise, while those languages that allow their periphrastic perfect to

---

118 Accordingly, German denotes a futurate interpretation in cases like *Im nächsten Jahr fliege ich nach Norwegen* ('I will fly to Norway next year.', lit. in.the next year fly I to Norway), whereas this is restricted to scheduled events in English: *Next year, I *(will) fly to Norway* (cf. König & Gast 2009: 84f.).

combine with positional adverbials (such as German) include a time span that ends at TT, languages that do not (such as English) necessarily include TT and thus allow it to extend after TT (cf. Larsson 2009: 82). Given the role of posteriority (TSit < TT), which is either brought in by implication (on the basis of a perfective eventuality) or encoded on HAVE, cross-linguistic distinctions would have to be associated with distinct ingredients in the present approach, which seems to be a bit of a stretch. Rather, the relation between TU and TT should take centre stage here, ideally.

We will assume that the properties of the adverbial modifier are the decisive factor here. In this respect, we may for instance follow what Klein (1992: 527) refers to as 'the scope solution' in assuming that the adverbial in English (but not in German) interacts with the tense of the finite auxiliary. Crucially, positional time adverbials – reminiscent of but virtually contrary to the adverbials in universal perfects – are assumed to make up an interval for TT which excludes TU (rather than including it) by virtue of preceding it in English (cf. Breul & Wegner 2017: 50). This is problematic in terms of leading to a 'clash' in that TT is *per definitionem* bound to include TU in the present tense, whereas the adverb has to exclude TU (cf. Klein 1992: 527, 1994: 132; von Stechow 2008: 146f.), which is why the example in (154a) is ungrammatical.[119] In German, grammaticality ensues in such cases because adverbials like *gestern* ('yesterday') in (154b) do not semantically interact with tense information, but rather with the situation on the basis of which the past participle is formed (cf. Breul & Wegner 2017: 50f.). While there is no difference here with respect to the assumption that TT includes TU, i.e. the denotation of present tense information, a clash does not occur and the underlying situation is part of a time span that comprises TU, as desired (cf. Breul & Wegner 2017: 50f.).[120] Eventually, the scope solution allows us to do without substantial differences concerning the semantics of the periphrastic perfect in languages exhibiting the present perfect puzzle as opposed to those that do not. Crucially, there is no distinction in terms of a present tense auxiliary signalling that TT includes TU, but rather the

---

[119] Note that Klein (1992: 527) eventually does not subscribe to this view, because it "must include an in-depth analysis of various types of (temporal) adverbials and an analysis of how these adverbials interact with the remainder of the clause". A proper discussion of these aspects exceeds the confines of the present work.

[120] While the assumption that the past participle grants the adverbial access to the denotation of the embedded verb form might be considered to be problematic, additional evidence for the scope solution comes from syntactic factors that we will not review here (cf. Breul & Wegner 2017: 51f.).

observable differences are solely based on distinctions concerning the scope of temporal adverbials.

Another cross-linguistic difference that has received a lot of attention concerns what is often referred to as 'loss of the preterite' ('Präteritumsschwund') in German (cf. König & Gast 2009: 87f.).[121] In fact, in German, but not in English, a periphrastic perfect like (155a) may (but need not) elicit the same interpretation as the simple past in (155b).

(155) a. Jack ist (gestern)   im   Wald verschwunden.
        Jack is (yesterday) in.the forest disappear.PTCP
        'Jack (has) disappeared in the forest (yesterday).'
   b. Jack verschwand   (gestern)   im   Wald.
        Jack disappear.PTCP *(yesterday) in.the forest*
        'Jack disappeared in the forest (yesterday).'
   c. Jack has disappeared in the forest.

While the English counterpart in (155c) infers that the disappearing-event is completed and its result state still obtains, the situation in the structurally analogous (155a) is different. In fact, the German variant may either elicit a perfect interpretation similar to its English counterpart or it may denote a situation resembling the simple past and hence interpretationally virtually indistinguishable from (155b), where the result state need not necessarily hold, i.e. Jack might as well have turned up again (cf. Vater 2002: 355fn2; see also Rothstein 2008: 147).[122] In this respect, the German perfect may be said to "oscillate[] between a tense interpretation and aspect interpretation" (Klein 1994: 111). Actually, on the basis of this interpretational similarity the periphrastic perfect in German has almost entirely replaced the German preterite, which marks the eponymous loss of the preterite (cf. Zeller 1994: 79). According to Behaghel (1924: 271), this process began as early as in Early Old High German and, indeed, the simple past is largely restricted to specific verbs (*sein* 'be', *haben* 'have', *müssen* 'must', *können* 'can' *heißen* 'to be called', etc.) and special contexts today (cf. Löbner 2002: 369; König & Gast 2009: 87). This development is most prevalent in Upper German (southern Bavarian and Alemannic), where "the process of replacing Past by Perfekt is almost complete" (Löbner 2002: 369; see also

---

[121] See also Ehrich & Vater (1989: 103f.) for a discussion of the loss of the preterite in Danish.
[122] This also becomes clear in cases in which a past tense reading is forced by the contextual embedding, as in Rothstein's (2008: 30) example *Peter hat gerade gespült, als ich heimkam* ('Peter was doing the dishes when I got home.', lit. Peter has just do-the-dishes.PTCP when I home-came).

Abraham 1992: 12).¹²³ However, the observable interchangeability does not work both ways: as König & Gast (2009: 87) as well as Rothstein (2008: 119) point out, a past tense may not serve as a substitute for a present perfect in contexts in which a result is bound to be denoted. The same also holds vice versa, i.e. the present perfect may not substitute a preterite in contexts in which a result may not come about (cf. Lohnstein 2011: 252f.).¹²⁴ While the perfect thus covers interpretations evoked by the simple past, it apparently does not forfeit its (intrinsic) compositional semantics (cf. Lohnstein 2011: 252). Nonetheless, the unexpected possibility of a lack of a result in examples like (155a) needs to be accounted for, i.e. the perfect has to be allowed to occur as a tense which comes quite close to the preterite (or past) tense (cf. Musan 1999: 6f.).

There are numerous approaches as to how to deal with this capability of the periphrastic perfect in German.¹²⁵ A major strand of approaches assumes the periphrastic perfect to be ambiguous in German, i.e. the constructional pattern accidentally is homophonous, but associated with different meanings (cf. Musan 1999: 6). Proponents of this view are, amongst others, Wunderlich (1970), Bäuerle (1979), and Ballweg (1988: 109f.), who claim that a single construction is associated both with perfect as well as past tense semantics (cf. Zeller 1994: 81). In contrast to these accounts, there have been numerous attempts at explaining the flexibility of the present perfect construction in terms of a single semantic representation. Zeller (1994: 81), for instance, claims that the perfect does

---

123 This development cross-linguistically is quite common. Accordingly, Bybee & Dahl (1989: 68f.) assume the following universal grammaticalisation path: resultative > present perfect > past tense (cf. Gillmann 2011: 204).

124 This can be seen in pairs of examples like the following, taken from Lohnstein (2011: 253):

(i) a. Sobald Peter angerufen hat, gehen wir ins Schwimmbad.
        *once   Peter call.*PTCP *has, go we into.the swimming.bath*
        'As soon as Peter has called, we go to the swimming bath.'
    b. *Sobald Peter anrief, gehen wir ins Schwimmbad.
        once   Peter called, go we into.the swimming.bath

(ii) a. Peter suchte das Buch, bis er es fand.
        Peter searched the book, until he it found
        'Peter searched for the book, until he found it.'
    b. *Peter suchte das Buch, bis er es gefunden hat.
        *Peter   searched the book, until he it find.*PTCP *has*

125 See Ehrich (1992: 88–92) and Zeller (1994: 80f.) for overviews of the different approaches to the (non-)identity of perfect and past tense interpretation on the basis of the periphrastic perfect construction.

not possess two meanings, but two different uses of a single form and its corresponding basic meaning. In a similar vein, Musan (1999: 7) takes a pragmatic perspective, arguing that perfect semantics is vague and hence inherently allows for a wide spectrum of different uses to be determined pragmatically. Under this view, the perfect construction is not inherently semantically or syntactically ambiguous, but there are only some vague components in semantics which are specified with the help of pragmatics, hence eliciting distinct functions and meanings (cf. Musan 1999: 48f.). As Löbner (2002: 369f.) points out, the identity-assumption necessitates that the tense of the construction must be 'present' all the time, whereas the ambiguity assumption (that he opts for) suggests that it "contribut[es] present tense in its present perfect function and past tense in the functions it has taken over from the Past." While the latter view appears to be desirable at first sight, there are substantial counter-arguments against the ambiguity claim. First, Zeller (1994: 80) has a point in claiming that associating a complex construction like the periphrastic perfect with a simple meaning like tense is at least counter-intuitive. Second, the general principle that language does not allow for total synonymy would be violated by the assumption of ambiguity (cf. Rothstein 2008: 25). Third, the present perfect and the preterite are not always interchangeable, i.e. there are specific contexts in which the present perfect does not elicit the reading that the simple past evokes, as we could see above (cf. Rothstein 2008: 26). This is unexpected under the assumption that the two are ambiguous (cf. Rothstein 2008: 26). Additionally, the latter is challenged by the fact that certain predicates mark exceptions to the use of a periphrastic perfect for a past tense, as hinted at before. Hence, an ambiguity-approach to the loss of the preterite is apparently misled, which is also claimed by Klein (2000: 362) and Rathert (2004: 43). Rather, what we have is yet another perfect reading restricted to languages like German: the preterite perfect (cf. Rothstein 2008: 119) or narrative use of the perfect (cf. König & Gast 2009: 86). This is also concluded by Zeller (1994: 81), who claims that the perfect has different readings rather than different meanings. However, this still leaves the question of how to reconcile the possibility of the lack of a result state with the perfect semantics discussed before. In the present approach, this is grammatically imposed in the case of past participles derived from simple changes of state and strongly implied by the interaction of posteriority (on HAVE) with telic predicates.

As we definitely cannot do justice to the intricate discussion of how the preterite perfect reading may be derived from the monosemous semantics of the periphrastic perfect, we will simply follow Rothstein's (2008: 125) suggestion that it stems from factors orthogonal to the intricate compositional properties of the periphrastic perfect. In fact, Rothstein (2008: 165) puts forth a discourse-driven account, where the eventual choice of a preterite perfect reading is strongly contingent on the time set up by the discourse.[126] This point is referred to as the Discourse time point (D) and establishes an anaphoric relation to the following event time (cf. Rothstein 2008: 165). The relation between D and the underlying event time eventually determines whether an interpretation indistinguishable from the simple past, i.e. the preterite perfect, is triggered or one of the other (proper) perfect readings comes about. In fact, the former arises "when (D) is simultaneous to the final Subinterval of the event time denoted by the present perfect, and a perfect reading when (D) is located after the event time" (Rothstein 2008: 165). This is somewhat reminiscent of the modification by positional time adverbials in that D directly picks out the underlying event in preterite perfect contexts. This would then account for the fact that a correlation between the absence of the present perfect puzzle and the loss of the preterite has often been remarked (cf. König & Gast 2009: 86f.). Eventually, then, a preterite reading is contextually triggered and a result is not asserted since D is simultaneous to a point in time where this result has not been triggered yet. Thus, in a case like *Peter ist gerade angekommen als ich telefonierte* ('Peter just arrived when when I phoned.', lit. Peter is just arrive.PTCP when I phoned) it is not the result state that matters, but rather the event phase that led to it. While this certainly leaves countless issues with respect to the loss of the preterite and the preterite perfect to future research, it indicates that it is principally possible to retrieve an interpretation resembling the simple past from a monosemous periphrastic perfect. Hence, these observations regarding cross-linguistic distinctions do not challenge the compositional approach to the periphrastic perfect laid out in the present section.

This concludes our discussion of the compositional semantics of the periphrastic perfect as based on the defective perfectivity contributed by the past participle and the posteriority introduced by HAVE. Accordingly, the syntactic and semantic properties of both the periphrastic passive as well as the analytic perfect have now been laid out against the backdrop of past participial identity. Hence, we are finally in a position to return to the major divergent and polymorphous realisations of past participles, as introduced in chapters 2.4 and 2.5, for a brief take on how these are accounted for in the present approach. Subsequently, what remains to be addressed before we turn to some concluding remarks are the properties of bare instantiations of past participles.

---

[126] See also Ehrich (1992: 106f.) for an approach based on the contextual fixation of TT and Lohnstein (2011: 252f.) for the role of contextual factors for determining temporal deixis.

4.2.4 Grasping divergent realisations and polymorphy

Now that we have seen how the properties of past participial morphology interact with their structural context in order to give rise to the periphrastic passive and the analytic perfect, we may return to the phenomena introduced in chapters 2.4 and 2.5. These phenomena, namely the divergent realisations commonly referred to as PPP, IPP, and PPI as well as the occurrence of agreement morphology, still demand to be technically accounted for in the context of the present approach. Given that important insights have been drawn from these contexts, it is not surprising that this turns out to be possible in a fairly straightforward fashion. Accordingly, let us now turn to each of them in turn in chapter 4.2.4.1 and 4.2.4.2, respectively, starting with the divergent morphological realisation of past participles in the context of verbal preposing in English and verbal clusters in other West Germanic languages.

4.2.4.1 Morphologically divergent occurrences

Recall that the characteristic property of the PPP is that a preposed participle may be realised as an infinitival (or plain) form, while this does not elicit any interpretational effects. Accordingly, the example in (156a), taken from Breul (2014: 470), is interpreted like a common HAVE-perfect despite lacking past participial morphology.

(156) a. The only way to battle this menace is town by town, county by county, and state by state, *and fight they have*.
 b. [W]hy lift entire paragraphs from a 1946 Life magazine article so successful that it was excerpted in Reader's Digest unless you actually plan to be caught? *And *catch/caught she was*, in the most public way...

As we have seen, the preposed verb may (optionally) be realised as an infinitival form only when occurring as part of a HAVE-perfect, as in (156a), but crucially not in passive counterparts, like the one in (156b) (cf. Breul 2014: 453).

While theoretical approaches to the PPP are quite scarce, Urushibara (1997), Oku (1996; 1998), and Breul (2014) provide accounts that are worthy of discussion. As briefly touched upon in chapter 2.5.1, Urushibara (1997: 130) assumes that the morphological form of a perfective participle is post-syntactically determined under string-adjacency of the head of a VP with HAVE. This entails that whenever the condition of string-adjacency is not met, the participial morpheme may not be spelled out (cf. Urushibara 1997: 130, 141). This fails to account for the fact that the PPP is optional and is not compatible with the identity of past participles, as there is no reason for why this should not carry over to passive cases. Additionally, the perfective participial marker boils down to a piece of ornamental morphology here (cf. Breul 2014: 455). This assumption, however, is highly dubious since this piece of morphology may virtually only be missing in this specific context and there is no stage in language acquisition that systematically exhibits participial constructions without the associated morphological marking (cf. Breul 2014: 455). Finally, what may empirically be held against an analysis based on string-adjacency is the fact that cases in which this is clearly disrupted by the presence of some intervening element, e.g. negation (NegP) or *wh*-movement, do not permit the PPP (cf. Oku 1998: 24f.). This is why Oku (1998: 24f.) substantially weakens the assumption of string-adjacency so as to hold only with respect to elements that never appear in adjacent positions throughout their syntactic derivation. This requires him to proclaim that the "'fronted' VP is base-generated in its surface position and lowers to the complement position of the Aux/Infl in the LF component, to satisfy the selectional property of the Aux/Infl" (Oku 1998: 28). The optionality of the PPP is then accounted for by claiming that in addition to base-generating the VP in clause-initial position, there is an option to move it there, in which case participial morphology is able to appear (cf. Oku 1998: 29). Given that this stipulates (optional) VP-lowering at LF as a means to satisfy selectional requirements (cf. Breul 2014: 456), this approach is just as problematic as Urushibara's (1997) alternative.[127] Given that these approaches to the PPP are quite problematic and do not match the conclusions drawn in the present work, we will rather side with Breul (2014) and adopt an approach based on impoverishment.

Embick & Noyer (2007: 311) point out that the morphological operation of impoverishment allows "a feature of a morpheme [to be] deleted in a specific context; after deletion the morpheme in question escapes the insertion of any vocabulary item requiring that feature". Applying this to the PPP, Breul (2014: 463) suggests that the past participial feature typically spelled-out as a morphological marker in canonical cases may be deleted when it is dislocated out of a position that is locally c-commanded by the perfect auxiliary *have* (cf. Breul 2014: 463). In other words, a feature responsible for the realisation of past participial morphology is deleted in a context in which its VP has been preposed (cf. Breul 2014: 463). Given that this deletion applies post-syntactically, the interpretation

---

[127] Oku (1996: 284f.) provides an alternative account that does without a focus on string-adjacency (be it at PF or in syntax) and instead emphasises on the properties of the remnant VP-trace, which unfortunately turns out to be no less prolematic. In fact, the main assumption here is that the remnant trace of a VP may participate in feature-checking with HAVE, whereas its preposed copy does not undergo this feature-checking and is therefore not morphophonologically realised as a past participle (cf. Oku 1996: 288). This is highly dubious in terms of being forced to stipulate that the copy of an element lacks the feature specifications of its trace.

of such constructions is identical to contexts in which there is no deletion.[128] Breul (2014: 463) formalises the application of impoverishment in the case of the PPP as in (157a), but remains cautious with respect to the precise properties of the participial feature that is deleted. Based on the previous discussion, we can pinpoint the constitutive feature that is deleted as well as specify the relevant contribution of the perfect auxiliary that makes impoverishment possible in the first place and hence arrive at the modified formalisation in (157b).

(157) a. [F̶p̶a̶r̶t̶] contained in Part is deleted (i.e. [F̶p̶a̶r̶t̶] → ø]) iff Part moves out of the local c-command domain of Aux[perf].[129]
 b. iAsp[def-perf] contained in Asp is deleted (i.e. iAsp[def-perf] → ø) iff Asp moves out of the local c-command domain of an Aux containing iAsp [posterior].

As a result of this feature-deletion, it is not possible anymore to associate the feature-bundle with the appropriate phonological form, which is why – as proposed by Halle & Marantz (1993: 133f.) – a null exponent is inserted. This exponent "is the default for those cases where there is no specified and listed phonological representation for an abstract syntactic terminal" (Breul 2014: 463). In the participial contexts at hand, this results in the realisation of the past participial item as a plain form of the verb (cf. Breul 2014: 463). While this suffices for a technical account, we have actually also seen that there is a sound conceptual basis to the observation that impoverishment is only possible in the context of HAVE.

What we could see throughout the present work is that all the relevant information for a passive interpretation reside in the past participial morpheme. With respect to perfect information, on the other hand, the situation is different in that both HAVE as well as the participial element contribute aspectual information.[130] In fact, HAVE introduces posteriority and the past participle contributes defective perfectivity. The presence of relevant perfect information

---

128 Such a PF-based analysis at first sight seems to diminish the explanatory power of the PPP, IPP and PPI and hence seems to contradict the conclusions drawn from these phenomena in section 2.5. However, this may be shown to be crucially misguided once we focus on the role of semantic recoverability as a necessary condition.

129 Breul (2014: 463) alternatively spells this out for non-identity approaches in terms of the following condition: "[F̶p̶a̶r̶t̶] contained in Part$_{perf}$ is deleted (i.e. [F̶p̶a̶r̶t̶] → ø]) iff Part$_{perf}$ is not locally c-commanded by Aux[perf]".

130 This is in line with Breul's (2014: 465) following conclusion: "the feature complex which is responsible for the interpretation of a clause as having perfect tense is located either in the perfect auxiliary alone or in the perfect auxiliary in combination with the feature equipment of the participle". The present work argues in favour of the latter variant.

on HAVE thus arguably is a necessary condition for the application of past participial impoverishment. This is in line with the assumption that a general requirement on impoverishment is that its application is only licit if it does not bar the "the recovery of what is associated with the exponent semantically" (Breul 2014: 465).[131] This may be construed from the perspective of parsing: just like in the context of ellipsis, the omission of morphophonological material is only possible if the intended interpretation may still reasonably be taken to be recoverable. Thus, impoverishment is barred in the case of BE, as there are no relevant features on the passive auxiliary that could serve to convey a passive interpretation. Rather, all of those actually reside in the past participle, which lexically marks an external argument for existential binding and hence is able to give rise to a passive interpretation all on its own (cf. Breul 2014: 465). In a nutshell, HAVE suffices to signal a perfect interpretation by means of denoting that the embedded eventuality precedes TT (posteriority). Futhermore, it facilitates an active interpretation by means of being capable of licensing an external argument (by virtue of recovering the semantic role marked for existential binding).[132] The auxiliary BE, by contrast, is semantically vacuous and crucially does not grant the recovery of passive semantics in the context of an impoverished past participle, which is why ungrammaticality ensues. Eventually, then, while the underlying syntactic derivation and its computation at LF are identical in PPP-contexts and those that do not feature impoverishment, it is the presence of HAVE that makes LF-recovery possible in the case of a HAVE-perfect that features an impoverished form. The crucial point here is that despite being a PF-phenomenon, impoverishment underlies semantic restrictions (in order to ensure recoverability) and these are what eventually grants important insights into the distribution of information in past participial periphrases, as suggested in chapter 2.5. The same line of argumentation carries over to the second divergent realisation that we considered, namely the IPP in languages like German.

Strongly reminiscent of the PPP, the IPP realises a plain form instead of a past participle in special contexts, namely if it is part of a verb cluster, as observable in (158).

---

[131] Note that this may also be taken to be fulfilled by merely attributing a signalling function to HAVE. However, assuming that HAVE just signals a perfect interpretation without a semantic contribution is conceptually weak.

[132] Note that the signalling effect of the auxiliary in PPP-contexts cannot be reduced to its argument structural contribution, since unaccusative predicates readily allow for impoverishment in the context of HAVE, although the perfect auxiliary does not contribute to the expression of argument structure here, as we have seen in (111): *This dessert was made out of the desire for the warm weather to just arrive. And arrive it has.*

(158) a. dass er den Film hat sehen dürfen/ *gedurft
  that he the movie has see.INF *may*.INF/ *may*.PTCP
  'that he was allowed to watch the movie'
 b. dass das Mädchen lachen *hören/ gehört wurde
  that the girl laugh.INF hear.INF/ hear.PTCP *become*
  'that the girl was heard laughing'
 c. dass das Mädchen sitzen *bleiben/ geblieben ist
  that the girl sit.INF remain.INF/ remain.PTCP *be*
  'that the girl remained sitting'

Just like with the PPP, the insertion of an infinitival form instead of a past participle in verbal clusters is restricted to the perfect, as in (158a), yet this is occasionally even obligatorily enforced in Standard German, unlike the optionality attested for the PPP in English.[133] To be precise, apart from a very limited set of exceptions that we will return to shortly, the IPP cross-linguistically only occurs in the context of HAVE, i.e. WERDEN-passive as well as BE-perfect instantiations as those in (158b) and (158c) are bound to overtly carry participial morphology (cf. Haider 2003: 104, Vogel 2009: 312). This raises the question of how to technically account for the observable facts, which is often closely tied to the issue of what triggers the IPP. There are basically two factors that are typically identified as playing an important role here: the existence of a complex verb cluster and the presence of the past participial prefix GE-.

While the present discussion definitely cannot do justice to the former factor of verbal clusters, it is commonly held that the nature of such clusters is an important ingredient of an insightful approach to the IPP (cf. Hinterhölzl 2009: 192).[134] In fact, in order for an infinitival form to be inserted instead of a past participle, there at least has to be a combination of a (modal) verb selecting a bare infinitive (cf. Bader & Schmid 2009: 178f.). This combination is in turn embedded under HAVE in the case of the IPP, which seems to be a triggering factor reminiscent of VP-preposing in the context of the PPP in English.[135] In

---

133 In fact, whether or not the IPP is obligatory hinges on the precise nature of the restructuring element in German: modals enforce the IPP and this usually also holds for the causative variant of *lassen* ('let'), whereas its continuative counterpart and verbs of perception like *sehen* ('see') or *hören* ('hear') as well as benefactives like *helfen* ('help') permit optionality (see Schmid 2002; Bader & Schmid 2009; Bader 2014).

134 See, for instance, Wurmbrand (2006) and Bader & Schmid (2009: 182) for the complex questions raised by verbal clusters and some routes to how they may be answered.

135 Cluster-formation may be accounted for in a variety of different ways. As Hinterhölzl (2009: 192) points out, there are for instance approaches that analyse these as adjunction structures derived by head movement (see Evers 1975; Rutten 1991) as well as those that derive such

addition, there is arguably another essential ingredient for the instantiation of the IPP, namely the presence of the participial marker GE-.[136] As we have seen, what is striking about the availability of the IPP is that it is delimited to those (West) Germanic languages that exhibit (a rough equivalent of) this prefix in their past participle formation (cf. Ørsnes 2008: 124). In fact, we can generalise with respect to Germanic that those languages that show the IPP also use GE- (Schmid 2002: 91), which is not available in languages like English and Frisian as well as the Scandinavian languages (cf. Lange 1982: 174).

In an attempt to technically grasp the IPP, Hinterhölzl (2009: 199) emphasises the combination of these two factors and concludes that the IPP arises since "verb cluster formation blocks (parts of) the participial morphology", namely the participial prefix (see also Vanden Wyngaerd 1994; 1996; Hinterhölzl 1998: 65f.). In a similar vein, Schmid (2002: 9) claims that the insertion of an infinitival form instead of a properly inflected past participle is a repair strategy that is employed as a last resort. The same intuition is emphasised by Askedal (1991: 21), who claims that highly complex verb clusters (e.g. comprising two modals and a verbal complement) are only possible due to the application of the IPP.[137] In order to grasp the incompatibility of GE- and a verb cluster,[138] Hinterhölzl (2009: 200) proposes a syntactic account based on designated functional heads for the participial pre- and suffixes (Asp1 and Asp2), where the position of the prefix (Asp2) is occupied by the restructuring element of a verbal cluster, thus blocking the insertion of the prefix, which in turn leads to a (last resort) spell-out as an infinitival. Accordingly, this purely structural approach manages to account for why the IPP is triggered in verbal complexes comprising a participial prefix, but it

---

structures by means of phrasal movement (see Hinterhölzl 1999; 2009; Koopman & Szabolcsi 2000). Additionally, some accounts (see e.g. Haider 1994) try to do without displacement and instead analyse verb clusters to come about via base generation (cf. Schmid 2002: 85f.). We will abstract away from such intricate technical issues for the present purposes, but acknowledge that the precise nature of these may lie at the core of triggering the IPP.

136 Note that all of the restructuring verbs allowing for the formation of verbal clusters feature the participial prefix *ge-* in German: e.g. *gesollt* (lit. shall.PTCP), *gekonnt* (lit. can.PTCP), *gewollt* (lit. want.PTCP), *gemusst* (lit. must.PTCP), *gedurft* (lit. may.PTCP), *gelassen* (lit. let.PTCP), *geblieben* (lit. remain.PTCP), *gehört* (lit. hear.PTCP), *gesehen* (lit. see.PTCP), *geholfen* (lit. help.PTCP).
137 Haider (2011: 254f.) even denies that repair strategies suffice to render such cases grammatical, but rather points out that they gain in acceptability, yet remain ungrammatical.
138 Note that there are also verbal clusters featuring a passive construction embedded under a modal, as in *dass das Auto hat repariert werden müssen* ('that the car had to be repaired', that the car has repair.PTCP become must), taken from Bader & Schmid (2009: 209). Here, the passive auxiliary properly governs the participial form *repariert* ('repaired'), which realises its past participial morphology, whereas the perfect auxiliary selects the modal *müssen* ('have to', lit. must), which may not be realised in its properly inflected form *gemusst* ('had to').

does so at a high cost. In fact, it relies on independent functional projections for the participial pre- and suffix and it has to stipulate that dependent infinitives occupy the same position as participial prefixes. This is then bound to be different in cases that optionally allow for proper participial morphology to be realised, e.g. clusters featuring verbs of perception like *sehen* ('see') or *hören* ('hear'). A further theoretical extension of such an approach is the requirement for a semantic repair mechanism that takes care of the proper interpretation by means of copying the semantic features associated with the participial prefix (cf. Hinterhölzl 2009: 213f.). Given these drawbacks, let us now turn to what an approach to the IPP based on the proposals made in the context of the PPP may look like.

While the PPP is triggered in case a participle is displaced out of the local c-command domain of the perfect auxiliary, in the case of the IPP it is the morphological reluctance to realise past participial morphology with GE- as part of a verbal cluster in the context of HAVE that arguably serves as a trigger. In other words, since the IPP only occurs in languages featuring GE- for past participle formation and solely shows up in the context of verbal clusters, which intrinsically require the presence of a (modal) verb bearing GE-, both morphological as well as structural complexity are at issue here. While we cannot provide a fine-grained structural analysis for these triggering factors, let us assume – in analogy to the PPP – that what is triggered is impoverishment of the participial form at PF. This may sketchily be formalised as in (159).[139]

(159) *i*Asp[def-perf] contained in Asp is deleted (i.e. *i*Asp[def-perf] → ø) iff Asp realises a prefix and is part of a verb cluster locally c-commanded by an Aux containing *i*Asp[posterior].

This impoverishment operation captures that the plain realisation of a past participle is restricted to verbal clusters featuring a restructuring verb usually derived via circumfixation, i.e. featuring the prefix GE-. Just like in the context of the PPP, what needs to be stressed here is that this is a PF-phenomenon that does not have an immediate effect on LF and hence might be critised for not providing any relevant insights. However, an externalisation-based analysis where there are semantic restrictions on recoverability that delimit the range of which

---

[139] This preliminary attempt at sketching the triggering factors for impoverishment in the case of the IPP neglects the optionality that occasionally arises with restructuring elements other than modals. A general intuition with respect to such cases, e.g. verbs of perception and benefactives, is that these are on the verge of (modal-like) restructuring elements and lexical verbs, where only the former induce a verbal cluster, triggering the IPP.

morphophonological material may be deleted, arguably renders this criticism unfounded.

Some further support for the validity of the two factors comes from diachronic and synchronic observations. Diachronically, the role of GE- finds support in that contexts exhibiting the IPP initially evoked prefixless participles (e.g. in Early New German) (cf. Hinterhölzl 2009: 199f.). This suggests that only the partipial prefix was left unrealised in earlier stages while impoverishment automatically elicits the insertion of a default exponent (bare infinitives) in more modern stages. The role of the verbal cluster may in turn be seen in in the examples in (160), based on Askedal (1991: 18f.).

(160) a. Loslassen hat er sie nie   können/   ?gekonnt.
        let.go   *has he her never* *could*.INF/ *could*.PTCP
        'Let go of her, he has never been able to.'
    b. Er hat sie nie   loslassen können/   *gekonnt.
        he has her never let.go   *could*.INF/ *could*.PTCP
        'He has never been able to let go of her.'

While the application of the IPP is obligatory in Standard German, as observable in (160b), displacing the main verb out of the verbal cluster, as in (160a), considerably weakens the unacceptability of participial morphology on the restructuring verb. This emphasises the structural nature of the IPP, which is strongly rooted in the underlying syntactic configuration (cf. Askedal 1991: 18f.). On the other hand, the fact that the IPP still applies in contexts in which the phonological integrity of a verbal cluster is disrupted by displacement shows that its trigger lies beyond the shallow incompatibility of a verbal cluster and GE- at PF. In fact, as we will see in the discussion of the PPI, the intricate structural interaction of a verbal cluster and a complex morphological form may even have to be supplemented by a third essential factor. This is the general strive for cluster-internal harmony, which induces the desire to mark the constitutive ingredients with the same morphological marker in order to convey the tight relation of the elements within a verbal cluster. Eventually, an approach based on impoverishment allows us to take such factors seriously, while doing without semantic repair mechanisms or the like. To be precise, it is once more just a PF-operation that takes care of deleting participial morphology, but only in case the semantic recovery of the intended interpretation is not challenged. This demands phonological late-insertion but no supplementary theoretical enhancements.

Similar to what we have seen in the case of the PPP, what is striking is that impoverishment is only possible if the participial element in question is governed by HAVE. While this is at first sight not very surprising given that most of the restructuring verbs are atelic and hence rely on the presence of HAVE, verbal clusters may also be formed with *lassen* ('let') and *bleiben* ('remain'),[140] where a clear opposition comes about with respect to the application of the IPP, as observable in (161) and (162).

(161) a. dass er sie hat schlafen *gelassen/ lassen
    that he her has sleep   let.PTCP/   *let*.INF
    'that he has let her sleep'
  b. dass sie schlafen gelassen/ *lassen wurde
    that she sleep   let.PTCP/ *let*.INF *became*
    'that she was allowed to remain sleeping'

(162) dass er stehen geblieben/   *bleiben   ist
    that he stand   remain.PTCP/ *remain*.INF *is*
    'that he remained standing'

These examples further explicate the point that has briefly been made with respect to the examples in (158) already: impoverishment is only possible in the context of HAVE, as instantiated in (161a), whereas the corresponding passive structure in (161b) formed with WERDEN does not allow for the IPP. In a similar vein, while *bleiben* ('remain') in (162) also takes an infinitival complement and thus forms a verbal cluster embedded under an auxiliary, it does not allow for impoverishment since it is governed by BE rather than HAVE. These observations suggest that the IPP – though triggered by configurational factors – has a semantic basis in that impoverishment is only possible if semantic recoverability is granted. Accordingly, the presence of an auxiliary that introduces relevant perfect information is a necessary (though of course not a sufficient) condition for the application of impoverishment as in (159). Even if past participial morphology is not properly instantiated in these cases, the intended interpretation may be recovered, unlike with BE and WERDEN, where there is no relevant passive or perfect information on the auxiliary and impoverishment thus bars recoverability. In other words, both past participles introducing an argument that is existentially bound (to be realised as WERDEN-passives) as well as those that bear perfectivity (to occur with BE), contain information that cannot be recovered when the participial morphology is not properly spelled-out. This naturally

---

[140] Recall that *bleiben* ('remain') denotes a simple change between two identical states (cf. Strobel 2007: 109).

bars impoverishment, as this operation underlies the restriction to the effect that nothing may be deleted that cannot be recovered.

As indicated before, what underlines the perfect-contribution of HAVE is not only that the IPP is not available whenever the perfect auxiliary is elided (cf. Ørsnes 2008: 125), but also the preposing of the perfect auxiliary. In fact, HAVE may (and occasionally even has to for independent reasons) leave its canonical clause-final position and phonologically move past the verbal cluster in Standard German (cf. Hinterhölzl 1998: 62).[141] Strikingly, the same kind of movement operation is observable in just one further context: verbal clusters governed by the future-auxiliary *werden* ('will') (cf. Haider 2003: 110). These instantiations of displacement may be argued to be carried out in order to aid interpretation, i.e. recoverability, so as to provide a relevant clue to how to deal with the cluster of infinitival forms before even encountering them in parsing (cf. Bærentzen 2004: 137f.).[142] This operation is usually not enforced, except in modal cases of the IPP, which are arguably affected by prescriptive rules. Rather, it is typically optional, although experimental data (see Bader & Schmid 2009; Bader 2014) show that preposing is usually (more or less strongly) preferred in both future and IPP-perfect cases. Crucially, with respect to the latter, there is a neat correlation between the application of the IPP and the availability of preposing: whenever participial morphology is introduced, preposing is illicit.[143] Thus, both the future configuration in (163a) and its IPP-perfect counterpart in (163b) are grammatical, whereas the counterpart featuring participial morphology in (163c) is not.

(163) a. dass er das Mädchen wird singen hören
      that he the girl   will sing   hear
      'that he will hear the girl sing'

---

[141] There is a large degree of dialectal variation concerning the acceptability of the IPP, which is often strongly contingent on word order (see Bader & Schmid 2009; Hinterhölzl 2009; and Vogel 2009: 319, amongst others).

[142] This is in line with the externalisation-driven account of semantic recoverability: the IPP simplifies the structure morphologically, but at the expense of the overt expression of the participle, which supposedly makes it more difficult to derive the associated interpretation. This is what allows the auxiliary to be preposed in order to provide relevant cues as early as possible.

[143] Note once more that this does not universally hold true. In fact, there are languages in which the IPP is not accompanied by HAVE-preposing, e.g. Afrikaans and West Flemish, which make use of extraposition instead (cf. IJbema 1997: 148). Additionally, even in German the availability of preposing, just like the IPP itself, is contingent on the properties of the particular restructuring predicate that is employed and subject to dialectal variation (cf. Bader & Schmid 2009: 180; Bader 2014). We will leave such intricate issues to future research.

b. dass er das Mädchen hat singen hören
   that he the girl will sing hear.INF
   'that he has heard the girl sing'
c. *dass er das Mädchen hat singen gehört
   that he the girl will sing hear.PTCP

This leaves numerous further issues for future research, e.g. concerning the nature of preposing and the precise role of distinct kinds of restructuring elements as well as parametric variation. The main point for the present purposes is that preposing is only possible because the auxiliary HAVE denotes perfect properties (in analogy to the future properties denoted by the German future auxiliary).

In a nutshell, semantic recoverability as granted by HAVE is a necessary condition for the application of impoverishment. This operation is primarily triggered by the interference of a verbal cluster with a morphologically complex participial form whose realisation features GE- (cf. Schmid 2002: 89), though arguably supplemented by a general strive for cluster-internal unity. Although these structural prerequisites could not be discussed sufficiently, the most important conclusion is that the IPP eventually boils down to an instance of impoverishment that only goes through if the underlying interpretation is properly recoverable. While this consistently holds for passive constructions, it apparently is challenged by cases of the IPP with the perfect auxiliary *zijn* ('be') in Dutch (as well as some similar cases in Bernese German and West Frisian). However, as we have seen before, these cases actually arise in the context of particular aspectual verbs (as in *is blijven staan*, lit. is remain.INF stand.INF, *is gaan zwemmen*, lit. is go.INF swim.INF, and *is komen werken*, lit. is come.INF work.INF). Given their exceptional characteristics, the predicates that undergo impoverishment here are likely to be lexically supplemented with a sense of completion, which is why recoverability of a perfect interpretation is granted in spite of the absence of both participial morphology as well as HAVE. This leaves the discussion of one further divergent realisation of past participial morphology that in a sense is basically a photographic negative of the IPP.

While the IPP is triggered by the realisation of the participial prefix GE- if it is part of a verbal cluster, the PPI occurs in similar contexts in languages whose past participles do not include a prefix. However, in contrast to the IPP, which could be shown to realise infinitival morphology on what is interpreted as a past participial form, the PPI does not only feature a properly inflected past participle but (optionally) also realises past participial morphology on an element that is interpreted as an infinitival. This is observable in the Norwegian example in (164), taken from Wiklund (2001: 201), which we have encountered before.

(164) Jeg hadde villet   lest/   lese   boka.
      I   had   want.PTCP read.PTCP/ read.INF book.the
      'I had wanted to read the book.'

As we have seen, Norwegian (like Swedish) only allows for the PPI in certain variants and the phenomenon is absent in the standard language (cf. Schmid 2002: 112), whereas Faroese and Frisian generally permit an additional instantiation of past participial morphology. Quite generally, the occurrence of the superfluous participial morpheme is typically optional, reminiscent of its impoverishment languages exhibiting IPP. Strikingly, the syntactic configuration in which the PPI may occur is identical to what we have seen in IPP-contexts, namely a complex verbal cluster consisting at least of a main verb embedded under a restructuring (modal) verb, which in turn is selected by the perfect auxiliary HAVE.[144] Passive variants of the PPI are just as absent as perfect variants with BE in exponents exhibiting auxiliary alternation. Just like in the context of the PPP and the IPP, this raises two questions, namely how the PPI may be grasped technically and whether there is a semantic basis in terms of recoverability.

At the core of previous approaches to the PPI lies the question of how the perfect auxiliary interacts with elements within a verbal cluster so as to trigger the realisation of an additional instance of past participial morphology on a form that is expected to surface as an infinitive. As we have briefly seen above, den Dikken & Hoekstra (1997: 1058f.) for instance provide a purely morphosyntactic approach to the PPI and assume that the phenomenon is based on multiple feature-checking of VPs that have to move through the specifier position of a functional head (eventually occupied by the auxiliary) in order to receive participial morphology. The main intuition in this approach is that it is the auxiliary alone that eventually introduces the aspectual information associated with past participial constructions, which is grasped in terms of multiple verbal elemens being allowed to check their (uninterpretable) features on the basis of the auxiliary (cf. den Dikken & Hoekstra 1997: 1068f.). Though appealing, what is problematic about this is that associating aspectual properties solely with the auxiliary renders past participial morphology ornamental and hence raises the question of why participial morphology is introduced in the context of a composite perfect at all rather than being systematically missing.

---

[144] Similar to what we have seen in the context of the IPP, the PPI is not restricted to featuring verbal clusters made up out of two verbal elements under a single auxiliary, but there may in fact even be three participial forms out of which only one is semantically interpreted as a participle (cf. den Dikken & Hoekstra 1997: 1068–1070).

An alternative account may be found in Wiklund (2007), who argues that the PPI arises as a consequence of a mechanism called 'participle copying' (Wiklund 2007: 7), which is claimed to be "*top-down, syntactic,* and *local*" (Wiklund 2007: 35). While this mechanism is unfortunately not spelled out in detail, Wurmbrand (2012a: 156) criticises that it assumes that the verbal forms in a given cluster end up with interpretable participial features. This is empirically inadequate in that it necessitates perfect semantics to occur on both past participial forms, despite the fact that only one form is eventually interpreted as a past participle (cf. Wurmbrand 2012a: 156). Wurmbrand (2012a) tries to circumvent this problem by resorting to Pesetsky & Torrego's (2007) dissociation of valuation and interpretability and the application of Reverse Agree. These assumptions allow her to assume that the direction of valuation of a participle and its auxiliary is parameterised in terms of whether the auxiliary values the participle or vice versa, the latter of which is what we find in languages with GE- (cf. Wurmbrand 2012a: 154).[145] Accordingly, "the feature value [T: perf] resides in AUX in Frisian, Scandinavian, and English, whereas in German, PART is inserted with the valued [T: perf] feature" (Wurmbrand 2012a: 160). This accounts for parasitic participles, where the perfect auxiliary contains an interpretable perfect (tense-)feature, which values the uninterpretable counterparts on both the embedded modal as well as the main verb, thus giving rise to past participial morphology on both of them (cf. Wurmbrand 2012a: 156f.). The alternative case without a parasitic participle is accounted for by assuming that an (empty) infinitival head is around, which contains an interpretable tense-feature with an infinitival value that values the lower main verb (cf. Wurmbrand 2012a: 156f.). These considerations provide an interesting morphosyntactic account of the PPI-data and the typological differences with respect to the presence of a participial prefix. However, attributing the prefix interpretable properties is debatable and subscribing to this approach comes at the cost of being forced to adopt Pesetsky & Torrego's (2007) valuation-framework. Additionally, this account does not readily provide an explanation for the IPP, but rather assumes that this is quite unlike the PPI by virtue of being a PF-phenomenon (cf. Wurmbrand 2012b: 130; see also Zwart 2007). Given these drawbacks, let us briefly sketch an alternative in analogy to the impoverishment operations that we have seen in the context of the PPP and the IPP above.

---

[145] This is tied to the characteristic property of languages like German, to form their participles with the help of a participial prefix, which is taken to be "*lexically valued* as a participle" (Wurmbrand 2012a: 160).

4.2 The syntax and semantics of past participles — 287

Since the contexts in which we find IPP and PPI are virtually identical, namely verbal clusters embedded under an auxiliary necessitating the presence of a past participle (either realised with or without a participial prefix), it is tempting to assume that the core of their explanation is at least remotely similar. As we have seen in the context of the IPP, impoverishment serves as a rescue mechanism in order to allow for the realisation of a participial element that would otherwise be realised in a morphologically complex way, i.e. as a circumfix, as part of a syntactically complex configuration. This does not have any effect on LF in that the plain form in question is properly interpreted as a past participle and the IPP-variant is hence semantically identical to one without impoverishment. The latter criterion crucially has to carry over to contexts in which a superfluous participle is realised, since this form is eventually interpreted just like its infinitival counterpart. The interference of a complex participial form and a verbal cluster cannot be at issue in the case of the PPI, though, as there is no prefix in languages exhibiting parasitic participles. Rather, as indicated before, elements within a verb cluster apparently tend to carry the same morphological inflection while not giving rise to the same interpretation. This factor, which additionally motivates the application of impoverishment in IPP-contexts, serves as a trigger for the application of a mechanism that is familiar from the DM-literature: ornamental morphology (cf. Embick & Noyer 2007: 305f.). This operation allows us to "introduce syntactico-semantically unmotivated structure and features which 'ornament' the syntactic representation" (Embick & Noyer 2007: 305). One variant of this process allows for morphophonological material to be copied from another syntactic object in what is called feature copying: "A feature is present on a node X in the narrow syntax is [sic!] copied onto another node Y at PF" (Embick & Noyer 2007: 309). Crucially, while what is copied is a morphosyntactic feature, this variant of feature copying is a postsyntactic PF-operation that does not have any effect on LF, as desired. Thus, a feature leading to the introduction of participial morphology is (phonologically) copied from the participial form governed by the perfect auxiliary onto all other constitutive verbs of the given cluster.[146] This leads to a clear demarcation of the participants in the verbal cluster. Eventually, similar to impoverishment, the PF-mechanism in

---

146 In a similar vein, Hinterhölzl (2009: 210f.) assumes that the repair-operation deriving the IPP is also capable of deriving the PPI: instead of spelling out "the default morphology of an infinitive[,] one can also imagine that the entire feature matrix, including its formal feature is copied on to [sic!] the higher head." This is accompanied by a semantic repair mechanism that eliminates the copied semantic feature at LF (cf. Hinterhölzl 2009: 211). Adopting ornamental morphology, we can do without this (somewhat redundant) semantic repair mechanism.

question may be sketched out as in (165), in analogy to impoverishment in (159).[147]

(165) *i*Asp[def-perf] contained in Asp is copied onto an element containing uT [non-fin] (i.e. ø → *i*Asp[def-perf]) iff Asp is part of a verb cluster locally c-commanded by an Aux containing *i*Asp[posterior].

This feature copying operation thus takes care of copying the participial morphology onto the infinitival element(s) within the verbal cluster, thus deriving the PPI. To be precise, the infinitival form is supplemented by the main aspectual feature *i*Asp[def-perf], which triggers the morphological realisation of past participial morphology. The successful application of this operation bears the advantage of clearly marking the verb cluster as a structural unit, similar to what we have seen in the case of the IPP. Accordingly, by virtue of imposing morphological uniformity, both the PPI as well as the IPP facilitate interpretational clarity by marking a verbal cluster. The strategy of how this is achieved is virtually opposed in the case of the two phenomena: constructions that are morphologically complex undergo impoverishment, whereas a fairly simple morphological derivation allows for ornamental morphology in terms of feature copying at PF.

This leaves the issue of recoverability, i.e. of how a configuration that instantiates the PPI can be assured to give rise to the same interpretation as a counterpart that does without ornamental morphology. Actually, this follows naturally from the present theory since HAVE suffices to indicate the licensing of an external argument (which is shared between main verb and modal). With respect to the perfect interpretation, it is clear that the superfluously marked form cannot trigger perfectivity all on its own, since the verb on which it occurs is atelic in the examples at hand.[148] The auxiliary HAVE cannot be held responsible for denoting that the (sub-)event of the main verb lies in the past either, as it only interacts with the participial element it governs, namely the restructuring modal. This imposes restrictions on word order, which needs to mark the relation

---

[147] Note that the problem of intervening elements that den Dikken & Hoekstra (1997: 1065) bring up against a phonological account of assimilation (or 'participle harmony') does not apply to (165) as all that matters is the structural presence within a verbal cluster, i.e. embedding of a main verb under a restructuring verb.

[148] This leaves the question of whether the ornamental morphology may also appear on unaccusatives as this may potentially convey an improper interpretation by virtue of erroneously signalling perfectivity, as laid out above. While a short survey does not bring forth any such cases, we will leave this issue to future research. Even if this turns out to be true, though, it need not necessarily be problematic as the parser may well identify the superfluous participial affix as a piece of ornamental morphology that does not have any semantic effect.

between the auxiliary and its participial complement (the restructuring verb), as this may not sufficiently be achieved by morphological marking alone. Eventually, the superfluously marked form in these contexts does not erroneously induce argument suppression nor does it trigger perfectivity. This leaves the explanation for why passive and BE-perfect instances may not make use of the PPI. With the former, the PPI would wrongly convey that both elements in the verbal cluster are to be interpreted as a passive, since this information is unequivocally associated with the past participle in the absence of HAVE (if the underlying verb bears an external argument). Something similar holds for BE-perfect cases where both verbs forming the embedded cluster would potentially qualify for conveying a perfective situation. Given these issues in terms of recoverability, the integrity of the verbal cluster can be signalled by spelling out the participial morphology twice only in the context of HAVE. While the intricate structural properties certainly demand a more fine-grained investigation in future research, the PF-mechanisms of impoverishment and ornamental morphology eventually allow us to account for the PPP, IPP and PPI. Most important for our present purposes in this context, as we have seen, is that there is only one context in which semantic recoverability is granted, namely the occurrence of a divergent realisation in the local c-command domain of HAVE.

4.2.4.2 Past participial agreement

Before concluding the discussion on the syntax and semantics of the periphrastic passive and perfect, let us briefly return to how the occurrence of past participial (object-)agreement that we have seen in (North) Germanic and Romance above may technically be grasped in the present approach. With respect to Slavic non-identity languages, which morphologically mark the distinction between passive and perfect on the participial element in the context of a single auxiliary (BE), what we could see was that past participial agreement with the surface subject regularly occurs in both cases. This could be accounted for by claiming that all of the arguments are introduced in the local domain of both passive and perfect participles, whereas this is distinct in identity-languages (cf. Broekhuis & Migdalski 2003: 3), where HAVE plays a crucial role in licensing external arguments. The usual case in identity languages is what we can see in (166), based on Thráinsson (2007: 9).

(166) a. Maður   var   bitinn   af hundi.
        the.man.NOM.M.SG *was* *bite*.PTCP.M.SG *by the.dog*
        'The man was bitten by the dog.'
    b. Hundurinn hefur bitið   manninn.
        the.dog   *has* *bite*.PTCP *the.man*
        'The dog has bitten the man.'

Icelandic consistently shows past participial agreement with the surface subject in cases with *vera* ('be') and *verða* ('become'), as observable in (166a), while using an invariant form in the context of *hafa* ('have'), as in (166b). This pattern is shared by all other identity languages exhibiting past participial agreement, although there is a highly restricted set of exceptions in Romance that we will return to shortly. Thus, just like with the divergent realisations we have just revisited, HAVE is the odd man out by virtue of blocking agreement where other auxiliaries generally permit it.[149] The reason for this may of course not be found in semantic recoverability on the basis of the contribution of posteriority though, but rather stems from the perfect auxiliary's capacity of licensing an external argument. This becomes obvious once we turn to the exceptional cases of past participial agreement with HAVE. The examples in (167) that we have already encountered before (cf. Franco 1994: 247, Bjorkman 2011: 155, and Rowlett 2007: 227, respectively) show the major contexts in which this shines through.

(167) a. Gianni l' ha   *mangiato/ mangiata.
       Gianni it.F has eat.PTCP/   eat.PTCP.F
       'Gianni has eaten it.'
   b. La maison que les filles on peint/   peinte.
      the house that the girls have paint.PTCP/ paint.PTCP.F
      'The house that the girls have painted.'
   c. Quelles maisons avez-vouz repeintes?
      which   houses have-you repaint.PTCP.PL
      'Which houses did you repaint?'

The Italian example in (167a) features a cliticised direct object with which the past participle obligatorily agrees in 3rd person contexts and optionally agrees elsewhere (cf. Muxí 1996: 127; Belletti 2006: 495f.). The French fronted direct objects in (167b) and (167c) also provide instances in which there is past participial object-agreement in the context of HAVE (cf. Rowlett 2007: 226f.). Even though something similar is barred in Italian, these contexts show that there is a highly restricted set of contexts in which past participial agreement with HAVE

---

149 Recall that past participial agreement is, of course, subject to parameterisation and hence agreement need not always occur with auxiliaries other than HAVE. Furthermore, even though this is a special case, it is not always a matter of all or nothing, as for instance observable in Danish, where stative passives optionally feature agreement, whereas eventive passives do not allow for agreement morphology to be realised at all.

may occur. As Lois (1990: 244) points out, such cases only crop up in auxiliary alternating languages, though.

The HAVE-contexts in (167) crucially share with their non-HAVE counterparts in Romance but also in Germanic and elsewhere that they involve phrasal movement of the underlying object that the past participial form eventually overtly agrees with (cf. Bjorkman 2011: 154). A prototypical HAVE-construction in which there is no movement is strictly barred from exhibiting past participial agreement cross-linguistically. This suggests that past participle agreement in identity languages universally marks "a reflex of the displacement of the nominal projection determining agreement" (Belletti 2006: 495).[150] Hence, structures featuring passives or unaccusatives may readily exhibit agreement in the Scandinavian languages and Romance, while some exponents of the latter occasionally also entertain participial object-agreement in case the direct object is moved via *wh*- or clitic movement (cf. Franco 1994: 256; Bjorkman 2011: 154). While approaches based on designated agreement projections may resort to movement through AgrOP, which is not instantiated in case the object remains *in situ*, the present feature-driven account has done without such designated projections thus far. Instead, we may take as our starting point Bjorkman's (2011: 155) assumption that past participial object-agreement is contingent on Reverse Agree.[151] Assuming this entails that "Agreement can be established only when the element with valued features c-commands its target" (Bjorkman 2011: 155). This accounts for the restriction that past participial object-agreement is only possible if the internal argument moves out of the participial phrase and through a position in which agreement may be established, whereas "external arguments are generated in too high a position to establish that relationship" (Bjorkman 2011: 156).

---

150 Note that the universal applicability of this claim is challenged by some Romance exponents, e.g. Occitan and dialects of southern Italian, where the direct object agrees with the participles in the context of HAVE despite staying *in situ* (cf. Belletti 2006: 502). This is for instance observable in the Italian example *Maria ha conosciute le ragazze* ('Maria has known the girls.', lit. Maria has known.F.PL the girls.F.PL) (cf. Belletti 2006: 502). This indicates that past participles may generally also exhibit agreement with their object, although this is usually disregarded as there is no need to mark a relation that retains locality at PF, something we will turn to shortly.
151 As we could briefly see in (130) above, this operation is a 'reversed' form of the standard feature-interaction operation (an unvalued element c-commands its valued counterpart) in terms of an element β bearing a valued feature c-commanding a syntactic object α that bears an unvalued counterpart. As we have seen, this theoretical extension is called for in the context of the valuation of tense features as well.

As the present approach relies on φ-features in terms of holding them accountable for the formal necessity of introducing arguments, we cannot simply claim that there is no agreement between the participle and its object in cases in which the latter is not moved out of the participial domain. Rather, we will assume that the overt morphophonological realisation of past participial object-agreement is only called for in cases in which the object is displaced out of the participial domain.[152] Crucially, then, Reverse Agree only matters in so far as the feature distribution on the basis of which morphologically marking past participial object-agreement at PF is triggered is bound to include a valued interpretable feature c-commanding its valued uninterpretable counterpart. In other words, Reverse Agree does not apply, but the configuration in which participial object-agreement is instantiated at PF is contingent on an *i*φ-feature which (asymmetrically) c-commands its *u*φ counterpart. Eventually, then, past participial object-agreement applies as tentatively sketched in (168).

(168)

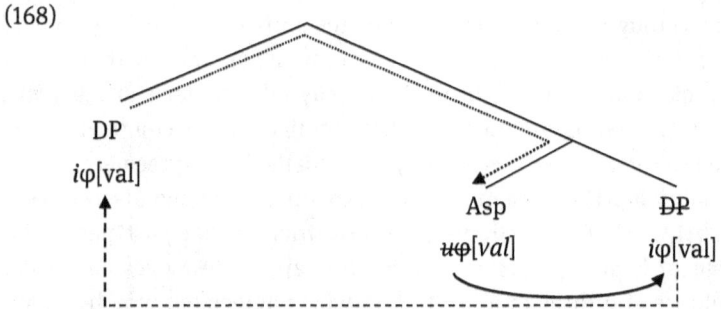

This arguably suffices to technically account for the general mechanism behind the overt instantiation of past participial object-agreement. The lack of past participial agreement with an external argument, on the other hand, follows from the fact that the external argument simply does not establish an agreement-relation by virtue of valuing v's (and Aux's) but crucially not Asp's φ-feature. Eventually, then, the syntactic valuation of φ-features is a necessary but not a sufficient condition for the overt morphological expression of agreement at PF. This raises numerous questions. In fact, although the general conceptual basis for spelling out participial agreement only in case the object is displaced appears to be clear, namely that a relation between the participle and its object is marked in order to maintain interpretational clarity, the precise PF-mechanisms behind

---

[152] In cases in which it is not necessary (or possible) to mark agreement, the participial form is spelled out with a default exponent at PF. This is typically (but not necessarily) the participial form without an agreement marker or the 3rd person neuter marker.

this remain to be discussed. Furthermore, what is striking with respect to parametric variation[153] is that participial object-agreement with HAVE is restricted to a small set of contexts in languages exhibiting auxiliary alternation. This raises the question of why HAVE-only languages never allow for agreement to be spelled out in the context of HAVE especially considering the fact that they comprise a large number of contexts that potentially qualify for this (namely HAVE-perfect contexts based on unaccusatives). Quite generally, the present account for the agreement-data also raises the intricate issue of what determines the immediacy of spelling out formal features at PF. We will have to leave these (and further) interesting questions to future research, but may, in conclusion, briefly focus on the role of the auxiliary in contexts of object-agreement.

While languages like English and German also exhibit the structural configuration in (168), they do not possess the capability to overtly mark agreement on the past participial form in periphrastic contexts. However, what is marked is that the direct object agrees with the auxiliary, as observable on the basis of plural marking with *The girls were chased* and *Die Mädchen sind verschwunden* ('The girls have disappeared.', lit. the girl.PL is.PL disappear.PTCP). This is technically grasped with the help of a *u*φ-feature on Aux, which is valued on the basis of the internal argument that moves through Spec, Aux. This raises the question of what happens in such cases in languages marking participial object-agreement. In contrast to languages like Icelandic and Danish, which possess an invariant auxiliary, languages like Italian, French and Romanian also exhibit surface subject agreement with the auxiliary. This leads to agreement chains in unaccusative and passive cases, as we can see in the Romanian example in (169), taken from Soare (2007: 174).[154]

(169) Căpșunile   sînt culese.
      the.strawberries are picked.PTCP.PL
      'The strawberries are picked.'

Here, not only the past participle, but also the auxiliary verb exhibits overt agreement morphology. This provides support for some of the technical assumptions laid out in the present work, namely that φ-features are inherently stored on nominal

---

153 See Kayne (1989), Lois (1990), Muxí (1996: 127f., 137f.), Franco (1994: 256f.), Friedeman & Siloni (1997), Caponigro & Schütze (2003), den Dikken (1994: 66f.), and Belletti (2006: 499f.), amongst others, for more detailed investigations of the parameterisation of participial agreement.
154 Recall that we have seen a similar case from Latin before: *Feminae captae sunt* ('The women have been seized.'). Even more complex cases for instance come to the fore in French examples like *Les voitures ont été lavées* ('The cars were washed.', lit. the.PL car.PL have.PL be.PTCP wash.PL).

expressions and may value several unvalued (and uninterpretable) counterparts on past participles as well as auxiliaries. In other words, φ-features allow for agreement-chains, where the determination of which of the integral parts receive an overt spell-out depends on independent factors like the presence of finite tense information (in the domain of T) or displacement out of a local domain (participial object-agreement).

Generally speaking, we may conclude that differences concerning the overt realisation of participial agreement can be traced back to the assumption that the morphological realisation of agreement is a means to signal relations between verbs (or auxiliaries) and their arguments. In identity languages, this is most notably called for in case the argument in question undergoes displacement and – at least in terms of overt phonological expression – gives up its local relationship with the verb to which it is interpretively related. In non-identity languages, on the other hand, the past participial morphology suffices to indicate interpretational differences, which is why the past participial forms may generally realise agreement morphology with the external argument in perfect cases and the internal argument in passive cases (cf. Iatridou et al. 2001: 235). Accordingly, in non-identity languages like Bulgarian "the uniform BE perfect is accompanied by uniform participial agreement with the subject, including underived subjects" (Bjorkman 2011: 156). This shows that the different properties of the morphologically distinguishable past participles in non-identity languages evoke further distinctions in grammatical behaviour,[155] the range and specifics of which remain to be worked out in future research.

This concludes our discussion of the syntax and semantics of the periphrastic passive and the analytic perfect in terms of an approach to the substantial identity of past participles in passive and perfect contexts. In the next section, we will briefly look over the rim of the tea cup by considering whether these assumptions may also be transferred to bare participial uses. Accordingly, we will consider whether a radical identity approach to past participles (i.e. one holding for all verbal and adjectival past participles) is a licit as well as insightful undertaking and, if this turns out not to be the case, which differences need to be granted. This discussion will eventually bring us back to the more general categorial considerations that have accompanied the discussion of past participles since day one.

---

[155] What seems to be at the core of proper participial subject-agreement in the case of morphologically distinct perfect participles is that there is no suppression of the external argument. Therefore, this argument need not be introduced by an auxiliary but may readily be licensed by the participle, which hence establishes a direct relation in terms of valuing its φ-features (cf. Broekhuis & Migdalski 2003: 3).

4.3 Bare instances and the category of past participles

Now that the major properties of past participial formation have been identified and a case for their substantial identity in periphrastic constructions has been made, what remains to be discussed is whether this identity carries over to bare instantiations. While the null hypothesis is that this question deserves an affirmative answer, the availability of adjectival instantiations laid bare in chapter 2.2 shows that additional properties might have to be attributed to past participial forms in order to allow them to occur in specific contexts. Accordingly, the underlying questions that the present chapter is briefly going to tackle in chapter 4.3.1 and 4.3.2 respectively are the following: How do the basic properties of past participial morphology shine through in their bare realisations? Which additional properties, if any, need to be attributed to past participial forms in order to account for their occurrence in syntactic configurations in which they show up without an accompanying auxiliary (e.g. in a prenominal position or with the copula BE)? What are the theoretical implications of these considerations for the category of past participles?

4.3.1 Bare past participles in resultative and eventive configurations

The arguably most prototypical adjectival occurrences of past participles appear in the context of the copula BE.[156] In fact, the participles in configurations like those in (170) and (171) are commonly taken to forfeit most of their eventive (verbal) properties.

(170) a. The house is built.
 b. The boy is (sloppily) combed.

(171) a. Das Haus ist gebaut.
 the house is build.PTCP
 'The house is (in the resultative state of having been) built.'
 b. Der Junge ist (schlampig) gekämmt.
 the boy is (sloppily) comb.PTCP
 'The boy is (in the resultative state of having been) combed (sloppily).'

---

[156] Note that this claim neglects the class of elements that Embick (2003; 2004) calls 'stative (passive) participles' (i.e. items like *sunken, shrunken, shaven* and *blessèd*), as these arguably boil down to fully-fledged adjectives rather than adjectival instances of deverbal past participles, as briefly touched upon in chapter 2.4.3.

As we could see on numerous occasions by now, these cases are usually referred to as 'stative passives'. However, they are actually not properly passive, i.e. crucially lack an external argument that is existentially bound.[157] Rather, the external argument is absent altogether (see Kratzer 1994; 2000; Rapp 1998; Meltzer-Asscher 2011). Evidence for this claim comes from the occurrences in (172) and (173). While English is subject to a large degree of homonymy, German employs distinct lexemes for the passive auxiliary (WERDEN) and the copula (BE), thus overtly distinguishing eventive and stative passives. Accordingly, evidence from German rather than English is presented.

(172) a. *Das Haus ist von Peter gebaut.
    the house is by Peter build.PTCP
 b. *Das Haus ist sorgfältig gebaut.
    the house is carefully build.PTCP

(173) a. *Das Haus ist gebaut, um es zu vermieten.
    the house is build.PTCP in.order it to rent
 b. Das Haus wurde gebaut, um es zu vermieten.
    the house became build.PTCP in.order it to rent
    'The house was built in order to rent it.'

The data presented in (172) show that adverbial modification by BY-phrases is barred in stative passives and the same holds for proper agent-oriented (eventive) modifiers. Both of these observations point to the absence of an external semantic role in the interpretation of these copular constructions. This claim finds support in the observation that control into purposes clauses is not available in stative passives, but properly functional in eventive passives due to the availability of an existentially bound external argument (cf. Rapp 1998; Roßdeutscher & Kamp 2010). An additional observation in support of this claim may be found in the fact that stative passives like those in (170b) and (171b) permit reflexive readings (see Kratzer 1994), unlike their eventive counterparts in (174), which are bound to exhibit disjoint reference.

(174) a. The boy is being combed.
 b. Der Junge wird gekämmt.
    the boy becomes comb.PTCP
    'The boy is (being) combed.'

---

[157] Accordingly, the term stative passive, as indicated before, is a misnomer.

The eventive passives in (174) force an interpretation under which some implicit agent crucially distinct from the raised internal argument serves as the causer of the eventuality. Their stative passive counterparts in (170b) and (171b), on the other hand, allow for the boy to be the agent of the event that eventually leads to the resultative state of him (i.e. the same referent) being combed. This diagnostic, however, only works with a subset of predicates allowing for a reflexive reading in the first place, namely only those that are naturally reflexive (cf. Kemmer 1993).

This drawback leads Alexiadou, Gehrke & Schäfer (2014: 130) to neglect the relevance of employing disjoint reference as a test. Likewise, McIntyre (2013) and Bruening (2014) put into question using control into purpose clauses as a relevant indicator and adduce some counter-evidence. The example in (175), taken from Alexiadou, Gehrke & Schäfer (2014: 129), for instance, shows that it is occasionally possible to find control into purpose clauses with stative passives.

(175) Die Partition ist versteckt, um ein versehentliches Löschen
*the partition is hide.*PTCP *in.order an unintended erasing*
der Dateien zu verhindern.
the data to prevent
'The partition is hidden in order to avoid that it gets deleted by mistake.'

Similar objections may be raised concerning the ban on agentive BY-phrases and agent-oriented modifiers. As a matter of fact, traditional German examples like those in (176) show that these diagnostics are not without exception either (see Maienborn 2007: 97f.).

(176) a. Der Brief ist mit roter Tinte geschrieben.
*the letter is with red ink write.*PTCP
'The letter is (in the resultative state of having been) written with red ink.'
b. Das Bild ist von da Vinci gemalt.
*the picture is by da Vince draw.*PTCP
'The picture is (in the resultative state of having been) drawn by da Vinci.'

However, as shown in Rapp (1997; 1998), Maienborn (2007; 2011), McIntyre (2013), Bruening (2014) and Gehrke (2015), there are clear restrictions on when such exceptions go through. In (176a), the adverbial phrase modifies the resultative state of writing a letter rather than the action that leads to it. The example in

(176b), in turn, requires the DP introduced as part of the BY-phrase to be non-referential and to derive a well-established kind (cf. Gehrke 2015: 923), as the ungrammaticality of the examples in (177) makes clear.

(177) a. *Das Bild ist von Peter gemalt.
 the picture is by Peter draw.PTCP
 b. #The article is written by Peter (vs. The article is written by Chomsky.)

In fact, the modifiers used here are prosodically, syntactically and semantically special (cf. Maienborn 2007: 99f.; Jacobs 1993; 1999; Gehrke 2013). Gehrke (2015: 919) accounts for this on the basis of pseudo-incorporating event-related modifiers into the participle. This is taken to be necessary as the adjectivisation of the participles in question is assumed to existentially bind the event variable and the event is thus forced to remain in the kind domain (see also Gehrke 2012; 2013). This finds support in the fact that the exceptional cases are not eventive in the sense of forcing disjoint reference nor do they allow for control into purpose clauses, as the example in (178) makes clear (see also Gehrke 2015: 905).

(178) a. *Das Bild ist von da Vinci gemalt, um den Papst zu beeindrucken.
 the picture is by da Vinci draw.PTCP, in.order the pope to impress
 b. *The article is written by Chomsky to impress Kayne.

Leaving the precise mechanics of this operation aside for the purposes of the present chapter, what this shows is that there may well be persuasive analyses for these exceptions that hold independent factors responsible. An initiator of the result denoted by the adjectival past participle may occasionally be pseudo-incorporated or conceptually reconstructed. This grants weak recourse to the constitutive event, but does not prohibit the structural absence of an external argument and thus a CAUSE in the event structure of the participial element.[158] Accordingly, the adjectval participles occurring in stative passives are exempt from the passivisation operation in (131). Given the complementary nature of passivisation and (defective) perfectivity as triggered by the past participle, the absence of an external argument enables the availability of a

---

[158] As Gehrke (2015: 907) puts it, "[i]t is standardly assumed that the external argument of the underlying verb is not syntactically active in adjectival passives, however it can be conceptually given."

perfective denotation, if the underlying eventuality is a simple change of state. Strikingly, this is even a prerequisite for the formation of stative passives: the adjectival past participles in these configurations have to attribute a result state to some referent. As Bresnan (1995: 12f.) puts it, "[t]he state denoted by the adjective appears to be the result state of the eventuality denoted by the participle".

In the tradition of Embick (2004), we may thus call the adjectival participles that occur in stative passives 'resultative participles'. While the underlying predicate usually needs to denote a change of state on the basis of its event structural representation, this denotation may also contextually be imposed upon atelic events, as observable in (179).

(179) a. The baby carriage is pushed.
 b. Der Kinderwagen ist geschoben.
    the baby.carriage is push.PTCP
    'The baby carriage is (in the resultative state of having been) pushed.'

According to Anagnostopoulou (2003: 14) such examples – derived from atelic causative predicates – become grammatical "when uttered in a factory that produces baby carriages and the workers' job is to push baby carriages to test their wheels". The interpretation that ensues is what Kratzer (2000) refers to as the 'job-is-done reading'. Accordingly, the two prerequisites for the formation of stative passives are in line with the contribution of the past participial morpheme: the external argument is formally absent and a result comes about on the basis of a simple change of state. Whenever the requirement for a simple change of state is not lexically met, it has to be imposed on the event pragmatically or else a stative passive may not be formed.

This raises the question of how to technically account for the formation of stative passives, where the more fine-grained task is to determine the contribution of the copula and the source of the adjectival character of the participial element it combines with. First of all, we need some (word-syntactic) means to attribute adjectival properties to the deverbal past participle. This primarily boils down to a mechanism that grants the direct association of the internal semantic role of the underlying verb with the (independently licensed) argument in question. To this end, following Meltzer-Asscher (2012: 168), we assume that whenever a given past participial adjunct is directly associated with a nominal governor, its internal thematic role is lexically marked for λ-abstraction, i.e. for the semantic association with a referent. This entails that whenever a past participle occurs in adjunct function, the internal thematic role can and need not syntactically be assigned (cf. Meltzer-Asscher 2012: 178).¹⁵⁹ Accordingly, Meltzer-Asscher (2012: 178) claims that this argument is "λ-abstracted over, and the resulting function applies to the subject argument", where 'subject' neutrally refers to the nominal element that the predicate is associated with. Taking this for granted, past participles associated with their internal arguments through a direct semantic relation rather than by virtue of realising them (word-)syntactically are formed by an operation along the lines of (180) (see McIntyre 2013: 27 and Bruening 2014: 385 for further approaches based on λ-abstraction).

(180) Marking the internal argument for λ-abstraction
When a given adjectival affix attaches to a past participle in word syntax, it marks the verb's internal semantic role, viz. any θ-role to be assigned to an argument in AspP not marked for inherent case, for λ-abstraction. This marking renders the internal θ-role inactive for syntactic purposes by means of rendering the associated feature-value unavailable.

Reminiscent of the existential binding rule in (131), this operation assures that the affected argument is dealt with semantically rather than syntactically. Accordingly, the *i*θ-feature associated with the lexically-marked argument is kept from playing any role in (phrasal) syntax. As the presence of a suitable internal semantic role is a necessary requirement for the formation of an 'adjectival past participle' (unlike the presence of an external role for past participial formation), this may be grasped by virtue of the presence of *u*θ on the adjectival functional head.¹⁶⁰ This naturally accounts for why adjectival participles may not be derived from those predicates that only have an external argument (i.e. unergatives as in *Der Vater ist gehustet/*The father is coughed or *der gehustete Vater/*the coughed father) or those that bear an internal argument that is marked for dative case (*Der Mann ist geholfen*, lit. the man is help.PTCP or

---

159 This holds most clearly for copular constructions and prenominal positions, but in terms of modifying a nominal governor arguably also in postnominal and adverbial distribution, as to be discussed shortly.

160 This emphasises that the framework laid out in chapter 1.2 does justice both to lexicalist as well as DM-assumptions. It complies with lexicalism in that the 'conversion' is effected by a lexical (i.e. word-syntactic) operation, but it also complies with DM in that this follows "from the syntactic-environment in which the root ultimately realized as a participle appears" (Embick 1997: 97). In this latter sense, then, lexical operations are taken to be based on the inventory of mechanisms supplied by syntax, although the semantic ingredients the terminal elements bring with them also play an important role, as observable in the operations on argument structure in (131) and (180).

der geholfene Mann, lit. the help.PTCP man): only those internal semantic roles that are not associated with inherent case may undergo λ-abstraction.

Technically speaking, the lexical marking of the internal argument for λ-abstraction is thus induced by a functional element which adds a layer to the word-syntactic formation of past participles (cf. (119)). In other words, this combination with a functional head in word syntax assures that the core adjectival function of attributing a property may be fulfilled in terms of directly relating a predicate to an argument (see Lieber 1980; Kratzer 1994; amongst others, for approaches based on zero-affixation).

(181)

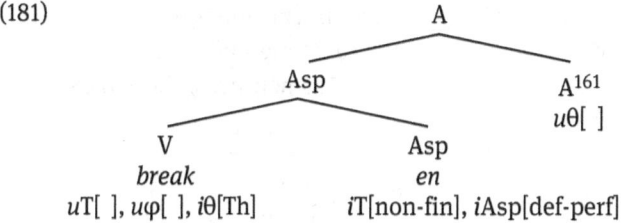

Beside the requirement for the direct association with an internal argument, evidence for the assumption that this process harks back to a lexical (i.e. word-syntactic) process comes from the oft-cited ability of past participles associated with a nominal governor via (181) to be modified by *un-* as in *unopened* and *unresolved* (see, amongst many others, Siegel 1973; Wasow 1977; Levin & Rappaport 1986). Additionally, as we have seen in passing in chapter 2.4, participles readily participate in the formation of adjectival compounds like *well-written, deeply-rooted* and *densely-populated*. These two mechanisms add to the stative character of adjectival past participles and thus emphasise the presence of a resultative state (viz. an anticausative change of state), which is why they may only occur in stative contexts like the stative passive. If one thus does not want to stipulate that both compounding as well as the attachment of derivational affixes like *un-* happen in (phrasal) syntax (e.g. by assuming a functional head), one has to assume that there is a lexical operation converting a past participle into an 'adjectival' element.

---

161 Note that the assumption that the A-head's $u\theta$ binds the verbal $i\theta$[Th] but leaves corresponding $u\varphi$ intact goes against the standard view according to which adjuncts do not bear any uninterpretable (and unvalued) features. Given that bare past participles may carry agreement morphology – consider *die geöffneten Briefe* ('the opened letters', lit. *the open.*PTCP.PL *letter.*PL) in German as well as stative passives in Danish – and the fact that the mechanism of adjunction still remains mysterious, it does not appear to be much of a stretch to violate this.

This leaves the role of the copula in the formation of stative passives. While the operation in (180) accounts for the adjectival characteristic of attributing a property, this is primarily an argument structural operation. In fact, the flexibility of less stative occurrences of adjectival past participles that we will turn to shortly suggests that it should not be held responsible for the restrictions imposed upon stative passives. Rather, this is where the copula comes in: it morphologically encodes finiteness and establishes a direct predicational relation in a clausal context. This copular head may have to be phonologically spelled out, as in Romance and Germanic languages, but can also remain without a phonological form, as in Turkish (consider *Claire öğrenci* 'Claire is a student.', lit. Claire student) (cf. Aygen 2009). The representation in (182) shows the derivation of an adjectival past participle embedded in a stative passive construction, viz. *Das Haus ist gebaut* ('The house is built.') in German.

(182)

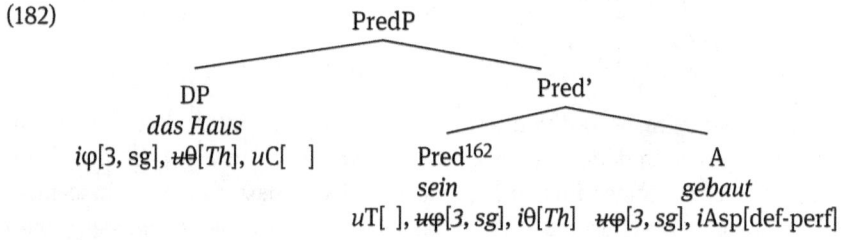

Without dwelling on the technical details, let us assume with Meltzer-Asscher (2012: 155f.) that a copula is introduced in a predicational phrase, PredP.[163] This is based on Bowers' (1993; 2001) assumption of a Pred-head and Baker's (2003) claim that adjectives do not assign θ-roles to their specifiers. Accordingly, past participles lexically marked for λ-abstraction in copular constructions are introduced as

---

162 While the presence of *i*θ[*Th*] is contestable and primarily included for technical reasons that we will return to shortly, the copula technically is quite impoverished by virtue of containing only *u*T and *u*φ. Semantically, the core meaning of the copular construction is attributing a stative property to a subject-referent (cf. Welke 2008: 127f.). Hence, copulas are maximally unrestricted in terms of which elements they establish a predicational relation for: the property denoted by the copula may be an adjective (*is tall*), another (generic) nominal expression (*is a doctor*), a prepositional phrase (*is in Paris*), or an adjectival past participle as in the case above.
163 Meltzer-Asscher (2011: 45, 2012: 168f.) assumes that associating the past participle with a referent generally requires the presence of a functional head, we will – prematurely, of course – assume here that PredP is only necessary in those contexts in which a stative reading is forced, hence stative passives, stative perfects and all English (but only some German) prenominal past participles. In other words, PredP is responsible for mediating the attribution of a state, which is necessary in clausal contexts and (more or less) optional in other distributions.

complements of predicational heads. This functional head mediates function application (i.e. providing a value for the semantically open λ-abstracted expression) and introduces the referent to which the participial property is attributed in its specifier position. This accounts for the traditional externalisation of the internal argument (see Borer 1984; Levin & Rappaport 1986; McIntyre 2013; Bruening 2014). The combination of a copular and its relational complement then suffices for the assignment of a θ-role to the argument in Spec, Pred (cf. Lohndahl 2006: 47). This is captured here by means of granting the copula an $i\theta$-feature that has been retrieved from the adjectival past participle (in analogy to HAVE in the context of a lexically-marked external role).[164] In formal syntactic terms, what is most remarkable here is that on top of the suppression (or deletion) of the external semantic role in the formation of an 'adjectival' past participle, the A-head's $u\theta$ binds the verbal $i\theta$[Th] but leaves corresponding $u\varphi$ intact (see (180)). Crucially, PredP's role of attributing a property to a referent also triggers semantic consequences. As it may only attribute a stative property, it forces stativisation in terms of existentially binding the event variable of the adjectival past participle (in the sense of Gehrke 2015: 919) and attributes the stative property to the argument introduced in its specifier position (cf. Pross 2018: 28). In fact, PredP picks out the perfective state from a resultative BECOME-phase and flattens the event by attributing this state to the referent in question. Hence, it is contingent on the absence of an eventive CAUSE.

These structural considerations carry over to other stative (or stativised) contexts. Accordingly, the requirement for a resultative state is also attested in the stative perfect configurations in (183) and the adjectival participles in the complement position of the raising verbs *seem* and *remain* in (184).

(183) a. Sie hat die Augen verbunden.
        she has the eyes   tie.PTCP
        'She has her eyes tied.'
     b. She has her eyes tied.

(184) a. This song seems well-written.
     b. The window remained broken.

---

[164] Alternatively, DP and A form a (potentially symmetrical) small clause, before the DP is displaced to Spec, Pred (see Moro 2000: 41). This, however, is bound to stipulate a way to account for the valuation of the θ-feature on DP, as this is syntactically unavailable since its value has lexically been marked for λ-abstraction.

These occurrences share with stative passives that they bar agentive BY-phrases and agent-oriented modifiers, do not enforce disjoint reference and do not permit control into purpose clauses. Accordingly, they lack an external argument just like their stative passive counterparts. Furthermore, they also exhibit the requirement for a simple change of state, which is a prerequisite for the denotation of a resultative state. The major difference with respect to the stative passives, then, is the fact that the Pred-head is not spelled out phonologically, as it does not serve to morphologically spell out finiteness.[165]

The stative occurrences we have just considered mark the adjectival pole of past participial occurrences that are not accompanied by auxiliaries. Most relevant for the present purposes is that the past participial affix may be taken to be one and the same in stative constructions as well as in the eventive occurrences, i.e. passive and perfect periphrases, that have formed the core of the present work. In fact, what allows the participial morpheme to denote a resultative state is the absence of an external argument and the presence of a simple change of state. This thus follows naturally from the core properties attributed to past participles so far and accounts for why such 'resultative participles' may show up in stative environments, i.e. in predicational relations as mediated by a stativising PredP. The fact that the argument structure of the adjectival participles is not syntactically realised demands the presence of an alternative means to deal with the internal semantic role: λ-abstraction as triggered by an (empty) adjectival head. In a nutshell, we trace the special characteristics of stative adjectival occurrences of past participles back to the presence of independent functional heads, rather than holding the presence of a distinct participial head responsible for their special characteristics.

Turning to adnominal occurrences of past participles, the same resultative properties also seem to carry over to prenominal instantiations in English. In fact, the prenominal position is reserved for resultative participles like the ones in (185) – alongside proper adjectives, including the class of Embick's (2003; 2004) 'stative participles' – in English.[166]

(185) a. the shaved boy
  b. a half-built house
  c. the unwritten letter

---

[165] Note that this requires us to assume that there are at least two variants of PredP, given that an overt spell-out is never attested in Romance and English in adnominal positions and the stative perfect. Furthermore, uT may not be valued here and the availability of an $i\theta$-value potentially leads the derivation to crash.

[166] Just like with stative passives, apparently atelic prenominal instances like *the pushed cart* are occasionally licit, but only if the context induces an anticausative (change of state) interpretation (i.e. a job-is-done reading).

Given that these instances also behave like stative configurations with respect to the diagnostics discussed above, it seems safe to conclude that they are derivationally equivalent.[167] Once more, the predicational stativiser Pred does not receive an overt spell-out, as it need not morphologically spell out finiteness. Furthermore, the referent that the adjectival participle is associated with via λ-abstraction is introduced independently, which is why it suffices for PredP to occupy the specifier position of N in order to attribute its result state to the nominal referent.

However, there are also more eventive occurrences of past participles that are not accompanied by auxiliaries. One of these is the postnominal use in English, as instantiated in the examples in (186).

(186) a. the girl (recently) seen by Jack
 b. the game (surprisingly) lost by Donald
 c. the house (currently) built by Bill
 d. the boy (longingly) admired by Linnea

While their prenominal counterparts give rise to an individual-level interpretation, these postnominal past participles elicit a stage-level interpretation. Furthermore, as these examples show, both agentive BY-phrases as well as agent-oriented modifiers are permitted in these eventive cases, which points to the presence of an (implicit) external argument. Unlike with their stative counterparts, there is also no requirement for a resultative state, as the concurrency of the participial situation in (186c) and (186d) shows. This suggests that there is no stativising PredP involved in these configurations and thus no requirement for an anticausative (resultative) participle is to be found.[168]

Such postnominal occurrences of eventive participles are often analysed as reduced relatives. In the analyses put forth by Kayne (1994) and Cinque (1999; 2003; 2005a; b) they boil down to impoverished CPs, where a copy of the participle's internal argument is attracted by an empty complementiser and the resulting CP

---

[167] Note that they also share with stative passives that unaccusative predicates are reluctant to occur in this position in English. However, these are not necessarily ungrammatical but only highly disregarded, which Klein (2010: 1239–1241) traces back to competition with the periphrastic HAVE-perfect. German readily allows unaccusatives in both constructions.

[168] Note that Meltzer-Asscher (2011: 94f.) proposes an alternative analysis which holds that adjectival participles are always stative but eventive properties may be brought in by implication: "when confronted with a θ-role but no appropriate event to accommodate it (namely, when the semantic representation includes the conjunct Agent(s,x) or Cause(s,x)), the semantic component reconstructs an event in which the Agent or the Cause has taken part, and this event is interpreted as causing the state denoted by the adjective."

occurs as the complement of a determiner. In a similar vein, Cecchetto & Donati (2015), on the other hand, assume that reduced relatives are the output of a relabelling operation, where the nominal copy is merged with VP to form an NP, which then serves as the complement of a determiner.[169] The latter analysis is arguably superior in terms of doing without the stipulation that determiners take CPs as their complements (and only do so in the case of reduced relatives). However, both types of approaches share a central shortcoming: given the dual role of the internal argument, they are both forced to violate the θ-criterion (see Chomsky 1981) in that two semantic roles are assigned to one and the same argument. The dissociation of the stativising PredP, which is restricted to stative contexts, and the argument structural function of the adjectival head allows us to do without such shortcomings.

Eventive occurrences of bare past participles may be taken to boil down to adjectival past participles in the sense that an empty A-head merges with the past participle and the internal argument is thus taken care of by means of λ-abstraction.[170] This adjectival past participle may directly modify a given nominal

---

169 These two types of analyses are structurally sketched out in (i) and (ii).

(i)
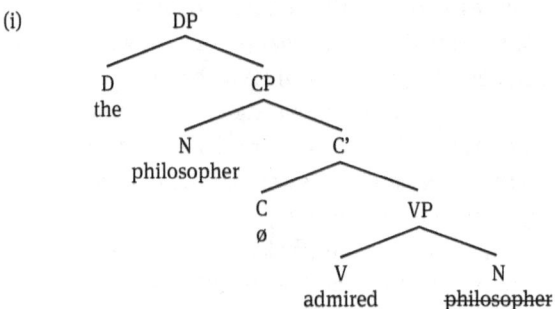

(ii)
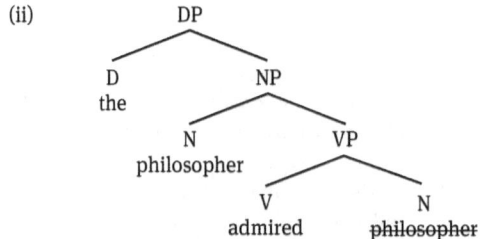

170 The adjectival properties of postnominal participles shine through in Italian, where they may show superlative morphology: *un uomo amatissimo da tutti* ('a man most loved by everyone', lit. a man loved.much by everyone) (cf. Cecchetto & Donati 2015: 78).

referent without any intervening mediator, which is why there is no requirement for a (resultative) state and thus the event structure of the underlying predicate is fully eventive and may feature an external argument. In other words, the passivizing operation in (131) readily kicks in as such cases are not anticausative. This accounts for the unrestricted application of eventive modifiers in postnominal positions, which readily house agentive BY-phrases and agent-oriented adverbs. The internal argument crucially is the only argument licit for undergoing λ-abstraction as triggered by A, since the external argument is marked for existential binding by the past participial morphology, which is introduced prior to the adjectival head. What is attributed to the nominal referent that is co-referential with the internal argument of the past participle is an 'eventive property'.[171]

Some further support for these claims comes from the occurrence of proper adjectives in postnominal positions and the interpretational differences they bring in, as observable in (187) and (188).

(187) a. the visible stars
b. the stars visible

(188) a. the present members
b. the members present

Similar to what was indicated above with respect to past participles, prenominal occurrences of derived as well as non-derived adjectives are restricted to individual-level readings, whereas those in postnominal distribution exhibit stage-level readings (see Carlson 1977; Higginbotham 1983).[172] As König & Gast (2009: 180) point out, "preposed adjectives denote permanent properties while postposed attributes describe temporal properties of the referents". Accordingly, the interpretational difference between (187a) and (187b) is that the stars in question are permanently visible in the former whereas they are only temporarily visible (e.g. because you can only see a part of the night sky through your bedroom window) in the latter. With (188a) and (188b), this shift in meaning is even more extreme as *present* may either

---

[171] Note that Sleeman (2014) applies this term to what she perceives to be prenominal instantiations of eventive participles, something we will return to shortly.

[172] What complicates things is that copular constructions are usually ambiguous between stage- and individual-level readings: *The stars are visible*. This is occasionally disambiguated in Romance, e.g. in Spanish where there are two distinct copulas, *ser* and *estar* ('be'). What is interesting in this context is that some adjectival elements like *present* in (188) unexpectedly only allow for a stage-level interpretation in copular instantiations and some (like *former*) only allow for a prenominal, but crucially no postnominal or copular occurrence (cf. Bolinger 1967).

mean 'actual'/'current' as in the former case or it may merely express the presence of a given individual as in the latter (see Alexiadou et al. 2007: 296f. for a more detailed investigation of the intricate properties of postnominal modification).

What complicates things is that the neat distributional differences that pertain to English do not necessarily carry over to other languages. Rather, there is parametric variation which has both kinds of past participial configurations converge in the prenominal position in German, for instance. This is observable in the examples in (189).

(189) a. ein rasierter Mann
    a shave.PTCP *man*
    'a shaved man'
  b. ein gelöstes Problem
    a solve.PTCP *problem*
    'a solved problem'
  c. das gegenwärtig von Thilo gespielte Turnier
    the currently by Thilo play.PTCP *tournament*
    'the tournament currently played by Thilo'
  d. die von drei Pferden über den Platz gezogene Kutsche
    the by three horses across the square draw.PTCP *carriage*
    'the carriage drawn by three horses across the square'

While the examples in (189a) and (189b) seem to give rise to a resultative state, (189c) and (189d) are interpreted in an eventive fashion and may do without a resultative component.[173] As we have seen before, there is also some room for stage-level interpretations to shine through in the restricted case of prenominal modification in English. This has recently been suggested by Laskova (2007: 134) and Sleeman (2011: 1569f.), who attest eventive properties for prenominal past participles, as in *the evacuated house*. However, given the fact that the diagnostics of stative properties are still met in these contexts, this is likely to be merely a consequence of implication, which infers eventive properties and thus allows for a concurrency-reading. We will thus maintain that there is a clear distinction

---

[173] The availability of a resulative state accounts for mismatches like *der erhaltene Brief* ('the obtained letter', lit. the receive.PTCP letter) vs. **Der Brief wurde erhalten* ('The letter was obtained.', the letter became receive.PTCP). The latter contains an insufficient amount of Proto-Agent properties and hence does not allow for existential binding (thus a passive interpretation), whereas the former is grammatical because *erhalten* ('obtain') is stripped of its external argument (which thus cannot be existentially bound), but allows for a resultative interpretation.

4.3 Bare instances and the category of past participles — 309

between pre- and postnominal occurrences in English, which converges in the prenominal position in German.[174]

The structural representations in (190) tentatively sketch the properties of the syntactic configurations of eventive pre- and postnominal occurrences of past participles in German and English, respectively.

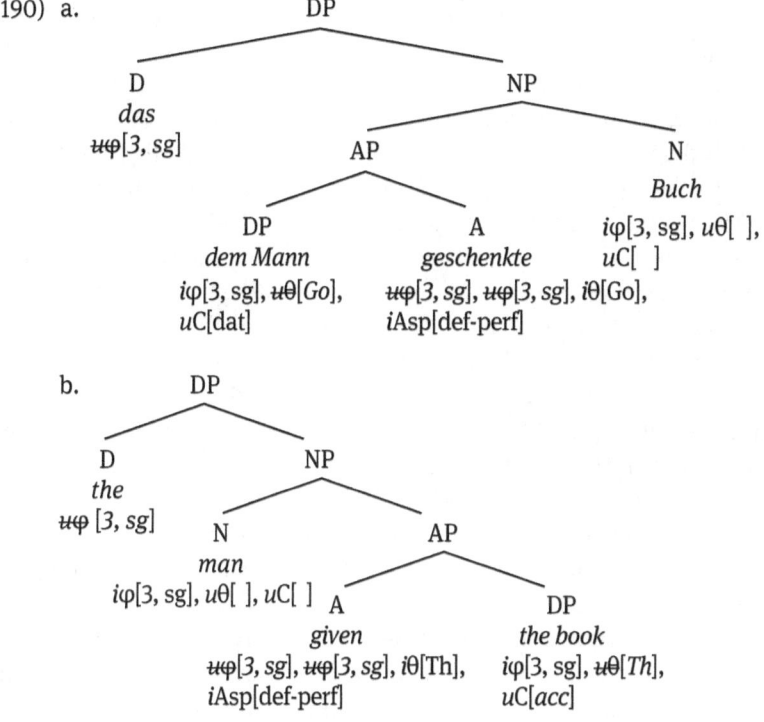

(190) a.

b.

---

174 An interesting complication that arises in German is that (manner of) motion predicates, which are arguably lexically associated with an endpoint (to different degrees), give rise to prenominal past participles. This can only be reconciled with (180), if the sole argument is conceptualised as an internal one.

(i) a. das *(nach Hause) gerannte Mädchen
       the   to   home   run PTCP girl
   b. das *(in den Raum) getanzte Mädchen
       the into the room dance.PTCP girl
   c. das *(zum Beckenrand) geschwommene Mädchen
       the to.the pool.edge swim. PTCP   girl

In contrast to their periphrastic counterparts which may form a proper BE-perfect, even fully lexicalised participles of motion verbs like *gerannt* ('run') demand the presence of an overt endpoint, which indicates that there are fine-grained differences regarding the factors responsible for triggering a periphrastic perfective and those triggering an adnominal resultative.

These structures featuring bare past participles derived from ditransitive predicates follow naturally from the technical properties identified so far. In the German prenominal construction in (190a), the $u\varphi$-feature associated with the dative-marked recipient is saturated first and, in turn, the dative argument values its $u\theta$-feature on the basis of the past participle's valued counterpart. The $u\varphi$-feature belonging to the lexically-marked internal argument is valued once the AP housing the past participle adjoins to the nominal element it modifies. The $u\theta$-feature on the modified noun is then independently valued by the main clause's predicate. The derivation of the postnominal use in (190b) proceeds in a similar fashion, although there is one important difference in flexibility. Based on the lack of inherent case, both the recipient as well as the theme are licit targets for the λ-abstraction mechanism in (180). In the present case, *the book* receives default (accusative) case and values its $u\theta$-feature on the basis of the past participle's $i\theta$-counterpart, which in turn values its associated $u\varphi$-feature with the help of the argument it licenses. This leaves the second instance of $u\varphi$ that is associated with the semantic role lexically marked for λ-abstraction. This feature is valued on the basis of its $i\varphi$-counterpart on the noun that is modified by the adjectival past participle. In the alternative derivation of *the book given to him*, on the other hand, it is the Theme-role that is lexically marked. Accordingly, *the book* is postmodified in this case. However, given that default case arguably generally cannot be realised on arguments introduced in verbal specifier positions (i.e. those associated with inherent case in other languages), a case-assigning preposition has to be introduced.

The major distinction between the resultative participles that show up in stative contexts and their eventive counterparts concerns the amount of event structure. This has repercussions on how straightforward the two-fold properties attributed to the past participial morpheme shine through: the absence of an external argument in stative configurations leads to anticausativity and perfective semantics in case the verbal root denotes a change of state, i.e. bears telic properties. The properties of eventive participles are more intricate, as there is no PredP enforcing restrictions on the amount of event structure in terms of requiring the presence of a resultative state. Given that periphrastic occurrences of eventive participles range between perfectivity and imperfectivity depending on the event structure of the predicates they are derived from, this is *per se* also expected from eventive properties. The examples in (191) and (192) show that this expectation is borne out on the basis of prenominal instantiations in German and postnominal ones in English (see also Rapp & von Stechow 2015: 289).

(191) a. ein (von vielen) geliebter Filmstar
       a   by   many   love.PTCP *film.star*
       'a film star loved by many'
    b. eine (von Dr. Evil) gestreichelte Katze
       a   by   Dr. Evil   stroke.PTCP *cat*
       'a cat stroked by Dr. Evil'
    c. ein angekommener Zug
       an arrive.PTCP   *train*
       'a train arrived at the station'
    d. ein verschwundenes Mädchen
       a   disappear.PTCP *girl*
       'a girl disappeared from the scene'

(192) a. a film star loved by many
    b. a cat stroked by Dr. Evil
    c. a train arrived at the station
    d. a girl disappeared from the scene

While the atelic predicates in the (a) and (b) examples of (191) and (192) allow for both an imperfective (as expected on the basis of the aspectual contribution of the past participle) as well as a perfective reading (somewhat surprisingly), their (anticausative) telic counterparts in (c) and (d) only allow for the latter. In an attempt to account for this, Rapp & von Stechow (2015: 289) in their discussion of prenominal participles in German claim that the past participle is always simultaneous with the modified noun and anteriority readings in the case of telic verbs merely stem from the supplementary presence of a PERF-operator. While this marks an easy way out, it certainly cannot shake off a strongly stipulative flavour. What this attempt shows is that it apparently is exceptionally difficult to account for the mixed properties of prenominal participles in German[175] and – despite the absence of homonymy with stativised resultative participles – a similar conclusion may be drawn from the postnominal cases in (192).

A way to determine whether the eventive participles in question permit a perfective or imperfective reading is by means of introducing the adverbial modifiers *kürzlich/recently* and *gegenwärtig/currently*. In line with the two-fold contribution of past participles put forth in the present work, telic

---

[175] Note that resorting to an explanation based on the structural ambiguity of resultative participles and eventive properties is not a solution, either: the instances that are interpreted in a perfective fashion would be expected to be anticausative, a prediction that is (unfortunately) not borne out, though.

anticausatives (simple changes of state) only permit readings under which the eventuality has come to an end. Accordingly, modification by *kürzlich/ recently* is always possible, whereas inserting *gegenwärtig/currently* does not give rise to a simultaneity-reading, as the examples in (193) and (194) show.[176]

(193) a. ein kürzlich/*gegenwärtig angekommener Zug
       a recently/currently   arrive.PTCP   *train*
       'a train recently arrived'
   b. ein kürzlich/#gegenwärtig verschwundenes Mädchen
       a recently/currently   disappear.PTCP *girl*
       'a girl recently disappeared'

(194) a. a train recently/*currently arrived at the station
   b. a girl recently/*currently disappeared from the scene

Furthermore, what complies with the imperfectivity of past participles derived from predicates that are not simple changes of state is that both proper atelic predicates like the ones in (a) and (b) examples of (191) and (192) as well as telic causatives (accomplishments) give rise to concurrency readings with *gegenwärtig/currently*. This is shown in (195) and (196).

(195) a. ein kürzlich/gegenwärtig gegessener Apfel
       a recently/currently   eat.PTCP   *apple*
       'an apple recently/currently eaten'
   b. ein kürzlich/gegenwärtig gebautes Haus
       a recently/currently   build.PTCP   *house*
       'a house recently/currently built (by Jack)'

(196) a. an apple recently/currently eaten (by Jack)
   b. a house recently/currently built (by Jack)

What is somewhat surprising about these cases is that they also permit the situation to have ended and hence also modification by *kürzlich/recently*. We will return to this shortly.

---

[176] Note that *gegenwärtig* ('currently') crucially only denotes that the resultative state (rather than the constitutive event) currently holds in these cases, if they denote a target (rather than a resultant) state. Modification by *currently* is barred in English as the postnominal distribution does not elicit a resultative state.

4.3 Bare instances and the category of past participles — 313

A further complication is that there is also a class of telic predicates that bars an imperfective reading: achievements, which are *per definitionem* punctual in nature. This is shown by the examples in (197) and (198).

(197) a. der kürzlich/*gegenwärtig gefundene Schlüssel
    the recently/currently   find.PTCP *key*
    'the key recently found'
  b. das kürzlich/*gegenwärtig erkannte Mädchen
     the recently/currently   recognise. PTCP *girl*
     'the girl recently recognised'

(198) a. the key recently/*currently found (by Peter).
  b. the girl recently/*currently recognized (by Bill).

These telic predicates only permit a perfective interpretation and may not be modified by *gegenwärtig/currently*.

We are thus left with two challenges: (i) how can causative telic and atelic predicates gain a perfective interpretation given the assumption that this does not stem from the participial morpheme, and (ii) why are telic achievements – despite being causative, which is what allows them to take part in imperfective passives – always perfective. With respect to the former issue, what is striking is that not just overt adverbial modification but also the temporal make-up of the superordinate clause plays a vital role in terms of determining whether or not a perfective or an imperfective reading comes about. The examples in (199) and (200) emphasise this.

(199) a. Der von Thilo gelesene Ratgeber wird ihm vermutlich erst auf Seite
     *the by Thilo read.*PTCP *guide*   *will him probably*   *only on page*
     243 den entscheidenden   Tipp   geben.
     243 the crucial   *hint*   *give.*
     'The guide read by Thilo will probably not give him any new insights until he reaches page 243.'
  b. Der von Thilo gelesene Ratgeber hatte ihn schnell gelangweilt.
     *the by Thilo read.*PTCP *guide*   *had him quickly bored*
     'The guide read by Thilo soon had him bored.'

(200) a. The guide read by Thilo will probably not give him any new insights until he reaches page 243.
  b. The guide read by Thilo soon had him bored.

This indicates that the imperfective reading is the more natural one, although contextual factors may imply the posteriority of TT with respect to the participial eventuality, TSit. This is reminiscent of the periphrastic perfect with HAVE, where the perfect auxiliary introduces posteriority. This leaves issue (ii), i.e. the question of why transitive achievements can *not* be imperfective. A reason for this may be found in the conceptual nature of achievements as punctual changes of state: a reading in which the participial event TSit is simultaneous with the overall situation (i.e. TT) is barred by the punctuality of TSit. In fact, in order for simultaneity to obtain, TSit has to sufficiently stretch out in time so as to include (or overlap with) TT, which is not possible with this kind of predicate.

Taking stock, we have now seen that resultative participles differ from eventive ones in terms of their functional embedding: the former are word-syntactically merged with an A-head and then introduced in PredP, which imposes restrictions on the amount of event structure that is permitted, whereas the latter are also adjectival but not restricted in terms of event structure due to the absence of PredP. English encodes a clear-cut distributional distinction by having eventive participles only in postnominal position, whereas resultative ones occur prenominally as well as in stative contexts (e.g. stative passives). In German, on the other hand, this neat distributional division breaks down due to the absence of a postnominal position: eventive and resultative participles converge in prenominal position (apart from their occurrence in stative configurations).

There is one additional distribution which may house eventive past participles, although there is room for structural ambiguity reminiscent of the prenominal position in German: adverbial clauses. Usually, adverbial instantiations of past participles are adjoined to the C-domain of a given main clause. This distribution does not in and of itself impose any structural restrictions, but depending on whether a stative or an eventive participle is realised, PredP may be around and impose the restrictions discussed before. The examples in (201) and (202) show the two kinds of realisations, where the examples in (a) and (b) mark resultative uses and (c) and (d) are eventive ones.

(201) a. Rasiert   sieht der Mann zehn Jahre jünger   aus.
shave.PTCP *looked the man ten   years younger* PARTICLE
'Shaved, the man looks ten years younger.'
b. Gegessen stellte der Kugelfisch sich als ungefährlich heraus.
eat.PTCP *turned the blowfish*   SELF *as harmless*   PARTICLE
'Eaten, the blowfish turned out to be harmless.'

c. Von seiner Mutter getragen   fühlte sich der Junge sicher.
   by   his   mother carry.PTCP *felt*   SELF *the boy   safe*
   'Carried by his mother, the boy felt safe.'
d. Am   Bahnhof angekommen hielt   der Zug   vollständig.
   at.the station   arrive.PTCP *stopped the train completely*
   'Arrived at the station, the train soon came to a complete halt.'

(202) a. Shaved, the man looks ten years younger.
 b. Eaten, the blowfish turned out to be no harm.
 c. Carried by his mother, the boy felt safe.
 d. Arrived at the station, the train soon came to a complete halt.[177]

With respect to the eventive uses, the adverbial diagnostics just discussed carry over to the adverbial distribution in a straightforward manner.

Based on the distributional flexibility of bare past participles discussed in the present section, the distinct distributional types may be summed up as in (203), in analogy to the overview in (38) above.

(203)

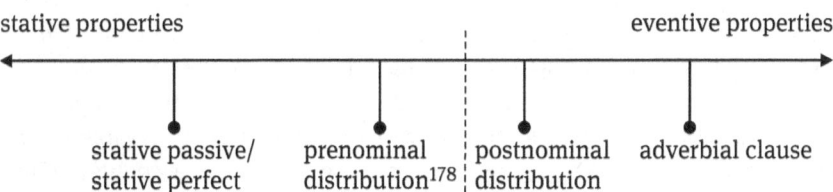

This view deviates from many traditional works on verbal and adjectival (past) participles in that it is not assumed that the contexts in (203) differ in terms of whether or not their bare past participles undergo the operation in (180). Rather, a 'verbal' reading may be attributed to 'adjectival' participles to different degrees depending on the amount of eventivity granted by a particular structural embedding and hence attributable to the past participle. These differences should primarily be tracked by distinctions in the fine-grained structural make-up of

---

177 Note that in the case of adverbial past participles it is typically, but not necessarily, the subject of the main clause that supplies this value. The attested example *Arrived at the office, the publisher sent down for him by Laurence, the boy with spots*, for instance has *him* provide the value, as becomes clear when considering the immediate context (cf. Breul & Wegner 2017: 7).
178 Note that this only holds for English prenominals, whereas the German ones are as flexible as the English postnominal occurrences and allow for a large amount of 'eventive' properties.

the underlying predicates in terms of their event structure, first and foremost the presence of a CAUSE.

Before we move on with some theoretical implications of the present approach to bare past participles, let us briefly regard one particularly interesting occurrence of adverbial instantiations: the so-called absolute clauses (or absolute constructions). Some relevant examples of this construction are given in (204) and (205).[179]

(204) a. Den   Drachen   erschlagen,   ruhte   der Ritter sich aus.
         the.ACC *dragon*.ACC *slay*.PTCP,   rest   the knight SELF PARTICLE
         'The dragon slain, the knight took his rest.'
    b. Den   Rasen gemäht, wandte der Gärtner   sich seinen Lilien
       the.ACC *lawn mow*.PTCP, turned the gardener SELF his   lilies
       zu
       PARTICLE
       'The lawn mowed, the gardener turned to his lilies.'

(205) a. The dragon slain, the knight took his rest.
    b. The lawn mowed, the gardener turned to his lilies.

Past participles in absolute clauses are necessarily interpreted as resultatives and based on anticausative changes of state, which once again is in line with the aspectual properties attributed to past participles in the present work.[180] As suggested in chapter 2.2.3, the fact that the internal arguments are apparently properly licensed and receive accusative case, as clearly observable in the German examples in (204), suggests that these are eventive configurations. However, as there is no external argument and thus no case-assigning v around, this preliminary conclusions seems to have been misguided. Rather, these configurations also seem to structurally correspond to stative configurations, i.e. there should be an adjectival past participle which is introduced by PredP, which is in line with the lack of eventive modification. This leaves the question of case-assignment. A potential reconciliation for this property comes from the fact that

---

179 Note that there are numerous kinds of absolute constructions that do not involve a participle: consider *The match over, the fans went home* or *(With) her hands behind her back, she was waiting for the surprise*.

180 Note that these also occur in Romance, e.g. in French (*une fois le problème résolu*, lit. one time the problem solved) and Catalan (*un cop solucionat el problema*, lit. one time solved the problem 'once the problem has been solved') (cf. Hofherr 2017: 233). This supports the claim that the properties of past participles identified in the present work and their role in periphrastic, adnominal and adverbial distributions are shared by Germanic and Romance languages.

English exhibits exceptional word order (OV) and occasionally licenses the preposition *with* on top of the absolute clause, as in (206).

(206) a. With the dinner served at 6 pm, the guests turned to their rooms before 9.
b. With the bomb defused, the soldiers were ready to head home.

The preposition, potentially always null in German and optionally also in English, may be held responsible for case assignment, which accounts for why it is not the German default (nominative) case that comes to the fore here. Crucially, then, absolute clauses boil down to predicational (stative) structures, which do not allow for the instantiation of a CAUSE. This, in turn, precludes a passive interpretation. These two aspects once more appear to be tightly interwoven in that the past participle denotes a simple change of state and hence conveys a perfective reading (thus inducing a result) in the absence of an atelic CAUSE-phase. Leaving much of the discussion of absolute clauses pending here, this brief discussion allowed us to adduce some further evidence for the properties of past participles identified before. In conclusion of the present chapter, let us briefly regard some implications for the category of past participles.

4.3.2 Categorial considerations

In terms of their underlying category, past participles are derivative of a single lexical (part of speech) category. In fact, they always retain a certain amount of verbal properties in terms of making recourse to a verbal event. These may be veiled behind a resultative state, though, if they are introduced by an adjectival functional head in word syntax. Nevertheless, it is unnecessary (and from the point of view of lexical economy even undesirable) to assume the existence of a designated 'cognitive lexical part-of-speech category', as Rauh (2017: 119) puts it, for (past) participles. Rather, these are lexically modified verbs that allow for insertion into syntactic contexts in which prototypical verbs are not to be expected.[181] A reason for this may be found in that lexically adding non-finiteness and aspectual information (which allows for the denotation of a resultative state) to the verbal element makes it more time-stable (cf. Givón 1979). Thus, the participial status as a deverbal category suggests that an item of this kind

---

181 Evidence for this comes from the fact that – unlike any of the other core categories (i.e., e.g., nouns, verbs, and adjectives) – the category 'participle' does not exhibit forms that are primarily affiliated with this category in the first place (cf. Weber 2002: 211). In other words, participles are inherently 'derived' from other items.

inherently belongs to the lexical core category 'verb', but once it attains past participial morphology, some of its prototypical verbal properties are lost, namely not just in terms of inflecting for tense, but also regarding the expression of argument structure. These 'deficiencies' may either be made up for by an auxiliary or – with the help of λ-abstraction as triggered by an adjectival head – allow the participial element to occur as an adjunct. In the latter case, it may exhibit more or less adjectival properties depending on the structural context, i.e. the presence of PredP, and the absence of an eventive CAUSE. The flexibility triggered by past participle formation thus accounts for their designation as 'middle words' (cf. Weber 2002: 198f., 211) – oscillating between verbs and adjectives. While cognitive linguists (see Langacker 1991; Rosch and Mervis 1975; Lenz 1993: 63f., 70f., 73f.) trace this categorial fuzziness back to a prototype theory of categories (cf. Aarts 2007: 27), we may simply derive the categorial flexibility from processes that verbs undergo in past participle formation. This allows us to maintain clear-cut Aristotelean categories in the lexicon, which are diffused in terms of their syntacticosemantic properties by word-formation processes and the particular properties of syntactic configurations.[182]

With respect to the range of verbal and adjectival past participial uses, the relevant dimensions determining how much verbal properties are retained eventually are the following: (1) the semantic presence of a CAUSE (to be existentially bound or overtly realised with the help of HAVE) in the underlying event structure, (2) the presence of an adjectival head (A) governing λ-abstraction, (3) the presence of a predicational phrase (PredP) enforcing stative properties upon a structural configuration. Given these distinctions, it is not surprising that Ross (1972) takes perfect participles to be more verbal than passive participles, since the latter regularly appear in adjectival distributions (cf. also Bresnan 1982). Perfect participles, on the other hand, are quite restricted in this respect, which is why discussions revolving around the category of past participles typically focus on passive participles (cf. Aarts 2007: 52). As has been shown in the present work, however, the distinction between passive and perfect(ive) participles is not substantial. Rather, it stems from the properties of a single kind of element, the past participle, which amalgamates diathetic and aspectual properties. In other words, the distinction between (verbal) passive and perfect(ive) participles is epiphenomenally derived from the basic properties of past participles and their

---

182 Cognitive categorisation (into 'lexical categories') is driven by the need to organise the lexicon and does not necessarily carry over to core grammar. As Aarts (2007: 205) puts it, the fuzzy boundaries occasionally exhibited between two categories are typically "the fall-out of the way grammarians have set up their grammatical descriptions, and not a property of the grammatical system itself".

interaction with their structural environment. With respect to adjectival past participles, there is one crucial distinction, though, namely the presence of a functional head that triggers λ-abstraction. However, this does not *per se* bear consequences for the amount of eventivity that is retained (although it prevents an adjectival past participle from being licit in core verbal distributions). Instead, differences in eventivity arguably are externally imposed, namely by the presence of a stativising functional head in syntax. This Pred-head demands the presence of a resultative state, which may only come about if the underlying situation has been rendered perfective by past participial morphology, i.e. if the underlying event structure boils down to a simple (anticausative) change of state.

Eventually, participles cognitively exhibit fuzzy boundaries in that they occupy the outer rims of both the category of verb and adjective in terms of a prototype theory of the cognitive organisation of lexical categories (cf. Rauh 2017: 118). However, this is not equalled by proper grammatical fuzziness, as past participles are not stored in the lexicon – once they are, they are forced to forfeit their verbal characteristics – but derived (in word-syntax). This is in line with the assumption that "on grounds of elegance and economy, in setting up a system of parts of speech, ideally the number of postulated categories is maximally restricted" (Aarts 2007: 10), ideally seven plus minus two in the tradition of Miller (1956) (cf. Rauh 2017: 125f.). Though stemming from a single lexical category, past participles give rise to numerous syntactic categories, which are eventually determined on the basis of their feature representations (cf. Rauh 2010: 144).[183] Accordingly, in terms of their syntactic category, past participles are not 'true hybrids' since their feature set determines whether they show up in adjectival or in verbal distribution (cf. Aarts 2007: 233). This is in line with the assumption that the number of syntactic categories outruns the number of lexical categories by far, since even slight changes to the feature matrix of a given element or differences within the matrices of several items have an effect (cf. Rauh 2017: 105).[184] These considerations allow us to explain the observable properties without having to resort to core (lexical) categorial distinctions or distinct places of formation (lexicon vs. syntax). While a feature-based approach to syntactic categories is quite flexible, it is not without flaws, though. A central disadvantage, as Rauh (2010: 149) makes clear, is that it is quite hard to pinpoint "which features belong to the sets that are necessary and sufficient for the

---

183 This leads Aarts (2007: 33) to the following conclusion: as "syntactic categories are defined by making use of features, [...] the notion of syntactic category becomes epiphenomenal".

184 According to Rauh (2010: 137), differences in syntactic category may even be based on the changes evoked by feature-checking, as observable in the case of finite and non-finite verbs that occupy different positions from one another and hence belong to different (syntactic) categories.

description of syntactic categories, i.e. how to specify how detailed a feature specification must be." This shows that much work remains to be done in feature-based approches, first and foremost with respect to the clear identification of a restricted set of features and their ability to combine in order to make up lexical items.

This concludes our tentative discussion of the intricate properties of past participles in bare uses. The main conclusion to be drawn from the behaviour of bare past participles is that these are based on the same forms as those employed in periphrastic constructions. However, past participles in bare uses are supplemented by a functional head in order to allow for the direct association with a referent. This does not necessarily evoke a stative interpretation, though. In fact, in order to enforce a stative reading, a functional head (Pred) has to mediate the attribution of a property, which is in turn contingent on the presence of a past participle that denotes a perfective situation and thus features a result. While this follows naturally in the case of unaccusatives, it demands the deletion of the external argument in (telic) transitive cases, which are thus rendered anticausative. Accordingly, the contribution of the past participial morpheme opens the flood gates for a broad variety of interpretations oscillating between strongly verbal and strictly adjectival. However, additional presuppositions (A, lack of a CAUSE, PredP) are necessary in order to shift the participial interpretation towards the adjectival end of the spectrum. While this certainly demands more detailed investigations, we will stick to the central issue of past participial (non-)identity here and therefore turn to the conclusions that may be derived from the present work in the subsequent chapter.

5 Conclusion

The present work investigated the issue of whether the participial forms that are used in passive and perfect constructions in Germanic and Romance are substantially distinct or rather syntacticosemantically identical. While the non-identity view suggests that designated passive participles have to be distinguished from syntacticosemantically distinct perfect(ive) participles that are just accidentally homophonous, the assumption of substantial identity does with a single kind of participle, the past participle. Based on the cross-linguistic data introduced in chapter 2 and the discussion of previous approaches in chapter 3, it could be shown that there is virtually no evidence for the non-identity of past participles in Germanic and Romance languages that do not make a proper morphophonological distinction. Instead, the relevant synchronic behaviour as well as the diachronic development of past participial forms clearly point to the substantial identity of the participial elements in passive and perfect instances. As none of the previous approaches to past participial identity sufficiently accounts for the data, a novel account of the substantial identity of past participles was laid out in chapter 4. This approach rests upon the assumption of what was called the amalgamation hypothesis, viz. the claim that past participles conflate diathetic and aspectual information. To be precise, the diathetic contribution consists of the (syntactic) suppression of an external argument, which follows from the lexical marking of the external semantic role (if present) for existential binding. In terms of its aspectual contribution, the past participle conveys what was termed 'defective' (or event-structure sensitive) perfectivity. This is a kind of perfectivity that is crucially different from its counterpart in aspectual languages by virtue of merely sufficing to induce the completion of a situation in case the underlying eventuality denotes a simple change of state.[1] These contributions are observable in an unfiltered fashion in BE-perfect and passive contexts (formed with BE or WERDEN). The perfect auxiliary HAVE, however, crucially affects the properties of the participial constructions it forms. In fact, HAVE contributes posteriority, which allows those past participles that cannot convey perfectivity on their own to denote a perfect interpretation after all. Additionally, this auxiliary is special in terms of its ability to license an external argument whose θ-role has been marked for existential binding. Accordingly, HAVE induces an active interpretation on the basis of a past participle that bears passive characteristics.

---

[1] Accordingly, 'past' participles eventually turn out to be 'underspecified passive-perfective' participles.

As pointed out in terms of a tentative extension to auxiliaryless cases, the aspectual and diathetic contributions of the past participle also shine through in bare instantiations. These arguably demand the supplementary presence of a functional head. This ingredient lexically marks an internal argument (not associated with inherent case) for λ-abstraction and hence allows for the direct modification of a nominal referent, which does not necessarily enforce core adjectival properties, though. Nevertheless, some caution is in order here, since bare cases may crucially be affected by stativisation (e.g. in stative passives) and its requirement for a resultative state, which may only be met with an anticausative event structure. Whenever there is a simple change of state, this allows defective perfectivity to induce a resultative state and renders the participial suppression of an external argument ineffective by virtue of the absence of an external semantic role.

As we could see in chapter 2, apart from the general behaviour of past participial forms in their wide range of occurrences, evidence for these proposals concerning past participial identity comes from synchronic observations of divergent realisations. The unexpected morphological behaviour of past participial forms in the phenomena known as PPP, IPP and PPI is crucially restricted to perfect contexts with HAVE. Underlined by the fact that the rare exceptions to this pattern (e.g. in Dutch) are restricted to BE-perfect cases in which the verbal element is likely to be lexically associated with a sense of completion, these contexts could be shown to provide support for the assumption that HAVE comprises relevant perfect information. This allows for the semantic recovery of a proper perfect interpretation in the absence of participial morphology and accounts for why its superfluous presence does not have an interpretive effect. In the case of the passive and the BE-perfect, on the other hand, all the relevant information for a passive or perfect interpretation is stored in the participle. Hence, its impoverishment prevents the semantic recovery of a proper perfect or passive interpretation and its superfluous presence on a further element in a verbal cluster cannot be kept from faultily inducing such an interpretation. While synchronic agreement-data (e.g. in Romance and North Germanic) at first sight appear to challenge this conclusion concerning past participial identity, these could be shown to be contingent on the particular synctactic configuration rather than the distinction between perfect and passive. In fact, past participial object-agreement may only ever be realised in identity-languages if an object is moved out of the participial domain, regardless of whether the participle is a 'perfect participle' or a 'passive participle'. Furthermore, the identity of past participles on the basis of an element that suppresses the external argument and denotes perfectivity only with a simple change of state is supported by diachronic data: the past participial form diachronically started out as a deverbal adjective that bore resultative meaning and was anticausative in nature. Throughout its grammaticalisation in the periphrastic passive and the analytic perfect, this element lost some of its core-adjectival properties, e.g. the presence of λ-abstraction and the requirement for the presence of a result. In turn, it regained the implicit presence of a CAUSE (in case the underlying predicate includes an external semantic role). Despite these developments towards more verbality, past participles remain defective in the sense that they are non-finite forms that carry aspectual information and hence demand the presence of an auxiliary (HAVE, BE, or WERDEN) in order to form the core of a clause.

The discussion of previous approaches to past participial (non-)identity in chapter 3 likewise failed to bring forth major arguments for the non-identity of passive and perfect(ive) participles. Rather, it presented a broad range of approaches to past participial identity and managed to point to their problems and merits. This provided us with the means to settle for an amalgamation approach to the basic meaning of past participles for the present work. To be precise, previous approaches attributing the perfect and passive denotation solely to the auxiliaries involved as well as those claiming that the participle is either perfect(ive) or passive in nature are incompatible with the cross-linguistic data. Instead, these clearly point to the conflation of both of these syntacticosemantic ingredients in a single past participial form, although they occasionally require relevant (diathetic and aspectual) contributions by the auxiliary HAVE. Nevertheless, the previous approaches that were discussed provided essential insights and presented some useful mechanisms that were eventually adopted for the purposes of the present approach (most importantly the intuition behind θ-merger and the importance of verbal aktionsart or event structure for the contribution of perfectivity).

Chapter 4 presented a compositional approach to past participial identity by first tying together the empirical and theoretical insights gained from the discussion in chapters 2 and 3. Subsequently, the syntax and semantics of the prototypical participial constructions, i.e. the periphrastic passive and the analytic perfect, was carved out by virtue of presenting a theoretical account of the properties of past participles and the auxiliaries they interact with. This discussion had us face some intricate issues in the domain of the passive as well as the perfect. In the former, we for instance had to deal with the properties of impersonal and dative passives and laid bare the semantic requirement for a sufficient amount of Proto-Agent properties. The discussion of the perfect, in turn, had to account for the complex properties of the distinct readings that the periphrastic perfect may give rise to. This automatically brought us to some supposedly problematic parametric contrasts concerning the present perfect puzzle and the apparent interchangeability of the present perfect and the simple past in

German, both of which were touched upon in passing. Subsequently, we could see that the technical properties introduced in the present approach are sufficient to account for the observations about past participial object-agreement and the divergent realisations discussed in chapter 2. This discussion of the central syntacticosemantic properties of past participial periphrases was then rounded off by extending the scope to bare instantiations, which could be shown to be based on the same participial morphemes. However, these have to be supplemented by a functional head governing λ-abstraction, although this alone does not enforce stativity. Rather, it is the absence of a CAUSE in the event structure of the underlying predicate that governs the possibility of a stative reading by virtue of coinciding with the instantiation of a resultative state. In certain syntactic contexts (namely whenever the adjectival participle is embedded under PredP) the presence of such a resultative state may be forced, giving rise to stative characteristics that may bar recourse to some, but crucially not all, eventive aspects of the constitutive event. In terms of their category, it could eventually be concluded that past participles are always deverbal elements, which may only lexically (i.e. in word-syntax, in the present account) differ in terms of their ability to be directly associated with a nominal governor in semantics, thus attributing a property to the referent in question. This entails that it is superfluous to assume that past participles make up a designated lexical category, but rather attributes the properties that make them oscillate between verbs and adjectives to their verbal heritage, which may more or less strongly be retained (depending on the presence of a CAUSE, A, and PredP).

In addition to the identity-languages primarily discussed in the present work, we occasionally also came across languages that do in fact make a principled distinction between passive and perfect(ive) participles. These languages feature passive participial forms that morphologically differ from perfect participial items, and this difference is crucially mirrored by syntacticosemantic non-identity. This is for instance observable in Bulgarian (and some other South Slavic languages), where a difference on the basis of the auxiliary is not called for, as the participles sufficiently convey all the relevant grammatical distinctions. Accordingly, these languages characteristically employ only BE, which adds to the assumption that BE is semantically vacuous, whereas HAVE contributes relevant information. As a matter of fact, there are two exceptional exponents of Slavic, namely Macedonian and Kashubian, which are subject to the grammaticalisation of a HAVE-perfect. As a consequence, the substantial distinction between passive and perfect(ive) participles collapses, i.e. what we find is a change towards past participial identity. Directionally opposed to this development, even Germanic exhibits an apparent odd man out which potentially qualifies as a proper non-identity language, namely Swedish. As we could see, this Scandinavian language diachronically exploited a phonologically-conditioned diversion of two participial forms, which now show substantial distinctions in behaviour: the supine and the past participle. Since this is a fairly recent development and HAVE is still properly employed, the effects of this diversion are relatively minor and it remains to be seen in how far Swedish may step out of the Germanic paradigm and approximate the properties of proper non-identity languages. However, first tendencies are already observable, for instance in the fact that the supine regularly does without its perfect auxiliary HAVE in finite embedded clauses. The case of Swedish shows that languages resorting to past participial non-identity may cross-linguistically differ from identity-languages to varying extents (see Wegner 2017). In a nutshell, Slavic languages like Bulgarian dissociate a perfect participle from a passive participle. Hence, distinctions on the basis of the auxiliary are superfluous, which is why the semantically vacuous auxiliary BE is always employed in participial contexts. In proper identity-languages, on the other hand, such distinctions are indispensable, as a passive and a perfect interpretation may not sufficiently be induced for all kinds of verbal predicates on the basis of the participial form alone. Swedish, as an exception ranging between the two extremes, is still strongly related to the Germanic paradigm of identity languages by virtue of being non-aspectual in nature. In fact, the relevant properties usually attributed to HAVE potentially are increasingly absorbed by the supine.

These distinctions show that the issue of past participial identity adds to the assumption of (ontological) linguistic minimalism by virtue of showing that there is a tendency towards grammatically exploiting morphological distinctions, whereas their absence motivates the introduction of independent means. Accordingly, Germanic and Romance diachronically made the best out of their (limited) morphological means by virtue of grammaticalising resultative deverbal adjectives towards allowing them to form an analytic passive and a periphrastic perfect. This coincided with the auxiliarisation of HAVE, BE and WERDEN for distinct purposes, where only the first is bound to substantially contribute to the intended interpretation. This has as its consequence that some kinds of verbal predicates are in complementary distribution in terms of their properties with respect to participial formation: (telic) unaccusative predicates may only ever give rise to perfective participles, whereas causative (di-)transitive and unergative predicates may only elicit imperfective passive participles (unless they are rendered anticausative by independent means). This leaves the class of atelic two-place unaccusatives, which are usually ruled out by virtue of violating the principle of Full Interpretation in that they neither sufficiently convey passive nor perfective meaning. However, in the context of HAVE, they are readily possible, which shows that perfect meaning is compositionally derived and participial morphology is not just ornamental in cases in which it fails to denote proper perfectivity. Eventually, then, rather than storing two designated participial morphemes, grammar opts for employing independent means to derive distinct concepts on the basis of one and the same form. These boil down to a sensitivity to the properties of the underlying predicate, on the one hand, and the external contribution by auxiliaries, on the other. This arguably approximates the SMT in that superfluous distinctions are avoided. In addition to these broad theoretical conclusions with respect to the general claims of minimalist frameworks, we could see that questions of identity are often difficult to discuss in proper anti-lexicalist frameworks. In fact, such approaches often rely on the dissociation of aspectual and diathetic information, which they distribute over designated functional heads. This renders it quite knotty to do justice to the assumption of substantial past participial identity unless one clearly defines the confines of the participial 'template'. Such problems do not arise in the present moderate reconciliation of anti-lexicalist ideas (in terms of the existence of word-syntax) with the existence of designated lexical items that come equipped with certain syntacticosemantic properties.

Besides the precise workings of the theoretical framework that was adopted, there are numerous interesting issues laid bare in the present work that have to be left to future research. These for instance concern the precise delineation of the grammatical properties of identity and non-identity languages and their specific synchronic as well as diachronic characteristics. A proper starting point besides a fine-grained look at non-identity languages like Bulgarian may be found in the properties of Swedish, which should be investigated in a detailed fashion against the backdrop of its supposed non-identity. Furthermore, the scope of the investigation of past participial (non-)identity could be extended to language families other than Germanic, Romance and Slavic in a principled fashion. With respect to the identity languages primarily addressed in the present work, what remains to be discussed in detail are the properties of bare instantiations, especially those of absolute constructions (e.g. issues of linearisation, their semantic properties as well as their general 'defectiveness') and the grammatical distinctions of resultative and eventive past participles. Additionally, the formal discussions in the present work have raised some central theoretical questions such as those pertaining to agreement morphology: the claim that past participial object-agreement may only be spelled-out if the internal argument moves out of the participial domain brings up the question of why this is almost never observable in the context of HAVE. In fact, what is quite curious is that HAVE-only languages apparently never exhibit past participial object-agreement with unaccusative predicates. Furthermore, given that the overt spell-out of agreement morphology is dissociated from the valuation of φ-features, this raises the intricate issue of what generally determines the immediacy of spelling out formal features at PF. In a similar vein, the PF-mechanisms of impoverishment and ornamental morphology that have been employed in the present work demand a fine-grained investigation with respect to their structural triggers. This discussion should focus on verbal clusters and their interaction with participial morphology, where special attention has to be paid to effects on word order and the exceptional case of aspectual verbs in Dutch. Another technical concern is the application of default valuation that we had to resort to in the context of impersonal passives (default φ-feature valuation) and ditransitive constructions (default case assignment). Moreover, the semantic properties of the periphrastic perfect in identity-languages certainly call for a more fine-grained discussion on the basis of the compositional characteristics introduced in the present work (including cross-linguistic differences such as the interchangeability of the preterite and the present perfect as well as the present perfect puzzle). Finally, the semantic vacuity attested for BE in the present work raises the question of whether the same auxiliary is also employed in present participial (progressive) periphrases. This is *per se* desirable especially in the case of English and German, where the sensitivity of BE to perfective as opposed to imperfective past participles could be said to bar it from forming the progressive in German. However, this leaves several questions unanswered and is cross-linguistically challenged by languages like Danish, which employ BE in order to denote a perfect as well the progressive. Eventually, the domain of past participial (non-)identity (and the countless areas of grammatical research it connects with) is a very fruitful testing ground for a broad variety of theoretical concerns. In fact, a similar range of insights arguably may also cross-linguistically be gained from several other domains that allow for the principled investigation of (non-)identity on the basis of alleged homonymy.

References

Aarts, Bas. 2007. *Syntactic gradience: The nature of grammatical indeterminacy*. Oxford: Oxford University Press.
Abney, Steven. 1987. The English noun phrase in its sentential aspect. PhD dissertation. Cambridge, MA: Massachusetts Institute of Technology.
Abraham, Werner. 1986. The grammar of German *haben*. *Groninger Arbeiten zur Germanistischen Linguistik* 26: 99–125.
Abraham, Werner. 1991. Aktionsartsemantik und Auxiliarisierung im Deutschen. In: Elisabeth Feldbusch, Reiner Pogarell & Cornelia Weiß (eds.). *Neue Fragen der Linguistik*. Tübingen: Max Niemeyer. 125–33.
Abraham, Werner. 1992. Event structure accounting for the emerging periphrastic tenses and the passive voice in German. In: Garry W. Davis & Gregory K. Iverson (eds.). *Explanation in historical linguistics*. Amsterdam: John Benjamins. 1–16.
Abraham, Werner. 1998. Perfektpartizip: seine angebliche Passivbedeutung im Deutschen. *Groninger Arbeiten zur Germanistischen Linguistik* 42: 154–68.
Abraham, Werner. 2000. Das Perfektpartizip: seine angebliche Passivbedeutung im Deutschen. *Zeitschrift für germanistische Linguistik* 28: 141–66.
Abraham, Werner. 2006a. Introduction: Passivization and typology: Form vs. function – a confined survey into the research status quo. In: Werner Abraham & Larisa Leisiö (eds.). *Passivization and typology: Form and function*. Amsterdam: John Benjamins. 1–27.
Abraham, Werner. 2006b. The compositional nature of the analytic passive: Syntactic vs. event semantic triggers. 'Argument Hypothesis' vs. 'Aspect Hypothesis'. In: Werner Abraham & Larisa Leisiö (eds.). *Passivization and typology: form and function*. Amsterdam: John Benjamins. 462–501.
Ackema, Peter. 1995. Syntax below zero. PhD dissertation. Utrecht: University of Utrecht.
Ackema, Peter. 1999. *Issues in morphosyntax*. Amsterdam: John Benjamins.
Ackema, Peter & Marelj, Marijana. 2012. To have the empty theta-role. In: Martin Everaert, Marijana Marelj & Tal Siloni (eds.). *The theta system: Argument structure at the interface*. Oxford: Oxford University Press. 227–50.
Ackema, Peter & Neeleman, Ad. 2007. Morphology ≠ syntax. In: Gillian Ramchand & Charles Reiss (eds.). *The Oxford handbook of linguistic interfaces*. Oxford: Oxford University Press. 325–52.
Ackerman, Farrell & Webelhuth, Gert. 1998. *A theory of predicates*. Stanford, CA: CSLI Publications.
Adger, David. 2003. *Core syntax: A minimalist approach*. Oxford: Oxford University Press.
Åfarli, Tor. 2009. Passive and participle agreement in Norwegian dialects. *Groninger Arbeiten zur Germanistischen Linguistik* 49: 167–81.
Åfarli, Tor A. 1989. Passive in Norwegian and in English. *Linguistic Inquiry* 20: 101–8.
Åfarli, Tor A. 1992. *The syntax of Norwegian passive constructions*. Amsterdam: John Benjamins.
Akmajian, Adrian & Wasow, Thomas. 1975. The constituent structure of VP and AUX and the position of the verb BE. *Linguistic Analysis* 1: 205–45.
Alexiadou, Artemis. 2014. Roots don't take complements. *Theoretical Linguistics* 40: 287–97.
Alexiadou, Artemis, Anagnostopoulou, Elena & Everaert, Martin (eds.). 2004. *The unaccusativity puzzle: Explorations of the syntax-lexicon interface*. Oxford: Oxford University Press.

Alexiadou, Artemis, Anagnostopoulou, Elena & Sevdali, Christina. 2014. Opaque and transparent datives, and how they behave in passives. *The Journal of Comparative Germanic Linguistics* 17: 1–34.
Alexiadou, Artemis, Gehrke, Berit & Schäfer, Florian. 2014. The argument structure of adjectival participles revisited. *Lingua* 149: 118–38.
Alexiadou, Artemis, Haegeman, Liliane & Stavrou, Melita. 2007. *Noun phrase in the generative perspective*. Berlin: de Gruyter.
Alkire, Ti & Rosen, Carol. 2010. *Romance languages: A historical introduction*. Cambridge: Cambridge University Press.
Allen, Cynthia. 1995. *Case marking and reanalysis: Grammatical relations from Old to Early Modern English*. Oxford: Clarendon Press.
Anagnostopoulou, Elena. 2003. Participles and voice. In: Artemis Alexiadou, Monika Rathert & Arnim von Stechow (eds.). *Perfect Explorations*. Berlin: de Gruyter. 1–36.
Anderson, Gregory D. S. 2006. *Auxiliary verb constructions*. Oxford: Oxford University Press.
Anderson, John M. 1989. Periphrases and paradigms. In: Bengt Odenstedt, Gunnar Persson & Mats Rydén (eds.). *Instead of flowers: Papers in honour of Mats Rydén on the occasion of his sixtieth birthday, August 27, 1989*. Stockholm: Almqvist & Wiksell. 1–10.
Anderson, John M. 2000. Auxiliaries as a morphological class. In: Geert E. Booij, Christian Lehmann & Joachim Mugdan (eds.). *Morphology: An international handbook on inflection and word-formation* (HSK 17.1). Berlin: de Gruyter. 808–20.
Andréasson, Maia, Karlsson, Susanna, Magnusson, Erik & Tingsell, Sofia. 2002. Har/hade-bortfall. Hur finit är ett naket supinum? In: Björn Melander, Ulla Melander Marttala, Catharinga Nyström, Mats Thelander & Carin Östman (eds.). *Svenskans beskrivning 26. Förhandlingar vid Tjugosjätte sammankomsten för svenskans beskrivning. Uppsala den 25–26 oktober 2002*. Uppsala: Hallgren & Fallgren. 67–74.
Aronoff, Mark. 1994. *Morphology by itself: Stems and inflectional classes*. Cambridge, MA: MIT Press.
Askedal, John O. 1991. „Ersatzinfinitiv/Partizipersatz" und Verwandtes: Zum Aufbau des verbalen Schlußfeldes in der modernen deutschen Standardsprache. *Zeitschrift für germanistische Linguistik* 19: 1–23.
Aygen, Gülşat. 2009. How many manifestations of 'copula' can a language employ? *Dil ve Edebiyat Dergisi / Journal of Linguistics and Literature* 6: 15–30.
Bader, Markus. 2014. Das Verb *lassen* im Deutschen: Zum Zusammenspiel von Auxiliarinversion und Ersatzinfinitiv. *Zeitschrift für Sprachwissenschaft* 33: 1–44.
Bader, Markus & Häussler, Jana. 2013. How much *bekommen* is there in the German *bekommen* passive. In: Artemis Alexiadou & Florian Schäfer (eds.). *Non-canonical passives*. Amsterdam: John Benjamins. 115–40.
Bader, Markus & Schmid, Tanja. 2009. Verb clusters in colloquial German. *The Journal of Comparative Germanic Linguistics* 12: 175–228.
Bærentzen, Per. 2004. Formale und semantische Unschärfen in vielgliedrigen Verbalkomplexen: Der Ersatzinfinitiv und anderes. *Tidsskrift for sprogforskning* 2: 127–39.
Baker, Mark. 1988. *Incorporation: A theory of grammatical function changing*. Chicago: The University of Chicago Press.
Baker, Mark. 2003. *Lexical categories: Verbs, nouns, and adjectives*. Cambridge: Cambridge University Press.
Baker, Mark, Johnson, Kyle & Roberts, Ian. 1989. Passive arguments raised. *Linguistic Inquiry* 20: 219–51.

Ballweg, Joachim. 1988. *Die Semantik der deutschen Tempusformen: Eine indirekte Analyse im Rahmen einer temporal erweiterten Aussagelogik*. Düsseldorf: Schwann.

Ballweg, Joachim. 1989. Preterite, (present-)perfect and future. In: Werner Abraham & Theo Janssen (eds.). *Tempus – Aspekt – Modus: die lexikalischen und grammatischen Formen in den germanischen Sprachen*. Tübingen: Max Niemeyer. 85–101.

Barner, David & Bale, Alan. 2002. No nouns, no verbs: psycholinguistic arguments in favour of lexical underspecification. *Lingua* 112: 771–91.

Basilico, David. 2008. The syntactic representation of perfectivity. *Lingua* 118: 1716–39.

Bäuerle, Rainer. 1979. *Temporale Deixis, temporale Frage*. Tübingen: G. Narr.

Bauke, Leah S. 2014. *Symmetry breaking in syntax and the lexicon*. Amsterdam: John Benjamins.

Bech, Gunnar. 1983 [1955]. *Studien über das deutsche Verbum infinitum* (2nd edn.). Tübingen: Max Niemeyer.

Beedham, Christopher. 1981. The passive in English, German, and Russian. *Journal of Linguistics* 17: 319–27.

Beedham, Christopher. 1998. The perfect passive participle in Russian: A review of *Participial passive and aspect in Russian* by Maaike Schoorlemmer (1995). Review article. *Lingua* 105: 79–94.

Behaghel, Otto. 1899. Ich habe geschlafen. *Zeitschrift für Deutsche Philologie* 32: 64–72.

Behaghel, Otto. 1924. *Deutsche Syntax. Band II: Die Wortklassen und Wortformen*. Heidelberg: Winter.

Behaghel, Otto. 1928. *Deutsche Syntax. Band III: Die Satzgebilde*. Heidelberg: Winter.

Belitschenko, Iwan. 1980. Zu Besonderheiten der temporalen Bedeutungen der Partizipien im Deutschen im Vergleich zu den Temporalbedeutungen der finiten Verbalformen. *Wissenschaftliche Zeitschrift der Humboldt-Universität zu Berlin, Ges. – Sprachw. Reihe* 29: 375–78.

Belletti, Adriana. 2006. (Past) participle agreement. In: Martin Everaert & Henk C. van Riemsdijk (eds.). *The Blackwell companion to syntax*. Malden, MA: Blackwell. 493–521.

Belletti, Adrianna & Rizzi, Luigi. 1988. Psych-verbs and theta-theory. *Natural Language and Linguistic Theory* 6: 291–352.

Belvin, Robert. 1993. The two causative haves are the two possessive haves. *MIT Working Papers in Linguistics* 20: 19–34.

Belvin, Robert. 1996. Inside events: The non-possessive meanings of possession predicates and the semantic conceptualization of events. PhD dissertation. Los Angeles: University of Southern California.

Benincà, Paola. 1989. Introduction. In: Paola Benincà (ed.). *Dialect variation and the theory of grammar*. Dordrecht: Foris. 1–8.

Bentley, Delia. 2006. *Split intransitivity in Italian*. Berlin: de Gruyter.

Benveniste, Émile. 1960/1966. 'Être' et 'avoir' dans leurs fonctions linguistiques. In: Benveniste, Émile (ed.). *Problèmes de linguistique générale*. Paris: Gallimard. 187–207.

Berman, Ruth A. 1980. On the category of auxiliary in Modern Hebrew. *Hebrew Annual Review* 4: 15–37.

Bertacca, Antonio. 2010. Present-day English irregular verbs revisited. *Poznań Studies in Contemporary Linguistics* 46: 127–54.

Bierwisch, Manfred. 1990. Verb-cluster formation as a morphological process. In: Geert E. Booij & Jaap van Marle (eds.). *Yearbook of morphology 1990*. Dordrecht: Kluwer. 173–99.

Binnick, Robert. 1991. *Time and the verb: A guide to tense and aspect*. Oxford: Oxford University Press.

Bjerre, Anne & Bjerre, Tavs. 2007. Perfect and periphrastic passive constructions in Danish. *Nordic Journal of Linguistics* 30: 5–53.
Bjorkman, Bronwyn M. 2011. BE-ing default: the morphosyntax of auxiliaries. PhD dissertation. Cambridge, MA: Massachusetts Institute of Technology.
Blevins, James P. 2003. Stems and paradigms. *Language* 79: 737–67.
Blevins, James P. 2006. Passives and impersonals. In: Keith Brown & Anne Anderson (eds.). *The encyclopedia of language and linguistics* (2nd edn.). Amsterdam: Elsevier. 236–39.
Bloch, Bernard. 1947. English verb inflection. *Language* 47: 399–418.
Bloomer, Robert. 1994. *System-congruity and the participles of Modern German and Modern English: A study in natural morphology*. Hamburg: Buske.
Bloomer, Robert. 1999. The nonmorphological isolation of strong and irregular past participles: Also a factor in the formation of weak participles? *Folia Linguistica* XXXIII: 287–94.
Boas, Franz. 1911. *Handbook of American Indian languages*, Part I. Washington, DC: Smithsonian Institution.
Boeckx, Cedric. 2006. *Linguistic minimalism: Origins, concepts, methods, and aims*. Oxford: Oxford University Press.
Borer, Hagit. 1998. Deriving passive without theta roles. In: Steven Lapointe, Diane Brentari & Patrick Farrell (eds.). *Morphology and its relation to phonology and syntax*. Stanford, CA: CSLI Publications. 60–99.
Borer, Hagit. 2003. Exo-skeletal vs. endo-skeletal explanations. In: John Moore & Maria Polinsky (eds.). *The nature of explanation in linguistic theory*. Chicago: University of Chicago Press. 31–67.
Borer, Hagit. 2004. The grammar machine. In: Artemis Alexiadou, Elena Anagnostopoulou & Martin Everaert (eds.). *The unaccusativity puzzle: Explorations of the syntax-lexicon interface*. Oxford: Oxford University Press. 288–331.
Borer, Hagit. 2005a. *Structuring sense. Volume 1: In name only*. Oxford: Oxford University Press.
Borer, Hagit. 2005b. *Structuring sense. Volume 2: The normal course of events*. Oxford: Oxford University Press.
Borer, Hagit. 2013. *Structuring sense. Volume 3: Taking form*. Oxford: Oxford University Press.
Borer, Hagit. 2014. Wherefore roots? *Theoretical Linguistics* 40: 343–59.
Borik, Olga. 2002. Aspect and reference time. PhD dissertation. Utrecht: University of Utrecht.
Borik, Olga & Gehrke, Berit. to appear. Imperfective past passive participles in Russian. In: Denisa Lenertová, Roland Meyer, Radek Šimík & Luka Szucsich (eds.). *Advances in formal Slavic linguistics 2016*. Berlin: Language Science Press.
Börjars, Kersti, Vincent, Nigel & Chapman, Carol. 1997. Paradigms, periphrasis and pronominal inflection: A feature-based account. In: Geert E. Booij & Jaap van Marle (eds.). *Yearbook of morphology 1996*. Dordrecht: Kluwer. 155–80.
Bourns, Stacey Katz. 2013. *Contextualized French grammar: A handbook*. Boston, MA: Heinle.
Bowers, John. 1993. The syntax of predication. *Linguistic Inquiry* 24: 591–656.
Bowers, John. 2001. Predication. In: Mark Baltin & Chris Collins (eds.). *The handbook of contemporary syntactic theory*. 299–333.
Bresnan, Joan. 1978. A realistic transformational grammar. In: Morris Halle, Joan Bresnan & George A. Miller (eds.). *Linguistic theory and psychological reality*. Cambridge, MA: MIT Press. 1–59.
Bresnan, Joan. 1982. *The mental representation of grammatical relations*. Cambridge, MA: MIT Press.

Bresnan, Joan. 1995. Lexicality and argument structure. Invited paper given at the Paris Syntax and Semantics Conference, October 12–14, 1995. <https://web.stanford.edu/~bresnan/paris.pdf>, accessed on January 4, 2017.

Breul, Carsten. 2004. *Focus structure in generative grammar: An integrated syntactic, semantic and intonational approach*. Amsterdam: John Benjamins.

Breul, Carsten. 2008. On a contrast between English and German copular sentences. *Zeitschrift für Anglistik und Amerikanistik* 56: 237–54.

Breul, Carsten. 2014. The perfect participle paradox: some implications for the architecture of grammar. *English Language and Linguistics* 18: 449–70.

Breul, Carsten & Wegner, Dennis. 2017. German and English past participles in perfect and passive contexts: An identity view. *Sprachwissenschaft* 42: 1–58.

Brinker, Klaus. 1971. *Das Passiv im heutigen Deutsch: Form und Funktion*. München, Düsseldorf: Max Huber Verlag, Pädagogischer Verlag Schwann.

British National Corpus [BNC]. Accessed throughout 2015 from http://corpus.byu.edu/ created and maintained by Mark Davies.

Broekhuis, Hans & Corver, Norbert. 2015. *Syntax of Dutch. Volume 2: Verbs and verb phrases*. Amsterdam: Amsterdam University Press.

Broekhuis, Hans & Migdalski, Krzysztof. 2003. Participle fronting in Bulgarian as XP-movement. In: Leonie Cornips & Paula Fikkert (eds.). *Linguistics in the Netherlands 2003*. Nijmegen: Meertens Institute / University of Nijmegen. 1–12.

Broekhuis, Hans & van Dijk, Kees. 1995. The syntactic function of the auxiliaries of time. In: Marcel Den Dikken & Kees Hengeveld (eds.). *Linguistics in the Netherlands 1995*. Amsterdam: John Benjamins. 37–48.

Bruening, Benjamin. 2014. Word formation is syntactic: Adjectival passives in English. *Natural Language & Linguistic Theory*. 32: 363–422.

Burzio, Luigi. 1986. *Italian syntax: A government-binding approach*. Dordrecht: Reidel.

Bybee, Joan L. 1985. *Morphology: A study of the relation between meaning and form*. Amsterdam: John Benjamins.

Bybee, Joan L. & Dahl, Östen. 1989. The creation of tense and aspect systems in the languages of the world. *Studies in Language* 13: 51–103.

Caha, Pavel. 2009. The nanosyntax of case. PhD dissertation. Tromsø: University of Tromsø.

Caponigro, Ivano & Schütze, Carson T. 2003. Parametrizing passive participle movement. *Linguistic Inquiry* 34: 293–307.

Carlson, Gregory N. 1977. Reference to kinds in English. PhD dissertation. Amherst, MA: University of Massachusetts, Amherst.

Carstairs-McCarthy, Andrew. 1994. Inflection classes, gender, and the principle of contrast. *Language* 70: 737–88.

Carstairs-McCarthy, Andrew. 2005. Basic terminology. In: Pavol Štekauer & Rochelle Lieber (eds.). *Handbook of word-formation*. Dordrecht: Springer. 5–23.

Cecchetto, Carlo & Donati, Caterina. 2010. On labeling: Principle C and head movement. *Syntax* 13: 241–78.

Cecchetto, Carlo & Donati, Caterina. 2015. *(Re)labeling*. Cambridge, MA: MIT Press.

Chomsky, Noam. 1957. *Syntactic structures*. The Hague: Mouton.

Chomsky, Noam. 1981. *Lectures on government and binding*. Dordrecht: Foris Publications.

Chomsky, Noam. 1986. *Knowledge of language*. Westport: Praeger.

Chomsky, Noam. 1993. A minimalist program for linguistic theory. In: Ken Hale & Samuel Jay Keyser (eds.). *The view from Building 20: Essays in linguistics in honor of Sylvain Bromberger*. Cambridge, MA: MIT Press. 1–52.
Chomsky, Noam. 1995a. Bare phrase structure. In: Gert Webelhuth (ed.). *Government and binding theory and the minimalist program*. Oxford: Blackwell. 385–439.
Chomsky, Noam. 1995b. *The minimalist program*. Cambridge, MA: MIT Press.
Chomsky, Noam. 2000. Minimalist inquiries: the framework. In: Roger Martin, David Michaels & Juan Uriagereka (eds.). *Step by step: Essays on minimalist syntax in honor of Howard Lasnik*. Cambridge, MA: MIT Press. 89–155.
Chomsky, Noam. 2001. Derivation by phase. In: Michael Kenstowicz (ed.). *Ken Hale: A life in language*. Cambridge, MA: MIT Press. 1–52.
Chomsky, Noam. 2004. Beyond explanatory adequacy. In: Adriana Belletti (ed.). *Structures and beyond: The cartography of syntactic structures* (vol. 3). Oxford: Oxford University Press. 104–31.
Chomsky, Noam. 2005. Three factors in language design. *Linguistic Inquiry* 36: 1–22.
Chomsky, Noam. 2007. Approaching UG from below. In: Uli Sauerland & Hans-Martin Gärtner (eds.). *Interfaces + recursion = language? Chomsky's minimalism and the view from syntax-semantics*. Berlin: de Gruyter. 1–30.
Chomsky, Noam. 2008. On phases. In: Robert Freidin, Carlos P. Otero, Maria Luisa Zubizarreta (eds.). *Foundational issues in linguistic theory: Essays in honor of Jean-Roger Vergnaud*. Cambridge, MA: MIT Press. 134–66.
Chomsky, Noam. 2013. Problems of projection. *Lingua* 130: 33–49.
Chomsky, Noam. 2015. Problems of projection: Extensions. In: Elisa Di Domenico, Cornelia Hamann & Simona Matteini (eds.). *Structures, strategies and beyond: Studies in honour of Adriana Belletti*. Amsterdam: John Benjamins. 3–16.
Christensen, Kirsti Koch & Taraldsen, Knut Tarnald. 1989. Expletive chain formation and past participle agreement in Scandinavian dialects. In: Paola Benincà (ed.). *Dialect variation and the theory of grammar*. Dordrecht: Foris. 53–83.
Cinque, Guglielmo. 1999. *Adverbs and functional heads*. Oxford: Oxford University Press.
Cinque, Guglielmo. 2003. The prenominal origin of relative clauses. Paper presented at the NYU Workshop on Antisymmetry and Remnant Movement, Oct. 31–Nov. 1, 2003.
Cinque, Guglielmo. 2005a. The dual source of adjectives and phrasal movement in the Romance DP. Manuscript. University of Venice.
Cinque, Guglielmo. 2005b. Deriving Greenberg's Universal 20 and its exceptions. *Linguistic Inquiry* 36: 315–32.
Collins, Chris. 2002. Eliminating labels. In: Samuel D. Epstein & T. Daniel Seely (eds.). *Derivation and explanation in the minimalist program*. Oxford: Blackwell. 42–64.
Comrie, Bernard. 1976. *Aspect*. Cambridge: Cambridge University Press.
Comrie, Bernard. 1985. *Tense*. Cambridge: Cambridge University Press.
Corpus of Contemporary American English [COCA]. Accessed throughout 2015 from http://corpus.byu.edu/ created and maintained by Mark Davies.
Coseriu, Eugen. 1976. *Das romanische Verbalsystem*. Tübingen: G. Narr.
Coussé, Evie. 2011. On ambiguous past participles in Dutch. *Linguistics* 49: 611–34.
Cowper, Elizabeth. 1989a. Perfective [-en] IS passive [-en]. In: E. Jane Fee & Kathryn Hunt (eds.). *Proceedings of the eighth West Coast Conference on Formal Linguistics*. Stanford, CA: Stanford Linguistics Association by the Center for the Study of Language and Information, Ventura Hall, Stanford University. 85–93.

Cowper, Elizabeth. 1989b. Thematic underspecification: The case of 'have'. *Toronto Working Papers in Linguistics* 10: 85–93.
Cowper, Elizabeth. 2005. The geometry of interpretable features: Infl in English and Spanish. *Language* 81: 10–46.
Curme, George O. 1935. *A grammar of the English language. Volume 1: Parts of speech*. Boston: Heath.
Dahl, Östen & Velupillai, Viveka. 2013a. Tense and aspect: General introduction. In: Matthew S. Dryer & Martin Haspelmath (eds.). *The world atlas of language structures online*. Leipzig: Max Planck Institute for Evolutionary Anthropology.
Dahl, Östen & Velupillai, Viveka. 2013b. The perfect. In: Matthew S. Dryer & Martin Haspelmath (eds.). *The world atlas of language structures online*. Leipzig: Max Planck Institute for Evolutionary Anthropology.
Dahl, Östen & Velupillai, Viveka. 2013c. Perfective/imperfective aspect. In: Matthew S. Dryer & Martin Haspelmath (eds.). *The world atlas of language structures online*. Leipzig: Max Planck Institute for Evolutionary Anthropology.
Dal, Ingerid. 2014 [1952]. *Kurze deutsche Syntax auf historischer Grundlage* (4th edn.). Revised by Hans-Werner Eroms. Berlin: de Gruyter.
Dammel, Antje. 2012. Partizipien II zwischen Flektiertheit und Unflektiertheit: Deutsch, Afrikaans, Schwedisch und oberdeutsche Sprachdialekte im Sprachkontrast. In: Björn Rothstein (ed.). *Nicht-flektierende Wortarten*. Berlin: de Gruyter. 247–74.
Davidson, Thos. 1874. The grammar of Dionysios Thrax: Translated from the Greek. *Journal of Speculative Philosophy* 8: 326–39.
de Saussure, Ferdinand. 1969 [1916]. *Cours de linguistique générale*. Charles Bally & Albert Sechehaye (eds.). Paris: Payot, 1969.
de Vos, Mark. 2001. Afrikaans verb clusters: A funtional-head analysis. Master's thesis. University of Tromsø.
Demirdache, Hamida & Uribe-Etxebarria, Myriam. 2007. The syntax of time arguments. *Lingua* 117: 330–66.
den Dikken, Marcel. 1994. Auxiliaries and participles. *Proceedings of NELS* 24: 65–79.
den Dikken, Marcel & Hoekstra, Eric. 1997. Parasitic participles. *Linguistics* 35: 1057–89.
Depraetere, Ilse. 1995. On the necessity of distinguishing between (un)boundedness and (a)telicity. *Linguistics and Philosophy* 18: 1–19.
Depraetere, Ilse. 1996. *The tense system in English relative clauses: A corpus-based analysis*. Berlin: de Gruyter.
di Sciullo, Anne-Marie & Williams, Edwin. 1987. *On the definition of word*. Cambridge, MA: MIT Press.
Diedrichsen, Elke. 2002. Zu einer semantischen Klassifikation der intransitiven *haben-* und *sein-*Verben im Deutschen. In: Graham Katz, Sabine Reinhard & Philip Reuter (eds.). *Sinn und Bedeutung 6. Proceedings of the sixth meeting of the Gesellschaft für Semantik*. Osnabrück: University of Osnabrück. 37–52.
Dowty, David. 1979. *Word meaning and Montague grammar. The semantics of verbs and times in generative semantics and in Montague's PTQ*. Dordrecht: Reidel.
Dowty, David. 1991. Thematic proto-roles and argument selection. *Language* 67: 547–619.
Drijkoningen, Frank. 1989. *The syntax of verbal affixation*. Tübingen: Max Niemeyer.
Dryer, Matthew S. 1982. In defense of a universal passive. *Linguistic Analysis* 10: 53–60.

Eckardt, Regine. 2011. Grammaticalization and semantic change. In: Heiko Narrog & Bern Heine (eds.). *The Oxford handbook of grammaticalization.* Oxford: Oxford University Press. 389–400.

Ehrich, Veronika. 1992. *Hier und jetzt: Studien zur lokalen und temporalen Deixis im Deutschen.* Tübingen: Max Niemeyer.

Ehrich, Veronika & Vater, Heinz. 1989. Das Perfekt im Dänischen und Deutschen. In: Werner Abraham & Theo Janssen (eds.). *Tempus – Aspekt – Modus: Die lexikalischen und grammatischen Formen in den germanischen Sprachen.* Tübingen: Max Niemeyer. 103–32.

Eisenberg, Peter. 1994. Die Syntax des Mittelwortes: Läßt sich die Kategorisierung der Partizipien einzelsprachlich rechtfertigen? In: Daniel Bresson & Martine Dalmas (eds.). *Partizip und Partizipialgruppen im Deutschen.* Tübingen: G. Narr. 69–90.

Eisenberg, Peter. 1999. *Grundriss der deutschen Grammatik.* Stuttgart: Metzler.

Eisenberg, Peter, Smith, Georg & Teuber, Oliver. 2001. Ersatzinfinitiv und Oberfeld: ein großes Rätsel der deutschen Syntax. *Deutsche Sprache* 3: 242–60.

Embick, David. 1997. Voice and the interfaces of syntax. PhD dissertation. Pennsylvania: University of Pennsylvania.

Embick, David. 2000. Features, syntax, and categories in the Latin perfect. *Linguistic Inquiry* 31: 185–230.

Embick, David. 2003. Locality, listedness and morphological identity. *Studia Linguistica* 57: 143–69.

Embick, David. 2004. On the structure of resultative participles in English. *Linguistic Inquiry* 35: 355–92.

Embick, David & Noyer, Rolf. 2007. Distributed morphology and the syntax-morphology interface. In: Gillian Ramchand & Charles Reiss (eds.). *The Oxford handbook of linguistic interfaces.* Oxford: Oxford University Press. 289–324.

Emonds, Joseph. 2000. *Lexicon and grammar: The English syntacticon.* Berlin: de Gruyter.

Emonds, Joseph. 2006. Adjectival passives. In: Martin Everaert & Henk C. van Riemsdijk (eds.). *The Blackwell companion to syntax.* Malden, MA: Blackwell. 16–60.

Emonds, Joseph. 2013. Indirect passives and the selection of English participles. *Lingua* 125: 58–75.

Engel, Ulrich. 1988. *Deutsche Grammatik.* Heidelberg: Groos.

Epstein, Samuel D., Kitahara, Hisatsugu & Seely, Daniel. 2016. Phase cancellation by external pair-merge of heads. *The Linguistic Review* 33: 87–102.

Erdmann, Oskar. 1886. *Grundzüge der deutschen Syntax nach ihrer geschichtlichen Entwicklung* (vol. 1). Stuttgart: J.G. Cotta'sche Buchhandlung.

Evans, Nicholas. 2000. Kinship verbs. In: Petra M. Vogel & Bernard Comrie (eds.). *Approaches to the typology of word classes.* Berlin: de Gruyter. 103–72.

Evers, Arnold. 1975. The transformational cycle in Dutch and German. PhD dissertation. Utrecht: University of Utrecht.

Evers, Arnold. 2003. Verbal clusters and cluster creepers. In: Pieter A. M. Seuren & Gerard Kempen (eds.). *Verb constructions in German and Dutch.* Amsterdam: John Benjamins. 43–90.

Fabb, Nigel. 1984. Syntactic affixation. PhD dissertation. Cambridge, MA: Massachusetts Institute of Technology.

Fadlon, Julie. 2014. The psycholinguistics of verbal diathesis: The transitive-unaccusative alternation. PhD dissertation. Tel Aviv: Tel Aviv University.

Fanselow, Gisbert. 1987. *Konfigurationalität: Untersuchungen zur Universalgrammatik am Beispiel des Deutschen.* Tübingen: G. Narr.

Fanselow, Gisbert. 2000. Optimal exceptions. In: Barbara Stiebels & Dieter Wunderlich (eds.). *Lexicon in focus*. Berlin: Akademie Verlag. 173–209.
Fanselow, Gisbert. 2003. Zur Generierung der Abfolge der Satzglieder im Deutschen. *Neue Beträge zur Germanistik* 112: 3–47.
Faucher, Eugène. 1994. Partizip oder Adjektiv? Partizip oder Infinitiv?: Benennungs- und Abgrenzungsfragen. In: Daniel Bresson & Martine Dalmas (eds.). *Partizip und Partizipialgruppen im Deutschen*. Tübingen: G. Narr. 1–19.
Filip, Hana. 2011. Aspectual class and aktionsart. In: Claudia Maienborn, Klaus von Heusinger & Paul Portner (eds.). *Semantics: An international handbook of natural language meaning*. Berlin: de Gruyter. 1186–217.
Forsgren, Kjell-Åke. 2000. Wortart, syntaktische Funktion, syntaktische Kategorie. In: Geert E. Booij, Christian Lehmann & Joachim Mugdan (eds.). *Morphology: An international handbook on inflection and word-formation* (HSK 17.1). Berlin: de Gruyter. 665–73.
Franco, Jon. 1994. On the absence of Spanish past participial object clitic agreement: The AGRo parameter in Romance. *Anuario del Seminario de Filología Vasca 'Julio de Urquijo' Donostia-San Sebastián*. 28: 247–62.
Friedemann, Marc-Ariel & Siloni, Tal. 1997. Agr$_{object}$ is not Agr$_{participle}$. *The Linguistic Review* 14: 69–96.
Gabrielson, A. 1967. *Engelsk grammatik för universitet och högskolor* (4th edn.). Stockholm: Svenska Bokförlaget.
Gallego, Ángel J. 2010. *Phase theory*. Amsterday: John Benjamins.
Garey, Howard B. 1957. Verbal aspects in French. *Language* 33: 91–110.
Gehrke, Berit 2012. Passive states. In: Violeta Demonte & Louise McNally (eds.). *Telicity, change, and state: A cross-categorial view of event structure*. Oxford: Oxford University Press. 185–211.
Gehrke, Berit. 2013. Still puzzled by adjectival passives? In: Raffaella Folli, Christina Sevdali & Robert Truswell (eds.). *Syntax and its limits*. Oxford: Oxford University Press. 175–91.
Gehrke, Berit. 2015. Adjectival participles, event kind modification and pseudo-incorporation. *Natural Language and Linguistic Theory* 33: 897–938.
Gillmann, Melitta. 2011. Die Grammatikalisierung des *sein*-Perfekts. *PBB (Beiträge zur Geschichte der deutschen Sprache und Literatur)* 133: 203–34.
Gillmann, Melitta. 2015. Auxiliary selection in closely related languages: The case of German and Dutch. In: Rolf Kailuweit & Malte Rosemeyer (eds.). *Auxiliary selection revisited: Gradience and gradualness*. Berlin: de Gruyter. 333–58.
Giorgi, Alessandra & Pianesi, Fabio. 1997. *Tense and aspect: From semantics to morphosyntax*. Oxford: Oxford University Press.
Givón, Talmy. 1979. *On understanding grammar*. New York: Academic Press.
Gönczöl-Davies, Ramona. 2008. *Romanian: An essential grammar*. New York: Routledge.
Graves, Nina. 2000. Macedonian: A language with three perfects? In: Östen Dahl (ed.). *Tense and aspect in the languages of Europe*. Berlin: de Gruyter. 479–94.
Grewendorf, Günther. 1989. *Ergativity in German*. Dordrecht: Foris.
Grewendorf, Günther. 1995. Präsens und Perfekt im Deutschen. *Zeitschrift für Sprachwissenschaft* 14: 72–90.
Grimm, Jacob. 1837. *Deutsche Grammatik*, vol. 4. Göttingen: Dieterichsche Buchhandlung.
Grimshaw, Jane. 1990. *Argument structure*. Cambridge, MA: MIT Press.
Guéron, Jacqueline. 2007. On tense and aspect. *Lingua* 117: 367–91.
Gunkel, Lutz. 1999. Causatives in German. *Theoretical Linguistics* 25: 133–59.

Gunkel, Lutz. 2003. *Infinitheit, Passiv und Kausativkonstruktionen im Deutschen*. Tübingen: Stauffenburg.
Gzella, Holger. 2011. Northwest semitic in general. In: Stefan Weninger (ed.). *The semitic languages: An international handbook*. Berlin: de Gruyter. 425–51.
Haegeman, Liliane. 1985. The *get*-passive and Burzio's generalization. *Lingua* 66: 53–77.
Haegeman, Liliane & Lohndal, Terje. 2010. Negative concord and (multiple) agree: a case study of West Flemish. *Linguistic Inquiry* 41: 181–211.
Haider, Hubert. 1984. Was zu haben ist und was zu sein hat: Bemerkungen zum Infinitiv. *Papiere zur Linguistik* 30: 23–36.
Haider, Hubert. 1986. Fehlende Argumente: vom Passiv zu kohärenten Infinitiven. *Linguistische Berichte* 101: 3–33.
Haider, Hubert. 1994. Fakultativ kohärente Infinitivkonstruktionen im Deutschen. In: Anita Steube & Gerhild Zybatow (eds.). *Zur Satzwertigkeit von Infinitiven und Small Clauses*. Berlin: de Gruyter. 75–106.
Haider, Hubert. 2003. V-clustering and clause union: Causes and effects. In: Pieter A. M. Seuren & Gerard Kempen (eds.). *Verb constructions in German and Dutch*. Amsterdam: John Benjamins. 91–126.
Haider, Hubert. 2010. *The syntax of German*. Cambridge: Cambridge University Press.
Haider, Hubert. 2011. Grammatische Illusionen: Lokal wohlgeformt – global deviant. *Zeitschrift für Sprachwissenschaft* 30: 223–57.
Hale, Kenneth & Keyser, Samuel J. 1991. *On the syntax of argument structure*. Cambridge, MA: Massachusetts Institute of Technology (Lexicon Project Working Papers).
Hale, Kenneth & Keyser, Samuel J. 1993. On argument structure and the lexical expression of syntactic relations. In: Ken Hale & Samuel Jay Keyser (eds.). *The view from Building 20: Essays in linguistics in honor of Sylvain Bromberger*. Cambridge, MA: MIT Press. 53–109.
Hale, Kenneth & Keyser, Samuel J. 2002. *Prolegomenon to a theory of argument structure*. Cambridge, MA: MIT Press.
Halle, Morris & Marantz, Alec. 1993. Distributed morphology and the pieces of inflection. In: Ken Hale & Samuel Jay Keyser (eds.). *The view from Building 20: Essays in linguistics in honor of Sylvain Bromberger*. Cambridge, MA: MIT Press. 111–76.
Halle, Morris & Marantz, Alec. 1994. Some key features of distributed morphology. *MIT Working Papers in Linguistics* 21: 275–88.
Harley, Heidi. 2014. On the identity of roots. *Theoretical Linguistics* 40: 225–76.
Harley, Heidi & Noyer, Rolf. 1999. Distributed morphology. *Glot International* 4: 3–9.
Harris, Zellig S. 1946. From morpheme to utterance. *Language* 22: 161–83.
Harris, Zellig S. 1951. *Methods in structural linguistics*. Chicago: The University of Chicago Press.
Harris, Zellig S. 1954. Distributional structure. *Word* 10: 146–62.
Haspelmath, Martin. 1990. The grammaticization of passive morphology. *Studies in Language* 14: 25–72.
Haspelmath, Martin. 1994. Passive participles across languages. In: Barbara A. Fox & Paul J. Hopper (eds.). *Voice: Form and function*. Amsterdam: John Benjamins. 151–77.
Haspelmath, Martin. 2000. Periphrasis. In: Geert E. Booij, Christian Lehmann & Joachim Mugdan (eds.). *Morphology: An international handbook on inflection and word-formation* (HSK 17.1). Berlin: de Gruyter. 654–64.
Haspelmath, Martin. 2002. *Understanding morphology*. London, New York: Arnold; Oxford University Press.

Hawkins, Roger. 1985. Errors in the use of French past participles by foreign speakers and their implications for a model of morphology. *Lingua* 67: 171–88.
Heinz, Wolfgang & Matiasek, Johannes. 1994. Argument structure and case assignment in German. In: John A. Nerbonne, Klaus Netter & Carl J. Pollard (eds.). *German in head-driven phrase structure grammar*. Stanford, CA: Center for the Study of Language and Information. 199–236.
Helbig, Gerhard & Buscha, Joachim. 1970. *Deutsche Grammatik: Ein Handbuch für den Ausländerunterricht*. Leipzig: Enzyklopädie.
Helland, Hans P. & Pitz, Anneliese. 2012. Open adjuncts: participial syntax. In: Cathrine Fabricius-Hansen (ed.). *Big events, small clauses: The grammar of elaboration*. Berlin: de Gruyter. 93–130.
Heyse, Johann Christoph August. 1886 [1838]. *Theoretisch-praktische Deutsche Grammatik oder Lehrbuch der deutschen Sprache* (24th edn., edited by Otto Lyon). Hannover: Hahn.
Higginbotham, James. 1983. Logical Form, binding and nominals. *Linguistic Inquiry* 14: 395–420.
Higginbotham, James. 1985. On semantics. *Linguistic Inquiry* 16: 547–93.
Hinrichs, Erhard W. & Nakazawa, Tsuneko. 1998. Third construction and VP extraposition in German: An HPSG analysis. In: Erhard Hinrichs, Andreas Kathol & Tsuneko Nakazawa (eds.). *Complex predicates in nonderivational syntax*. San Diego: Academic Press. 115–57.
Hinterhölzl, Roland. 1998. The syntax of IPP-constructions and the structure of the lower Middlefield in Westgermanic. *U. Penn Working Papers in Linguistics* 5: 59–70.
Hinterhölzl, Roland. 1999. Restructuring infinitives and the theory of complementation. PhD dissertation. Los Angeles: University of Southern California.
Hinterhölzl, Roland. 2006. The phase condition and cyclic spell-out: Evidence from VP-topicalization. In: Mara Frascarelli (ed.). *Phases of interpretation*. Berlin: de Gruyter. 237–59.
Hinterhölzl, Roland. 2009. The IPP-effect, phrasal affixes and repair strategies in the syntax-morphology-interface. *Linguistische Berichte* 218: 191–215.
Hoeksema, Jacob. 1988. A constraint on governors in the West Germanic verb cluster. In: Martin Everaert, Arnold Evers, Riny Huybregts & Mieke Trommelen (eds.). *Morphology and modularity: In honour of Henk Schultink*. Foris: Dordrecht. 147–61.
Hoekstra, Eric. 1997. Analysing linear asymmetries in the verb clusters of Dutch and Frisian and their dialects. In: Dorothee Beermann, David LeBlanc & Henk van Riemsdijk (eds.). *Rightward movement*. Amsterdam: John Benjamins. 153–70.
Hoekstra, Teun. 1984. *Transitivity: Grammatical relations in a government-binding theory*. Dordrecht: Foris.
Hoekstra, Teun. 1986a. Passives and participles. In: Frits Beukema & Aafke Hulk (eds.). *Linguistics in the Netherlands 1986*. Dordrecht: Foris. 95–105.
Hoekstra, Teun. 1986b. Deverbalization and inheritance. *Linguistics* 24: 549–84.
Hoekstra, Teun. 2003 [1986]. Verbal affixation. In: Rint Sybesma, Sjef Barbiers, Marcel den Dikken, Jenny Doetjes, GertJan Postma & Guido Vanden Wyngaerd (eds.). *Arguments and structure: Studies on the architecture of the sentence*. Berlin: de Gruyter. 95–124.
Hoekstra, Eric & van Koppen, Marjo. 2013. Holland and Utrecht: Morphology and syntax. In: Frans Hinskens & Johan Taeldeman (eds.). *Language and Space. An international handbook of linguistic variation. Vol. 3: Dutch* (HSK 30.3). Berlin: de Gruyter. 418–442.
Hofherr, Patricia Cabredo. 2017. Voice and voice alternations. In: Elisabeth Stark & Andreas Dufter (eds). *Manual of romance morphosyntax and syntax*. Berlin: de Gruyter. 230–71.
Höhle, Tilmann. 2006. Observing non-finite verbs: Some 3V phenomena in German. In: Patrick Brandt & Eric Fuß (eds.). *Form, structure and grammar: A festschrift presented to Günther Grewendorf on occasion of his 60th birthday*. Berlin: Akademieverlag. 55–77.

Höhle, Tilman N. 1978. *Lexikalistische Syntax: Die Aktiv-Passiv-Relation und andere Infinitkonstruktionen im Deutschen*. Tübingen: Max Niemeyer.
Höhle, Tilman N. 1992. Über Verum-Fokus im Deutschen. In: Joachim Jacobs (ed.). *Informationsstruktur und Grammatik* (Linguistische Berichte. Sonderheft 4 / 1991–1992). Opladen: Westdeutscher Verlag. 112–41.
Hole, Daniel. 2002. Er hat den Arm verbunden – Valenzreduktion und Argumentvermehrung im *haben*-Konfigurativ. In: Japanische Gesellschaft für Germanistik (ed.). *Grammatische Kategorien aus sprachhistorischer und typologischer Perspektive. Akten des 29. Linguisten-Seminars (Kyoto 2001)*. München: Iudicium. 167–86.
Horgan, Dianne. 1978. The development of the full passive. *Journal of Child Language* 5: 65–80.
Hornstein, Norbert. 1990. *As time goes by*. Cambridge, MA: MIT Press.
Hornstein, Norbert. 2001. *Move! A minimalist theory of construal*. Oxford: Blackwell.
Huddleston, Rodney D. 1984. *Introduction to the grammar of English*. Cambridge: Cambridge University Press.
Huddleston, Rodney D. 2002. The verb. In: Rodney D. Huddleston & Geoffrey K. Pullum (eds.). *The cambridge grammar of the English language*. Cambridge: Cambridge University Press. 71–212.
Hutchinson, Amélia P. & Lloyd, Janet. 1996. *Portuguese: An essential grammar*. London: Routledge.
Iatridou, Sabine. 2003. A little bit more on the English perfect. In: Artemis Alexiadou, Monika Rathert & Arnim von Stechow (eds.). *Perfect explorations*. Berlin: de Gruyter. 133–52.
Iatridou, Sabine, Anagnostopoulou, Elena & Izvorski, Roumyana. 2001. Observations about the form and meaning of the perfect. In: Kenneth L. Hale & Michael J. Kenstowicz (eds.). *Ken Hale: A life in language*. Cambridge, MA: MIT Press. 189–238.
IJbema, Aniek. 1997. Der IPP-Effekt im Deutschen und im Niederländischen. *Groninger Arbeiten zur germanistischen Linguistik* 40: 137–63.
Irurtzun, Aritz. 2007. The grammar of focus at the interfaces. PhD dissertation. Alava, Biskaia & Gipuzkoa: University of the Basque Country.
Israel, Michael, Johnson, Christopher & Brooks, Patricia J. 2000. From states to events: The acquisition of the English passive participles. *Cognitive Linguistics* 11: 103–29.
Jacobs, Joachim. 1993. Integration. In: M. Reis (ed.). *Wortstellung und Informationsstruktur*. Tübingen: Niemeyer. 63–116.
Jacobs, Joachim. 1994. Das lexikalische Fundament der Unterscheidung von obligatorischen und fakultativen Ergänzungen. *Zeitschrift für germanistische Linguistik* 22: 284–319.
Jacobs, Joachim. 1999. Informational autonomy. In: Peter Bosch & Rob van der Sandt (eds.), *Focus: Linguistic, cognitive, and computational perspectives*. Cambridge: Cambridge University Press. 56–81.
Jaeggli, Osvaldo A. 1986. Passive. *Linguistic Inquiry* 17: 587–622.
Jespersen, Otto. 1924. *The philosophy of grammar*. London: Allen & Unwin.
Julien, Marit. 2007. On the relation between morphology and syntax. In: Gillian Ramchand & Charles Reiss (eds.). *The Oxford handbook of linguistic interfaces*. Oxford: Oxford University Press. 209–38.
Kamp, Hans & Ryle, Uwe. 1993. *From discourse to logic*. Dordrecht: Kluwer.
Kathol, Andreas. 1991. Verbal and adjectival passives in German. In: Jonathan D. Bobaljik & Tony Bures (eds.). *Papers from the third Student Conference in Linguistics* (MIT Working Papers in Linguistics 14). Cambridge, MA: Massachusetts Institute of Technology. 115–30.

Kathol, Andreas. 1994. Passives without lexical rules. In: John A. Nerbonne, Klaus Netter & Carl J. Pollard (eds.). *German in head-driven phrase structure grammar*. Stanford, CA: Center for the Study of Language and Information. 237–72.
Kathol, Andreas. 1998. Constituency and linearization of verbal complexes. In: Erhard Hinrichs, Tsuneko Nakazawa & Andreas Kathol (eds.). *Complex predicates in non-derivational syntax*. New York: Academic Press. 221–70.
Kaufmann, Ingrid. 1995. O- and D-predicates: A semantic approach to the unaccusative-unergative distinction. *Journal of Semantics* 12: 377–427.
Kayne, Richard. 1989. Facets of Romance past participle agreement. In: Paola Beninca (ed.). *Dialect variation and the theory of grammar*. Dordrecht: Foris. 85–104.
Kayne, Richard. 1994. *The antisymmetry of syntax*. Cambridge, MA: MIT Press.
Kemmer, Suzanne. 1993. *The middle voice*. Amsterdam: Benjamins.
Kiparsky, Paul. 2013. Towards a null theory of the passive. *Lingua* 125: 7–33.
Kiss, Tibor. 1992. Variable Subkategorisierung. Eine Theorie unpersönlicher Einbettungen im Deutschen. *Linguistische Berichte* 140: 256–93.
Kjellmer, Göran. 2003. On nonoccurring perfective have in Modern English. *Studia Neophilologica* 75: 11–20.
Klein, Wolfgang. 1992. The present perfect puzzle. *Language* 68: 525–52.
Klein, Wolfgang. 1999. Wie sich das deutsche Perfekt zusammensetzt. *Zeitschrift für Literaturwissenschaft und Linguistik (LiLi)* 113: 52–85.
Klein, Wolfgang. 2000. An analysis of the German Perfekt. *Language* 76: 358–82.
Klein, Wolfgang. 2010. On times and arguments. *Linguistics* 48: 1221–53.
Klein, Wolfgang. 1994. *Time in language*. London, New York: Routledge.
Klingvall, Eva. 2011. On past participles and their external arguments. *Working Papers in Scandinavian Syntax* 87: 53–80.
König, Ekkehard & Gast, Volker. 2009. *Understanding English-German contrasts* (2nd edn.). Berlin: Erich Schmidt.
Koopman, Hilda & Szabolcsi, Anna. 2000. *Verbal complexes*. Cambridge: MIT Press.
Kratzer, Angelika. 1994. The event argument and the semantics of voice. Manuscript. Amherst: University of Massachusetts, Amherst.
Kratzer, Angelika. 1996. Severing the external argument from its verb. In: Johan Rooryck & Laurie Zaring (eds.). *Phrase structure and the lexicon*. Dordrecht: Kluwer. 109–37.
Kratzer, Angelika. 2000. Building statives. In: Lisa Conathan, Jeff Good, Darya Kavitskaya, Alyssa Wulf & Alan Yu (eds.). *Proceedings of the twenty-sixth annual meeting of the Berkeley Linguistic Society*. Berkeley, CA: Berkeley Linguistics Society. 385–99.
Krifka, Manfred. 1998. The origins of telicity. In: Susan Rothstein (ed.), *Events and grammar*. Dordrecht: Kluwer. 197–235.
Kunze, Jürgen. 1996. Plain middles and *lassen* middles in German: reflexive constructions and sentence perspective. *Linguistics* 34: 645–95.
Landau, Idan. 2010. *The locative syntax of experiencers*. Cambridge, MA: MIT Press.
Langacker, Ronald W. 1991. *Foundations of cognitive grammar. Volume 2: Descriptive application*. Stanford, CA: Stanford University Press.
Lange, Klaus P. 1982. Ersatzinfinitiv und Oberflächenprofil. *Zeitschrift für germanistische Linguistik* 10: 173–86.
Larson, Richard K. 1988. On the double object construction. In: *Linguistic Inquiry* 19: 335–91.
Larsson, Ida. 2009. *Particles in time: The development of the perfect tense in Swedish*. PhD dissertation. Göteborg: University of Göteborg.

Larsson, Ida. 2015. The HAVE/BE alternation in Scandinavian: Perfects, resultatives and unaccusative structure. In: Rolf Kailuweit & Malte Rosemeyer (eds.). *Auxiliary selection revisited: Gradience and gradualness*. Berlin: de Gruyter. 145–82.
Laskova, Vesselina. 2007. Verbal participles and the prenominal position in English. *Rivista di grammatica generativa* 32: 125–40.
Lebeth, Kai. 1994. *Morphosyntaktischer Strukturaufbau: Die Generierung komplexer Verben im HPSG-Lexikon eines Sprachproduktionssystems*. Hamburg: Universität Hamburg.
Łęcki, Andrzej M. 2010. *Grammaticalisation paths of* Have *in English*. Frankfurt am Main: Lang.
Leiss, Elisabeth. 1992. *Die Verbalkategorien des Deutschen: Ein Beitrag zur Theorie der sprachlichen Kategorisierung*. Berlin: Walter de Gruyter.
Lenz, Barbara. 1993. Probleme der Kategorisierung deutscher Partizipien. *Zeitschrift für Sprachwissenschaft* 12: 39–76.
Levin, Beth & Rappaport Hovav, Malka. 1995. *Unaccusativity: At the syntax-lexical semantics interface*. Cambridge, MA: MIT Press.
Levin, Beth & Rappaport, Malka. 1986. The formation of adjectival passives. *Linguistic Inquiry* 17: 623–61.
Lie, Svein 1994. Partisipper = Adjektiver. In: Jens Allwood, Bo Ralph, Paula Andersson, Dora Kós-Dienes & Åsa Wengelin (eds.). *Proceedings of the fourteenth Scandinavian Conference of Linguistics and the eighth Conference of Nordic and General Linguistics, August 16–21, 1993. General Session 2*. Göteborg: Institutionen för Lingvistik. 247–58.
Lieber, Rochelle. 1980. On the organization of the lexicon. PhD dissertation. Cambridge, MA: Massachusetts Institute of Technology.
Lieber, Rochelle. 1983. Argument linking and compounds in English. *Linguistic Inquiry* 14: 251–85.
Lieber, Rochelle & Baayen, Harald. 1997. A semantic principle of auxiliary selection in Dutch. *Natural Language and Linguistic Theory* 15: 789–845.
Lightfoot, David. 1979. Rule classes and syntactic change. *Linguistic Inquiry* 11: 83–103.
Lindqvist, Axel. 1944. Über einen Fall von syntaktischer Assimilation. *Studia Neophilologica* 16: 277–85.
Lindstedt, Jouoko. 2000. The perfect: Aspectual, temporal and evidential. In: Östen Dahl (ed.). *Tense and aspect in the languages of Europe*. Berlin: de Gruyter. 365–84.
Ljunggren, Ragnar. 1934. Supinum och dubbelsupinum. PhD dissertation. Uppsala: Uppsala University.
Löbner, Sebastian. 2002. Is the German Perfekt a perfect perfect? In: Ingrid Kaufmann & Barbara Stiebels (eds.). *More than words: A festschrift for Dieter Wunderlich*. Berlin: Akademie Verlag. 369–92.
Lockwood, William B. 1977. *An introduction to Modern Faroese*. Munksgaard: Copenhagen.
Lødrup, Helge. 1996. The theory of complex predicates and the Norwegian verb få 'get'. *Working Papers in Scandinavian Syntax* 57: 76–91.
Lohndahl, Terje. 2006. The phrase structure of the copula. *Working Papers in Scandinavian Syntax* 78: 37–75.
Lohnstein, Horst. 2011. *Formale Semantik und natürliche Sprache*. Berlin, New York: de Gruyter.
Lois, Ximena. 1990. Auxiliary selection and past participle agreement in Romance. *Probus* 2: 233–55.
Lübbe, Anja & Rapp, Irene. 2011. Aspekt, Temporalität und Argumentstruktur bei attributiven Partizipien des Deutschen. *Zeitschrift für Sprachwissenschaft* 30: 259–99.
Lundquist, Bjørn. 2013. The category of participles. In: Roy Iordăchioaia & Kaori Takamine (eds.). *Categorization and category change*. Newcastle upon Tyne: Cambridge Scholars. 11–32.

Lyons, Christopher. 1995. Voice, aspect, and arbitrary arguments. In: John C. Smith & Martin Maiden (eds.). *Linguistic theory and the Romance languages*. Amsterdam: John Benjamins. 77–114.

Maienborn, Claudia. 2007. Das Zustandspassiv: Grammatische Einordnung – Bildungsbeschränkung – Interpretationsspielraum. *Zeitschrift für germanistische Linguistik* 35: 83–114.

Maienborn, Claudia. 2011. Strukturausbau am Rande der Wörter: Adverbiale Modifikatoren beim Zustandspassiv. In: Stefan Engelberg, Anke Holler, Kristel Proost (eds.). *Sprachliches Wissen zwischen Lexikon und Grammatik*. Berlin: de Gruyter. 317–43.

Marelj, Marijana. 2013. Experiencing linking: Psych verbs at the interface. In: Elly van Gelderen, Michaela Cennamo & Jóhanna Barðdal (eds.). *Argument structure in flux: The Naples-Capri Papers*. Amsterdam: John Benjamins. 135–68.

Marillier, Jean-François. 1994. Was sind Partizipien? Kritische Stellungnahme am Beispiel des sogenannten Partizips 2. In: Daniel Bresson & Martine Dalmas (eds.). *Partizip und Partizipialgruppen im Deutschen*. Tübingen: G. Narr. 19–32.

Martin, Roger & Uriagereka, Juan. 2000. Some possible foundations of the minimalist program. In: Roger Martin, David Michaels & Juan Uriagereka (eds.). *Step by step: Essays on minimalist syntax in honor of Howard Lasnik*. Cambridge, MA: MIT Press. 1–29.

Marvin, Tatjana. 2003. Past participles in reduced relatives: A cross-linguistic perspective. *Linguistica* 43: 141–60.

McCawley, J. 1971. Tense and time reference in English. In: Charles J. Fillmore & D. Terence Langendoen (eds.). *Studies in linguistic semantics*. New York: Holt, Rinehartand Winston. 96–113.

McCoard, Robert W. 1978. *The English perfect: Tense choice and pragmatic inferences*. Amsterdam: North-Holland.

McFadden, Thomas. 2007. Default case and the status of compound categories in distributed morphology. *U. Penn Working Papers in Linguistics* 13: 225–38.

McFadden, Thomas & Alexiadou, Artemis. 2010. Perfects, resultatives, and auxiliaries in earlier English. *Linguistic Inquiry* 41: 389–425.

McIntyre, Andrew. 2013. Adjectival passives and adjectival participles in English. In: Artemis Alexiadou & Florian Schäfer (eds.). *Non-canonical passives*. Amsterdam: John Benjamins. 21–42.

Meltzer-Asscher, Aya. 2011. Adjectives and argument structure. PhD dissertation. Tel Aviv: Tel Aviv University.

Meltzer-Asscher, Aya. 2012. The subject of adjectives: Syntactic position and semantic interpretation. *The Linguistic Review* 29: 149–89.

Merchant, Jason. 2011. Aleut case matters. In: Etsuyo Yuasa, Tista Bagchi, & Katharine P. Beals (eds.). *Pragmatics and autolexical grammar: In honor of Jerry Sadock*. Amsterdam: John Benjamins. 382–411.

Merkes, Peter Wilhelm. 1895. Der neuhochdeutsche Infinitiv als Teil einer umschriebenen Zeitform: historisch-grammatische Betrachtungen. PhD dissertation. Göttingen: University of Göttingen.

Meurers, Walt D. 2000. Lexical generalizations in the syntax of German non-finite constructions. PhD dissertation. Tübingen: University of Tübingen.

Michaelis, Laura A. 2006. Tense in English. In: Bas Aarts & April McMahon (eds.). *The handbook of English linguistics*. Malden, MA: Blackwell. 220–43.

Michaelis, Laura A. & Ruppenhofer, Josef. 2001. *Beyond alternations: A constructional model of the German applicative pattern*. Stanford, CA: CSLI Publications.

Migdalski, Krzysztof. 2006. *The syntax of compound tenses in Slavic.* Tilburg: University of Tilburg.

Migdalski, Krzysztof. 2010. Diachronic impoverishment of the auxiliary and participle movement in Slavic. In: Petr Karlík (ed.). *Development of language through the lens of formal linguistics.* München: LINCOM Europa. 129–36.

Mikkelsen, Line. 2005. *Copular clauses: Specification, predication and equation.* Amsterdam: John Benjamins.

Miller, Georg A. 1956. The magical number seven, plus or minus two: Some limits on our capacity to process information. *The Psychological Review* 63: 81–87.

Mitchell, Bruce. 1985. *Old English syntax.* Vol. 1. Oxford: Clarendon.

Mittwoch, Anita. 1988. Aspects of English aspect: On the interaction of perfect, progressive, and durational phrases. *Linguistics and Philosophy* 11: 203–54.

Mittwoch, Anita. 2008. The English resultative perfect and its relationship to the experiential perfect and the simple past tense. *Linguistics and Philosophy* 31: 323–51.

Moro, Andrea. 2000. *Dynamic antisymmetry: Movement as a symmetry-breaking phenomenon.* Cambridge, MA: MIT Press.

Mortelmans, Tanja, Boye Kasper & van der Auwera, Johan. 2009. Modals in the Germanic languages. In: Björn Hansen & Ferdinand de Haan (eds.). *Modals in the languages of Europe: A reference work.* Berlin: de Gruyter. 11–70.

Müller, Gereon. 2015. *Structure removal: A new approach to conflicting representations.* Manuscript. Leipzig: University of Leipzig. 1–60.

Müller, Natascha, Schmitz, Katrin, Cantone, Katja & Kupish, Tanja. 2006. Null arguments in monolingual children: A comparison of Italian and French. In: Vincent Torrens & Linda Escobar (eds.). *The acquisition of syntax in Romance languages.* Amsterdam: John Benjamins. 69–93.

Müller, Stefan. 1999. *Deutsche Syntax deklarativ: Head-Driven Phrase Structure Grammar für das Deutsche* (2nd edn.). Tübingen: Max Niemeyer.

Müller, Stefan. 2001. The passive as a lexical rule. In: Daniel P. Flickinger & Andreas Kathol (eds.). *Proceedings of the HPSG-2000 Conference.* Stanford, CA: CSLI Publications. 247–66.

Müller, Stefan. 2002. Blockaden und Deblockaden: Perfekt, Passiv und modale Infinitive. In: David Reitter (ed.). *Tagungsband TaCoS 2002, Potsdam.* Potsdam: University of Potsdam. 4–12.

Müller, Stefan. 2007. *Head-Driven Phrase Structure Grammar: Eine Einführung.* Tübingen: Stauffenburg.

Müller, Stefan & Ørsnes, Bjarne. 2013. Passive in Danish, English, and German. In: Stefan Müller (ed.). *Proceedings of the twentieth International Conference on Head-Driven Phrase Structure Grammar.* Stanford, CA: CSLI Publications. 140–60.

Musan, Renate. 1998. The core semantics of the perfect. *ZAS Papers in Linguistics* 10: 113–45.

Musan, Renate. 1999. Die Lesarten des Perfekts. *Zeitschrift für Literaturwissenschaft und Linguistik* 113: 6–51.

Muxí, Isabel. 1996. Optional participial agreement with direct object clitics in Catalan. *Catalan Working Papers in Linguistics* 5: 127–45.

Narita, Hiroki. 2011. Phasing in full interpretation. PhD dissertation. Cambridge, MA: Harvard University.

Neeleman, Ad. 1994. Complex predicates. PhD dissertation. Utrecht: University of Utrecht.

Neeleman, Ad & van de Koot, Hans. 2002. Bare resultatives. *Journal of Comparative Germanic Linguistics* 6: 1–52.

Nerbonne, John. 1985. *German temporal semantics*. Ann Arbor: University of Michigan Press.
Neubauer, Kathleen & Clahsen, Harald. 2009. Decomposition of inflected words in a second language: An experimental study of German participles. *Studies in Second Language Acquisition* 31: 403–35.
Öhl, Peter. 2009. Die Entstehung des periphrastischen Perfekts mit haben und sein im Deutschen: eine längst beantwortete Frage? *Zeitschrift für Sprachwissenschaft* 28: 265–306.
Oku, Satoshi. 1996. Perfective participle paradox in English VP-fronting. In: Antony Dubach Green & Virginia Motapanyane (eds.). *Proceedings of the thirteenth Eastern States Conference on Linguistics '96 (ESCOL)*. Ithaca: Cornell University. 282–93.
Oku, Satoshi. 1998. A theory of selection and reconstruction in the minimalist perspective. PhD dissertation. Connecticut: University of Connecticut.
Ørsnes, Bjarne. 2008. Form und Funktion bei der Verwendung des Ersatzinfinitivs im Deutschen: Zum Gebrauch des Ersatzinfinitivs bei Fügungen mit Modalverb und Direktionalerganzung. *Acta Linguistica Hafniensia: International Journal of Linguistics* 40: 121–58.
Oštir, Alja Lipavic. 2010. Grammaticalization and language contact between German and Slovene. In: Nomachi Motoki (ed.). *Grammaticalization in Slavic languages: From areal and typological perspectives* (2nd edn.). Sapporo: Slavic Research Center. 27–48.
Ott, Dennis. 2012. *Local instability: Split topicalization and quantifier float in German*. Berlin: de Gruyter.
Panã Dindelegan, Gabriela. 2013. *The grammar of Romanian*. Oxford: Oxford University Press.
Panagiotidis, Phoevos. 2002. Against category-less roots in syntax and word learning: Objections to Barner and Bale (2002). *Lingua* 115: 1181–94.
Pancheva, Roumyana. 2003. The aspectual makeup of perfect participles and the interpretations of the perfect. In: Artemis Alexiadou, Monika Rathert & Arnim von Stechow (eds.). *Perfect explorations*. Berlin: de Gruyter. 277–306.
Pancheva, Roumyana & von Stechow, Arnim. 2004. On the present perfect puzzle. In: Keir Moulton & Matthew Wolf (eds.). *Proceedings of the annual meeting of the North Eastern Linguistic Society* (NELS) 34. Amherst, MA: GLSA, 469–83.
Parsons, Terence. 1990. *Events in the semantics of English: A study in subatomic semantics*. Cambridge, MA: MIT Press.
Paul, Hermann. 1957. *Deutsche Grammatik, vol. 4*. Halle: Max Niemeyer.
Perlmutter, David. 1978. Impersonal passives and the unaccusative hypothesis. In: Berkeley Linguistic Society (eds). *Proceedings of the first annual meeting of the Berkeley Linguistic Society*. 157–89.
Pesetsky, David. 1995. *Zero syntax: Experiencers and cascades*. Cambridge, MA: MIT Press.
Pesetsky, David & Torrego, Esther. 2002. Tense, case, and the nature of syntactic categories. In: Jacqeline Guéron & Jacqueline Lecarme (eds.). *The syntax of time*. Cambridge, MA: MIT Press. 495–537.
Pesetsky, David & Torrego, Esther. 2006. Probes, goals and syntactic categories. In: Yukio Otsu (ed.). *Proceedings of the seventh Tokyo Conference on Psycholinguistics*. Tokyo: Hituzi Syobo. 25–60.
Pesetsky, David & Torrego, Esther. 2007. The syntax of valuation and the interpretability of features. In: Simin Karimi, Vida Samiian & Wendy Wilkins (eds.). *Phrasal and clausal architecture*. Amsterdam: John Benjamins. 262–94.
Peyronel, Stella & Higgins, Ian. 2006. *Basic Italian: A grammar and workbook*. New York: Routledge.

Pinkster, Harm. 1987. The strategy and chronology of future and perfect tense auxiliaries in Latin. In: Martin Harris & Paolo Ramat (eds.). *The historical development of auxiliaries*. Berlin: de Gruyter. 193–223.

Platzack, Christer. 1989. The Swedish supine: An active verb form or the non-agreeing form of the past participle? In: Dany Jaspers, Wim Klooster, Yvan Putseys & Pieter Seuren (eds.). *Sentential complementation and the lexicon: Studies in honour of Wim de Geest*. Dordrecht: Foris. 305–19.

Poitou, Jacques. 1994. Morphologische Analyse und Kategorisierung der Partizipien. In: Daniel Bresson & Martine Dalmas (eds.). *Partizip und Partizipialgruppen im Deutschen*. Tübingen: G. Narr. 109–20.

Pollard, Carl J. 1994. Toward a unified account of passive in German. In: John A. Nerbonne, Klaus Netter & Carl J. Pollard (eds.). *German in head-driven phrase structure grammar*. Stanford, CA: Center for the Study of Language and Information. 273–96.

Pollard, Carl J. & Sag, Ivan A. 1987. *Information-based syntax and semantics*. Stanford, CA: CSLI Publications.

Portner, Paul. 2011. Perfect and progressive. In: Klaus von Heusinger, Claudia Maienborn & Paul Portner (eds.). *Semantics: An international handbook of natural language meaning* (HSK 33.2). Berlin: de Gruyter. 1217–61.

Potashnik, Joseph. 2012. Emission verbs. In: Martin Everaert, Marijana Marelj & Tal Siloni (eds.). *The theta system: Argument structure at the interface*. Oxford: Oxford University Press. 251–78.

Pountain, Christopher J. & Kattân-Ibarra, Juan. 1997. *Modern Spanish grammar: A practical guide*. New York: Routledge.

Primus, Beatrice. 2010. Event-structure and individuation in impersonal passives. In: Patrick Brandt & Marco García García (eds.). *Transitivity*. Amsterdam: John Benjamins. 209–33.

Primus, Beatrice. 2011. Das unpersönliche Passiv: Ein Fall für die Konstruktionsgrammatik. In: Stefan Engelberg, Anke Holler & Kristel Proost (eds.). *Sprachliches Wissen zwischen Lexikon und Grammatik*. Berlin: de Gruyter. 285–313.

Pross, Tillmann. 2018. What about lexical semantics if syntax is the only generative component of the grammar? A case study on word meaning in German. *Natural Language and Linguistic Theory* 2018: 1–47.

Pustejovsky, James. 1991. The syntax of event structure. *Cognition* 41: 47–81.

Quintin, Hervé. 1994. Zur morphosyntaktischen und semantischen Einordnung von deutschen Partizipien und Partizipialsätzen. In: Daniel Bresson & Martine Dalmas (eds.). *Partizip und Partiziplalgruppen im Deutschen*. Tübingen: G. Narr. 91–107.

Radford, Andrew. 1997. *Syntax: A minimalist introduction*. Cambridge: Cambridge University Press.

Radford, Andrew. 2009. *An introduction to English sentence structure*. Cambridge: Cambridge University Press.

Radford, Andrew, Atkinson, Martin, Britain, David, Clahsen, Harald & Spencer, Andrew. 2009. *Linguistics: An introduction* (2nd edn.). Cambridge: Cambridge University Press.

Ramchand, Gillian C. 2008. *Verb meaning and the lexicon: A first phase syntax*. Cambridge: Cambridge University Press.

Rapp, Irene. 1997. *Partizipien und semantische Struktur: Zu passivischen Konstruktionen mit dem 3. Status*. Tübingen: Stauffenburg.

Rapp, Irene. 1998. Zustand? Passiv? Überlegungen zum sogenannten „Zustandspassiv". *Zeitschrift für Sprachwissenschaft* 15: 231–65.

Rapp, Irene. 2001. The attributive past participle: Structure and temporal interpretation. In: Caroline Féry & Wolfgang Sternefeld (eds.). *Audiatur Vox Sapientiae: A Festschrift for A. v. Stechow*. Berlin: Akademie. 392–409.
Rapp, Irene & Arnim von Stechow. 2015. The temporal orientation of prenominal past participles in German. In: Christian Fortmann, Anja Lübbe & Irene Rapp (eds.). *Situationsargumente im Nominalbereich*. Berlin: de Gruyter.
Rathert, Monika. 2004. *Textures of time*. Berlin: Akademie Verlag.
Rauh, Gisa. 2000a. Wi(e)der die Wortarten! Zum Problem linguistischer Kategorisierung. *Linguistische Berichte* 184: 485–507.
Rauh, Gisa. 2000b. Don't call it 'X'! or: Why X does not represent grammatical categories. In: Hero Janßen (ed.). *Verbal projections*. Tübingen: Max Niemeyer. 1–21.
Rauh, Gisa. 2010. *Syntactic categories: Their identification and description in linguistic theories*. Oxford, New York, NY: Oxford University Press.
Rauh, Gisa. 2016. Linguistic categories and the syntax-semantics interface: Evaluating competing approaches. In: Jens Fleischhauer, Anja Latrouite & Rainer Osswald (eds.). *Exploring the syntax-semantics-pragmatics interface*. Düsseldorf: Düsseldorf University Press. 15–56.
Rauh, Gisa. 2017. Parts of speech vs. syntactic categories: The case of English adverbs. In: Sandra Döring & Jochen Geilfuß-Wolfgang (eds.). *Probleme syntaktischer Kategorisierung: Einzelgänger, Außenseiter und mehr*. Tübingen: Stauffenburg. 101–38.
Reichenbach, Hans. 1947. *Elements of symbolic logic*. New York: Macmillan & Co.
Reinhart, Tanya. 2002. The theta-system: An overview. *Theoretical Linguistics* 28: 229–90.
Reis, Marga. 1979. Ansätze zu einer realistischen Grammatik. In: Klaus Grubmüller, Ernst Hellgardt, Heinrich Jellissen & Marga Reis (eds.). *Befund und Bedeutung: Zum Verhältnis von Empirie und Interpretation in Sprach- und Literaturwissenschaft*. Tübingen: Max Niemeyer. 1–21.
Reis, Marga. 2001. Bilden Modalverben im Deutschen eine syntaktische Klasse? In: Reimar Müller & Marga Reis (eds.). *Modalität und Modalverben im Deutschen*. Hamburg: Buske. 287–318.
Remberger, Eva-Maria. 2006. *Hilfsverben: Eine minimalistische Analyse am Beispiel des Italienischen und Sardischen*. Tübingen: Niemeyer.
Reuland, Eric J. 1983. Government and the search for AUXes: A case study in cross-linguistic category identification. In: Frank Heny & Barry Richards (eds.). *Linguistic categories: Auxiliaries and related puzzles, Vol. II: The scope, order, and distribution of English auxiliary verbs*. Dordrecht: Reidel. 99–168.
Richards, Marc. 2015. Minimalism. In: Tibor Kiss & Artemis Alexiadou. *Syntax – Theory and analysis: An international handbook* (HSK 42.2). Berlin: de Gruyter. 803–38.
Ritter, Elizabeth & Rosen, Sara Thomas. 1997. The function of *have*. *Lingua* 101: 295–321.
Roberts, Ian G. 1984. Verbal case and auxiliary selection with participles. *Wiener linguistische Gazette* (Supplement 3): 216–20.
Roberts, Ian G. 1985. Absorption parameters and the passive in UG. Paper presented at GLOW 8, Brussels. Abstract in *GLOW Newsletter* 14: 71–73.
Roberts, Ian G. 1987. *The representation of implicit and dethematized subjects*. Dordrecht: Foris.
Robinson, Orrin W. 1992. *Old English and its closest relatives: A survey of the earliest Germanic languages*. Stanford, CA: Stanford University Press.
Rosch, Eleanor & Mervis, Carolyn B. 1975. Family resemblances: Studies in the internal structure of categories. *Cognitive Psychology* 8: 573–605.
Rosen, Sara T. 1990. *Argument structure and complex predicates*. New York: Garland.

Ross, John R. 1972. The category squish: Endstation Hauptwort. In: Paul M. Peranteau, Judith N. Levi & Gloria C. Phares (eds.). *Papers from the eighth regional meeting of the Chicago Linguistics Society*. Chicago: Chicago Linguistic Society. 316–28.

Roßdeutscher, Antje & Kamp, Hans. 2010. Syntactic and semantic constraints on the formation and interpretation of *ung*-nouns. In: Artemis Alexiadou and Monika Rathert (eds.). *Nominalisations across languages and frameworks*. Berlin: de Gruyter. 169–214.

Rothstein, Björn. 2007. Einige Bemerkungen zum Partizip II in *Das Pferd hat die Fesseln bandagiert*. In: Ljudmila Geist & Björn Rothstein (eds.). *Kopulaverben und Kopulasätze: intersprachliche und intrasprachliche Aspekte*. Tübingen: Max Niemeyer. 285–98.

Rothstein, Björn. 2008. *The perfect time span: On the present perfect in German, Swedish and English*. Amsterdam: John Benjamins.

Rothstein, Susan. 2001. *Predicates and their subjects*. Dordrecht: Kluwer.

Rouveret, Alain & Vergnaud, Jean-Roger. 1980. Specifying reference to the subject: French causatives and conditions on representations. *Linguistic Inquiry* 11: 97–202.

Rowlett, Paul. 2007. *The syntax of French*. Cambridge: Cambridge University Press.

Rutten, Jean. 1991. Infinitival complements and auxiliaries. PhD dissertation. Amsterdam: University of Amsterdam.

Ruys, Eddy. 2010. Expletive selection and CP arguments in Dutch. *Journal of Comparative Germanic Linguistics* 13: 141–78.

Ryu, Byong-Rae. 1997. *Argumentstruktur und Linking im constraint-basierten Lexikon: ein Zwei-Stufen-Modell für eine HPSG-Analyse von Ergativität und Passivierung im Deutschen*. Tübingen: University of Tübingen.

Salvi, Giampaolo. 1987. Syntactic restructuring in the evolution of Romance auxiliaries. In: Martin Harris & Paolo Ramat (eds.). *Historical development of auxiliaries*. Berlin: de Gruyter. 225–36.

Şandor, Mihaela. 2008. Zur Grammatikalisierung der doppelten Perfektformen. In: Roxana Nubert (ed.). *Temeswarer Beiträge zur Germanistik* (Band 6). Temeswar: Mirton. 29–46.

Savova, Milena. 1989. On the invariant meaning of English past participles. *Philologia* 21–22:68–77.

Schäfer, Florian. 2013. Passives of reflexive verbs: The repair of a Principle A violation. In: Patrick Brandt & Eric Fuß (eds.). *Repairs: The added value of being wrong*. Berlin: de Gruyter. 335–64.

Schallert, Oliver. 2014. IPP-constructions in Alemannic and Bavarian in comparison. In: Günther Grewendorf & Helmut Weiß (eds.). *Bavarian syntax: Contributions to the theory of syntax*. Amsterdam: John Benjamins. 247–304.

Schlief, Anne-Kathrin. 2012. Untersuchungen zum morphsyntaktischen Status des Partizips II beim ‚Partizipialen Haben-Konfigurativ'. In: Björn Rothstein (ed.). *Nicht-flektierende Wortarten*. Berlin: de Gruyter. 300–27.

Schmid, Tanja. 2002. *West Germanic IPP-constructions: An optimality theoretic approach*. Stuttgart: Universität Stuttgart.

Schrodt, Richard. 2004. *Althochdeutsche Grammatik II: Syntax*. Tübingen: Max Niemeyer.

Schütze, Carson T. 2001. On the nature of default case. *Syntax* 4.3: 205–38.

Seely, T. Daniel. 2006. Merge, derivational c-command, and subcategorization in a label-free syntax. In: Cedric Boeckx (ed.). *Minimalist essays*. Amsterdam: John Benjamins. 182–217.

Shibatani, Masayoshi. 1985. Passives and related constructions: A prototype analysis. *Language* 61: 821–48.

Siddiqi, Daniel. 2009. *Syntax within the word: Economy, allomorphy and argument selection in distributed morphology*. Amsterdam: John Benjamins.
Siegel, Dorothy. 1973. Non-sources for un-passives. In: John P. Kimball (ed). *Syntax and semantics* II. New York: Seminar Press. 301–317.
Siewierska, Anna. 1984. *The passive: A comparative linguistic analysis*. London: Croom Helm.
Siewierska, Anna. 1988. The Passive in Slavic. In: Masayoshi Shibatani (ed.). *Passive and voice*. Amsterdam: John Benjamins. 243–89.
Sigurðsson, Halldór Ármann. 1989. Verbal syntax and case in Icelandic. PhD dissertation. Lund: University of Lund, Department of Scandinavian Languages.
Siloni, Tal. 1997. *Noun phrases and nominalizations: The syntax of DPs*. Dordrecht: Kluwer.
Sleeman, Petra. 2011. Verbal and adjectival participles: Position and internal structure. *Lingua* 121: 1569–87.
Sleeman, Petra. 2014. From participle to adjective in Germanic and Romance. In: Petra Sleeman, Freek van de Velde & Harry Perridon (eds.). *Adjectives in Germanic and Romance*. Amsterdam: John Benjamins. 171–98.
Smith, John C. 1995. Agreement between past participle and direct object in Catalan: The hypothesis of Castilian influence revisited. In: Jacek Fisiak (ed.). *Linguistic change under contact conditions*. Berlin: de Gruyter. 271–90.
Smolka, Eva, Zwitserlood, Pienie & Rösler, Frank. 2007. Stem access in regular and irregular inflection: Evidence from German participles. *Journal of Memory and Language* 57: 325–47.
Soare, Elena. 2007. Morphosyntactic mismatches revisited: The case of the Romanian supine. *Acta Linguistica Hungarica* 54: 173–92.
Sorace, Antonella. 2000. Gradients in auxiliary selection with intransitive verbs. *Language* 76: 859–90.
Spencer, Andrew. 2001. The paradigm-based model of morphosyntax. *Transactions of the Philological Society* 99: 279–313.
Squartini, Mario. 1998: *Verbal periphrases in Romance: Aspect, actionality, and grammaticalization*. Berlin: de Gruyter.
Stechow, Arnim von & Sternefeld, Wolfgang. 1988. *Bausteine syntaktischen Wissens: Ein Lehrbuch der generativen Grammatik*. Opladen: Westdeutscher Verlag.
Steele, Susan. 1999. Auxiliaries. In: Keith Brown & Jim Miller (eds.). *Concise encyclopedia of grammatical categories*. Amsterdam: Elsevier. 49–56.
Sternefeld, Wolfgang. 1984. On case and binding theory. In: Jindřich Toman (ed.). *Studies in German grammar*. Dordrecht: Foris. 231–85.
Sternefeld, Wolfgang. 1995. Voice phrases and their specifiers. *FAS Papers in Linguistics* 3: 48–85.
Stone, Gerald. 2002. Cassubian. In: Bernard Comrie & Greville G. Corbett (eds.). *The Slavonic languages*. London: Routledge. 759–94.
Strandskogen, Åse-Berit & Strandskogen, Rolf. 1995 [1986]. *Norwegian: An Essential Grammar*. Translated by Barbara White. London & New York: Routledge.
Strobel, Sven. 2007. Die Perfektauxiliarselektion des Deutschen: Ein lexikalistischer Ansatz ohne Unakkusativität. Doctoral dissertation. Stuttgart: University of Stuttgart.
Struckmeier, Volker. 2007. *Attribute im Deutschen: zu ihren Eigenschaften und ihrer Position im grammatischen System*. Berlin: Akademie Verlag.
Svartvik, Jan & Sager, Olof. 1996. *Engelsk universitetsgrammatik* (2nd edn.). Stockholm: Almqvist & Wiksell.
Svenonius, Peter. 2012. Look Both Ways: Outward-looking allomorphy in Icelandic participles. <http://ling.auf.net/lingbuzz/001519>, accessed on December 19, 2015.

Sybesma, Rint & Vanden Wyngaerd, Guido. 1997. Realizing end points: The syntax and semantics of Dutch *ge* and Mandarin *le*. In: Jane Coerts & Helen de Hoop (eds.). *Linguistics in the Netherlands 1997*. Amsterdam: John Benjamins. 207–18.

Teuber, Oliver. 2005. *Analytische Verbformen des Deutschen. Syntax, Semantik und Grammatikalisierung*. Hildesheim: Georg Olms.

Thieroff, Rolf. 1994. Perfect and pluperfect in German. In: Co Vet & Carl Vetters (eds.). *Tense and aspect in discourse*. Berlin: de Gruyter. 99–113.

Thieroff, Rolf. 2000. On the areal distribution of tense aspect categories in Europe.
In: Östen Dahl (ed.). *Tense and aspect in the languages of Europe*. Berlin: de Gruyter. 265–305.

Thráinsson, Höskuldur. 2007. *The syntax of Icelandic*. Cambridge: Cambridge University Press.

Toman, Jindřich. 1986. A (word-)syntax for participles. *Linguistische Berichte* 105: 367–408.

Urushibara, Saeko. 1997. Facets of the English past participle. In: Masatomo Ukaji, Toshio Nakao, Masaru Kajita & Shuji Chiba (eds.). *English linguistics: A festschrift for Akira Ota on the occasion of his 80th Birthday*. Tokyo: Taishukan. 130–46.

Valentin, Paul. 1994. Über Nicht-Partizipien und Partizipien im heutigen Deutsch. In: Daniel Bresson & Martine Dalmas (eds.). *Partizip und Partizipialgruppen im Deutschen*. Tübingen: G. Narr. 33–46.

van den Wyngaerd, Guido. 1988. Passive and the analysis of auxiliary verbs. In: Peter Coopmans & Aafke Hulk (eds.). *Linguistics in the Netherlands 1988*. Dordrecht: Foris. 159–68.

Vanden Wyngaerd, Guido. 1994. IPP and the structure of participles. *Groninger Arbeiten zur germanistischen Linguistik* 37: 265–76.

Vanden Wyngaerd, Guido. 1996. Participles and bare argument structure. In: Werner Abraham, Samuel David Epstein, Höskuldur Thráinsson & C. Jan-Wouter Zwart (eds.). *Minimal ideas*. Amsterdam: John Benjamins. 347–363.

Vater, Heinz. 2002. 'Sein' + participle construction in German. In: Ingrid Kaufmann & Barbara Stiebels (eds.). *More than words: A festschrift for Dieter Wunderlich*. Berlin: Akademie Verlag. 355–68.

Vater, Heinz. 2013. On participles of German verbs borrowed from English. In: Holden Härtl & Susan Olsen (eds.). *Interfaces of morphology: A festschrift for Susan Olsen*. Berlin: Akademie Verlag. 249–62.

Vendler, Zeno. 1967. *Linguistics in philosophy*. Ithaca: Cornell University Press.

Vennemann, Theo. 1987. Tempora und Zeitrelation im Standarddeutschen. *Sprachwissenschaft* 12: 234–49.

Verkuyl, H. J. 1989. Aspectual classes and aspectual composition. *Linguistics and Philosophy* 12: 39–94.

Vierhuff, Tilman, Hildebrandt, Bernd & Eikmeyer, Hans-Jürgen. 2003. Effiziente Verarbeitung deutscher Konstituentenstellung mit der Combinatorial Categorial Grammar. *Linguistische Berichte* 194: 213–37.

Vincent, Nigel. 1987. The interaction of periphrasis and inflection: Some Romance examples. In: Martin Harris & Paolo Ramat (eds.). *Historical development of auxiliaries*. Berlin: de Gruyter. 237–56.

Vogel, Ralf. 2009. Skandal im Verbkomplex: Betrachtungen zur scheinbar inkorrekten Morphologie in infiniten Verbkomplexen des Deutschen. *Zeitschrift für Sprachwissenschaft* 28: 307–46.

von der Gabelentz, Georg. 1891. *Die Sprachwissenschaft: Ihre Aufgaben, Methoden und bisherigen Ergebnisse*. Leipzig: Weigel.

von Stechow, Arnim. 1990. Status government and coherence in German. In: Günther Grewendorf & Wolfgang Sternefeld (eds.). *Scrambling and barriers*. Amsterdam: John Benjamins. 143–99.
von Stechow, Arnim. 1996. The different readings of *wieder* 'again': A structural account. *Journal of Semantics* 13: 87–138.
von Stechow, Arnim. 1998. German participles II in distributed morphology. Manuscript. Tübingen: Universität Tübingen.
von Stechow, Arnim. 1999. Eine erweiterte Extended-Now-Theorie für Perfekt und Futur. *Zeitschrift für Literaturwissenschaft und Linguistik* 113: 86–118.
von Stechow, Arnim. 2008. Tenses in compositional semantics. In: Wolfgang Klein & Ping Li (eds.). *The expression of time*. Berlin: de Gruyter. 129–66.
Wanner, Anja. 2009. *Deconstructing the English passive*. Berlin: de Gruyter.
Ward, Gregory, Birner, Betty & Huddleston, Rodney. 2002. Information packaging. In: Rodney D. Huddleston & Geoffrey K. Pullum (eds.). *The Cambridge grammar of the English language*. Cambridge: Cambridge University Press. 1363–448.
Ward, Gregory L. 1988. *The semantics and pragmatics of preposing*. New York: Garland.
Warner, Anthony R. 1993. *English auxiliaries: Structure and history*. Cambridge: Cambridge University Press.
Wasow, Thomas. 1977. Transformations and the lexicon. In: Peter W. Culicover, Thomas Wasow & Adrian Akmajian (eds.). *Formal syntax*. New York: Academic Press. 327–60.
Weber, Heinrich. 2002. Partizipien als Partizipien, Verben und Adjektive: Über Kontinuität und Fortschritt in der Geschichte der Sprachwissenschaft. In: Adolfo Murguía (ed.). *Sprache und Welt: Festgabe für Eugenio Coseriu zum 80. Geburtstag*. Tübingen: G. Narr. 191–214.
Wegener, Heide. 1998. Der Kasus des EXP. In: Marcel Vuillaume (ed.). *Die Kasus im Deutschen: Form und Inhalt*. Tübingen: Stauffenburg Verlag. 71–84.
Wegner, Dennis. 2017. The exceptional status of the Swedish supine: on the parametric variation of past participial (non-)identity. *Working Papers in Scandinavian Syntax* 99: 1–29.
Welke, Klaus. 2008. Das Zustandspassiv: Pragmatische Beschränkungen und Regelkonflikte. *Zeitschrift für germanistische Linguistik* 35: 115–45.
Wheeler, Max W., Yates, Alan & Dols, Nicolau. 1999. *Catalan: A comprehensive grammar*. New York: Routledge.
Wiklund, Anna-Lena. 2001. Dressing up for vocabulary insertion: The parasitic supine. *Natural Language and Linguistic Theory* 19: 199–228.
Wiklund, Anna-Lena. 2007. *The syntax of tenselessness: Tense/mood/aspect-agreeing infinitivals*. Berlin: de Gruyter.
Williams, Edwin. 1981. Argument structure and morphology. *The Linguistic Review* 1: 81–114.
Williams, Edwin. 2007. Dumping lexicalism. In: Gillian Ramchand & Charles Reiss (eds.). *The Oxford handbook of linguistic interfaces*. Oxford: Oxford University Press. 353–82.
Wilmanns, Wilhelm. 1906. *Deutsche Grammatik, vol. 3*. Straßburg: Trübner.
Wolff, Roland A. 1981. German past participles and the simplicity metric. *Linguistics* 19: 3–13.
Wunderlich, Dieter. 1970. *Tempus und Zeitreferenz im Deutschen*. München: Huber.
Wunderlich, Dieter. 1997. Participle, perfect and passive in German. *Theorie des Lexikons* 99: 1–34.
Wunderlich, Dieter. 2012. Operations on argument structure. In: Claudia Maienborn, Klaus von Heusinger & Paul Portner (eds.). *Semantics: An international handbook of natural language meaning* (HSK 33.3). Berlin: de Gruyter. 2224–59.
Wurmbrand, Susanne. 2001. *Infinitives: Restructuring and clause structure*. Berlin: de Gruyter.

Wurmbrand, Susanne. 2004. Two types of restructuring: Lexical versus functional. *Lingua* 114: 991–1015.

Wurmbrand, Susanne. 2006. Verb clusters, verb raising, and restructuring. In: Martin Everaert & Henk van Riemsdijk (eds.). *The Blackwell companion to syntax*. Oxford: Blackwell. 227–341.

Wurmbrand, Susanne. 2016. Complex predicate formation via voice incorporation. In: Léa Nash & Pollet Samvelian (eds.). *Approaches to complex predicates*. Leiden: Brill. 248–90.

Wurmbrand, Susi. 2012a. The syntax of valuation in auxiliary-participle constructions. *Coyote Papers: Working Papers in Linguistics, Linguistic Theory at the University of Arizona* 20: 154–62.

Wurmbrand, Susi. 2012b. Parasitic participles: Evidence for the theory of verb clusters. *Taal en Tongval* 64.1: 129–56.

Yao, Xinyue & Collins, Peter C. 2012. The present perfect in world Englishes. *World Englishes* 31: 386–403.

Zaenen, Annie. 1993. Unaccusativity in Dutch: Integrating syntax and lexical semantics. In: James Pustejovsky (ed.). *Semantics and the lexicon*. Dordrecht: Kluwer. 129–61.

Zaenen, Annie, Maling, Joan & Thráinsson, Höskuldur. 1985. Case and grammatical functions: The Icelandic passive. *Syntax and Semantics* 24: 95–136.

Zagona, Karen. 1991. Perfective Haber and the theory of tenses. In: Héctor Campos & Fernando Martínez-Gil (eds.). *Studies in Spanish linguistics*. Washington: Georgetown University Press. 379–403.

Zeijlstra, Hedde. 2012. There is only one way to agree. *The Linguistic Review* 29: 491–539.

Zeller, Jochen. 1994. *Die Syntax des Tempus: zur strukturellen Repräsentation temporaler Ausdrücke*. Opladen: Westdeutscher Verlag.

Zieglschmid, Friedrich. 1929. Zur Entwicklung der Perfektumschreibung im Deutschen. *Language* 5: 7–75.

Zifonun, Gisela, Hoffmann, Ludger & Strecker, Bruno. 1997. *Grammatik der deutschen Sprache*. Berlin: de Gruyter.

Zimmermann, Ilse. 1999. Partizip II-Konstruktionen des Deutschen als Modifikatoren. *ZAS Papers in Linguistics* 14: 123–46.

Zwart, Jan-Wouter. 2007. Some notes on the origin and distribution of the IPP-effect. *Groninger Arbeiten zur Germanistischen Linguistik* 45: 77–99.

Index

absolute clause 72, 132, 174, 316, 317, 326
θ-absorption 137, 138, 154–156, 222
λ-abstraction 12, 299–302, 304–306, 310, 318, 322–324
accusative 25, 26, 29, 61, 82, 130, 151, 152, 162, 164, 165, 195, 205, 206, 219–221, 223, 232, 234, 235, 237, 310, 316
adjectival compound 75, 301
adjectival past participle 56, 62, 63, 68, 73–75, 77, 78, 96, 129, 131, 174, 294, 298–306, 310, 316, 319, 324
adnominal use of a past participle 63, 66–73, 77, 78, 165, 173, 174, 176, 304
adverbial use of a past participle 10, 55, 69, 70, 72, 73, 76, 174, 176, 314–316
aktionsart 11, 23, 29, 31, 33, 84–87, 126, 132, 145, 147, 150, 170, 183, 184, 209, 218, 241, 249, 252, 256, 263, 323
amalgamation 144, 148, 159, 160, 161, 168–170, 180, 321, 323
anticausative 11, 36, 74, 122, 124, 125, 301, 305, 307, 311, 316, 319, 320, 322, 323, 325
anti-lexicalism 16–20, 198, 250, 326
aspect 1, 3, 5, 7, 36, 50, 66, 87, 121, 143–146, 148–151, 158, 159, 164, 165, 167, 241, 244, 245, 249, 251, 259, 270
aspectual language 51, 183, 197, 253, 321
auxiliarisation 121, 123, 125–127, 131, 133, 167, 176, 325
auxiliary alternation 2, 11, 23, 31, 35, 38, 39, 41, 42, 46, 48, 52, 56, 59, 60, 80, 82, 84, 86, 96, 97, 129, 130, 132, 137, 175, 185, 189, 191, 193, 209–212, 243, 254, 257, 285, 293

bare past participial clause 70, 71, 105, 193
bare past participle 13, 68, 70–73, 76, 105, 165, 173, 176, 178, 193, 294, 306, 310, 315, 316, 320, 322
biased identity 143, 144, 148, 150, 152, 158, 159, 161, 163, 167–169
boundedness 149, 211, 225, 246, 247, 251, 252–254, 257

Bulgarian 9, 32, 34, 35, 51–54, 87, 89, 93, 98, 132, 171, 253, 266, 294, 324–326
Burzio's Generalization 25, 153, 220

case absorption 138, 152, 154–156, 164, 223
Catalan 45–48, 97
category 1, 6, 14, 22, 56, 63, 64, 66, 73, 74, 78, 79, 123, 132, 166, 219, 242, 295, 317–319, 324
concurrency 70, 90, 305, 308, 312
control into purposes clauses 296
copula 6, 37, 60, 62, 63, 69, 77, 81, 82, 108, 123, 125, 126, 129, 131, 149, 151, 174, 192, 193, 219, 235, 295, 296, 299, 301–303

Danish 36–38, 42–44, 61, 77, 95, 96, 111, 116, 126, 128, 228, 229, 268, 293, 327
dative 2, 18, 26, 27, 29, 31, 61, 65, 76, 80, 81, 123, 178, 211, 219, 230–235, 237, 300, 310, 323
decomposition 249, 252, 253
default case 21, 26, 47, 82, 151, 235, 237, 310, 327
default φ-feature valuation 21, 201, 202, 218, 228, 229, 327
defective perfectivity 12, 32, 184, 196, 212, 241, 243, 249, 253, 254, 258, 259, 263–266, 273, 276, 322
deponent verb 102, 119–121
designated argument 157, 224, 239
deverbal 7, 63, 74, 101, 122, 124–126, 128, 130, 131, 133, 169, 170, 175, 184, 204, 241, 252, 299, 317, 322, 324, 325
diachrony 1, 7, 18, 31, 35, 41, 61, 80, 86, 94, 101, 108, 121–125, 127, 130, 131, 133, 138, 140, 150, 167, 175, 184, 241, 244, 267, 281, 322, 325, 326
disjoint reference 177, 296–298, 303
Distributed Morphology 12, 17, 20, 120, 141, 195, 287
ditransitive predicate 21, 23, 25, 41, 80, 230, 231, 232, 234, 235, 310, 327

Dutch 40, 41, 60, 84, 85, 106, 108, 109, 111, 113, 118, 126, 129, 133, 202, 228, 284, 322, 327

endpoint 31, 41, 83, 84, 87, 179, 252, 254, 263
event structure 23, 87, 132, 140, 146, 160, 162, 169, 170, 183, 184, 208, 241, 242, 244, 246, 249, 252, 254, 255, 259, 263, 298, 307, 310, 314, 316, 318, 322–324
existential binding 11, 180, 189, 190, 197, 199, 206, 207, 209, 211, 212, 216, 221, 224, 226, 231, 238–241, 277, 300, 307, 321
experiential perfect 57, 262–266

Faroese 42, 115, 116, 285
feature-checking 15, 117, 285
FL 14, 32
French 37, 38, 45–49, 67, 71, 77, 84, 85, 97, 98, 128, 197, 268, 290, 293
Frisian 10, 42, 102, 110, 111, 114–116, 279, 284–286
Full Interpretation 225, 325

genitive 27
grammaticalisation 80, 86, 90, 121–125, 127, 128, 130, 131, 133, 175, 230, 242, 267, 323, 324
Greek 37, 38, 50, 55, 61, 78, 266

Hebrew 54
heterogeneity 1, 66, 147, 245, 259
homogeneity 66, 147, 161, 245, 259

Icelandic 8, 21, 35, 36, 42, 43, 95, 116, 128, 130, 193, 197, 202, 268, 290, 293
impersonal passive 18, 21, 58, 92, 201, 202, 223, 228, 229, 239, 327
impoverishment 20, 104, 105, 112, 114, 117, 118, 121, 133, 175, 185, 186, 275–277, 280–282, 284–289, 322, 327
individual-level 305, 307
Infinitivus pro Participio 10, 41, 101, 102, 106, 107, 109–119, 121, 185, 186, 188, 277–285, 287, 288

inherent case 2, 12, 18, 26, 27, 29, 31, 61, 76, 230–235, 237, 238, 300, 301, 310, 322
Italian 29, 37, 45–49, 60, 77, 82, 84, 85, 97, 98, 130, 197, 228, 290, 293

Kashubian 52, 53, 90, 324

Latin 6, 36, 37, 49, 50, 51, 62, 89, 119, 120, 121, 124, 126, 171, 241, 253
lexicalisation 84, 85, 126
lexicalism 12, 16, 18, 19, 22, 120, 195, 198
LF 18, 105, 226, 237, 239, 275, 277, 280, 287
locative verb 227
loss of the preterite 270, 272, 273

Macedonian 51–53, 55, 90, 324
Merge 15, 20–22
θ-merger 154–156, 170, 207, 323
Minimalist Programme 12, 14, 15, 17, 21, 31, 33, 217, 220, 326
morphomic level 139, 166
motion verb 83–86, 110, 126, 178, 179, 189

nominative 26, 29, 81, 174, 231–235, 237, 317
non-finite 5, 41, 64, 69, 77, 92, 93, 154, 159, 160, 173, 174, 180, 190, 196, 197, 200, 243, 251, 317, 323
non-identity 32, 44, 45, 54, 74, 87, 89, 90, 92, 94, 98, 122, 132, 134, 135, 137, 138, 140, 151, 166, 168, 169, 171, 289, 294, 321, 323, 324, 326
Norwegian 42, 43, 48, 71, 91, 96, 114–116, 185, 202, 223, 228, 268, 284

ornamental morphology 20, 104, 117, 118, 121, 133, 158, 165, 188, 275, 285, 287, 288, 326, 327

parameterisation 54, 149, 190, 201, 203, 216, 256, 268, 286
parasitic participle 10, 115, 116, 286, 287
participial subject-agreement 52, 98, 99, 294
Participium pro Infinitivo 10, 101, 102, 114 –119, 121, 185, 284–288

passivisation 42, 120, 131, 142, 150, 157, 220, 221, 223, 225, 228, 238–241, 298
past participial object-agreement 13, 43, 47–50, 77, 96–99, 132, 197, 218, 289–294, 322, 324, 326
past participial (non-)identity 2, 3, 7, 8, 11–13, 32, 34, 50, 54–56, 78, 79, 95, 101, 104, 107, 109, 112, 119, 121, 131, 133–135, 139, 143, 149, 160, 162, 166, 167, 169, 184, 250, 320, 323, 326, 327
Perfect(ive) Participle Paradox 10, 101–107, 109, 112, 116, 118, 119, 121, 185, 186, 274, 275, 277, 278, 280
PF 16, 18, 21, 22, 105, 117, 118, 277, 280, 281, 286–289, 292, 327
phrasal syntax 19, 21, 197, 198, 213, 234
Polish 51, 52
polymorphy 101, 132, 172, 219
Portuguese 38, 45, 46, 48, 97
posteriority 12, 159, 189, 191, 205, 208, 209, 211, 215, 242–244, 247–249, 251, 253–255, 257, 261, 263–265, 269, 272, 273, 276, 290, 314, 321
postnominal past participles 55, 63–65, 67–69, 72, 75, 76, 78, 90, 132, 305, 307–311, 314
PredP 302, 304–306, 310, 314, 316, 318–320, 324
prenominal past participles 56, 63–68, 75–78, 85, 177, 295, 304, 305, 307–311, 314
preposing 102, 103, 105, 113, 274, 278, 283, 284
present participle 1, 3, 5, 32, 55, 66, 67, 135, 140, 192, 327
present perfect puzzle 267–269, 273, 323, 327
pro 220, 222
progressive 1, 3, 120, 193, 327
Proto-Agent 27, 81, 160, 179, 180, 227, 233, 237, 239, 323
Proto-Patient 87, 160, 179, 189, 233
psych verb 26, 227

resultant state 12, 100
resultative participle 124, 299, 304, 310, 311, 314

resultative perfect 36, 58, 127, 261–264
Reverse Agree 217, 286, 291, 292
Romanian 45–48, 97, 293
root 18, 22, 101, 120, 141, 310
Russian 36–38, 51, 171, 241, 253

semantic recoverability 112, 118, 281, 282, 284, 289, 290, 322
semantic vacuity 11, 35, 41, 54, 116, 120, 134, 137, 143, 144, 149, 154, 158, 162–165, 167, 168, 181, 190–192, 243, 248, 258, 277, 324, 325, 327
simple change of state 87, 132, 170, 183–185, 188, 197, 205, 208, 211, 242, 243, 247, 253, 258, 299, 304, 317, 321, 322
Slovenian 35, 51, 53, 87, 90
Spanish 38, 45–48, 67, 82, 97, 128, 130, 228
stage-level 305, 307, 308
stative participle 65, 73, 304
stative passive 41, 42, 44, 57, 59, 60–62, 67, 73, 77, 78, 96, 99–101, 123–125, 129, 131, 165, 174, 175, 184, 192–194, 296–299, 301–304, 314, 322
stative perfect 61, 89, 123, 126, 127, 176, 184, 303
supine 9, 13, 45, 88, 91–95, 115, 132, 325
Supinum pro Infinitivo 115
suppression of the external argument 32, 160, 167, 174, 175, 178, 180, 185, 186, 189, 196, 221, 223, 239, 289, 303, 321, 322
Swedish 9, 13, 34, 38, 42–45, 54, 88, 90–95, 114–116, 126, 132, 171, 228, 268, 285, 324, 326
synthetic passive 36, 42, 43, 45, 50, 55, 78, 92

target state 100
tense 3, 4, 5, 7, 22, 38, 39, 54, 55, 74, 89, 93, 105, 106, 113, 117, 127, 128, 131, 143, 144, 146, 148–151, 158, 159, 163, 165, 167, 173, 190, 192, 193, 196, 201, 205, 218, 244, 248, 249, 251, 254, 255, 260, 266, 268–271, 286, 294, 318
terminology 3, 4, 12, 45, 66, 69, 135, 146, 262
Theme-unergative 27, 28, 178, 227, 255

Time of the Situation 191, 250, 252–257, 259, 264, 269, 314
Topic Time 191, 201, 205, 251, 252, 254–257, 259, 261, 264, 268, 269, 277, 314
two-place unaccusative 27–29, 86, 170, 187, 191, 208, 210, 211, 231, 253, 258, 325

un-affixation 75, 78, 100, 301
universal perfect 12, 37, 55, 57, 136, 147, 182, 188, 215, 245, 246, 248, 256, 261–263, 265, 266, 269
Utterance Time 146, 201, 251, 266

valuation 15, 21, 117, 196, 202, 213, 216, 217, 223, 286, 292, 326
verb cluster 102, 110–113, 116–118, 133, 186, 187, 274, 278–285, 287–289, 322, 327

weak perfectivity 259, 260
word-syntax 19, 20–22, 33, 194, 195, 204, 213, 215, 221, 243, 249, 299–301, 314, 317, 319, 324, 326

Yiddish 41, 111

www.ingramcontent.com/pod-product-compliance
Lightning Source LLC
Chambersburg PA
CBHW031752220426
43662CB00007B/379